RESTLESS SOUL

Sometimes the right path is the wrong choice

PART II

Charles Harrison Bell

His wife's ancestors and his married days

Godfrey Bell

His father's story

Order this book online at www.trafford.com/06-2017
or email orders@trafford.com

Most Trafford titles are also available at major online book retailers.

Note for Librarians: A cataloguing record for this book is available from Library and Archives Canada at www.collectionscanada.ca/amicus/index-e.html

Printed in Victoria, BC, Canada.

ISBN: 978-1-4251-0260-9

We at Trafford believe that it is the responsibility of us all, as both individuals and corporations, to make choices that are environmentally and socially sound. You, in turn, are supporting this responsible conduct each time you purchase a Trafford book, or make use of our publishing services. To find out how you are helping, please visit www.trafford.com/responsiblepublishing.html

Our mission is to efficiently provide the world's finest, most comprehensive book publishing service, enabling every author to experience success. To find out how to publish your book, your way, and have it available worldwide, visit us online at www.trafford.com/10510

Trafford PUBLISHING™

www.trafford.com

North America & international
toll-free: 1 888 232 4444 (USA & Canada)
phone: 250 383 6864 • fax: 250 383 6804
email: info@trafford.com

The United Kingdom & Europe
phone: +44 (0)1865 722 113 • local rate: 0845 230 9601
facsimile: +44 (0)1865 722 868 • email: info.uk@trafford.com

10 9 8 7 6 5 4

Chapter 12

MORE ROOTS: RAE'S FAMILY HISTORY

The Barrells, Sullys, Fitzers and Diamonds

We now need to step back in time once again, this time to trace Rae's roots on both her father and her mother's side.

Hilda Rae Barrell (called Rae – or "Girl" by her family) was soon to be Mrs Rae Bell and her family tree suddenly met up with mine. The origin of the family name of Barrell is ascribed to the Huguenots, the French protestants who were members of the Reformed Church established by John Calvin in 1550. An estimated 50,000 Huguenots fled to Britain to escape prosecution in Roman Catholic France, Barrells amongst them. But some were in Britain before that. The first record of the name Barrell was found in Herefordshire where they had settled from about 1400. But the comparatively large number of Barrells in Somerset suggests that they were of a stock separate from those in eastern England. Some were in Bristol and a great number were in Bath. Earliest records are of a Phillip Barrell and a Walter Barrell in 1297. Weston-super-Mare in particular and Somerset in general figure highly in Rae's roots – as Somerset does in mine (with the Perrott family in Shepton Mallet). William Henry Barrell, Rae's great great grandfather (c1796-c1850) lived in Weston-super-Mare in 1822 as proved by records of his presence at his son Henry William's baptism in 1822.

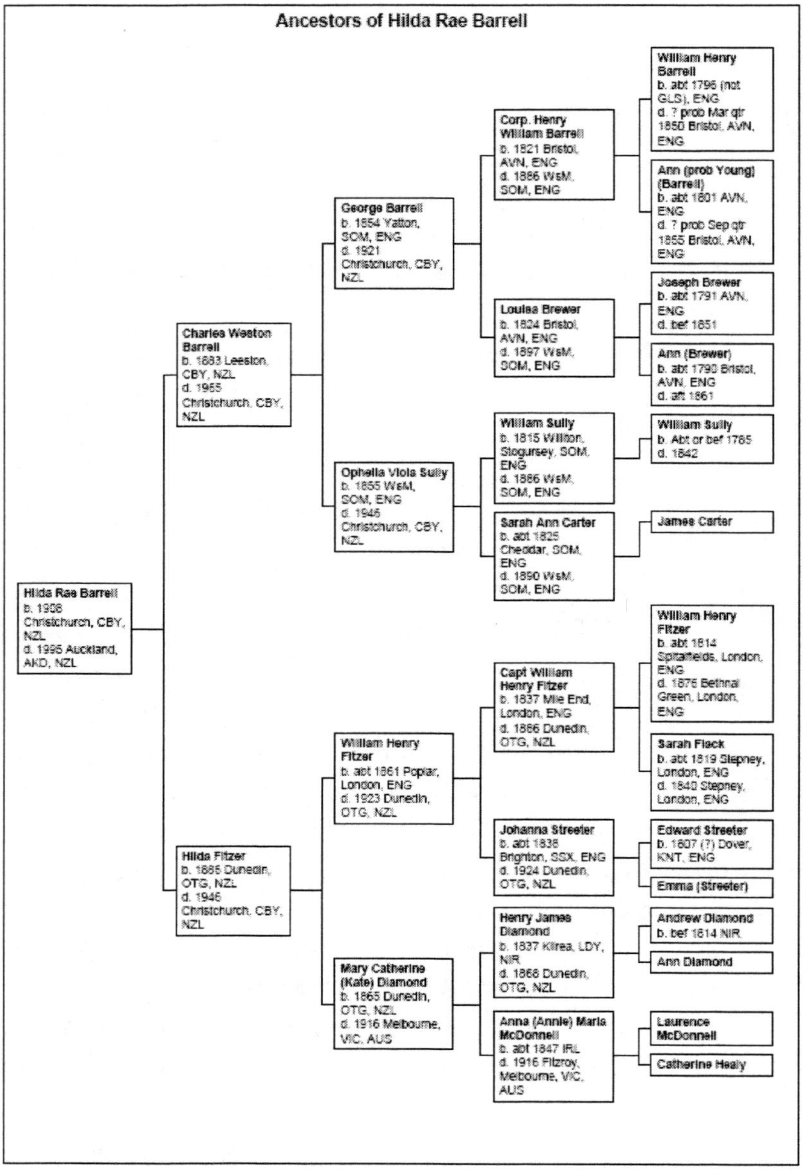

Rae's great great grandparents were Joseph and Ann Brewer (maiden name unknown), both born probably in or near Bristol about 1790 or 1791. Joseph was a butcher. They had thirteen children, eight daughters and five sons. Louisa was their sixth daughter born in 1824 in Bristol. She married Henry William[1] Barrell who was born in 1821 also in Bristol in Denmark Street, St Augustine's Parish[2]. Henry and Louisa, Rae's great grandparents, married in 1844 making the extraordinary combination of Barrell and Brewer![3] Henry William was baptised in Weston-super-Mare in the parish church of St John in Lower Church Road (as it is called today) on 2nd January 1822. The old Norman church was run-down and semi-derelict and it was demolished just one year later, to be replaced with a new parish church in 1824. In the new parish church two of Henry's children, Isabelle and Matilda Ann (Tilly) were baptised in 1860 and 1862 respectively.

Henry and Louisa had a large family of fourteen children[4] but some children died very young. While his mother was pregnant with Rae's grandfather, George, Louisa's eighth child, eight year old Ellen Louisa, died on 18 December 1853 just a few weeks *before* George was born. Two weeks *after* George was born (31 January 1854), Louisa lost another child, five year old Matilda Ann who died on 14 February 1854. To lose two children and give birth to one within a few weeks of each other must have been extraordinarily tough. Both George's sisters were buried in the Yatton Parish Church graveyard. It is for this reason that it seems likely that at that time this was the family church and to assume that George was also baptised there, even though no baptism record has yet been found to verify it.

---

1 There is some confusion as to whether he was Henry William or just Henry. Records are inconsistent.

2 A reference in a family Bible (courtesy Trish Hadden), refers to Henry William being born in St Augustine's Hospital, Denmark Street, but no hospital there or near there has been traced. Denmark Street however does exist (right in the centre of Bristol) and it was in the Parish of St Augustine's. The parish church of St Augustine the Less was damaged during the Blitz and has been demolished. Interestingly, Bristol Cathedral was founded as St Augustine's Abbey in 1140.

3 From *The Barrells of Durham Street*, Margaret Scott.

4 Although for many years it has been claimed that Henry and Louisa had 14 children, some records have failed to be found despite significant recent research. There may have been confusion and misunderstanding arising from duplicate names and dates or missing or badly written parish records. It is possible, although not certain, that they did in fact have only 11 or 12 children. - GB 2005

Another of George's sisters was Emily (Rae's great aunt) who in 1899 married (for a second time) Henry William (or William Henry – records vary) Twiggs. In 1918 Twiggs became Lord Mayor of Bristol.

A younger brother of George, Charles Edward Barrell (Rae's great uncle) married Annie J Lock. Charles and, it appears, his brothers-in-law, set up a grocer business in Bristol called Lock & Barrell. This is another interesting combination of family names as it is not too far removed from the popular expression of "lock, stock and barrel" – and as shop keepers Lock and Barrell were indeed interested in stock! Charles must have got on well with his in-laws as it appears that the Lock and Barrell families were living together in 1901. At the time of the 1901 census, when Charles was thirty-seven, they were sharing the same address of 74 Alma Road, Clifton, Bristol.

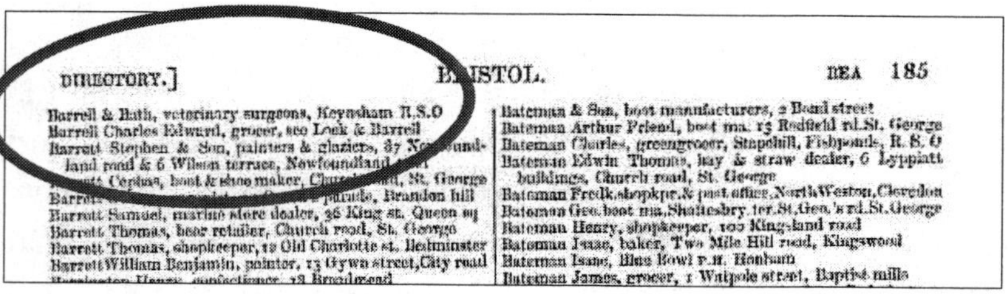

DIRECTORY.] BRISTOL. BEA 185

Barrell & Bath, veterinary surgeons, Keynsham R.S.O
Barrell Charles Edward, grocer, see Lock & Barrell
Barrett Stephen & Son, painters & glaziers, 87 Newfoundland road & 6 Wilson terrace, Newfoundland
Barrett Cephas, boot & shoe maker, Church road, St. George
Barrett Samuel, marine store dealer, 36 King st. Queen sq
Barrett Thomas, beer retailer, Church road, St. George
Barrett Thomas, shopkeeper, 12 Old Charlotte st. Bedminster
Barrett William Benjamin, painter, 13 Gywn street, City road

Bateman & Son, boot manufacturers, 2 Bond street
Bateman Arthur Friend, boot ma. 13 Redfield rd. St. George
Bateman Charles, greengrocer, Stapehill, Fishponds, R. S. O
Bateman Edwin Thomas, hay & straw dealer, 6 Lyppiatt buildings, Church road, St. George
Bateman Fredk. shopkpr. & post office, North Weston, Clevedon
Bateman Geo. boot ma. Shaftesbry. ter. St. Geo.'s rd. St. George
Bateman Henry, shopkeeper, 100 Kingsland road
Bateman Isaac, baker, Two Mile Hill road, Kingswood
Bateman Isaac, Blue Bowl p.h. Hanham
Bateman James, grocer, 1 Walpole street, Baptist mills

Extracts from the Bristol Commercial Directory 1889[1].
Entries show Charles Edward Barrell (above) and Lock and Barrell (below), grocers, in Imperial Parade, Alma Road, Clifton, Bristol.

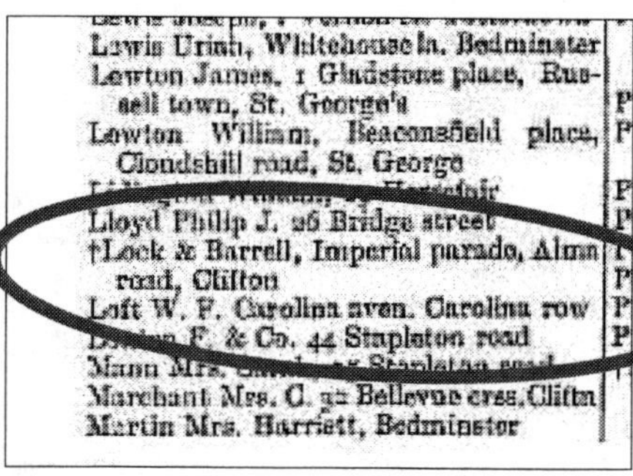

Lewis Uriah, Whitehouse la. Bedminster
Lewton James, 1 Gladstone place, Russell town, St. George's
Lewton William, Beaconsfield place, Cloudshill road, St. George
Lloyd Philip J. 26 Bridge street
†Lock & Barrell, Imperial parade, Alma road, Clifton
Loft W. F. Carolina aven. Carolina row
[illegible] F. & Co. 44 Stapleton road
Marchant Mrs. C. 92 Bellevue cres. Cliftn
Martin Mrs. Harriett, Bedminster

1 Research acknowledgement: Jennifer Jones.

George himself, Rae's grandfather, was born in 1854 in the parish of Yatton (near Bristol in north Somerset) and died in New Zealand in 1921 in Christchurch when Rae was thirteen. He married Ophelia Viola Sully and they had nine children, one of whom, the second son and fifth child, was Charles Weston (Rae's father, named after his mother's home town, Weston-super-Mare), born in Leeston, Canterbury, New Zealand, on 17 April 1883.

Henry William Barrell was a hairdresser when he married Louisa in 1844. According to a family Bible record, soon after he married he served as a Corporal of Artillery in the East India Company[1] and in 1845 he was stationed in the Warley Barracks married quarters in Great Warley, Essex.

The East India Company *(the Honourable East India Company (HEIC))*
From about 1600, large parts of India were administered by the Honourable East India Company which traded and raised revenue like a Government. Also, like a Government, they raised an Army to protect their interests and maintain the peace. Officers were enlisted from the UK and other ranks were recruited from both the UK and from amongst 'Native Indians'.

In effect, the HEIC was the Government of India and they maintained the Bengal, the Madras and the Bombay armies, all of which had units of cavalry, infantry, artillery and engineers. Despite this military presence in India, the British Government sent regiments to spend many years helping the HEIC to maintain order and protect the borders from foreigners – mainly the French and Portuguese, although the Russians also cast envious eyes at India and its neighbour Afghanistan.

Thus, during the 19th century, the HEIC was assisted in keeping the peace by British regiments on temporary postings (some of which could be for as long as 7 or 14 years), so that in effect there were two distinct military organisations (the Army of the HEIC and the British Army), in India until 1858. These two organisations continued to operate quite separately and maintained separate records.

[1] Research acknowledgement: Trish Hadden.

After the Indian Mutiny in 1857, the HEIC's function was taken over by the British Government and in 1860 the Indian Army was created and the HEIC army was disbanded. The new Indian Army still had British officers but other ranks were no longer brought out from the UK and so all ranks below that of commissioned officer were Indians. The Indian Army continued to operate independently of the British Army and this independence is reflected in modern archives.

Further research has established that Warley Barracks was used by the East India Company from 1843 when they transferred there from Brompton Barracks, Chatham, to house seven officers, twenty-one staff sergeants and eight hundred men. By the end of 1856, 2500 men had passed through the barracks and had been shipped to India. Training was initially for artillery and infantry but later included cavalry recruits. Henry Barrell was definitely one of the men at Warley Barracks but there is no evidence to suggest he went to India. His occupation was listed as "General Agent" which is, according to some sources who "know the military" a most unusual description of an army occupation and they were slightly at a loss to explain what it meant. Nonetheless, that is precisely what appears on the East India Company records for Rae's great grandfather. He was enlisted on 11 May 1843 at the age of twenty-one years six months and joined the Warley depot a week later.

It is fascinating to discover a personal description of an ancestor when no photograph, portrait or drawing is known to exist. The Warley records showed that Henry Barrell was 5'7" tall, had light brown hair, hazel eyes, fresh complexion and 525 visage[1]. He was discharged on 23 September 1851 being paid a discharge fee of £15. Henry had served in the EIC for 8 years and 135 days.

---

1 British Military Records of the time included a Regimental Description Book. This book described, amongst a host of other details, the soldier's complexion, the colour of his eyes and hair, the form (shape) of his visage (face) and whether he had any physical marks. What the "525" bit means in relation to the "form of his face" has not been established. The record of another soldier (unrelated) refers to "607 visage" so there is obviously a code, which has yet to be broken!

Henry and Louisa's first son after five daughters, Henry Joseph (who became known as Harry), was born in Warley, Essex, in 1850[1] and was baptised in Brentwood. After Henry left the East India Company in 1851 he returned to Bristol where he continued working as a hairdresser until 1854. At that time he gave up hairdressing for good and he joined the Bristol and Exeter Railway Company as a porter and booking clerk and worked at the Yatton railway station. The railway company was amalgamated into the Great Western Railway (GWR) and on 1 January 1876 Henry was officially employed by that company as a "booking porter" and then a "railway clerk" with a wage of 27/6 per week (today, £1.27)[2]. In 1861 Henry was living at 2 Queen's Terrace, Weston-super-Mare which suggests that by then he was working at the Weston-super-Mare railway station. In 1871 the family was living at 5 Camden Terrace[3], Weston-super-Mare. He resigned from the GWR in 1885 at the age of sixty-four but died within the year, at the same age on 10th September 1886 in Weston-super-Mare. Rae's great grandmother, Louisa, died on 3rd March 1897 at the age of seventy-three. Buried with them in the same grave in Weston-super-Mare is one of their fourteen[4] children, Matilda Ann (Tilly) Barrell, who died at the age of sixty-one in 1924. She was the second Matilda Ann of Henry and Louisa. She was named in memory of her sister who died at the age of five.

Ophelia, Rae's grandmother, was born on 4 May 1855 in Weston-super-Mare, Somerset. The name of this place was to become a great family name. Rae's father was named Charles Weston Barrell, his second daughter was named Annette Weston Barrell, his grandson was named Graeme Weston Barrell and our first son was, more unusually, given it as a first name, Weston Thomas Bell.

---

1 An error in one of the censuses suggests an alternative birth year was 1856 – but the almost certain conclusion is that 1850 is the correct year of birth.

2 Research acknowledgement: Richard Symonds.

3 Today, after Camden Terrace was re-numbered, it is no. 6

4 Evidence as to number of children inconclusive.

George and Ophelia were married in the Bristol Road Baptist Church, Weston-super-Mare on 17 August 1874. The church was right next door to where Ophelia lived at 1 Southside, Weston-super-Mare.

As if emigration was some kind of wedding present it seems, George and Ophelia emigrated to New Zealand just a month later leaving Gravesend, Kent (River Thames, London) on 18 September 1874 on the full-rigged iron 1,200 ton clipper ship *Geraldine Paget* with 380 New Zealand Government immigrants. Ophelia and George were among those immigrants on an assisted passage and paid £14-10s-0d each for their enormous trip to the other side of the world. The fact that they opted to travel on an assisted passage thereby taking an inferior cabin, is a little bit surprising as it appeared, certainly later on, that they were by no means "poor". The ship was built by a small Port Glasgow builder Lawrence Hill in 1870, and was operated by I & C Campbell. It was the *Geraldine Paget's* first voyage of three to New Zealand. They rounded the Cape of Good Hope on 20 November and arrived in Lyttelton just after Christmas on 27 December 1874 making it a journey of exactly one hundred days, port to port. Near the end of that long voyage, on 18 December, almost within sight of his new homeland, one of the immigrants, nineteen year old John White, fell into the sea and drowned after doing gymnastic feats on the jib guys.

The ship set off from London with more immigrants than arrived. Apart from John White, eleven died and many were sick: at one time there were twenty-seven cases of measles. The main causes of death were diarrhoea, convulsions, bronchitis and tuberculosis. Despite the age range of those who died being three months to thirty-eight years, most were just toddlers. Six died in as many days. And none of this takes into account plain old but frightful sea sickness which must have been severe in the primitive sailing ships. Whichever way you look at it, world-wide voyages in those days must have been barely survivable let alone comfortable.

George and Ophelia settled in Leeston in Canterbury for ten years. George had experience as a funeral director in England but he was also an experienced cabinetmaker and produced some extremely fine furniture. George established a "Cabinetmaker and Funeral Director" business during the ten years they lived in Leeston, and this business continued for some time after he left there to settle in Christchurch.

During the ten years that George and Ophelia lived in Leeston, six of their nine children were born, including Rae's father Charles Weston. Shortly after this the family travelled to Melbourne, Australia, where they stayed for eight months. The reason for this move is not exactly known, but it may have had something to do with George's next business enterprise which was the invention and manufacturing of steam washing machines. He returned to Christchurch in 1886 and established his business as a washing machine manufacturer in premises at 64 Manchester Street, Christchurch. He also had a shop at 133 Manchester Street, which he possibly rented out. An advertisement in the Christchurch Press in 1887 read:

> *Wanted Known - Barrell's Wonderful Patent Steam Washers are surprising everyone. Neighbours are envious; Laundry women indignant. Numbers keep their washing at home now. . . .*

Later he moved his business to 157 Victoria Street. There is no doubt that George Barrell was an enterprising and astute businessman. From washing machines he began buying and selling property as well as running a house-letting business. By the end of the 1890s he owned a lot of property in and around Christchurch, some of it particularly valuable: Percy Street, 79 East Belt, Riccarton, 55 Durham Street, 57 Durham Street, "corner house" Durham Street, 236 St Asaph Street, 57 Selwyn Street, 72 Fairfield Avenue, 73 Fairfield Avenue, 74 Fairfield Avenue, Richmond Terrace, Smallott Street off Colombo Street, City Malt House Colombo Road South, Wordsworth Street. In 1897 he bought a section in Addington Cemetery, from which he sold six graves. But the property of greatest significance was that which gave them the name, *The Barrells of Durham Street,* which Margaret Scott aptly used for her family history book. It is the property George and Ophelia owned and lived in at the corner of Durham and St Asaph Streets. It was a substantial section and there were already three houses on it at the time it was purchased. Presumably they lived at 53 Durham Street prior to the completion of their new home at what was listed then as 55 Durham Street, but which was much later to become no 221. Stables also had to be built since at that time they had no motorised vehicles for the undertaking business. All his other business interests aside, his name has always been associated with funeral directing. Although the first motor cars appeared in New Zealand in 1900, it was not until 1916 that George purchased the first motor hearse in Canterbury.

My first impressions of Rae's most social life style are reflected in that of her grandparents. George and Ophelia held wonderful Christmases in the Durham Street "corner house". A marquee was erected in the back garden and festooned with streamers and coloured lights. Huge Christmas trees bearing not only pine needles and decorations, but one Christmas, exciting scooters for each of the young grandsons, were typical of the extravagance showered on the large family (six sons, three daughters) which as the children married, of course, got larger. Each year, each married son was the recipient of a substantial goose and a side of lamb, prepared by Ophelia.

George was only twenty and Ophelia only nineteen when they married and set off from England for the other side of the world. But they were fortunate. They travelled extensively – which was rare indeed for new immigrants to New Zealand. Their short time in Melbourne was followed by two trips back to England and Europe. There are photographs of them in Ireland at the Gap of Dunloe, Killarney in 1908. On their second visit in 1912 a photograph shows them in St Mark's Square, Venice .

They also visited the Niagara Falls in North America. India was a port of call en route.

As much as the name "Barrells of Durham Street" was attached to the family due to their huge corner home there, so too was their strong support of and active participation in the Durham Street Methodist Church. George made substantial donations to the church and was a long time officer of it. On many occasions he represented the church at the annual Methodist Conference.

George Barrell died on 1st January 1921 after seven months of cancer of the oesophagus and was buried in Linwood Cemetery, Christchurch. He was relatively young at sixty-six years old and by then had lived in New Zealand for forty-six years. His death certificate records his occupation as an undertaker and his last residence was 221 Durham Street, Christchurch.

Rae's father showed signs of an enterprising nature from the age of thirteen when he built himself a rowing boat and charged his friends for rides on the Avon River until he had saved enough money for a deposit on his first section of land. His father loaned him the balance and thus began a lifelong and successful interest in property. A keen footballer and swimmer, when he was fifteen years old in 1898, Charles won a silver teapot[1] for winning a swimming race from Lyttelton to Diamond Harbour. He went on to swim in many competitions representing Canterbury. He was an outdoor man and enjoyed cycling, fishing, shooting and tramping. However, Charles also loved English literature and he became well versed in the classics. His particular love was Shakespeare and he quoted the plays frequently. He was as active in Durham Street Methodist Church as his father had been, a steward and a lay preacher. His sermons and children's talks often related to nature.

It was through the Durham Street Methodist Church and their shared interests in Bible Class and the Shakespearean

[1] See photo end of previous chapter.

Society, that Charles met Rae's mother Hilda Fitzer, who was born in Dunedin in 1885, two years his junior. Hilda was the only daughter and had four brothers. She had a little sister for a while who died at the age of one. Hilda's maternal family was Roman Catholic, but Hilda turned to Methodism. Considering her Roman Catholic background her allegiance to Methodism became almost surprisingly staunch and devout.

Hilda, elocutionist and dramatist (not surprising that she joined the Shakespearean Society), and Charles Weston Barrell were married in Christchurch at the Durham Street Methodist Church on 19 December 1907. According to the *New Zealand Gazette* Hilda was made a Justice of the Peace on 30 July 1945 – quite a distinction for a woman in those days. (Distinction or not, Hilda was to die an unhappy woman only six months later). She was also President of the Women's Christian Temperance Union at local, district and national levels and worked tirelessly, and perhaps almost obsessively for the cause all her life. This goes a long way to explaining Rae's own unflinching stance on teetotalism which has continued without abate or compromise all her life also. When on occasions she felt the pressure from friends or indeed from family, to compromise her view on alcoholic drink, Rae reverted, and still does, to a deep, obdurate loyalty to her mother and her mother's work. "When I think of what my mother went through for this cause, I could never, will never, turn my back on her work." If there was one thing I was to learn about Rae as we spent our lives together, it was her astonishingly deep sense of loyalty to everyone she loved. Often her loyalty blocked all sense of rationality, and if reasoned argument meant compromising that loyalty, then it was quite simple: reasoned argument would be put aside and the subject would not be discussed any further. It was not only born of obstinacy but also of kindness. One of her most common sayings has been, "If you are ever in doubt as to what to do or to say, choose the kinder thing" – a saying which I assume she learned from her own mother. Having said all that, there was a characteristic stubbornness in the Barrells, never seen more acutely than between the twins themselves! When Boy and Girl disagreed, that was the end of the road – disagreement!

Rae's ancestors on her mother's side of the family included the Fitzer and Diamond families. Rae's great great grandfather was William Henry Fitzer who was born in Spitalfields in London's East End about 1814. In fact, although quite a popular practice to pass on the father's name, it can get pretty confusing a generation or so later. Rae's great great grandfather was William Henry Fitzer (c1814 London – 1876 London), so was her great grandfather (1837 London – 1886 Dunedin), so was her grandfather (c1861 London – 1923 Dunedin), so was her uncle (1893 Melbourne – 1959 Sydney) and so was her cousin William (Billy) Henry Fitzer (c1927 Australia – 2004 Australia)! In all, there were *five* successive generations of William Henry Fitzers.

William Henry (b c1814) was a cooper as was one of his younger sons, this time named, no doubt for a bit of variety, Henry William as the first son had already taken William Henry! A cooper, who often worked for distillers, made or repaired vessels constructed of wooden staves or hoops, such as barrels, casks and tubs. According to the 1861 census, at the age of forty-six William Henry (b c1814) was living at 24 Foster Street, Bethnal Green, with his second wife, a second Sarah[1] and his second family. These children were Rae's half great great uncles and aunts.

The Fitzers for several generations lived in and around the London Spitalfields area including Bethnal Green, and in particular in Foster, Collingwood and Little Collingwood Streets. None of these streets remain today except for Collingwood Street where the original houses have been demolished and replaced with a large housing estate. The estate is huge and neighbouring streets (including Foster) were wiped out completely. The only way to find where these ancestors lived was to consult an old Victorian map of London's Bethnal Green which showed what the area looked like before streets were swallowed up by

---

1 Sarah Susanah Paul, dates of birth and death never verified, but married William Henry Fitzer 9th October 1842

developments in the 20th century. The sole remaining "Collingwood Street" sign is a lonely epitaph to the Fitzer families who lived in it and nearby.

William Henry Fitzer married three times. His first wife was a young seventeen year old girl, Sarah Flack[1]. They married in St Leonard's Church, Shoreditch, London. This church was probably founded in the 12th century and it is still going strong today. Its bells are famously commemorated in the rhyme *Oranges and Lemons* with the line: *When I grow rich, say the bells of Shoreditch.* Sarah, Rae's great great grandmother died tragically young. She had three children one after the other, and then she died at the age of only twenty-one. The death certificate records cause of death as "phthisis" – Greek for consumption (tuberculosis / TB).

William Henry's second wife was another Sarah, Sarah Susannah Paul, whom he married in 1842, six years after he married his first wife, at St Matthew's Parish Church, St Matthew's Row, Bethnal Green, . Although William Henry lived only until the age of sixty-two he outlived his second wife also, and married for a third time when he was fifty-eight. He married Eliza Ann Furlong[2] (nee Gooch) in 1872 at St John's Church, Bethnal Green, . Eliza was forty-six years old and William Henry died just four years later.

It must have been Sarah, his first wife, who either influenced or persuaded William to be baptised, because he was baptised a year after he was first married, on the 28 June 1837. In the long list of baptism records found amongst the ancestors on both sides of the family, this is perhaps one of the latest baptisms recorded. Most of course were baptised as infants.

William Henry's first Sarah's first born was Rae's great grandfather, another William Henry Fitzer[3]. He was born in Stepney in London's East End in 1837 and became a sea captain.

---

[1] Sarah Flack c1819 (London) – 1840 (London)

[2] Eliza Ann Furlong (nee Gooch) b c1826 (London) – d ?

[3] Captain William Henry Fitzer 1837 (London) - 1886 (Dunedin)

Rae's great grandmother Johanna Fitzer[1] (nee Streeter) was born in Brighton in 1838. Her other great grandfather, Henry James Diamond[2], was born, also in 1837, in County Derry, Northern Ireland. Surprisingly in light of the great Methodist household Rae was born into, many of the Diamonds were staunch Roman Catholics, with even two Diamond members of the extended family being nuns. In 1864 Rae's maternal great grandmother, Anna Maria Diamond (nee McDonnell)[3] , married Henry James Diamond in St Joseph's Roman Catholic Church in Dunedin, the first Roman Catholic church in Otago. Their first born, Mary Catherine Diamond, Rae's grandmother, was born in Dunedin in 1865. Many of the Fitzer and Diamond families settled or were born or buried in Dunedin, although the Diamonds were also strongly connected with Melbourne and Perth in Australia. Rae's grandmother, Mary Catherine (Kate) Diamond (m Fitzer)[4] , "Nan Fitzer", went to live in St Kilda Road, Melbourne and in 1916 died there a young but frail lady at the age of only fifty-one. Rae was not quite eight years old when she died. Extraordinarily, Mary Catherine died just three weeks after her mother Anna Maria Diamond (nee McDonnell) died – also in Melbourne although mother and daughter are buried in different cemeteries.

Mary Diamond's brother, Rae's great uncle Charles Diamond[5] was also born in Dunedin but married Lillian Fothergill of Ballarat, Victoria, Australia and settled in Australia. They moved to live in Mt Lawley, Perth, where Charles became Manager of the Commercial Bank of Australia[6]. They had seven children, all of whom were Roman Catholics. Remembering how Rae had been brought up with a strong and ill disguised anti-Roman Catholic prejudice, it is almost hard to credit that Rae had

---

1 Johanna Streeter c1838 (Brighton) - 1924 (Dunedin)

2 Henry James Diamond 1837 (Londonderry Northern Ireland) - 1868 (Dunedin)

3 Anna Maria McDonnell (m Diamond) c1837 (Ireland) - 1916 (Melbourne)

4 Mary Catherine (Kate) Diamond (m Fitzer) 1865 (Dunedin) - 1916 (Melbourne)

5 Charles Diamond 1868 (Dunedin) - 1954 (Perth)

6 The Commercial Bank of Australia ("CBA"), founded in Melbourne 1866, became Westpac Banking Corporation when it merged with the Bank of New South Wales in 1982.

so many Roman Catholic relatives. Charles Diamond died in Perth in August 1954 and his wife Lillian died only six weeks after him.

For some years Rae's great grandfather William Henry Fitzer was Chief Officer on the steam ship *Wellington*[1]. The ship was built in 1863 by Blackwood & Gordon in Glasgow, for the New Zealand Steam Navigation Company Limited of Wellington (which is probably the reason for its name). In 1871 she was sold to the New Zealand Steam Shipping Company of Wellington, running between Wellington, Port Chalmers (Dunedin – where Capt. William Henry Fitzer lived) and Onehunga. In 1876 she was taken over by the Union Steam Ship Co of New Zealand and then had a few more owners before finally being converted to a hulk. In 1913 she was sunk as a breakwater at Moehau, Coromandel. Although the records show it was sunk here, Moehau itself (other than Mount Moehau) has not been found on a map of the Coromandel. Further research revealed that the hulk of the *SS Wellington* was sunk as a breakwater at Paritiu, about forty five kilometres north of Coromandel, by the granite wharf and quarry[2]. Until a couple of years ago (c2004) her boiler was visible all the time but it has now sunk and can only be seen on a very low tide. There are other assorted pieces of pipe and metal still lying around both on and off shore. Perhaps one day a Fitzer descendant will want to go exploring and diving there to seek the remains of their ancestor's ship.

When William Fitzer handwrote his will on July 30th 1878 he was Chief Officer "on board the Steam Ship *Wellington*" and he also refers to himself as "of Wellington". This presumably means the home port of the ship he was on at the time as no evidence has been found that suggests he ever lived in Wellington. He died in Dunedin eight years later in 1886 at the age of forty-nine. Evidence as provided on the death certificates

---

1 There was also a "SS" Wellington, a sailing ship, built 1874, which brought immigrants to NZ. For the avoidance of doubt, W H Fitzer was Chief Officer on the *steam* ship Wellington.

2 Frustratingly though Paritiu also was not found on a map!

of both William and his wife Johanna, indicates that 1878 was the year that they formally settled in New Zealand and William's will made in July of that year would appear to endorse that.

Interestingly, William Henry Fitzer's death certificate records his occupation as a warehouseman. He must have retired from the sea – maybe due to ill health. Or the record is simply incorrect.

Funeral Notice for William H Fitzer:

Those who are desirous of attending the funeral of the late Captain W H Fitzer will kindly take notice that the Cortege will leave his late residence, Forbury Road[1], Caversham (near the Baptist Church) tomorrow Thursday 21 January 1886 at 2.30 o'clock for place of interment at the Southern Cemetery.

Transcript of the last Will and Testament of William Henry Fitzer, written in his own hand, July 30th 1878 (see following page):

This is the last Will and Testament of me William Henry Fitzer of Wellington in the Colony of New Zealand, Chief Officer on board the Steam Ship Wellington. I give, divide and bequeath all my [?] real and personal estate whatsoever and wheresoever situate unto my wife, Johanna Fitzer, absolutely and I appoint my said wife sole executor of this my will. In witness whereof I the said William Henry Fitzer have hereunto set my hand this 30th day of July one thousand eight hundred and seventy-eight.
(signed) William Henry Fitzer
Signed by the Testator as and for his last Will and Testament in the presence of us who in his presence at his request and in the presence of each other have here unto subscribed our names as witnesses.
(signed) ?? (signed) Thomas McGee

[1] 26 (now 35) Surrey Street, Caversham. There were two Forbury Roads at one time and this one was renamed Surrey Street in 1916.

The last will of William Henry Fitzer, Rae's great grandfather, written on board his ship, the steam ship Wellington, signed 30 July 1878. He was born in London and died in Dunedin in 1886 at the age of 49.

[See transcript on previous page.]

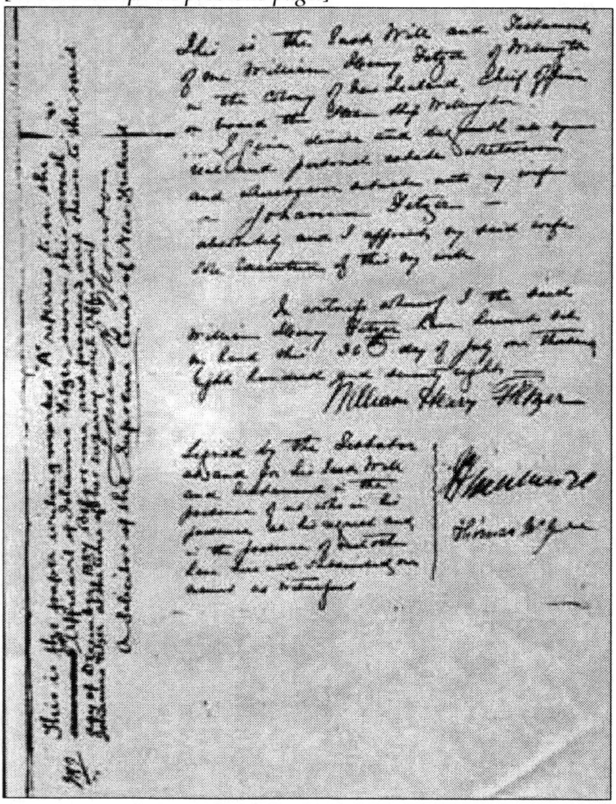

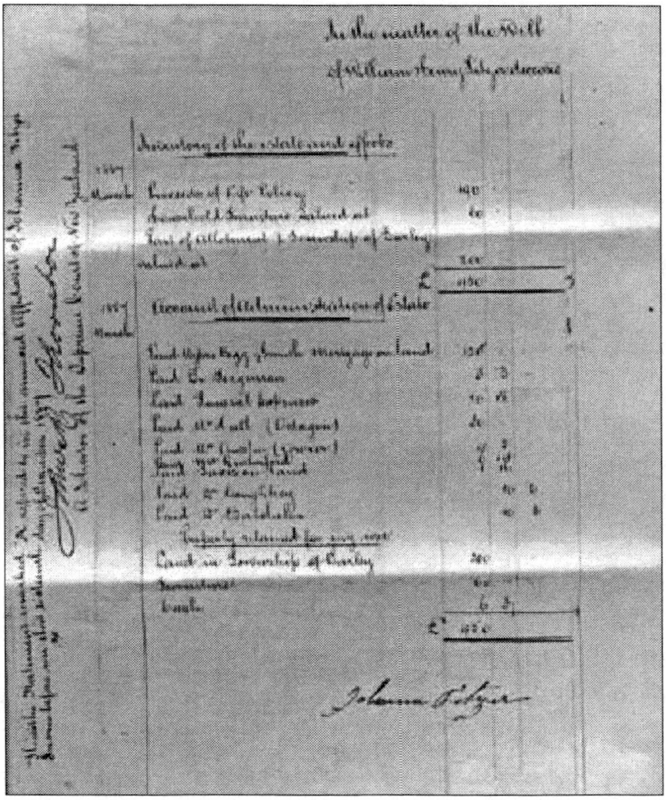
In the matter of the Will
of William Henry Fitzer deceased

Inventory of the estate and effects

Johanna Fitzer

The estate of Rae's great grandfather, Capt. William Henry Fitzer, who died in 1886, was valued at £450. It refers to his property in Darley (an area in Caversham, Dunedin, a name that has since vanished). This property is probably what is today 35 Surrey Street. The valuation has been signed by his widow, Johanna.

It is in the Diamond family history that there appears to be the catalyst for Rae's own mother to convert so passionately to Methodism and to teetotalism. Rae's maternal great grandmother, Annie Diamond[1] (Anna Maria nee McDonnell) married Henry James Diamond in 1864 when she was eighteen years old. She became a widow and a mother of three at the age

[1] The spelling of Anne Diamond's name varies from one official record to the other, let alone the varieties of how she was popularly known. She is recorded as Anna, Annie, Anne and Ann – and that is before the second name is considered which is also sometimes listed as the first name not the second – Maria and Mary. So the combinations seem endless!

of just twenty-two when Henry died four years later at the age of thirty-one on Christmas Day 1868. In 1866 Henry is understood to have been a hotel keeper. After he died Annie continued to work in and eventually run and own hotels and pubs in Dunedin.

Mrs Ann Diamond was listed as licensee of the Globe Hotel in Princes Street South (closed down 1903) from 1872 – 1876 and from 1881 – 1884. It was while she was at The Globe that she was convicted not once, but twice of "sly grogging"[1]. The fact that licensee records fail to show her name between 1876 and 1881 may well suggest that these were the years of her conviction of sly grogging.

Having apparently got her licence back in 1881, Annie was still heading for trouble. On the 22nd September 1884 she was declared bankrupt with net debts of £302 6s 0d. The official list of her liabilities are interesting to read. They include W. Lane & Co., and Thomson & Co which were both soft drink manufacturers, and Brown, Ewing & Co, a haberdashery and clothing store.

Her second pub, but third period as a publican was the Clarendon Hotel Maclaggan Street, from 1884 to 1888. Shortly after Annie became proprietor of it her daughter, Rae's grandmother, Mary Catherine Diamond, married William Henry Fitzer there in 1884. Maclaggan Street today is popularly known to be in a rather "less than savoury" area in Dunedin with several brothels in or near that street. Whether or not it had a similar reputation in the 1880s is unknown. What is known is that Annie Diamond was never far from financial ruin, pubs, alcohol or, for that matter, alcoholism. With both Annie, Hilda's grandmother, being a heavy drinker and her first son, Hilda's uncle Henry (Harry) James, becoming an alcoholic, it seems that the Diamond family was no stranger to alcoholism. This makes Rae's mother Hilda's efforts and staunch conviction that teetotalism was "the only answer", all the more poignant.

---

1 Illegally sold alcoholic drink.

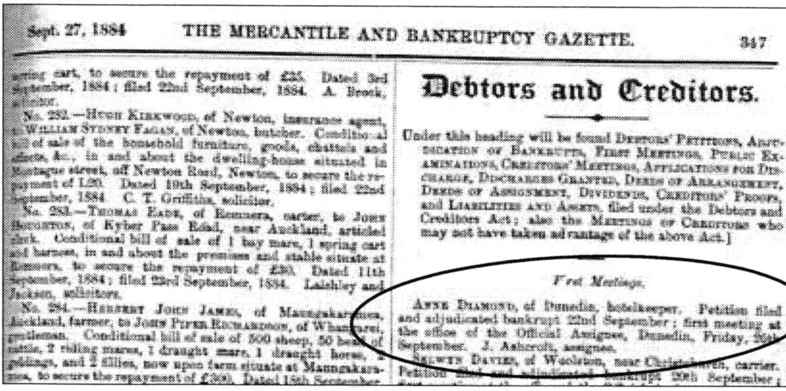

Sept. 27, 1884 THE MERCANTILE AND BANKRUPTCY GAZETTE. 347

spring cart, to secure the repayment of £25. Dated 3rd September, 1884; filed 22nd September, 1884. A. Brock, solicitor.

No. 282.—Hugh Kirkwood, of Newton, insurance agent, to William Sydney Fagan, of Newton, butcher. Conditional bill of sale of the household furniture, goods, chattels and effects, &c., in and about the dwelling-house situated in Montague street, off Newton Road, Newton, to secure the repayment of L20. Dated 19th September, 1884; filed 22nd September, 1884. C. T. Griffiths, solicitor.

No. 283.—Thomas Eade, of Remuera, carter, to John Boughton, of Kyber Pass Road, near Auckland, articled clerk. Conditional bill of sale of 1 bay mare, 1 spring cart and harness, in and about the premises and stable situate at Remuera, to secure the repayment of £20. Dated 11th September, 1884; filed 22nd September, 1884. Laishley and Jackson, solicitors.

No. 284.—Herbert John James, of Mangakaramea, Auckland, farmer, to John Piper Richardson, of Whangarei, gentleman. Conditional bill of sale of 500 sheep, 50 head of cattle, 2 riding mares, 1 draught mare, 1 draught horse, 2 geldings, and 2 fillies, now upon farm situate at Mangakaramea, to secure the repayment of £300. Dated 15th September ...

Debtors and Creditors.

[Under this heading will be found Debtors' Petitions, Adjudication of Bankrupts, First Meetings, Public Examinations, Creditors' Meetings, Applications for Discharge, Discharges Granted, Deeds of Arrangement, Deeds of Assignment, Dividends, Creditors' Proofs, and Liabilities and Assets, filed under the Debtors and Creditors Act; also the Meetings of Creditors who may not have taken advantage of the above Act.]

First Meetings.

Anne Diamond, of Dunedin, hotelkeeper. Petition filed and adjudicated bankrupt 22nd September; first meeting at the office of the Official Assignee, Dunedin, Friday, 26th September. J. Ashcroft, assignee.

Selwyn Davies, of Woolston, near Christchurch, carrier. Petition filed and adjudicated bankrupt 20th September; ...

The announcement of Anne Diamond's bankruptcy in 1884.

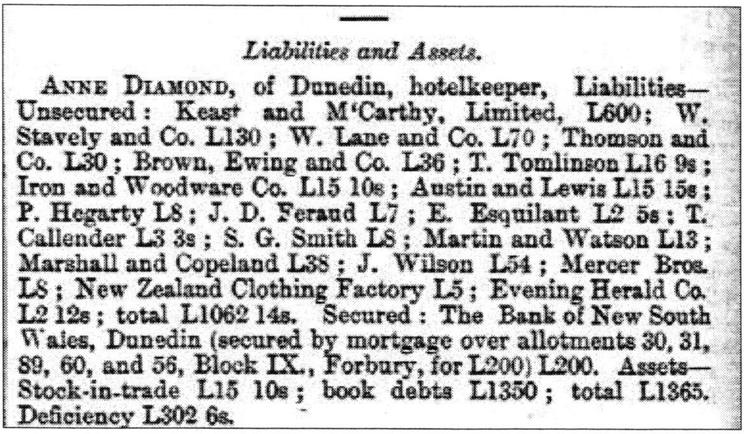

Liabilities and Assets.

Anne Diamond, of Dunedin, hotelkeeper, Liabilities—Unsecured: Keast and M'Carthy, Limited, L600; W. Stavely and Co. L130; W. Lane and Co. L70; Thomson and Co. L30; Brown, Ewing and Co. L36; T. Tomlinson L16 9s; Iron and Woodware Co. L15 10s; Austin and Lewis L15 15s; P. Hegarty L8; J. D. Feraud L7; E. Esquilant L2 5s; T. Callender L3 3s; S. G. Smith L8; Martin and Watson L13; Marshall and Copeland L38; J. Wilson L54; Mercer Bros. L8; New Zealand Clothing Factory L5; Evening Herald Co. L2 12s; total L1062 14s. Secured: The Bank of New South Wales, Dunedin (secured by mortgage over allotments 30, 31, 59, 60, and 56, Block IX., Forbury, for L200) L200. Assets—Stock-in-trade L15 10s; book debts L1350; total L1365. Deficiency L302 6s.

The list of Anne Diamond's assets and liabilities announced in The Gazette the same periodical as her bankruptcy in 1884, showed a net deficiency of £302 6s 0d. The "L" is how the £ sign was printed.

Despite the fact that there is a Clarendon Hotel in the same street in Dunedin today, the history of Annie Diamond's Clarendon is unclear. In the Stone's Dunedin Street directories for 1884 and 1885 the following entries appear.

1884 Diamond, A. Globe Hotel, Princes St.
1884 Clarendon Hotel. Proprietor W.Wishart
1885 Diamond, Anne. Clarendon Hotel, Maclaggan St.
1885 Clarendon Hotel. Proprietor A. Diamond

The name of Clarendon Hotel drops out of the directories in 1889 the year immediately after Annie was proprietor of it and the hotel seems to have vanished from all records. A hotel was built on the corner of Clark and Maclaggan Streets in 1902 and named The Shamrock (the successor to an original Shamrock built in 1862 further along Maclaggan on the corner of Rattray Street). Much later in 1936 the new Shamrock changed its name to the Clarendon – the Clarendon which still operates today. The reason for the change of name in 1936 is not known, but perhaps it is a reflection of the original hotel on that site, or at the very least, on the same street. Was the 1902 "new Shamrock" actually built on the site of Annie's original Clarendon? As yet, this has not been established.

At some point after 1888 Annie left Dunedin and New Zealand and went to Australia where she remained for the rest of her life. She went to live with or near her daughter Mary Catherine Fitzer. Annie was present at the births of her grandchildren, Vera Catherine Fitzer[1] in 1890 (who died just short of her second birthday) and William Henry Ross Fitzer (called Ross)[2][3] in 1893.

Rae's great grandmother Annie died in Fitzroy, Melbourne in 1916 at the age of sixty-nine and was buried in Coburg Cemetery: — . Rae's grandmother, Annie's daughter Mary Catherine, died just three weeks after her mother at the age of fifty-one. Mary Catherine (Kate) Fitzer is buried with her infant daughter Vera, in the Melbourne General Cemetery.

There are several stories of Diamonds in Melbourne and in Dunedin – even another Annie Diamond (who was also a hotelkeeper) and husband Patrick[4] – could he have been a cousin or brother of Annie's husband Henry? Despite research,

---

[1] Vera Catherine Fitzer 1890 (Melbourne) - 1892 (Melbourne)

[2] William Henry ROSS Fitzer 1893 (Melbourne) - 1959 (Sydney)

[3] Yet another William Henry Fitzer, fourth generation, albeit with the additional name this time of Ross!

[4] This Annie (nee Gleeson) and Patrick Diamond married in Melbourne in 1859, moved to Dunedin and then to Greymouth.

frustratingly in light of other similarities, no family connection has (yet?) been found.

As at January 1917, Rae's great uncle, her mother's uncle, Harry Diamond, was working for a John Robertson in Makauri but then he enlisted for the New Zealand Army on 6 February 1917 and embarked in Wellington on 26 April 1917 to fight in Western Europe. Private Henry James Diamond (46004 Canterbury Regiment) , a six foot tall, fair complexioned man with light brown hair and blue eyes, lost a leg in World War I. He was a wagon driver. He served overseas for 1 year 48 days and returned to New Zealand an invalid, disembarking at Devonport on 20 July 1918. He was formally discharged from the Army on 28 April 1920: "No longer physically fit for war service on account of wounds received in action." His official address on his discharge was given as Chalmers Military Hospital, Christchurch.

Either before or after his discharge[1], great uncle Harry spent some time in Rotorua at the Returned Servicemen's Hospital but at the invitation of his niece, Rae's mother, eagerly went to Christchurch to live in the Barrell home, under the watchful eye of Hilda. Harry was a "gentleman gambler" and heavy drinker and this incongruous member of the Barrell household, deeply at odds in his lifestyle (and a lapsed Roman Catholic) with the conservative and upright (and staunch Methodist) family in Riccarton, was nonetheless loved and cared for – typical, remarkably typical of the kind of woman Hilda Barrell was. He became for several years a part of the family and Rae and her twin lived daily with the arguments, the lies, the denials and at the same time love of their patient mother as she dealt with Harry's lack of money, his lack of control over drink and the hopelessness brought about by his passion for gambling. Harry was a perfect gentleman when he was sober. But when he went on the booze he would disappear. One day Rae's twin Charles, as he came out of Bible Class in Riccarton, found Harry

---

[1] Been unable to establish the sequence of these addresses.

in the gutter. His friends saw him first, "Charles isn't that your uncle?" Harry was bleeding and his clothes were torn. Charles went home and got his father to pick him up in his car. During these years, Hilda was working publicly against "the evils of drink". As she did this she cared lovingly for her own invalid, alcoholic uncle in her own home. Harry's health and mental stability suffered to the point that eventually he was admitted to Sunnyside Mental Hospital in Christchurch. Harry denied he was a Roman Catholic and would have nothing to do with priests until he asked for one when he was on his death bed. Hilda asked Father McGilligan to go and see him in Sunnyside "because Grandma Diamond would have wanted that". Harry never married and died on 8 May 1925[1], his will leaving everything to his niece Hilda[2] – a total of £204/16/7.

Rae was still sixteen when her "Uncle Harry" (in fact her great uncle) died of acute tuberculosis in Sunnyside Mental Hospital in Christchurch at the age of fifty-nine years. It is clear that not only did Rae's mother have a profound influence on Rae's own attitude to drink and gambling, so too, did Harry himself as she shared many of her younger years in the same household with him and had to confront the issues almost daily. The impact of the anguish and despair, his alcoholism, his gambling and his refusal to acknowledge any part of his Roman Catholic upbringing nor even show respect for this very Methodist home, registered sorely with Rae. For some time, Rae seemed to view Roman Catholicism as a church that actually promoted gambling and drinking and then showed little compassion for those who fell by the wayside. This, of course, is not correct, but in the adolescent mind of Rae it was a part of her own mother's conversion to Methodism that instilled an antipathy to that faith. In the meantime, Rae's ultra conservative

---

[1] This is according to his death certificate and his NZ Army and Probate records; but inexplicably his headstone in the Southern Cemetery in Dunedin is completely incorrect – showing his death as 8 Sep 1929.

[2] This Will dated 5 December 1923 with The Public Trust, contradicts the Probate record, which puzzlingly indicates he died intestate.

father looked at this man in his home with more tolerance than acceptance and sometimes with outright dismay. Somehow this man symbolised his "wife's family" and her background, and he was not endeared to it. It may go some way to explaining his harsh and insensitive remark, made in a moment of grief to May Pile (who married a Fitzer and had Fitzer children) at the time of his wife's death: "I am finished with the Fitzers now, thank goodness."[1]

---

1 May Pile (nee Scott), Hilda's sister-in-law, was first married to Hilda's brother Raymond Fitzer. See letter from May Pile – consult index.

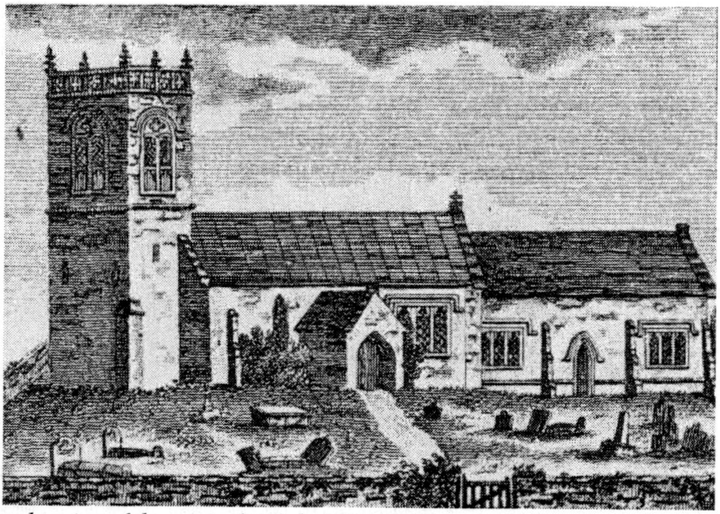

A line drawing of the original St John's Parish Church, Weston-super-Mare, which stood in the middle of a field. It was built in Norman times and demolished shortly after Rae's great grandfather Henry William Barrell was baptised there in 1822.

St John's Parish Church in Church Road Weston-super-Mare 1887. which, in 1824, replaced the old Norman parish church on the same site (above). The road was built two years later in 1826. Opposite is a row of terraced houses called Oriel Terrace built in 1847. The grounds of Glebe House are on the right. This is probably the same scene when Rae's great aunts were baptised in this church in 1860 and 1862.
Photo Francis Frith Collection Around Weston-super-Mare *by Sharon Poole*

St John's (the Parish Church of Weston-super-Mare) today, in Lower Church Road (formerly Church Road). Photo Kevin Taylor

Weston Bell, who was named after Weston-super-Mare through a family tradition started by George Barrell, stands outside St John's Parish Church where his great great aunts were baptised and where, on the same site, his great great grandfather Henry William Barrell was baptised. Photo Kathy Bell Sep 2004

Oriel Terrace today taken from in front of St John's Parish Church. The headstones of the church graveyard are in the foreground and the view looks across Lower Church Road to Oriel Terrace. On the building itself you can see a name plaque. The name has led to some confusion in researching the place of Henry William Barrell's baptism because it was believed that Oriel Terrace was a separate street. In fact St John's Parish Church "Oriel Terrace" is in Lower Church Road. It is possible that originally this road was popularly known as Oriel Terrace which led to some records showing St John's in this "terrace", but that was never an official street name. Photo Kathy Bell Sep 2004

William Henry Twiggs who was Lord Mayor of Bristol in 1918. (His birth name was Henry William but by the time he married he was calling himself William Henry. Photo courtesy Anthony Gregory

Lord Mayor William Henry Twiggs in 1918 with his family. Although the family members are unidentified, presumably one of these is his second wife, Rae's great aunt Emily Barrell, who William married in 1899. Photo courtesy Anthony Gregory

A cartoon from The Bristol Guardian *1st July 1916, depicting the second husband of Emily Barrell (c1847-1930) (Rae's great aunt), William H Twiggs, not long before he became Lord Mayor of Bristol.*
Image courtesy Amanda Gregory

St Mary's, Yatton Parish Church near Bristol. The church was known as "The Cathedral of the Moors". It is of Norman origin, possibly older, but the present building dates from the 1320s. A spire was added to the tower in the 1450s but the top half was taken off in 1595 and has never been replaced

Weston Bell stands in the grave yard of St Mary's Yatton Parish Church seeking the graves of his great great aunts who died as young children and were buried there in 1853 and 1854. In this church also, his great grandfather George Barrell was baptised in 1854[1]*. Photo Kathy Bell*

[1] Research not conclusive but this is an almost certain conclusion.

Yatton Railway Station c1900, where Rae's great grandfather, Henry William Barrell, worked as a railway porter/clerk from about 1854 after returning from Warley, Essex, where he served as a Corporal of Artillery in the East India Company.

Yatton Railway Station today. The footbridge is the same one that spanned the original broad gauge tracks – and the one that Rae's great grandfather would have undoubtedly walked across many times a day in his job at the station. (In the c1900 photo above it can just be made out at the far end of the platform.) The station may be a shadow of its former self, but in reality it has come full circle and once more resembles the station as designed by Brunel. It opened in 1841 as Clevedon Road with the name changing to Yatton in 1845.

No 5 (today no 6) Camden Terrace, Weston-super-Mare, where Rae's great grandparents Henry William and Louisa Barrell and five of their children, including her grandfather George Barrell, were living at the time of the 1871 census. This was just three years before George married Ophelia Sully and emigrated to New Zealand. William Brewer, George's older brother, also was living here. He married Ophelia's sister just after George married but died a few years later at the age of only 27. Photo Weston Bell

1 Southside, Weston-super-Mare as it is today. The home of Ophelia Sully until she married George Barrell in 1874 in the Bristol Road Baptist Church next door, the rear of which is seen here on the left. Photo Nicholas Hemens 2004

Part of the obscured headstone of Rae's great grandparents and her great aunt, Henry and Louisa Barrell's and Matilda Ann Barrell's grave in Weston-super-Mare cemetery. Photo Weston Bell 2004

In loving memory of Henry Barrell
who fell asleep in Jesus
10th September 1886 aged 64 years
Forever with the Lord.
Also of Louisa, Beloved wife of the above
who fell asleep in Jesus
3rd March 1897 aged 73 years
Parents dear are gone before us
Never shall their memory fade.
Loving thoughts will always linger
Round the spot where they are laid.

Matilda Ann Barrell, daughter of the above
Passed away March 30th 1924
Jesus said "Come unto Me"

The interior of Bristol Road Baptist Church, Weston-super-Mare, where Ophelia Sully married George Barrell in 1874, shortly before they left to emigrate to New Zealand.

Rae's grandparents George and Ophelia Barrell travelled the world at a time when those who settled in New Zealand rarely left its shores again. Seen here in St Mark's Square, Venice, 1913, when Ophelia was about 58 and George 59. Their granddaughter, Rae, was then 5 years old.

92 years later, Godfrey, George and Ophelia's great grandson, stands on the same spot where they stood in Venice. Nothing much has changed, except, perhaps, that the pigeons are not so fat! And Godfrey is not wearing a suit and hat as he should and, horrifyingly, in the crowd behind there are some women wearing trousers. Sept 2005. Photo: Nicholas Hemens

George Barrell and Ophelia (nee Sully)

George and Ophelia Barrell in June 1883 with their children George, Lucy, Eva, Kate and on Ophelia's knee, two month old Charles Weston Barrell, Rae's father.

Rae's grandmother, Ophelia Viola Barrell (nee Sully) 1855 (Weston-super-Mare) – 1946 (Christchurch)

Ophelia, 1937, aged 82 yrs

Barrell family, Christmas 1913 with George and Ophelia (having returned from Venice earlier that year), Hilda Barrell (kneeling by George) and the twins aged 5, Rae (standing between her grandparents) and Charles (on his grandfather's knee)

The Durham Street Methodist Church where Rae's parents married in 1907 is a Victorian Gothic building which opened on Christmas Day, 1864. It was the first stone church built on the Canterbury Plains, just 14 years after European settlement. The church was strongly supported by the Barrell family, both financially and spiritually. Rae's grandfather, father and twin brother were active officers in this church. George Barrell regularly represented it at the Annual Conference of the Methodist Church of New Zealand and her father Charles was a steward and lay preacher there. It was the venue for many Barrell family baptisms, marriages and funerals.

Durham Street Methodist Church and Sunday School c1900
Photo The History of Methodism in New Zealand, Rev William Morley pub 1900

The Trustees of Durham Street Methodist Church 1900
Rae's grandfather, George Barrell (46yo) is middle row, left. ,
Photo The History of Methodism in New Zealand, Rev William Morley pub 1900

Rae's parents, Charles Barrell and Hilda Fitzer married at Durham Street Methodist Church 19 December 1907. The groom sits and the bride stands! Charles's best man is his brother William and two of the bridesmaids sitting on the right are his sisters Eva and Kate.

Hilda and Charles Barrell with his siblings. Transcribed on back by Charles D Barrell (Rae's twin): "Uncle George, Aunt Kate, Uncle Arthur, Aunt Eva, Uncle Frank, Aunt Lily (Jane Lydia Fitzer), Mum, Dad, Annie."

Rae, 1933, aged 25 years

Rae's home, converted by her father himself from an old church, 130 Clarence Road, Riccarton Christchurch. Photo taken 1938. The family moved there from Peverel St/Clarence Rd corner in 1918 (when Rae was 10yo) and they did not move again. Rae's mother's funeral service was held in the house in 1946 and her father died there in 1965. The house was demolished in the late 1960s or early 1970s.

Rae's father, Charles Weston Barrell, date unknown, but probably about 1925 aged 42 years.

Charles Weston Barrell, 1963 aged 80 years. Visiting his daughter in Rangiora. (The only photo GB took of his grandfather. Godfrey later said he never once saw his grandfather Barrell out of a suit.)

Rae at "Phyllis's wedding 24 August 1940". Rae and Charles were engaged.

Rae, on left, on the boat returning from her holiday in Australia, 1939

Hilda with the new born twins, Hilda Rae (right) and Charles Durham who came to be known as "Boy" and "Girl". 1908

Barrell twins Rae (left) and Charles strapped in a seat c1909. This expression on Rae's face even as a babe, proved to be recognisable throughout her life (including the hands!).

Hilda and Charles Weston Barrell outside their home 130 Clarence Road, Riccarton, Christchurch

The twins with their mother, date unknown but probably about 1918. Twins aged about 10 years, Hilda about 33 years.

Boy and Girl, date unknown, but probably about 1924 (16 yo)

The twins with their parents at their first home, corner Peverel Street & Clarence Road, Riccarton, Christchurch. Rae lived there until she was 10. In 1918 they moved only a block or two further up to 130 Clarence Road.

Boy and Girl 1918 (10yo)

Boy and Girl at a Methodist Conference, Auckland, about 1958, aged about 50 years.

Boy and Girl – their last photo together, aged 81 years, Christchurch, Nov 1989

The sole surviving Fitzer family street (albeit with new housing estates) Collingwood Street, in Bethnal Green, east London. Other Fitzer family streets, such as Foster Street which was nearby, vanished altogether when the area was redeveloped mostly with council housing.

An image of the Fitzer family entry in the Bethnal Green 1861 census. The four lines show the entries for William Fitzer (Rae's great great grandfather), Sarah (his second wife), and children Lucy and Henry. William is shown as born in Spitalfields (London), Sarah in (St.)Georges East (London), and Lucy and Henry in Bethnal Green (London). William aged 46 and Henry aged 17, are both coopers. The first column (fourth line from the bottom) reads 24 Foster Street. Four more children are listed on the following page (not shown).

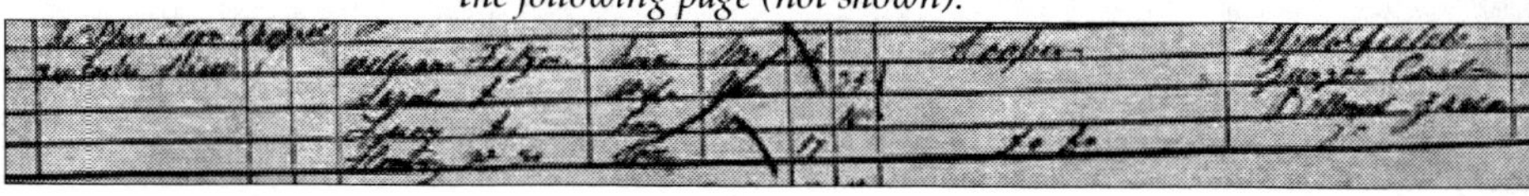

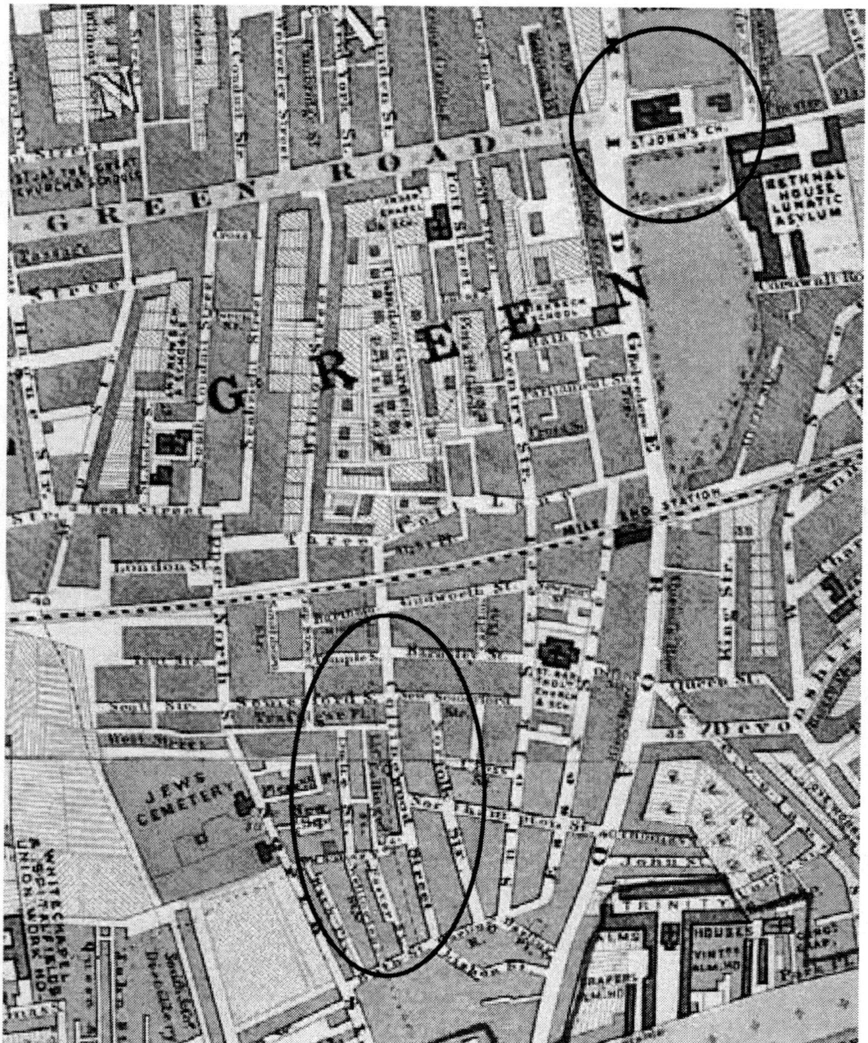

The map of Bethnal Green, London, as it was in 1862. St John's Church, where Rae's great great grandfather married his third wife is in top right (circled). Collingwood and Foster Streets where the Fitzers lived are in the lower middle of the map (both appear in the larger circle). Foster Street no longer exists today.

Reproduced with permission. Section from Edward Stanford's 6" to the mil. Library Map of London and its suburbs 1862 Sheets 7 & 1.

St Leonard's, Shoreditch, London, where Rae's great great grandparents, William Henry Fitzer (1814-1876) and his first wife, Sarah Flack, were married in 1836. She died just four years later after giving birth to three children. The church's bells are commemorated in the rhyme Oranges and Lemons: "When I grow rich, say the bells of Shoreditch".

After the death of his first wife, Rae's great great grandfather, William Henry Fitzer (1814-1876) married twice more. At the age of 28, he married Sarah Susannah Paul on 9 October 1842 in St Matthew's Parish Church, St Matthew's Row, Bethnal Green, London (above). Photo K Andersen 1999.
And in 1872 when he was 58 he married his third wife Eliza Ann Furlong (nee Gooch) in St John's, Bethnal Green, London (below). William died relatively young himself at the age of 62 but by then he had had three wives.

Kavanagh College, Dunedin, now stands on the site of the old St Joseph's Church where Rae's great grandmother married in 1864. The top of one of the towers of the present day St Joseph's Cathedral which was built lower down the hill, can just be seen and Dunedin harbour forms a backdrop. Although the 1863 landscape around the original St Joseph's appears rather grim on the next page, one can imagine that the uninterrupted view from here right across the harbour when the Diamonds married must have been magnificent.

St Joseph's Church built in 1862, the first Catholic church in Otago, was where Rae's great grandmother married in 1864.

St Joseph's Church, Dunedin, 1863.
The scene much as it would have been when Rae's great grandmother Anna Maria McDonnell married Henry James Diamond in 1864 in St Joseph's Church (St Joseph's "Brick Chapel" as it was known then). The church is indicated on the top of the hill and the site where St Joseph's Cathedral stands today is also marked. The brick chapel was the first Roman Catholic church in Otago and had only recently been completed when Anna and Henry were married there by Father PA Martin – the assistant to the first priest in the diocese, Father Moreau. The cathedral did not start to be built until 1878. The old St Joseph's Church was remodelled as a parish school building upon the opening of the Cathedral and was eventually demolished in the 1980s. Today Kavanagh College, a Roman Catholic secondary school, stands on the site. (See photo opposite.)
Acknowledgement: Marc Peyroux, St Joseph's Cathedral, Dunedin

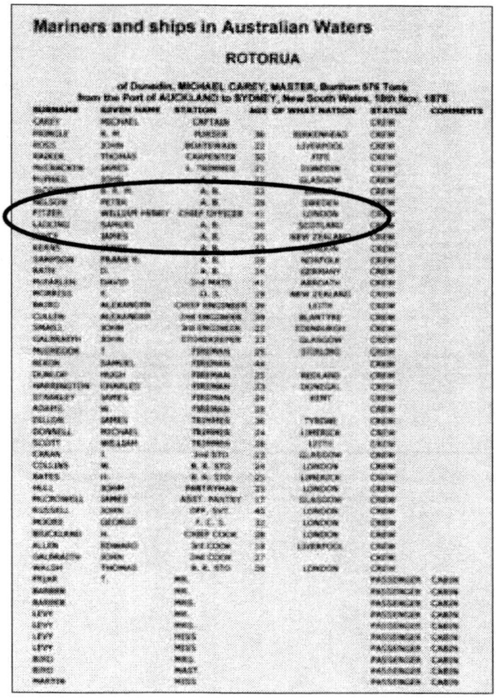

Mariners and ships in Australian Waters

ROTORUA

of Dunedin, MICHAEL CAREY, MASTER, Burthen 576 Tons
from the Port of AUCKLAND to SYDNEY, New South Wales, 18th Nov. 1878

SURNAME	GIVEN NAME	STATION	AGE	OF WHAT NATION	STATUS	COMMENTS

The Rotorua, *one of the ships Rae's great grandfather, William Henry Fitzer II (1837-1886), sailed on as Chief Officer. Pictured at Wellington, c1885. The (partial) Crew & Passenger List above shows him sailing from Auckland to Sydney 18th Nov 1878 just a few months after he made his will and apparently soon after he had settled in NZ with his wife. Note his age of 41 yrs and his birthplace as London. The* Rotorua *was built in 1876.*

Photo courtesy Museum of Wellington neg 4052.

The steam ship Wellington leaving Auckland Harbour about 1871. It was on this ship in 1878, that Rae's great grandfather, William Henry Fitzer II (1837-1886), Chief Officer, wrote his will. The ship ended its days in 1913, sunk as a breakwater at Moehau, Coromandel.

Painted by Thos. Robertson. The Hocken Library, University of Otago, Ref F H689[1]

Rae's grandfather, William Henry Fitzer III (c1861-1923) with three of his four sons, John, Tas (Tasman) and Bill (William Henry IV but with the additional name of Ross).

[1] A further image of the steam ship Wellington, an actual photograph, according to the archive records, is in the Auckland War Memorial Museum, ref W135. However, a recent search for it was unsuccessful.

Rae's great grandmother, Johanna Fitzer (nee Streeter) 1922, aged 84 years. Born in Brighton, England in 1838, she died in Dunedin in 1924.

Rae's grandmother at 43yo, with Boy and Girl, 1908. Mary Catherine (Kate) Fitzer (nee Diamond) was born in Dunedin in 1865 and died in 1916 in Melbourne at the young age of 51.

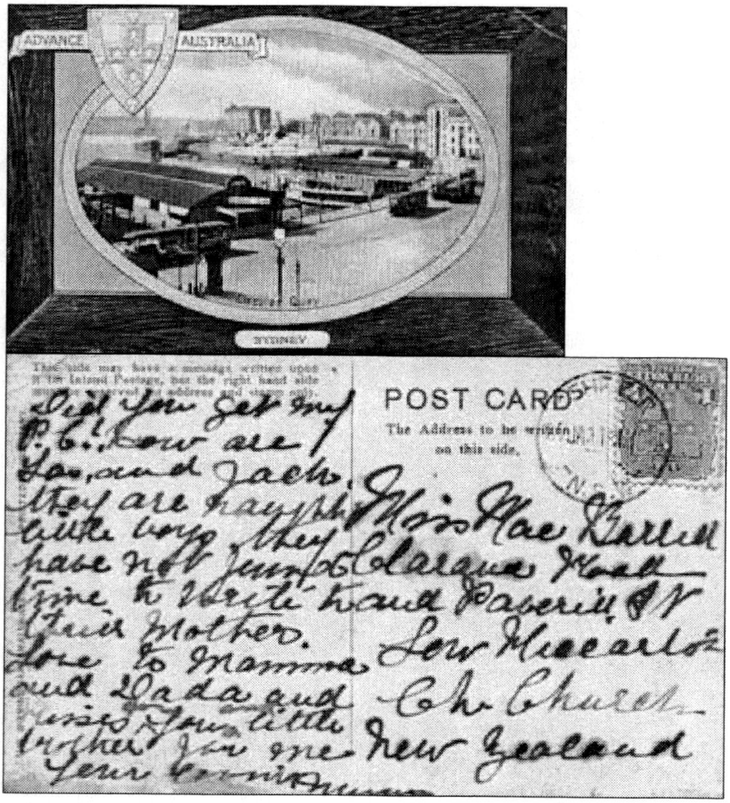

A postcard to 6 year old Rae from her grandmother Mary Catherine (Kate) Fitzer (nee Diamond). Posted in Sydney on January 27th 1914. Kate's two youngest sons (Jack then 12 years old and Tas 18 years old) must have gone to NZ for a holiday to stay with their sister and Kate's only daughter Hilda and family. Kate's youngest son Jack (later John Fitzroy) was only six years older than her granddaughter Rae. The card was written two years before Kate died in Melbourne at the age of 51.

The text reads:

Miss Rae Barrell, Clarence Road and Paverill [sic] St, Low Riccarton, ChChurch New Zealand. Did you get my P.C.? How are Tas and Jack, they are naughty little boys, they have not found time to write to their mother. Love to Mamma and Dada and kisses for you and little brother for me. Your loving Nana.

(It seems odd that she appears to have referred to Rae's twin as little brother – but who else could she mean?)

GLOBE HOTEL
Princes Street South, opposite the Market Reserve.
Licensees:

1872-1876	**Mrs Ann Diamond**
1877	**D. Harris**
1878-1880	**Alexander Owen**
1881-1884	**Mrs Ann Diamond**
1885-1892	**Joseph Reany**
1893	**John C. Bannatyne**
1894-1897	**Mary Bannatyne**
1899-1903	**James McKewen**

Closed June, 1903.

Globe Hotel, Princes Street South.

Rae's great grandmother Ann Diamond's first pub, The Globe, *Princes Street South, opposite the Market Reserve in Dunedin. Note in the listing of licensees (top) the break between 1876 and 1881 – probably the years when she had been convicted (twice) of sly grogging. She was declared bankrupt in 1884 when her listing disappears again.*
From Pubs Galore: History of Dunedin Hotels 1846-1984 *by Frank Tod.*

The Clarendon Hotel of today, 28 MacLaggan Street, Dunedin. Rae's great grandmother Anna (Annie) Maria Diamond (nee McDonnell) was proprietor of the original Clarendon in Maclaggan Street from 1884 to 1888 and her daughter, Mary Catherine (Kate), Rae's grandmother, married William Henry Fitzer there in 1884. The Clarendon photographed above was built in 1902 and until 1936 was known as The Shamrock. It has not been established if this "new Clarendon" was actually built on the same site as the old one, but it is possible. Photo Riley Bell 2005

The unmarked and undefined grave in Dunedin's Southern Cemetery of Rae's great grandfather Capt William Henry Fitzer. He died 19 January 1886 at the age of 49. It is not known whether a stone was ever erected or if it has since been destroyed or removed. Photo Riley Bell 2005

In the Southern Cemetery, Dunedin, on the left the tombstone of Henry James Diamond, Rae's great grandfather who died at the age of 31 on Christmas Day, 25 Dec 1868, just 4 years after he married and had had 3 children in that short time. On the right the headstone of his son Henry James, at the foot of his father's monument and at right angles to it, erected by the RSA. Photos Riley Bell 2005

HERE LIE THE REMAINS OF HENRY DIEMOND [sic]
WHO DEPARTED THIS LIFE 25TH DEC 1868 AGED 31 YEARS
NATIVE OF COUNTY DERRY, IRELAND
MAY HIS SOUL REST IN PEACE. AMEN.
THIS WAS ERECTED BY HIS WIFE ANNIA (sic) MARY
IN MEMORY OF HER BELOVED HUSBAND.

The stone leaves space below for a further inscription, undoubtedly intended for Anna Mary. However, she died in Melbourne in 1916 and is buried in the Coburg Cemetery there. Henry James, the first son of Henry and Anna and Rae's great uncle, lived in Rae's childhood home for many years and his presence there had a profound but sad impact on her. His headstone is very difficult to read and it also appears that the wrong month was inscribed. The correct date of his death is 8 May 1925. He died in Christchurch at the age of 58.

46004 PTE H J DIAMOND
CANTERBURY REGIMENT
DIED 8 / 9 /1925 [date incorrect]
NZEF

Chapter 13

MOVING TO THE SOUTH ISLAND

1941 - 1943

A Probationary Minister of Religion
First Appointment : Christchurch

John Wesley once said that the world was his parish, but we, his spiritual sons, were allocated only minute corners of it at the direction of the New Zealand Methodist Conference. Some corners of it looked greener than others in our eyes and we each hoped we would get the most green of them all. For me, a South Island corner had the biggest attraction because Rae lived in Christchurch.

The Conference announced the placements of its ministers by "readings of stationings". There was usually a first, second and third reading as adjustments were invariably made as time progressed before each placement was finalised and approved by all involved parties. On the first reading of stationing my name was put down for Taihape in the middle of the North Island. It was a big disappointment. Rae and I consoled ourselves that it was at least on the main trunk line which made it comparatively easy to travel when we wanted to visit each other. However, our delight knew no bounds when the final reading came out. This time my name was against "Richmond-Shirley", Richmond and Shirley being two separate suburbs of Christchurch itself, part of the Christchurch East Circuit consisting of four ministers covering eastern Christchurch. My appointment there was a pure coincidence. Although more senior ministers may be invited by Circuits to seek an appointment with them, younger ministers are at the entire disposal of Conference to place in any parish it may choose. There was not even any system in place where preferences could be expressed. Indeed, if any system operated at all, it was the exact opposite: a statement of preference by a young minister would have been viewed harshly.

Christchurch city's reputation was one of grace and culture which went back to its beginnings as a Church of England settlement of carefully selected immigrants. The stately cathedral in the Square stands witness to this heritage as do the well-established English trees and the charm of the River Avon which winds its way through the city's heart.

In my first year in Christchurch I boarded with a very kind elderly lady called, quite appropriately for the city, Mrs Grace, who looked after me like a son and this included giving me excellent meals. One evening, I recall, I was just finishing one such excellent dinner, when the phone rang. It was from friends, Mr and Mrs Clothier, asking me where I was. They had arranged the previous Sunday for me to come to dinner with them that night and they were waiting for me. I had completely forgotten but as I was so embarrassed I simply said I was on my way. I sat down and ate another full dinner without saying a word. I felt sick.

The two years at Richmond-Shirley were among the busiest I had experienced before or since, matched only, I would say, by my five years in another Richmond, this time in Nelson, an appointment which was still seven years away.

Both the Richmond and Shirley churches were fully operational with two services each and every Sunday, a Sunday School at each, Bible Classes, Boys Brigade, Girls Brigade, Men's Fellowship, weekly Fellowship studies, Ladies Guilds, Women's Missionary Auxiliaries and choirs. Apart from the minister being expected to look in on each group's normal activities regularly to show interest and give support, he was required to chair most of their formal meetings which were held weekly, monthly and/or annually.

April 1941: Charles visits Geraldine with Rae, attends psychology lectures, moves into lodgings and takes a spill on his bike; but also, as ever, wants to know more about the pigs, the milk, the farm, and gives advice to his youngest sister on how to fix the car engine.

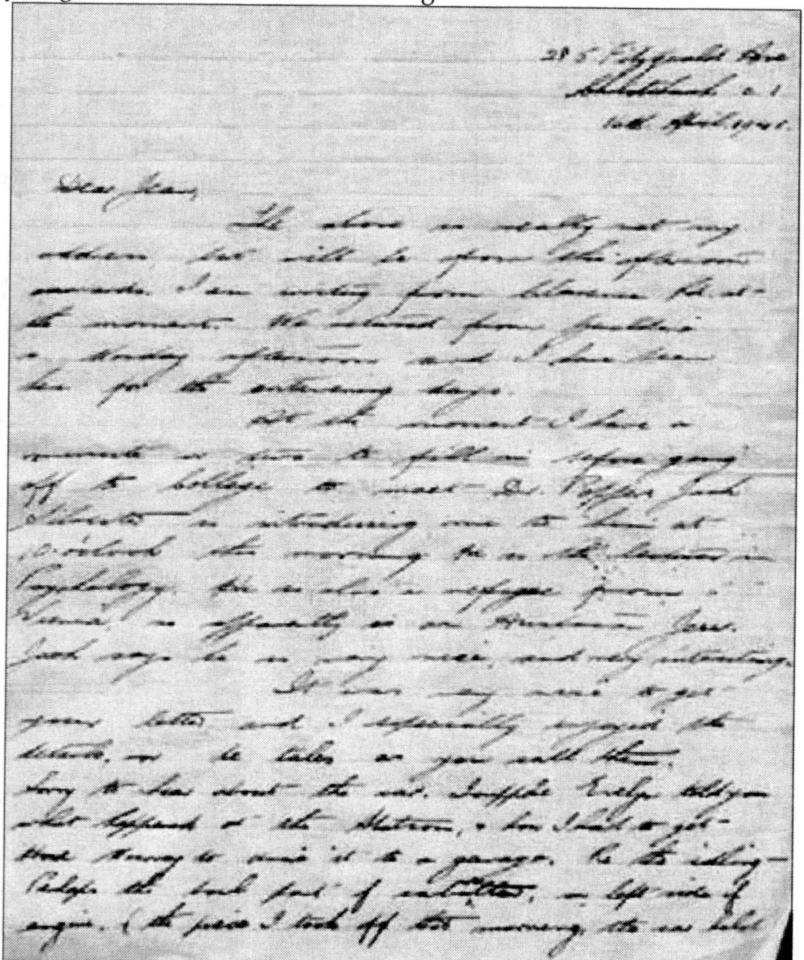

A letter from Charles to his youngest sister Jean, dated 16th April 1941. The image above illustrates his handwriting which didn't seem to change at all throughout his life and was typical of his style in the many hundreds of sermons he wrote by hand. Although there is nothing particularly significant in this letter, it was saved by Jean and now gives a snapshot of Charles's life in 1941. It was written on the day he was going to take up lodgings with Mrs Grace. A transcript of the complete letter follows.

285 Fitzgerald Ave
Christchurch c.1.
16th April 1941

Dear Jean

The above is really not my address, but will be from this afternoon onwards. I am writing from Clarence Rd at the moment. We returned from Geraldine on Monday afternoon and I have been here for the intervening days.

At the moment I have a minute or two to fill in before going off to College to meet Dr. Popper. Jack Silvester is introducing me to him at 10 o'clock this morning. He is the lecturer in Psychology. He is also a refugee from Vienna, so apparently is an Austrian Jew. Jack says he is very nice and very interesting.

It was very nice to get your letter and I especially enjoyed the details or the tales as you call them. Sorry to hear about the car. I suppose Evelyn told you what happened at the station and how I had to get Hood [?] Murray to drive it to a garage. Re the idling – perhaps the bowl part of the carburettor on left side of engine (the piece I took off that morning, the car held you and Dick up [?]) needs taking off and cleaning out. Again. It would pay to [?] the benzine pipe leading into the carburettor at the same place. I had it off once and it didn't go back too easily and it might just need an extra turn or it might be letting a drop of benzine out. What are they doing to the truck? Wouldn't spend more than necessary on it if I were you. By the way, there is a ring around the top of the bowl or carburettor, to keep it air tight, and it had a small break in it. That might be why the car is not idling. Better renew it anyway.

Have any of the pigs gone away yet? I'll be thinking of you in hot pursuit of the tawny[?] when the time comes. Don't forget that logging chain is to be returned to Reg Hosking. Was very interested in the letters from Betty and Shirley. They must be growing up fast when they can write letters even though they are directed by higher powers. Give them my love and also all the Jago's.

There might be a small demand for a speaker [?] at a mart but I'd put a 10/- reserve on it, at least. Perhaps 15/-. If it doesn't

sell at that, there's no hurry to get rid of it so it won't matter. Good idea to put a piece of the cord with it. It will help to sell it. Only just a short piece in. Won't get any more if you pack a long piece in. [??!]
Somewhere between here and the beginning I stopped and went to Varsity and was interviewed by some of the Professors. On the way out I had a spill on my byke [sic] but didn't do much damage. I had a very small suitcase and it caught between my knee and the handle bars and over I went. Took some skin off a knuckle and it looked a bit bloody. Hope I didn't shock the Professors and Doctors!!
Dr Popper is very nice and so are the others. Will start lectures on Friday most likely.
Saw Jack Silvester and he seems to be much the same.
We came back from Geraldine on Monday afternoon after a good holiday. The weather was somewhat inclement but it didn't worry us overmuch! On Sunday night we went to Jim McKeown's for tea. It's a great old place – typically a big farmer's place. A tremendous house, with many and large rooms. Outside were sheds galore, particularly granaries and stables. Before the last depression, at one time they had 10 to 18 men working full time on the place. Jack Scott has just bought a run of 5,000 acres up in the hills. To me it looks like the ranges around Mt. Egmont. Rises to 5,000 feet and already has some snow on it. Have to watch the weather before going to work on it because the clouds come down. He is running sheep on it.
Well folks the time is running out and I have to pack and go across to my new abode. Spent all yesterday shopping and getting my books over. They cost me £1-15-0 and I spent over £5 altogether and have still to get another [?]. Of course I'll be getting a refund on the books.
Goodbye for now. Kind regards to Dick – tell him that when the milk gets down to 50 gals he'll have to stop drinking it in his tea!!
All my love and also Rae's
Chas

On one occasion I dropped in on the Ladies Guild but my timing was not good. The 1940s were still the time of acute abashment between the sexes and there were subjects that women would be horrified to discuss in front of men: to do so would be viewed as the height of rudeness and indicative of poor upbringing. It was against such a social background that I listened to the President of the Ladies Guild talking of her recent trip to England and of the conditions prevailing there under the impact of war. As I sat down near the back of group she had come to the point where she was describing how people had to be evacuated from central London. A mother who had already started in labour, had had to have an injection to delay the birth until she could be evacuated to another hospital. But the President had not expected a male to be in the audience, let alone a single man to boot. To understand her embarrassment perhaps it is important to put her trial into context by remembering that at that time, fathers themselves were strictly banned from attending the birth of their own children (indeed the idea would have been repugnant to many women then). She was obviously ill at ease with the predicament but as she had committed herself to the tale she had to go on. This she did in a quite painful and protracted way, lurching and lilting around the tricky subject choosing her words so carefully that she stumbled and hesitated as she searched in vain for alternative ways of putting the same message across. "Ums" and "ahs" and "oh dear me's" and "well now's" punctuated every sentence and accompanied every flush of her cheeks. She reached the conclusion of her quite simple tale with much and obvious relief.

In addition to the two main churches in Richmond and Shirley was a small country church at Marshland. I was required to preach there at least once a month and to take a religious study lesson in the local school ("Bible-in-schools") once a week. There was also Bible-in-schools weekly at Richmond and Shirley Primary Schools and at Shirley Intermediate School. Of course there was all the normal pastoral work of visiting the homes of parishioners and hospitals, when parishioners or friends or relatives of parishioners were ill. Weddings and funerals were merely additional requirements, and delightful or as sad as each may have been, my week was usually crammed with meetings and duties filling each day from morning to ten at night. It was a seven day week. As a full time minister I realised there was no such thing as a weekend off, nor a Monday off (the nominated minister's day off by tradition – but which usually happened more by accident than by design), as people were still sick on that day too or in need of help in one way or other.

Students fresh from theological college were known as Probationary Ministers which meant we had to continue our studies for four years along with doing parish work. I studied theology and Greek and I found them an unwelcome extra burden, but I had little choice. They were mandatory if I sought to complete my training and to be ordained in four years time.

Being a university city (now the University of Canterbury but then still part of the University of New Zealand) I decided it was an opportunity to put my required studying time towards a Bachelor of Arts degree. Then part-time university students were required to take a minimum of two subjects (four papers) at a time. All this work wasn't helped by having only a bicycle for transport. Thankfully Christchurch was flat, but it also covered several kilometres. I had to cycle between churches, between parishioners' homes, between meetings, between hospitals, between schools and between university and home.

The World War raged on and the local authorities, in testing defence measures, periodically sounded an air raid siren. We all had to dash off and report at our allocated clearing stations. On the first occasion we just sat around. On the second occasion I took some study books with me for I could not afford to waste the time. The third and fourth time I decided not to go at all. Before the fifth time I got a ring from the organiser who wrapped me over the knuckles. "Irresponsible", he retorted disapprovingly, "for a man with your standing in the community, a minister, not to set an example of what we are trying to do for the community."

Although it had already begun to dawn on me in my Home Missionary days that a minister of religion is not an individual in his own right, now the reality was beginning to hit with a vengeance: a minister is A Figure in the Community. I had not quite prepared myself for a man of God being a man of the community. Quite unwittingly, I had voted to become a public figure. It was light years away from working alone with cows and sheep and crops in the paddocks on a farm. Despite the call to public duty in so many little ways which the life of a minister imposed on me, I remained shy all my life and would have avoided every speech or role of leadership had I had half the chance to do so.

Because of the war, the city authorities insisted that the churches blacked out all their windows for evening services. This we did at the Richmond Church but the Shirley congregation opted instead to have the evening service at four o'clock. This worked well except for me. I fell in for taking two evening services each Sunday one after the other whereas before I could physically only do one and the two parishes contented themselves with alternate evening services being taken by a lay preacher.

Letter extract from Charles to his mother, dated 15 Oct 1941, home address 285 Fitzgerald Avenue, Christchurch

> Dear Mother
> ....Rae has about 10 days annual leave still owing to her, and so she is going away for a trip to Geraldine, leaving here next Saturday. Christchurch will hardly seem the same without Rae here! It will be my first experience of it as such...
> ...They are talking of increasing my stipend by £20, which is very nice but will go nowhere if I have to rent a house. I should much sooner they gave me the Parsonage but it doesn't seem too likely...
> Love to all at Hawera and Stratford. Chas

Meanwhile, in this my first year, I was also trying to court my fiancée and even though Rae was wonderfully understanding, patient and supportive, I grew very tired. Above all else I wanted to marry. Although the Methodist Church then did not permit its probationary ministers to marry, in my tiredness I could think of nothing worse than remaining single. I longed for a proper home and I wanted Rae at the end of each busy day. As both she and I were older than the majority of students who may have wanted to marry during their probationary years, we put our case forward to the Conference asking for special leave to marry. Of course we had to wait for Conference to happen which was still months away – and so our engagement wore on regardless. At last, special leave to marry was granted.

We had been engaged almost two years when we married at the end of my first year as a probationary minister, on my thirtieth birthday, March 19th, 1942. It was a Thursday (convenient for the number of ministers involved and invited whose weekends were working days). Rae was thirty-three, and although she had holidayed in Melbourne, Australia (another manifestation of the yawning gap in our lifestyles) and spent a few months in Auckland, and travelled well in New Zealand on various short holidays, she was essentially still a girl from home. On that day, I took her off her father. I felt it. He felt it. Rae did too. Being the only daughter of a doting father, she was given away reluctantly. I was never allowed to forget that it was only from the kindness of my father-in-law's heart that he had bequeathed her to me!

We married in the Clarence Road (now Street) Methodist Church in Riccarton, Christchurch, Rae's local church, although her parents were more closely attached to the main Methodist Church in central Christchurch, usually simply known as "Durham Street". The Clarence Road church was small, that is compared with Durham Street, and as Rae's parents had planned a big wedding they were keen it should be conducted in Durham Street. Big wedding or not, unmoved by the size and stature of Durham Street, Rae insisted that she wanted to marry in her own church, and so it was. Her father had, however, helped established the Riccarton Methodist Church and, indeed, Rae herself had participated in the ceremony of the laying of the foundation stone for the new Sunday School building next to it, so it was still a very special church for both Rae and her father.

The church itself was established in 1908 (the year Rae was born) and it had grown rapidly. It was well supported by Rae's father financially and he was a named trustee on the title deeds of both the church and the parsonage at 15 Nelson Street. It is interesting to note that Clarence Street was financially strong at a time when the depression hit New Zealand generally. Yet in 1928 the new Clarence Street Sunday School Hall was opened and the whole thing had been paid off seven years later – no mean feat for small churches in those days.

It was a typical Christchurch nor'wester day: fine, hot, sunny blue skies, but with very strong, very warm winds blowing hard from across the Canterbury Plains. In every photograph Rae's veil is blowing wildly off or right across her face. The wedding was recorded on a cinefilm – one of the very latest and most "up to the minute" fads of the time. As often as not Rae is seen holding her hand to her head trying to hold her headgear in place, or with her head bowed as she walked into the wind. Despite, or maybe because of, Rae's large number of girlfriends, she chose family members for her three bridesmaids. One was my sister Evelyn, who at the time had a florist shop in the High Street in Hawera, and two were Rae's cousins, Doreen Barrell[1] and Valerie Barrell[2]. In good Methodist tradition, singing was loud and strong in the wedding ceremony, with three hymns: numbers 776 (*O Father, all creating*), 777 (*O perfect Love, all human thought transcending*) and 759 (*And now, O Father, mindful of the love*).

Evelyn did the flowers for the wedding. The colour theme was cream and scarlet with both Rae and all the bridesmaids wearing the same colour – cream. Rae wore her mother's

---

[1] Doreen Rosalie Barrell 1927-1947.

[2] Valerie Mary Barrell 1918 (NZ) - 1967 (Christchurch), dux of Geraldine Primary School, daughter of Arthur and Mary Barrell, married Graeme Mitchell (died), remarried David Vicars, died at age of 49 on 7 August 1967. She is buried in Waimarie Cemetery, Christchurch. Her headstone does not refer to either husband or to her married names.

wedding gown as well as the same necklace her mother wore on her wedding day[1]. The bridesmaids carried valotta lilies and Rae carried longiflorum lilies[2]. Evelyn, today, in recalling the wedding, says that she remembers particularly that Rae smiled all day long: "She never stopped smiling, you know what Rae is like."

Evelyn and my father were the only members of the family there. My mother was suffering from high blood pressure and was not well enough to attend. Gwen had four very young children. It was war time of course and during those years it was never easy to travel regardless of personal circumstances. The wedding breakfast was held at the Winter Gardens. I was nervous and gave a rather poor speech considering I was supposedly a confident sermoniser. My father on the other hand, although somewhat nervous amidst all this finery and money, spoke extremely well.

As I look back on it now, I *suppose* it was the nearest thing to a "society wedding" (New Zealand society that is) that one would expect to see in Christchurch. But at the time such an observation would have been meaningless to me. Admittedly, for me it was a rather grand and certainly overwhelming affair but in my heart, I was still from New Zealand Taranaki, not English Christchurch. Perhaps I was just naive. The Occasion was organised to the last detail. The Occasion had no expense spared. The Occasion directed me to do this, do that, be there, say this, wear that. In the end I let The Occasion take its course. I did what I was told to do. Throughout the weeks preceding The Occasion, the employed helpers seemed to treble and The House seemed to bulge with activity. My future mother-in-law organised her troops like an experienced commando and my

---

[1] Mum left this necklace to her granddaughter Hilary with the wish that she wore it too on her wedding day. Had this worked out, Hilary would have worn the same necklace her great grandmother wore on her wedding day. - GB

[2] Longiflorum lilies also known as Christmas or November lilies, and predominantly in the Northern hemisphere as Easter lilies.

future father-in-law signed the cheques without murmur: this, after all, was his one and only daughter.

No small part of this hive of activity leading up to the wedding, was, as anyone could well have guessed, the number of parties thrown for Rae. She was much feted being treated, as was the custom then, to many gift functions ("showers"). It seemed that each one of her endless list of friends wanted to give her a shower. She had her friends still loyal even from primary school days, her Public Trust friends (and they also gave a number of picnics in her honour), her church friends, friends she had met on the many and large Bible Class camps around the nation which Rae attended frequently (with Rae seeming to play a key organising or central role at each) and, finally, she had her sporting team friends. I cannot remember all the formal parties let alone the informal ones which seemed to go on ad infinitum. There were kitchen showers, dining room showers, washhouse showers, pantry showers, bathroom showers, showers, indeed, for every room of some imagined house. Going by the number of parties being held for it, this house must have been some rambling mansion in everyone's minds rather than a future humble Methodist parsonage.

Deciphered from Mum's 1942 Diary which was mostly written in shorthand, a list of some of the showers written at the back of her diary, and other diary entries, showed:

Hilda	24 Feb	Variety
Betty	26 Feb	Household
Gladys	27 Feb 8pm	Kitchen
Doreen	28 Feb 8pm	Preserves
Public Trust Junior Girls	2 March	Trousseau
Public Trust Senior Girls	3 March	Trousseau
Meryl	5 March 2.30	Wash house
Sadie	6 March 8pm	Pantry
Miss Cant	7 March 2.30	Bathroom & Medicine chest
Ida	7 March 9pm	Pantry

Shirley Bible Class	12 March	Party
Clarence Rd Bible Class	13 March	Trousseau
Lil & Maisie	14 March 10.30am	Afternoon
Lil W	14 March 2.30	Tins
Ola Roberts	16 March	Trousseau
Edgeware Rd Church	16 March	Gift presentation: carving set

I was slightly overwhelmed by and, if truth be known, slightly in awe of, the popularity of my wife to be. Being in the same city as my fiancée and being able to witness her lifestyle more closely than had been possible when I was in Auckland only served to endorse these feelings.

Rae's lifestyle was undoubtedly enviable to many. Her youthful years in the 1920s and 1930s, were the heyday for rich young ladies. She went to Wharenui Primary School, then to Christchurch Girls High School (and her twin to Christchurch Boys High School). After school she went to Gregg College where she learned her shorthand and secretarial skills – and had even more fun, mostly yet again as the centre of attention. She appeared to be captain of every sports team she entered (including her favourite sport of basketball) and was invariably leader of every church group she associated with.

She brought her confidence and wonderful sense of humour to the stage where she was quite simply "at home" as a character elocutionist. Acting was in the family on her mother's side. Her mother herself was an accomplished elocutionist and actress (as well as noted public speaker) and her mother's brother, Rae's Uncle John Fitzer who lived in Australia was also an actor and singer. He changed his name by deed poll to John Fitzroy as a more appropriate, he felt, stage name[1]. John also

[1] John (also called Jack) Fitzroy (Fitzer) 1902 (Melbourne) – 1991 (Brisbane), the last surviving member of Rae's mother's family. There is no grave or headstone as he left his body to the Medical School.

acted in New Zealand. At one time in his younger days he played a lead role in *Rose Marie*[1] in Christchurch.

Rae's style of elocution was very similar to that of the renowned British actress Joyce Grenfell who recorded many monologues, one of the favourites and most famous being her characterisation of a nursery school teacher which included the ominous line, *"George – don't do that"*[2]. In addition to secretarial college Rae studied elocution (following a similar programme to that of a modern day speech and drama course) culminating in 1935, when she was twenty-seven, with her passing her ATCL (Associate of Trinity College of London) examination. She recited often, holding the stage alone with confidence and ease to the delight – and prolonged applause – of many. Over these years Rae collected many hundreds of poems and monologues – all of which she has left to Godfrey, believing that if anyone would ever end up on the stage, he would[3].

With this background and interest in the English language and particularly in enunciation, all our children were subjected to correction in their speech, pronunciation, grammar, volume, tone, and advice on the selection of the best words: "Speak up, son, don't mumble." Enjoying acting as she did, later on she was happy to appear in several plays put on by the local parish for one reason or another. One I remember vividly and which she enjoyed particularly, was *World Without Men* put on in Matamata. She carried a small pet dog on stage (I think it was a poodle) and when the plot thickened to get rid of all males on earth, as the stage went dark all males in the world were dramatically removed – as planned. On the successful conclusion of the operation, the lights came on again only for Rae to find that not only had the men gone, but so, too, had her dog from her lap, which, sadly, was also a male. This, of course, had not been

---

[1] Based on the 1920s operetta of the same name, two films were made of Rose Marie as a musical – 1936 and 1954.

[2] Joyce Grenfell died in 1980.

[3] I now have these. All of them are dated – not that I have any intention of following Mum's footsteps! - GB

anticipated. Her anguished scream can still be remembered by the locals today, I am sure!

It was fun being Rae Barrell's friend and she attracted them like bees to a honey pot. Utterly spoiled by her father, there were more attractions than just her laughter. In the days when comparatively few families had cars, let alone young girls driving them, Rae was often allowed the use of her father's handsome automobile. Regularly, Rae would pile as many friends as she could cram in to the Essex[1] (little wonder she remembers it so well) and sail off around Christchurch with a giggling, heaving mass of noisy young ladies next to or behind her. On one occasion, with just such a manifest of passengers, she drove through Christchurch's Cathedral Square quite late at night for proper ladies. The noise and laughter emanating from the Essex as it went around Cathedral Square, not once, twice or even thrice, but more, might in this day and age have suggested the car load was drunk. But not at all. Rae herself had been brought up as a teetotaller and alcohol rarely – if ever – featured in her social circles. Suddenly, however, Rae was stopped by a traffic officer. As he opened the door, the officer was met by a car load of squealing girls – and had there been rules about overloading then, no doubt, would have faced their first charge for that. Rae sat behind the wheel, bright eyed. "Yes, officer. How can we help you? Are you in any trouble?" she asked mischievously, if not cheekily.

"Are you having fun Miss?" the officer enquired.

"We surely are, officer", replied the elegant 1930s Rae (money was no object for her father when it came to fashion either), "And we do hope you are too."

"I would have more fun, Miss, if you would turn your lights on. You have just gone round Cathedral Square four times with them off. May I suggest you turn them on before you go round again?"

---

[1] See photo of a similar Essex at end of Chapter 2

Totally un-deflated by this brush with the law, she hooted with laughter and told the officer that it was "A jolly good idea indeed!" She floated off with her girls still giggling madly and looking behind them through the oval rear window at the officer – and went around the Square again – with the lights on. It was, one might say, a thoroughly modern evening altogether!

All these friends and all these tales seemed to polarise the differences between this city "society" girl and me, whom I still considered to be the farmer boy from New Zealand's outbacks, minister or no minister. Politically, we were different too. Perhaps it was only to be expected that the Barrells were staunch Nationalists. My views were somewhat out of line with theirs. As it transpired, Rae was to become more sympathetic to the Labour cause, perhaps through the influence of my job, but I remember her warning me, "Politics must never be discussed with my father". I am sure she feared that she would be excommunicated were he ever to suspect that his beloved daughter just might not vote National. It transpired to be hard enough with Boy, her twin, who also all his life voted National and chastised Rae for even wavering in her political loyalties. Admittedly this was done in good humour (or dismay?), but nevertheless political views between the Bells and Barrells were poles apart and politics always remained a touchy subject.

Despite the differences I saw between us, we shared very similar values. Christianity, Methodism, views on alcohol, marriage, family cohesiveness, morals, education, work ethic. If anything, she was more inflexible in her values than I was. At times, in comparison with Rae, I was outright liberal. And as for her home and for socialising, it was always critically important to her that "the right thing be done". This attitude she learned entirely from her mother, the elegant, consummate hostess and home maker – at all costs.

As I look back now, it seems hard to credit that I was in quite such awe of both her and her home. Perhaps now as I am less impressionable, perhaps now as I am not quite so "fresh from the turnips", I may have viewed it all so differently. But then the perception *was* the reality – the social and financial gulf between us, through my eyes at least, seemed enormous. And across that gulf and through those eyes, Rae, was – and could be – nothing less than a film star. But, happily, that gulf between us, whether perceived or real, and as great as it appeared to me to be anyway, made no difference: I was madly in love with her, and spent half my time being thankful, and the other half being amazed, that she was in love with me.

My circle of friends included, predictably, ministers from Theological College: far fewer and, compared with Rae's circle of constantly laughing, constantly bubbling, constantly enthusiastic, constantly active, friends who seemed to move around the city of Christchurch together as a single pride of lionesses, much quieter! My minister friends were also my groomsmen and this contributed quite significantly to The Occasion's wedding party, for it was most unusual. Indeed, for many passers by on the wedding day, the sight must have been quite extraordinary: every man in the entire wedding party wore a white ministerial collar (the "dog collar"). To partner Rae's three bridesmaids I had my Best Man, Reverend Harold Brown[1] (who was living in Mt Eden, Auckland, at the time) and two groomsmen, Reverend Len Willing[2] and Reverend Henry Woolford. But that was not all: The Occasion truly *oozed* dog collars. My Superintendent Minister, Reverend James H Allen[3] and Rae's own Clarence Road minister, Reverend Archer O Harris[4], together conducted the wedding service. Rae's parents' minister from Durham Street, Reverend Ray Dudley[5], proposed one of the toasts as did another friend, Reverend Charles Hailwood[6]. And of course there were even more ministers among the guests.

---

[1] Usually signed himself as H Kilford Brown, as he did on Dad's Marriage Certificate. Interestingly, Dad also often signed himself C. Harrison Bell. - GB.

[2] Rev Len Willing, still living 2006

[3] Rev James H Allen 1891-1955

[4] Rev Archer O Harris 1885-1965

[5] Rev Raymond Dudley 1904-1963

[6] Rev Charles O Hailwood 1904-1991

Surrounded that day as I was by Rae's family and friends, by so many ministers, by Christchurch city itself, by cars, by cine cameras, by suits, by fine dresses, by flowers, by lavish food, by gifts, I could not have been physically further distanced from the farming community in Taranaki and my upbringing. But emotionally, I was not distanced at all. I was never distanced from my love for my family nor for farming and that was to follow me throughout my career.

Rae was surrounded with Charles's: her father, her one and only brother and her husband. She was one of only two children, twins (although many years later she was to have a half sister) and her twin brother and she were inseparable. Apparently, as a youngster she took great glee in announcing to one and all that she was, in fact, of course, very important as she was older than her brother. "By three minutes", she explained. Although she absolutely adored her "younger brother", after her mother had died years later and after our own family was complete, she occasionally mused that she had no mother, no sister and no daughter. I believe that she was genuinely sad about this. She was later, when her father remarried as a widower and had a child by his second wife, to have a half sister, Annette[1]. But Annette was so much younger than herself that the closeness she may have otherwise yearned with a sister could not be fulfilled. Of course, the very existence of Annette could not fail but to remind Rae of the tragic death of her mother. She longed to be close to Annette but found it hard to deal with her memories and pain. The situation was fraught with sadness which affected her father, his new wife and his new daughter. I think if Rae's mother had died in any other way everything would have been entirely different.

Perhaps Rae wondered if her daughters-in-law of the future (and even granddaughters?) would fill the gap. Maybe because of her isolation in her male dominated family at the time, as a young girl and young woman she appeared to compensate

---

1 Annette Weston Barrell

by having many girlfriends with whom she formed close and lasting relationships. Even in her final years, she remained in touch with all of them. As we moved from parish to parish, she made new friends easily and they too, still wrote to her in her old age.

On returning from our honeymoon, my laughing dancing brown-eyed new wife suddenly took seriously ill. She was prevented from being admitted to hospital only by the forceful viewpoint of her father who concluded that Rae would be much better off were she to come home (a reprieve for him?!). It was the first time I had seen Rae anything other than bubbling and I think I was shocked to discover that this angel was, after all, susceptible to human illnesses. My busy schedule continued to demand long hours every day – even with meetings in the evenings – and I could not give her the attention I so much wanted to. Therefore, it was with some relief that I acceded to my father-in-law's persistent suggestions that we both move in to live with them for as long as she remained ill – which transpired to be many weeks. It was certainly true that her parents could look after her much better than I, but their home was on the opposite side of Christchurch to my parish in Richmond and Shirley. I now had even longer bicycle journeys every day and the pressure continued to build.

Rae recovered to full health and our attention turned, at last, to setting up our first home. The normal practice was for a parish to supply a house for their minister, but as we had "broken the rules" by getting married during my probationary years, no house had been provided for us and we had to make our own arrangements. We found a place at 158 Edgeware Road[1], St Albans in Christchurch where a Mr and Mrs Dodge had just converted the upstairs of their house into a flat. The

---

[1] According to the address on a Life Insurance policy, a bonus notice was addressed to Rev CH Bell, 235 Fitzgerald Avenue, Christchurch. This was March 1944 and it was crossed out for redirection to Roxburgh. The same bonus notice dated March 1942 was addressed to 285 Fitzgerald Avenue. Therefore it appears Dad may have moved three times while in Christchurch, two addresses in Fitzgerald Avenue and one in Edgeware Road. Some confusion remains however.

approach to it was an outside flight of steps which my father-in-law regarded as a pretty poor show for his daughter. The engagement evenings in Rae's honour where gifts were lavished on her helped us enormously, and Rae with her sure knack for making any place into an attractive home put the gifts to good use here. We settled cosily and comfortably into our love nest and we stayed there from May 1942 until the following April when we were due to move to a new parish appointment.

The flat was some distance from our churches but the inevitable scroungers found their way to our door. I learned very quickly that one of the penalties of being a minister of religion in the local community is that you are expected to offer your home and your money to every waif and stray in the district. They sniff you out regardless of denomination. You are a minister. You are there representing love and charity. They need you. And you are supposed – and expected – to be nice to them and of course, as they see it, it is your job to be kind and generous.

One of our very first visitors of this type was unusually insistent. Rae was not used to such pestering and remembers this occasion vividly. He had come up the long flight of stairs and as Rae opened the door he was almost inside before she could speak. I was out at the time and she wasn't quite sure how to handle the situation. Excusing herself, she went through to the kitchen and out of the window threw not one but two tea towels in quick succession. Mrs Dodge's kitchen was directly beneath and luckily she saw them fall. As Rae had hoped, Mrs Dodge thought it was very strange and alarm bells began to ring. Much to Rae's relief Mrs Dodge paid a visit and between them managed to convince the visitor to leave but not without the women having to apply some physical force. The door was quickly slammed shut behind him. Over the years, Rae got used to this type of visitor, and handled them well – meaning assertively. Although she always treated them kindly they never ever got over the threshold again. Sometimes she could be quite sharp (sharper than me) and did not shy from offering rebukes. These were not always aimed just at waifs and strays.

Occasionally Rae would open the front door to be greeted by Mormons or Seventh Day Adventists or other "doorstep preachers". As they invariably launched into a well rehearsed line inviting her to consider Christ as her saviour, Rae would invariably launch into her own well rehearsed response. This was succinct: "You do realise, I suppose, that this is the Methodist Parsonage?" The abrupt question never received an answer as it was concluded with the swift, but well controlled, closing of the door – just a little short of a slam. This sort of thing annoyed Rae while somehow it didn't bother me at all.

Many of the church meetings would be held on the church premises but the preferred location was the parsonage itself when the minister's wife was expected to entertain, giving not only of her time and but also of her food. Usually food was served at crucial moments of boredom or tension when disagreements began to lead to some heated discussions. Rae was soon to discover that her new lifestyle as the parson's wife meant that her home was not to be considered her own, but rather the community's at large. She was being introduced to a lifestyle of interrupted meals and a home which offered precious little privacy. It was something akin to a community centre – not only the target of scroungers (by design) and doorstep preachers (by chance) but also to church groups (by expectation), and an endless stream of visitors and phone calls. Although Rae was not used to providing an open home to friends and strangers alike, morning, noon and night, she adapted to the role of supportive wife and on duty hostess, willingly and without a murmur of complaint (except for the Mormons et al, "Can you believe the cheek of it…?"). Despite the constant entertaining we had no staff or household assistance of any kind and this was an even bigger contrast to Rae's previous home and lifestyle: if there was ever a need for her mother's employed helpers, it was here, not there. Rae spent most of her day baking and cleaning in readiness for the inevitable door bell to ring. She always rose early, and eventually our later family was taught to rise early and make beds immediately, all because visitors may (and usually did) call early too. Unlike the privacy offered by her parents' home, Rae learned that the parsonage offered her none. For a girl who had come from a grand type of home by typical New Zealand standards of the time, and a family who had been lavishly attended to by domestic helpers, Rae was beginning to learn another side of life. I looked on anxiously, wondering how she would take to it. She took to it marvellously and my worries were ill founded.

My second year at Richmond-Shirley was a much happier one for me as I was married. I remained extremely busy but I felt better in myself and began to take the relentless schedule of meetings slightly more in my stride.

In one of my meetings at Shirley following a church service, one of the men was putting forth a point of view when another on the opposite side of the hall challenged him outright. An altercation ensued across the hall over the heads of the people. It proved to be my first challenge of calling a meeting to order in my capacity as Chairman. Being young and inexperienced in handling meetings, especially ones that got out of order, this moment was a memorable one. I rose to my feet and tried to tell them that they must address their remarks to the Chair but the first time I said that they were in such a rage with each other they either did not hear me or chose to appear not to hear me. I was desperately casting about in my mind as to what to do next while my congregation looked to their minister to regain control. The only thing I recall thinking after that was that this would not have happened on a farm. I could at least have rounded up sheep with a dog. So much more easily, so much more easily. I began to wonder exactly how much I was enjoying myself.

Anxious moments like that did not go away. In fact, they increased in those early years in the ministry. One came in a Shirley church evening service during the final hymn. Before the hymn had concluded, the organist suddenly stopped playing and turned around and glared down at the congregation. Of course as the organ halted suddenly so did the singing and the church fell abruptly into a tense silence. Everyone in the choir held their breath as they knew what was coming. The organist/choirmaster had taught them at choir practice that a particular rhythm in a well known hymn was always incorrectly sung. They were to sing it correctly at church this evening. But with the strength of the congregation voices dominating them, the choir, despite any efforts to the contrary it seemed, sang along with the popular but incorrect rhythm. The organist, who was always a blunt, outspoken man, interrupted the entire service most irreverently by bellowing out with a sharp edged tongue of anger and impatience: "It is not 1, 2,3. It is 1, 2 *AND* 3." The congregation and choir looked at him wide-eyed and there was not a sound in the whole church, which only a few moments earlier had been reverberating to the lofty singing of sincere voices turned to the heavens. I looked at him embarrassed and angry at the same time. The organist started playing again but the situation got worse when the music was greeted with a deathly hush. A few brave souls who dared to utter any sound at all, one by one began to offer some form of contribution. But as they did not want the organist to hear whether indeed they did get the rhythm right or wrong, they sang like strangled cats *eee*eeking out only a few thin, pathetic, sounds. For me and for the congregation, the service had been ruined and everyone left for home that evening feeling uncomfortable. The congregation had looked to me to do something about this unwelcome and inappropriate outburst. I did nothing. And as always in these awful moments, I wondered why I was a preacher man, or indeed if I had what it took to lead a diverse group of personalities, a diversity which, after all, was common to any parish. I had a hunch that Rae would have handled it better!

There was a sequel. Some of the Trustees had been unhappy with the organist's performances for quite a while and this incident proved to be the proverbial last straw. They informed me that they wanted a meeting and would be asking for his resignation. In fairness to him, I told the organist what was planned and he said he was grateful for being forewarned. I was content that he would offer his resignation voluntarily.

When the meeting came, he was roundly criticised by member after member. To my amazement he sat calmly and took it all in. He refused, however, to resign and afterwards said to me, "If it wasn't for you, I would have resigned." I could not believe it as I was the one who wanted his resignation perhaps more than the others. He had taken my warning as a friendly gesture to prepare him *not* to resign. I was not, I thought, making very many effective in-roads in managing people, congregations or organists. The same organist was still there when I left.

With the war raging on, anyone who expressed even the mildest sympathies for the pacifist argument was often treated with either overt or covert disrespect, if not outright contempt. In my Richmond (Christchurch) church I twice experienced such treatment. Not long before my arrival at the church, an elderly couple had had a son killed overseas. I did my best to be a kind, sympathetic and understanding pastor, visiting regularly and listening to their recital of the boyhood days of their adored son. Their grief was sad beyond words. I never ever passed on my personal view of the war and pacifism to this couple, but they learned from someone else that "perhaps Reverend Bell had pacifist sympathies". The couple immediately went to the church officials to complain. They were not prepared to be ministered by such a man and they were not prepared to listen to any explanation from me personally. Eventually, my Superintendent Minister, Reverend James Allen had to intervene. He assured them that Reverend Bell would not be removed and persuaded them (somehow) not to leave the church. My pastoral ties with them were re-established but rather tenuously. The tension remained.

In a second incident, at the beginning of a service, a choir member said to me, "My father-in-law will not be at church tonight because you do not pray for the soldiers, sailors and airmen." It was a difficult situation. The Methodist church, and I, did not laud war. The official view was that our faith and personal values did not support any patriotism that engendered, or could be seen to engender, belligerence in the peoples of this nation, or any nation. We were torn, deeply torn, that anyone should be at war at all and we rejected outright jingoistic supporters. I was not a pacifist, but I did have pacifist sympathies, and the pacifist movement was not insubstantial in the Methodist church in those days. In my own congregation there were parishioners who would leave the church if I supported the war ("Surely this is not consistent with our Christian beliefs?"). There were those who would leave if I did not support the war ("How can you expect to minister to us and not recognise the sacrifice we make for our country and for the world?"). From that point on, I decided to write out my prayers, choosing my words carefully. I did pray for the soldiers, sailors and airmen but I steered a middle ground. It appeared I achieved some mild success. No one left the church on the basis of omission or inclusion in my prayers and the father-in-law returned to the fold, seemingly satisfied.

But the whole issue remained, quite understandably, difficult, tense, sensitive and explosively divisive. In the parish, the minister was expected to walk the narrow line between the two arguments. Today, I view the cases of minority groups (racism, sexism and so on) with a great deal of compassion. I think it is a compassion born of experiencing the views of two entirely separate minority groups myself: one as a potential pacifist and the other as a lifelong committed teetotaller. I felt the crushing contempt of a majority view in the former case and the intolerant jeering of a majority view in the latter case. Perhaps there is even a third, that of Methodism itself, a minority denomination. Whether the minorities be moral, social, religious or political, people who belong to minority groups or support them with a passion do not have it easy. It is a character-forming, tough road. Almost strangely, I have found through my years in the ministry that people who have suffered judgements against them as a minority are more tolerant, more kind, more understanding and more supportive of a far greater and wider range of issues – and people – than those who have never been challenged to think through and support a passionate personal stand on anything at all.

Not all memories of Richmond-Shirley are of tense issues. One was of pure fear. The choirmaster of the Richmond (Christchurch) church lived on the Cashmere Hills. At the end of each year he entertained his choir in his home as a gesture of appreciation for their work. This year's choir party was held on an evening when I was at university but after my last lecture, tired as I was, as minister I was expected to put in an appearance. The Cashmere Hills were several kilometres from the university, but nevertheless I made it and turned up. After an enjoyable evening I set off for home, as usual on my bicycle. What I did not realise in the darkness was just how steep the Cashmere Hills road was even though I had pushed my bike up it earlier. I was riding a fixed wheel bike and in a matter of seconds it was travelling at a speed quite beyond my control and getting faster all the time in spite of back pedalling as hard as I could. In a moment or two I was considering whether I should throw myself off the bike or ride it out. The problem was that there was a crossroads at the foot of the hill and it would only require a car to be on it at the crucial moment and I would be thrown high into the air or go under its wheels. I was terrified. My guardian angel was on duty that night however. I shot through the intersection safely but at a speed that I reckon must have been defying the natural laws of a bicycle staying upright! I was moving so fast I thought that the speed could have taken me straight on into Christchurch's central Cathedral Square seven kilometres away, without any more pedalling. I thought I was safe but that night I dreamt about it and that was worse than the reality. In a dream one feels so powerless in the face of danger.

One week was exceptionally busy and Sunday arrived on me without a sermon prepared. I dipped into my box of old sermons, chose one hastily and preached it. After the service a church officer, Mr Huia Beaumont, said to me with an air of intrigue, "That was an altogether different sermon but on exactly the same Bible text as last week." Horror! A minister's gravest error! Throughout the sermon I had a vague feeling that there was something amiss but I told myself that it must be alright as the sermon I had selected came from a box of sermons I had preached in the North Island. I was therefore confident that there was no way I could be repeating the same sermon to the same congregation. I wasn't repeating the same sermon of course, but I did not think about checking that I was not repeating the same text. Despite feeling somewhat shame-faced, I was a little gratified that Mr Beaumont even noticed. No one else commented. Perhaps they didn't notice. And, if not, that was almost as bad I reflected. Not for the first time in my career, I wondered if I was wasting my time – did any one listen to sermons anyway?!

But some parishioners seemed to enjoy catching their minister out like that – in one way or another. In drawing up a list of subjects for study by a church group, I had put down "The Efficacy of Prayer" but it was printed as "The Efficiency of Prayer". One of the congregation's stalwarts and grand warriors got his teeth into this and wanted to know what I meant by the *efficiency* of prayer. I explained that it was a typing mistake but this did not satisfy him. He kept coming back at me about it accusing me of evading the question and implying I was unable to answer it. I am sure he was seeking a significant theological debate with his minister and he wanted it right now – in front of this audience. It is true that I was ill prepared for such a debate but the fact remained that this was not the intended topic and I stuck to my guns. But I felt challenged by him and uncomfortable. Throughout my ministry, I came to realise that every time I felt uncomfortable or felt that I responded inadequately to situations such as these, my mind quickly turned to the solace of farming – and to how much easier cows were to deal with! And every time in my private moments I asked myself again if I was really cut out for all this.

The time had come for us to move on. We were waiting for Conference's stationing list. The second reading had just come out and I was down to go to Cambridge – regarded as a rather attractive appointment. Standing in the group with me, as it was published, was a past President of Conference, a man who was prominent on the examination committee at the time I had been turned down in one of my earlier applications for the ministry itself. He must have been taken aback with this appointment for me while still only a probationary minister. With a certain degree of sarcasm, he commented, "Next appointment, Pitt Street, Charlie, no doubt." He was referring to Pitt Street Methodist Church in Auckland, a church looked upon as a top New Zealand appointment. He was probably satisfied that on the third reading, Charles Bell name was not next to either of these places, but Roxburgh in the deep south.

I greeted the end of my appointment in Christchurch with some relief as Roxburgh was a small, quiet town in Central Otago near the bottom of the South Island. I was sure it would be so much easier than my first two probationary years at Richmond-Shirley had proved to be. Many years later when I revisited a parishioner friend there, he recalled, "We really made things too tough for you, Charlie, didn't we?" I was surprised at the comment because I was not aware that I was handling anything other than average parish situations. Had they taken advantage of my youth or my inexperience or did they sense that I was really more of a country man than a townsman? Those two years were my very first in full time ministry. During them I got married, had had an ill wife for many weeks, had studied at university and had felt that I had cycled the breadth and length of Christchurch, down every street, a thousand times. Roxburgh, after Christchurch, I felt I could surely cycle around in half the time. I looked forward to the move south immensely, but I was aware that it would be Rae's first move away from her loved home town. She was also pregnant with our first child.

Rae and Charles's first home, 158 Edgeware Road, Christchurch May 1942 – March 1943

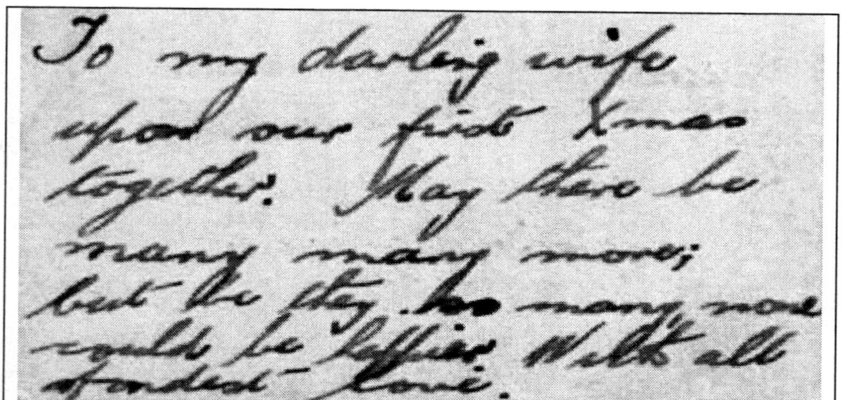

To my darling wife
upon our first Xmas
together. May there be
many many more;
but we stay. [illegible] many more
could be happier. With all
fondest love.

Christmas 1942: On the back of Dad's visiting card, with the Edgeware Road address – probably accompanying flowers – and carefully kept for 53 years by Mum, found after Mum died. - GB

Clarence Road (now Street) Methodist Church on the corner of Nelson & Clarence Streets, Riccarton, Christchurch, built in 1908. The very large windows at the front of the church, which show in Charles and Rae's wedding photos, were subsequently replaced with these smaller ones for structural reasons. These structural problems (the tile roof was too heavy for the walls) eventually led to the demise of the church, and it was demolished about 1977. It had lasted barely 70 years.

Rae, aged 19 in November 1927, participated in the ceremony of the laying of the foundation stone of the new Clarence Road Methodist Sunday School. Seen here with her uncle William ("Will") Barrell and ??. The stone was officially laid by J A Flesher, OBE, Vice President of the Methodist Conference in that year.

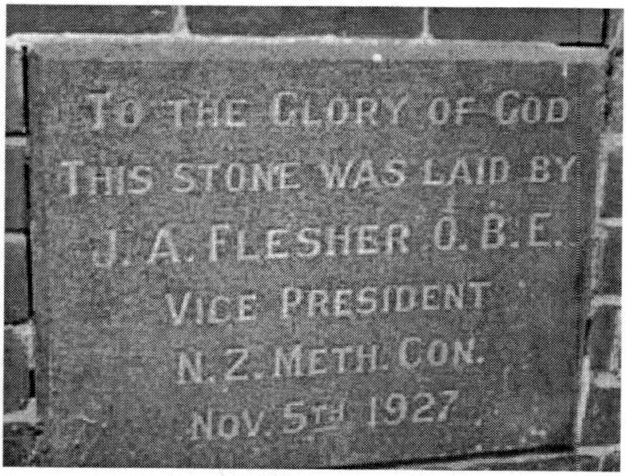

The foundation stone Rae helped to lay in 1927 for the Sunday School and which has now incorporated the new church. Photo Andrew Bell 2005

Lower Ricc Methodists forced to move

As the little church in Clarence St has been found to be unsound, services for Lower Riccarton Methodists are to be transferred to the Sunday school building adjoining.

The future of the church is in doubt and alterations are being made to the brick building to accommodate a chapel and social hall.

A group of long-standing members met at the home of Mrs Ida Vaughan, Straven Rd, to revive memories of the church's history, several having been present at the laying of the foundation stone by Mrs Joan Brown, of "Hatherton," Freyberg Ave (now the Rehabilitation League hostel).

The Rev Griffiths, Addington circuit superintendent, was the prime mover in forming a Methodist congregation.

Among the supernumeries and ministers who followed, the Rev W. T. Hooper held services in the open during the 1918 influenza epidemic, and was indefatiguable in visiting stricken people of all denominations, scrubbing their floors, and doing whatever he could to help.

A former president of the Methodist Church of New Zealand, the Rev J. D Grocott served the church for 15 years.

The present minister is the Rev Ian Clark.

Mrs Gertrude Dunn (nee Watson), of Brockworth Pl, was organist for five years prior to her marriage during World War 1.

A former church member and Sunday school superintendent, Mr T. W. Stephenson, a Christchurch butcher, lived in a large homestead with a long drive and ornamental lake on the present Shands Cres reserve, with his family of 17.

An early choirmaster, Mr Ernie James, of James's Shoe Store, Armagh St, was present with his three sisters at the laying of the foundation stone.

He lived in the brick house on the corner of Riccarton Rd and Deans Ave for many years, and died a few years ago well over 80 years of age.

Next Sunday at 2.30pm former members will have the opportunity to attend a special service and meet the present congregation.

Anyone needing transport should telephone Mr H. T. Francis, [illegible].

The local Riccarton newspaper forecasts the ultimate demise of the church building. Unfortunately the date this article appeared has not been established but it was probably mid to late 1970s.

The new Clarence Street Methodist Church as it is today (2005). The new church was the old Sunday School building (the foundation stone of which Rae helped lay in 1927) with an added extension. Photo Andrew Bell 2005

The pipe organ from the old church was kept. This is probably the organ played at Rae and Charles's wedding in 1942. Photo Andrew Bell 2005

Bridesmaids at Rae's home. L to R: Charles's sister Ev Bell, Rae's cousins Valerie Barrell and 15yo Doreen Barrell. (Doreen died 5 years later at 20 yo.)

A gaggle of Reverends! L to R: Henry Woodford, Charles, Len Willing, and Best Man Harold Brown

The hymn sheet for Charles & Rae's wedding, Thursday, 19 March 1942

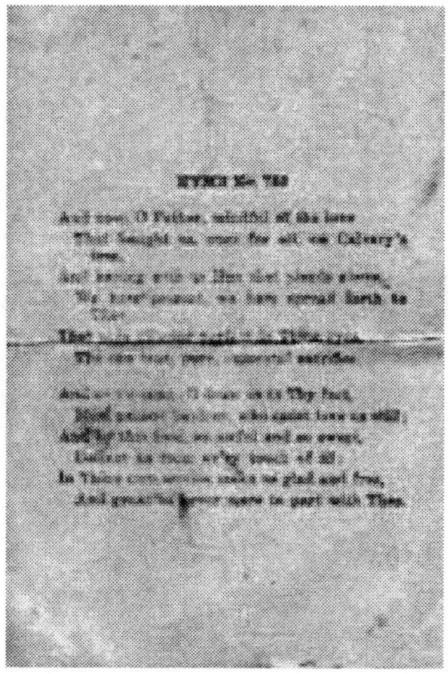

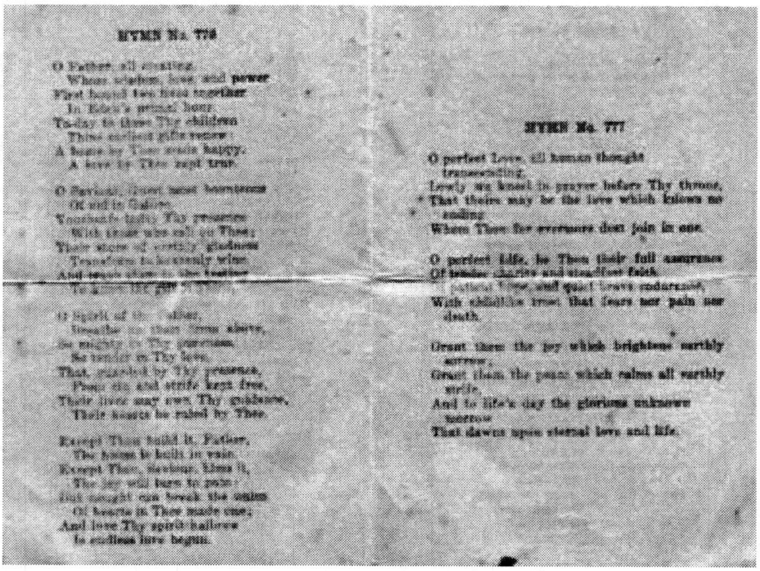

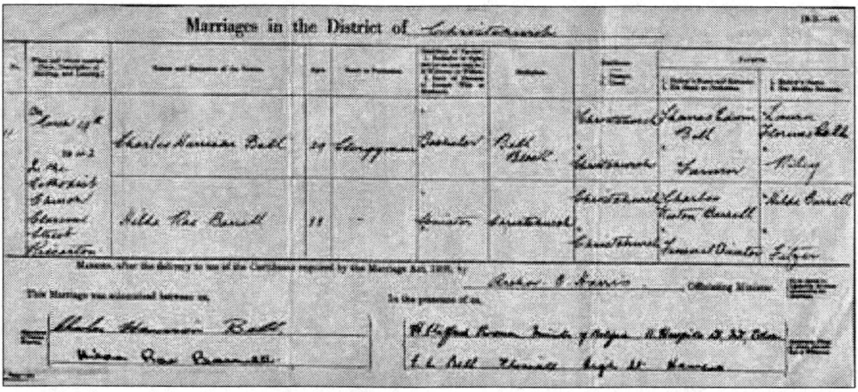
Marriages in the District of

Charles and Rae's marriage certificate, showing their signatures and those of the witnesses, friend Rev Harold Brown and sister Evelyn L Bell, then a florist in Hawera

Reverends Henry Woodford, Len Willing, Best Man Harold Brown, Charles, Rae, Charles's sister Evelyn, Rae's cousins Doreen Barrell, Valerie Barrell

Cutting the bottom layer of a 3 layer cake. The reception was held at the Winter Gardens (which no longer exists)

Rae with her parents Hilda and Charles at their home

Clarence Road (now Street) Methodist Church, Riccarton Christchurch, 19 March 1942. Although her father wanted Rae to marry in Durham Street Methodist Church, this was Rae's local church (in the same street as her home) and where she was highly involved. She herself participated in the ceremony of the laying of the foundation stone of the church's new Sunday School 15 years earlier.

More than 50 years later, Auntie Ev, Dad's sister and Mum's bridesmaid, in recounting the day to me, said, "Rae smiled all day long. She couldn't stop. You know what your mother was like." - GB

Chapter 14

IN THE FAR SOUTH

1943 - 1945

A Probationary Minister of Religion
Second Appointment : Roxburgh, Otago

Having completed two years of my probation ministry in a city, I was moved to do the remaining two in a country parish, although I believe the move was due as much to the exigencies of stationing as to any desirability to "round out" my probationary training. So we moved to Roxburgh in New Zealand's deep south, Central Otago, under the shadow of the Southern Alps. It has the driest and one of the sunniest (in summer) micro-climates in New Zealand and is a prolific fruit-growing region. In contrast, the region's winter climate is rigorous. The rest of Otago, outside the fruit growing region, is characterised by spreading tussock lands which for the settlers proved good for sheep farming, needing little development, and there were substantial areas of land suitable for cropping. However the early prosperity of Otago was based on lucrative earnings from gold mining in Central Otago in the 1860s. During the first fifty years of settlement in New Zealand, Otago was the most substantial and successful of all the provinces. The Otago province was an organised settlement under the aegis of the Otago Association, sponsored by the Free Church of Scotland.

Roxburgh is a small town in the Clutha Valley, about one hundred and fifty kilometres north west of Dunedin. It was originally populated by the gold miners but today it is most notable for its fruit growing and its hydro electric dam. Large quantities of quality pip and stone fruits and some berry fruits are grown on the flats alongside the Clutha River at Roxburgh and there is a canning factory not far from the town. When the Roxburgh Hydro Electric Power Station was built in 1956 (eleven years after we left there) on a narrow gorge in the Clutha River only ten kilometres north of the town, it was the largest station in New Zealand. It has now been surpassed in capacity by the Clyde Dam (which began in 1977 and was not completed until 1989).

All the activities that now sustain the town occur along the valley on the banks of the beautiful, dark, deep, almost threatening Clutha River which in my day, at the Roxburgh part of the river anyway, was known as the Molyneux River. There was some confusion in the use of the name Molyneux. It had been bestowed on some local harbour or river, although precisely which one is debatable, by Captain James Cook after his sailing master, Robert Molineux. The name of the river became popularly spelled "Molyneux" despite the Robert Molineux spelling. It was not that Molineux was some great character after whom a beautiful river should be rightly named. Indeed Molineux died at the age of twenty-five and, as James Cook described him, "he was unfortunately given. . . up to extravagancy and intemperance"[1]. Rightly or wrongly, the name Molyneux persisted in the affections of Central Otago people, and as late as the 1940s, perhaps longer, arguments would often arise as to which part of the river was properly the Clutha and which part the Molyneux. Officially speaking, however, Molyneux did not properly belong to the river at all and as each new bridge and dam project was devised, the official name

[1] Captain Cook's journals

gradually throttled its rival to death[1]. Like people's reputations, place-names rise and fall in importance with the tides of history. The Molyneux name rose from relative obscurity to some importance as the name of New Zealand's most powerful river and today it has almost vanished from the land[2]. Perhaps Robert Molineux was not destined to be remembered forever!

The Clutha discharges the largest volume of water of any river in New Zealand and is the country's second longest. It issues from Lake Wanaka and on its journey across Central Otago it is fed by the Hawea, the Kawarau and the Shotover Rivers. The Clutha and its tributaries were the centre of the Otago gold rush which started with Gabriel Read finding deposits by the Tuapeka River, a Clutha tributary. Without doubt, the Clutha River, is a dominant, and for me memorable feature of my days in Roxburgh and Central Otago. The grandeur of the great river is unquestionable. It is extremely deep, blue-green and seems to muscle its way past the arches of bridges, and hugs "beachless" banks from which tree branches hang low to touch its cold water. It surges past silently, a massive amount of water moving almost sedately, but with a force and speed that conveys not only a sense of rapid current, but also of whirlpools.

As you look west, wide, sweeping, treeless and fenceless hills form a dramatic backdrop and skyline to the town of Roxburgh. In a way they are most fitting as they are reminiscent of Scottish highlands and perhaps also of the high broad hills of England's Lake District. To the east, the dramatic impact fades as the hills move further back to frame the wider Clutha Valley.

In the valley are small settlements, all of them planted in acres of orchards of apples, pears, apricots, peaches and cherries. When spring arrives, the bare trees suddenly burst forth into blossom, a veritable fairyland of colours that reach as far as the eye can see.

---

[1] Dad referred only to the Molyneux: when I could not find it on the map I researched the history of the name for this explanation.

[2] *Names and Places in Southern New Zealand*, George Griffiths

Amidst the orchards are the occasional small, sod (pressed earth) houses. These are the relics of the days when the gold diggers opened up what had been a hard frost-bitten, inhospitable, intractable country to the first intrusion of civilisation. The first Methodist service ever held in Roxburgh was taken by one of these miners, a lay preacher from England's Cornwall. On his first Sunday there, he preached from standing on a stone on the edge of the river. The first Methodist Church built in Roxburgh was also made of pressed earth and it has survived the passage of time to this day: small, low-roofed, quaint, solid and charming.

To here we came in 1943 – and this appointment included a parsonage – our first church home. They were two very happy years for us and all the more memorable as we had our first children there. In September 1943 our first son, Weston Thomas, was born there followed nearly eighteen months later in March 1945, by our second son, Riley Charles. Weston was named after his maternal grandfather (Charles Weston Barrell) and his great grandmother, Ophelia Barrell's (nee Sully) home town, Weston-super-Mare in England where she was born and where his great grandparents were married. He now also shares his name with his half aunt Annette Weston Barrell and his cousin Graeme Weston Barrell. Thomas was his middle name after his paternal grandfather (with, of course, a nostalgic connection to the *Thomas Harrison* sailing ship which brought the Riley family to New Zealand in 1842.) Riley was named after the Riley family on his paternal grandparents side and Charles again after his maternal grandfather but also after me.

Roxburgh had been Reverend Tom Skuse's earliest appointment on arriving in New Zealand from Wales. That I had come into the ministry under his chaperoning when he was our Stratford minister and was now following his footsteps not only delighted him, but also gave me some more personal introductions to the parishioners here.

The parish was such a striking contrast to what we had left in Christchurch that for me Roxburgh was almost like a holiday.

To start with there were no evening meetings at all. The church membership was much smaller and we worked in close co-operation with the Presbyterians and shared the same buildings. One week the service would be Methodist, the next Presbyterian. When I preached in Roxburgh, the Presbyterian minister would preach in the country churches and the following Sunday the position would be reversed. This lightened the preaching burden and made for an economical use of buildings – and sermons!

The contrast was almost too great to let me be at ease with it, so I introduced some new things. I set up a weekly "Boys Club" for school boys. This proved to be very popular and earned me the gratitude of many parents. I also set in motion a week night Fellowship meeting and this found strong support from among the Presbyterians as well as Methodists. Of course there were no university lectures to attend, so I took up my next two subjects as an extramural student of the University of in Dunedin. A local school teacher was a student of Greek and she was ready to give me tuition, so I saw in this an ideal opportunity to get the degree requirements for a language behind me. I had already studied Greek at Theological College but this was strictly New Testament Greek and did not meet degree requirements.

Letter extract from Charles — just before Weston was born, and a time of serious University studies — Greek, history and philosophy – but worry about the Greek paper. Charles wrote home every week.

Roxburgh
11th Aug 1943

Dear Home Folk,
I'm reversing my usual procedure by writing to you at the beginning of the day's work instead of at the end. I'm afraid that is why I so often sound tired or complain of being tired. When I am fit and energetic I feel that the time is too precious to be spent on anything but swot – and Greek in particular. It's rather an exacting subject and unless one is wide awake it is well nigh impossible to do. I'm afraid that even my sermons get pushed into the background a little too much. I will be

relieved when all this swot comes to an end and I am able to give more attention to my circuit [parish] work...
...The Greek is monopolising my time these days, but Miss Curle [?] is quite pleased with my progress and is hopeful of my being able to make the grade. She wrote to Professor Adams and told him what she was doing with me and how we planned to get through a certain book in a fortnight. His reply was that if I could do that, nothing was impossible to me but I fear — !! Anyway the fortnight is up and the book is not finished... The other subjects are being neglected but if I made the grade in Greek I would be so pleased that I would not begrudge having to repeat history and philosophy. *[In fact he pulled out of Greek in the end – see letter from Rae below. – GB]*
Had a letter from the President yesterday saying that he hoped to be able to come through for [the church's] 80th Anniversary on Nov 7th [1943]. This will be very nice but make the burden of the celebrations heavier and that following night are degree exams!
Rae and I went to a party last night...I don't know whether Rae is lucky or not in being able to go out so much at this stage [Weston was due in a month's time].
...Had an excellent congregation on Sunday night, numbering 76 in all. The evening congregation has been growing over the weeks but last Sunday represents a great leap forward. Only hope that it is maintained.
...Heard from Henry Woolford and Harold Brown on Monday. Neither of them seem particularly thrilled with their new circuits [parishes] although quite happy. Harold was saying that the Kaeo people remember still our visit to them that night when I did that sketch of the lover and the rogue. Do you remember it? I know Ivy Hosking does, but not with a great deal of pleasure!
Well the precious minutes of freshness are slipping by, so I must away to swot. Cheerio for now. Love to you all and Coldstream too.
Love Chas

Letter extract from an excited new mother Rae to Charles's sisters (address Roxburgh, date Tuesday 19 Oct 1943). Weston just 5 weeks old; she talks of Charles as having an inferiority complex about his studies; as she writes he is in Dunedin sitting exams.

Dear Gwen and Evelyn and Jean [copies]

Note written as post script across top of letter: In a Greek exam paper (Probationers') returned today of Charl's, he has got 96% and remarks one on top "Excellent work". One last week on Theology 98%. *[These are not the university results as Charles in fact appeared to pull out of Greek that year – see below. They are probably Theological College ordination exam paper results. GB]*

...Charl, as you know, is in Dunedin and I told him that I would write so he would not be worrying if he did not have a chance to put pen to paper [himself].

... I was disappointed when Charl decided the other day to give up the idea of sitting Greek – I felt better to try and fail, but he said he had not covered nearly enough ground. The pity is that to get Greek he has neglected his other subjects. This year, in particular, he has a real inferiority complex about his exams, but maybe he will do better than he thinks... [1]

...One of the church men was going through to Dunedin for a holiday and said he would take his car if Charl would supply the petrol: that was easy and Charl was thrilled to bits, as he always lets Charl drive, so away they went on Saturday. I am fairly certain too that Charl would have the use of the car all the time in Dunedin as Mr Bloxham told me he would only be in Dunedin two days as he was going to Christchurch by train for his holiday.

...I am wondering about Gwen – am still anxious as to whether she had the appendicitis operation...

...Thank you for the £1 you sent Evelyn. It was very generous. The £1 sent by mother [Laura] was supposed to be from you all but it is appreciated and is with other money given the babe, and probably will go into a bank account or toward his [life] insurance.

...I have two girlfriends here from Christchurch with me: one is a Public Trust girl [Maisie] and the other a married girl [Betty]. It is far preferable to staying on one's own. I had made up my mind I would,

[1] There is confusion here. It appears Dad decided to pull out of Greek (that is, not sit the exam) but in later diary notes he says he failed it. Perhaps "giving up on Greek" was in his mind "failing it". Otherwise, he changed his mind and did in fact sit – and fail – the exam in Dunedin. - GB

despite several offers to stay at people's places, but I would not dream of that with a young babe, it would drive me mad. However, Charl was worrying about me being alone, so all has turned out for the best. I am feeling much better too now and the weather has at last changed to sunshine and is glorious. Weston Thomas is outside all day. Maisie brought a camera with her and took a snap of baby and me this morning and I have asked her if she would leave her camera here and Betty will take it back when she goes. Maisie leaves on Monday and Charl won't be back till Wednesday 27th or Thursday, and Betty will be here for three days after Charl's return [so] Charl can be taken with his son too.

...Now this son: he is a perfect darling and is growing every day. He cries a bit at times but goes for two days often without a murmur and then has a cross day... This morning I said to him, "Your Daddy is just at this moment in an examination room, now you give me a smile for him" and it was as funny as anything, Weston Thomas just cooed right out loud and smiled a beautiful smile as if he knew exactly what I was saying.

The Plunket Nurse may be here tomorrow and if she is I will tell you what weight he is. The biggest trouble of all is his hands. He just hates me tucking them in and yet I have them only loosely covered, but no, he fights like mad and bawls and as sure as eggs I can go and peep at him later and both hands will be out of the cover. Last night I put him down at 6pm and he cried and cried, so I left one hand half out and tucked the other one in tightly: if I don't he pushes the cover over his mouth. Twenty minutes later I crept into the room...and as I got near the bassinette I saw two sweet wee hands waving about and then I had a look at him and was received with wide open eyes and a real chuckle as if to say, "Hello Mum, I won, I've got both hands out". Gee I just laughed but had to give him a kiss, he looked so sweet.

...I told Weston Thomas that his Gran and Grandad and Aunties [from Taranaki] were coming to see him in January [1944] ...My Dad [from Christchurch] is coming next month or early in December for a week and I'm just overjoyed.

...the baby takes his food much too quickly sometimes and I try and make him have a rest now and then, but he goes "off the handle" properly...

Weston Thomas is being christened by the President of the Methodist Conference [effectively President of the Methodist Church – an annual

posting] (C H Olds[1]) in three weeks' time, Nov 7th, at the 80th anniversary celebrations of Roxburgh Church. My mother thinks Weston Thomas is a bit young [for christening yet] but it is a good opportunity. The christening gown which was presented to Durham Street Methodist Church[2], Christchurch, just prior to Graeme's [nephew Graeme Weston Barrell] christening (he was the first baby to wear it) , is being sent down. I did not think of it, but Mrs Ray Dudley did – it is a magnificent thing, and we will do our best to get loan of a camera, but the worst part will be getting a film.
I suppose I will have to have C H Olds staying here and it is a most inconvenient house, with a baby. However, I will manage.
...I must go and mow the lawns and Charl gave me instructions to look after his veges. He has such a lovely garden and is very proud of it.
...Charl is going to ring me up one night and I am already wishing it were tonight: he will be dying to know how his wee son is.
Much love to you all and a X each from the wee chap – how I wish you could see him – such a pet! - Rae

Roxburgh also gave me the opportunity to prepare my thesis of ten thousand words, a requirement for ordination some two years hence. I chose the theme of a doctrine of man and related the Biblical and theological teachings to my university philosophical studies, particularly on Plato. For me it was a most rewarding exercise and as well as moulding my own thinking it proved to be quite a reservoir of material for later sermons. Once, when the government's Youth Department was looking for a study for young people's weekend schools I was able to supply the thesis. I found this, too, rewarding and a source of satisfaction.

The multiplicity of religious denominations has always been a source of confusion and scandal to non-church people. Church people themselves have not been above vying with each other to gain support for their particular brand of "churchianity".

---

1 Rev Charles H Olds 1884-1969

2 Was this gown a gift to the church from the Barrell family? Why else was Graeme the first to wear it, and why was it in order to have it sent down to Roxburgh for Rae's son's christening? - GB

The fact is that there exists no theological nor Biblical foundation for such divisions or such rivalries. Fortunately, this has become increasingly recognised in the last century. Today, there is a greater acceptance that denominations only represent a deeper emphasis on particular aspects of the same truth, without denying the truth that is emphasised by other denominations. This represents my point of view and I have had no problem accepting and working closely with other churches. On the contrary, my patience was most tested where other denominations have perceived that their position is the only and true one and on these grounds sought to justify proselytising.

Roxburgh manifested a most successful interdenominational cooperation, which, then, was quite unconventional. Again, in contrast with Christchurch where my two main congregations were large enough to run a full programme of activities, all Methodist, in Roxburgh we were closely involved with the Presbyterian church and there was very little done that did not involve members of both denominations. Of course Otago and its neighbouring province, Southland, are commonly regarded as New Zealand's Scottish provinces. More pioneers who emigrated to New Zealand from Scotland settled here in the south than in any other part of the country. Hence it was that Scotland's traditional Presbyterian Church commanded a significant presence in these parts, and the Methodist church was much less strong. I discovered though that for twenty-five years the two denominations had been working in close cooperation. Leading lay men of the day in both churches had taken a long hard look at the folly of maintaining or trying to maintain two denominations at full force in a small community, and they saw the advantages of close cooperation for both congregations. While the church buildings remained invested in the denominations that had originally built them, they were regarded as at the disposal of either congregation. This avoided a duplication of church buildings except in Roxburgh itself where the two churches and the two ministers' residences already existed.

Perhaps one of the personal bonuses came from the arrangements for preaching – not least of which was having every second Sunday evening free. It was a highly efficient plan.

The circuit fell naturally into four areas. At the centre was Roxburgh itself. Roxburgh East was across the Clutha River. To the north was Coal Creek and to the south along the main road was Ettrick. I preached once a month at Miller's Flat, just a bit further south, but at that time no Methodist family lived in the area. For visiting purposes I allocated one week each month to each area and once a month I was able to call on almost all Methodist families associated with my congregations.

The preaching plan for each Sunday in the month would look something like this:

	1st Sunday	2nd Sunday	3rd Sunday	4th Sunday
1100	Pres minister; Roxburgh Pres church	Meth min.; Roxburgh Meth church	Pres min; Roxburgh Meth church	Meth min; Roxburgh Pres church
1100	Meth. Min.; Ettrick Meth ch	Pres min; Ettrick Meth ch	Meth min.; Ettrick Meth ch	Pres min; Ettrick Meth ch
1400	Meth min.; Coal Creek Meth ch	Pres min.; Miller's Flat Pres ch	Meth min.; Miller's Flat Pres ch	Meth min.; Coal Creek Meth ch
1400	Pres min; Miller's Flat Pres ch	Meth min.; Coal Creek Meth ch	Pres min.; Coal Creek Meth ch	Pres min.; Miller's Flat Pres ch
1900	Meth min.; Roxburgh Meth ch	Pres min.; Roxburgh Pres ch	Meth min.; Roxburgh Meth ch	Pres min.; Roxburgh Pres ch

For practical purposes it was intended that the congregation would be the same at each service irrespective of whether the Presbyterian or Methodist minister was preaching. But there were a few in each camp who felt they needed to go only to the services conducted by their own minister. These tended to be the people who were quick to support any new, strongly denominational minister who arrived on the scene full of zeal and whose initial idea would be to abandon the arrangement. But whatever attitude such ministers adopted, and however hard the malcontents applied pressure, they came up against a strong team in each church who were equally determined that the sharing arrangement survived. Notable among these interdenominationalists were the local doctor, Doctor Gilmour and an orchardist T P Michelle.

The Presbyterian minister in my time was Reverend Heggie, who unsurprisingly came from Scotland. He was one of those who was not too happy with the arrangement and he was rather unimpressed that he was expected to cooperate with the Methodists to such an extent. In New Zealand, although the Presbyterian Church was the largest in the parishes of Otago and Southland, the other denominations represented a far stronger contingent here than they ever did in Scotland and he was quite unused to having to take account of them. Moreover, the Methodists were a new breed to him, one he could not quite accept. He certainly could not comprehend that we held a theology that could produce pacifists such as that of Reverend O E Burton[1]'s ilk (who was currently in prison for his stated beliefs – see letter to me reproduced below). With his parish being the larger Mr Heggie found working with the Methodists something of an anathema to him and he was indignant at the prospect. An uneasy alliance continued. The Methodists were nearly unanimous in their acceptance of the cooperation but they fell into some of the pitfalls that are almost inherent in minority groups. One of these was the constant eagerness to assert one's presence as a safeguard against being overlooked. For one thing, they always reminded the Presbyterians that the Methodist church was the first church in Roxburgh (as Methodists often are – carrying the missionary torch high in their commitment to the faith). This was a futile if not puerile assertion and it achieved

---

1 Rev Ormond E Burton 1893-1974

nothing if it was quoted when an issue of cooperation between the churches needed resolving.

The Parsonage
22 Webb Street
Wellington
10 February 1942

Dear Bro Bell

Herewith the two assignments you sent to me. There were of course difficulties. I was able to receive your MS but not write out to you. In consequence, except for sending you a few notes, I wasn't able to do much to help you. Sorry you appear as only having the 9/10 marks for the first lot of work. The other will be counted unto you for righteousness just the same. Of course I fully understand how difficult the years of probation are. Someday I hope we shall have the Presbyterian system under which all academic work is completed before a man takes up pastoral work.

Your first lot of work was the best I had. I think it is a very good thing to be able to take a source document, sweep your mind clear of what someone else thinks and make your own independent précis. Unless one is able to do this one very often falls into traditional errors or comes under altogether undue influence.

The whole of the work was set to cover a good method of work to cover really any subject. Accurate précis and comparison of source documents, chronological arrangement of facts and opinions and from these a venture in independent thinking. I thought your essay not so good as the first assignment but this no doubt was due to a measure of haste at the end of the year. The first assignment was typed and very well arranged. It is one of my own regrets that I never learned to type with facility. Good mechanical methods save endless hours. As you can type I would suggest that you publish per medium cyclostyle some of your more important sermons to your congregation. One reason why I always have an essay and am very keen on thesis work as opposed to examination is that in the generation that is coming we all need to write more – and better. Radio and cheap duplicating processes are making this imperative.

Sorry to have been so little help this year but if there is anything I can do in the future let me know. I should be very glad.

Yours sincerely
O E Burton

The Methodists had in fact arrived with the first gold miners in the 1860s when some miners themselves were lay preachers. True to the John Wesley tradition, when the first Sunday came it was the Cornish lay preacher gold miner who stood at the river and conducted a service of worship. In contrast, no Presbyterian would take upon himself such a liberty. Therefore, although there were Presbyterians in the area, no service was held by them until an ordained minister could make the trip from an adjoining parish. Whether the Presbyterians dated their beginnings from when they were officially constituted a parish and had an ordained minister appointed or when an ordained minister preached a sermon in the area, I cannot now recall but in any case it was after the Methodist lay preacher had held that first service. Thus it was that the Methodists were not always discreet or diplomatic in mentioning it from time to time and I am now rather ashamed to admit, I fear that I was not without guilt in this matter either.

The local Presbyterian church officials were not happy with their new minister's disapproval of the cooperation with the Methodists and, together with many in the congregation, found fault with him. One of these officials was the Secretary of the local Electric Power Board and he had his office in the middle of the main street. I often dropped in on him and chatted and we shared together many church concerns. On one occasion when I called in, he said, "Charlie, I had a long session with Mr Heggie last night, talking over church matters and especially about those dealing with the interdenominational cooperation schemes. And I asked him why he could not be like Charlie Bell."

I was horrified and embarrassed. "I hope you didn't say that. That is surely adding fuel to the fire." Here was an older man, rich in experience and nearing retirement, being compared unfavourably with a young man only at the beginning of his ministry. My appointment to Roxburgh was destined to incur an uneasy relationship with the Presbyterian minister there despite being thrown together by the wishes of our congregations. The inevitable coolness between us, I am sorry to say, was never fully resolved.

Today, the Methodist Church and Presbyterian Church in Roxburgh have fully combined into the United Church. My Methodist church building is now a kindergarten/play centre.[1]

Despite some of the tensions between certain members of the two congregations, Rae and I were warmly received into the homes of many Presbyterian families. They were good to us and we formed many close friendships that carried into the years ahead. One of these was a Mr Nicholson, a local storekeeper. It was in the days when a political party called Social Credit was emerging and his name was put forward as a candidate. He asked me to go on his committee for the general election and we consulted together on the content of his speeches and their presentation. He did not succeed in winning the seat but he did score as high a count as any other Social Credit candidate nation-wide.

Next door to the parsonage was a strawberry farm and the owners, after despatching a load to the markets in Dunedin, often gave us any remaining punnets. Roxburgh in the summer was a land of cream and honey, of sunshine, delicious fresh fruits and views of orchards which stretched as far as the eye could see up the valley and alongside the great Clutha River, with the majestic Southern Alps in the distance lying as a painted backdrop to the entire scene.

Roxburgh offered me a longed for opportunity to get close to the land again. As a stone fruit growing area, nearly every farming family in the district owned orchards. When I visited my parishioners during the summer, I invariably found myself in the packing sheds where, chances were, every member of the family would be helping out with the packing of apricots, apples, cherries, peaches and pears. This generally meant I would go home with a case of tree-ripened fruit but most of all I delighted

---

[1] In Nov 1989, Weston and Riley visited Roxburgh with Mum and Dad: the old parsonage is still there in the main street opposite a hotel. I drove through the town for the first time myself in Jan 1995. - GB

in spending half an hour amongst the activity. I had been off the farm too long and these visits whetted my appetite for the life again. It was clear that I could not leave my love for farming behind me altogether and Roxburgh was the first parish where I brought a bit of my farm to the parsonage.

To the amusement of my parishioners, I purchased a house cow which I kept in a friend's paddock on the outskirts of town. So Roxburgh became a life of fruit and cream: delicious local fruit supplied copiously and generously by orchardist parishioners and great lashings of cream supplied by our very own cow – which of course, I milked – eagerly!

Under the pretext of getting to know my parishioners better, I enthusiastically offered to help them out with fruit picking. Indeed, my eagerness often not only surprised but bemused them as their minister joined the fruit pickers. Far from being an act of dedication to my parish, it was sheer joy for me. Working in the outdoors again! Milking our cow twice a day, picking fruit whenever I could!

On another occasion I quickly offered to help a young man with his haymaking. He was staggered that the local Methodist minister wanted to do this, but accepted the offer albeit with a slight air of incredulity. Although I was far from green as a farmer, this occasion introduced me for the first time to an extraordinary machine – a hay baler. It stood in the middle of the field and the hay was brought to it and forked in. Today's balers have developed into mobile units that can be towed around the paddock picking up the hay as they go and spitting out the bales behind, all neatly compacted and tied. Nevertheless, the stationary hay baler to which we had to trudge carrying the hay was still amazing enough to me. I enjoyed the haymaking immensely and when my few days of helping were over, I quietly and secretly recognised that my heart was heavy as I returned to routine parish duties.

The Coal Creek church was built of pressed earth in the days of the horse and gig – and probably at the time of the earliest gold rushes. To allow for tethering the horses and parking the gigs, they had made a liberal allowance of land around the building. Fallow land was too much for me to ignore. It was land was it not? And did I not have access to it? No, such a waste was sacrilege and true to my father's spirit, land must be productive. Every square inch of land to me was always a potential farm – and what other people and especially my later family – could never get over was how I simply could not pass by a piece of land. If it was not my career, it was an intense hobby. As usual, the burning question was, "Now, what can I do with this piece of land here?" I spent as much time and enthusiasm on this very serious project as I did considering the sermons for the next week or so. I was happy! I decided to buy ten lambs and fatten them for home killing. I hastily erected a fence that "would do" and shortly Coal Creek Methodist Church was surrounded with the minister's very own flock of ten sheep. There was little comment from the parishioners on this strange behaviour of their minister until one evening when I had a phone call to tell me that the lambs had got out and caused a motor car accident. At least one lamb had been killed. An offer was immediately forthcoming from one of my parishioners (who was no doubt desperate to save his minister's face) to buy the Coal Creek Methodist Church Sheep Farm on the spot. My venture into stock farming came to an abrupt end and my thankful parishioners considered, quite patiently they thought, that I could now resume my full time pastoral duties and pastoral care *of them* – which, after all, was much more appropriate, was it not? There was still the cow of course.

A lovely elderly lady from the church became particularly fond of Rae and took her under her motherly wing. One of the things she shared with Rae was her great skill in preserving fruit. When we eventually left Roxburgh it was with an enormous cupboard full of preserves and not until Rae was nearly eighty years old did she ever believe her year was normal without its preserving season. Through all those years, Rae rarely had fewer than one hundred jars of preserves of fruits or jams or vegetables. Maintaining that stock level seemed to become for her symptomatic of the right supply at any one time for any good mother and housewife to have at hand. It was often a point of conversation. "I have noticed we have only twenty-three jars of peaches left, Charlie – and it is only July. We will have to use more apricots for a while," and the internal calculator would work out how many more family meals were left between now and next bottling season.

Roxburgh gave me the chance to take up some gardening which I did with a relish. One year I had a wonderful crop of peas, more than we could eat. I decided to complement Rae's new skills and I undertook to preserve them. I stored them, rather triumphantly, in a top cupboard shelf. One day when Rae got out from a lower shelf in that same cupboard some new quality sheets which she had carefully stored from her glory box, she was shattered to find green stains right through them. My first proud efforts of preserving had turned to disaster! In my enthusiasm I had not stopped to learn that peas are particularly difficult to preserve and require some experience to do it successfully.

When I went to Roxburgh I had no car nor did the church. To get to my Sunday services, a local Methodist school teacher used her car to drive me and redeemed the time by getting her school preparation done. This suited her and it suited me. As she did not need to attend the afternoon service it meant she did not have to hear the same sermon repeated and it saved me from having to prepare a new one which I may otherwise have been obligated to do.

The church officials were conscious that it was their responsibility to supply transport for the minister and to this end they had established a car fund. The idea that at least one of them had was that the fund be treated as an investment and the interest therefrom should finance the transport costs. This particular individual wanted to lend the money to me to provide the car myself and then charge me interest on the loan. He was vexed when I did not agree.

Eventually I gave up looking for help from the church's car fund. At the end of that year, Conference had made no appointment to Cromwell, a small township some eighty kilometres north of Roxburgh, so it was put under my care. Now the need for a car was urgent and a parishioner undertook to give me a private, interest free loan. On Christmas Eve 1943, I hiked off to Dunedin. The minister presently at Maori Hill (Dunedin) had previously been in the motor business and had earlier been the minister at Cromwell. He was concerned for his former parish and anxious that I would indeed be able to meet my pastoral obligations there, so he wanted to help me select a good car – one that would not wear me out travelling over the rugged country to and from Cromwell. I had looked at and selected one or two small cars for his approval. He turned them both down quite unsatisfied and finally chose for me a V8 Ford Coupe (c1934 model) — a car I would never have thought of picking. What a delightful car it proved to be and I still think of it with some affection.

Our first child and son, Weston, was born six months after our arrival in Roxburgh. In our isolation from other Methodist ministers, the question of having him baptised created a small problem. When the Roxburgh church anniversary came round it was decided to invite the President of the Methodist Church, Reverend C H Olds, to visit and take the services. This was the opportunity I had been looking for, so we arranged for him not only to baptise Weston, but also four other babies in the parish.

For a time Weston seemed to suffer from some sort of claustrophobia. Rae could not even go into a shop without him immediately starting to scream the place down. In fact the shopkeepers got to know this so well that Mrs Bell was met on the street outside to get her order. At the baptism, the crowded church produced the same effect on Weston and his crying grew into a bellow and effectively drowned out all the words of the President, which I found exceptionally embarrassing. Fortunately, Weston was the first to be baptised and as soon as Mr Olds moved on to the second baby, a motherly soul rose up from the congregation, came forward, reached over Rae's shoulder, took Weston out of her arms and went outside. A great peace descended and the congregation heard the rest of the service. True to form, Weston stopped crying instantly he was taken out of the door. He was a gurgling, bubbly, happy baby for the rest of the day, which did nothing to appease Rae or me following his performance inside the church.

Roxburgh was a small community and living there gave me an insight to the interdependence that involves everyone. When the Otago University sent a WEA[1] officer to the area, he undertook to organise a drama evening. As a member of the local community, I felt some obligation when I was approached to take a part in a play. It was "An Interlude in Diplomacy" and I was cast as the Ambassador. I was sorry that Rae could not be part of it, actress as she was, but she was caring for her young son and was pregnant with the second. As for me, I was almost surprised that I enjoyed the experience. It was a relaxing break from my normal rounds and I found new friends outside the immediate church circle. The sense of community that belongs to these smaller towns was manifested by the packed local town hall for the noble performance. It was almost hard to believe by the size of the audience that there was anyone left at home for miles around.

At times I have thought the church has not been fully cognisant of the importance of the role of the ministers appointed to small and isolated places. As in my case in Roxburgh, the Conference often appointed probationary ministers who are young and inexperienced. Yet in that community the young probationers are seen *as* the Methodist Church and carry on their shoulders the aura and reputation of their denomination. In one instance, when Roxburgh had an official Vice-Regal visit, Rae and I were included on the guest list to meet Governor General

---

[1] Workers' Educational Association. WEAs came to NZ in 1915 with the goal of making learning opportunities available to those who missed out on such opportunities in earlier education.

Newall[1]. In the cities for a similar occasion the probationary minister would have been passed over without question. And in the smaller communities always on occasions such as Anzac Services the local minister would be among those participating and representing his denomination. In the cities, again, a more senior minister would undoubtedly have been selected to represent the church in any occasion representing the wider community.

Every Christmas and New Year the local camping ground was packed with caravans and tents. There was not a great deal for the visitors to do once they had arrived and settled down, a fact bemoaned by some of the locals. The second year I was there New Year's Eve fell on a Sunday, so I suggested to my congregation that we moved our evening service to the town hall and turn it into a community night for singing with only the briefest of sermons, and invite the local congregations and holiday makers alike. Of course, we were working with the Presbyterians so they had to be consulted. They were not at all sure that my suggestion was a good one. "For the Scots", they said, "you must realise that New Year is as important as Christmas. We are not at all sure we like your idea." I suggested a compromise of having our normal service first and following this with a straight out community sing song in the town hall. This was not acceptable to the Presbyterians either and it was fast becoming one of those occasions when the following rule needed to be applied: *when all else fails remind the Presbyterians that the Methodists were here first!* That was the temptation but I cannot recall if the reminder was actually delivered on that occasion or not. Of course it would not have made any difference even if it had been. In the end the Presbyterians and Methodists agreed to disagree. They elected to have their own version of observing the New Year while the rest of us carried on with the campers. I was happy (and relieved) that we packed the town hall to

---

1 Marshal of the RAF, Sir Cyril Louis Norton Newall, Governor General of New Zealand 1941-1946 (b1886-d1963)

capacity. It was a new role for me to be a sing-a-long leader in such a setting.

After my Boys Club had been operating for some time, I suggested that we held a camp. I had had experience of many Easter Camps with the Bible Class Movement of the Methodist Church, both as a member and as a leader. With the support of a young church member, Bert Bloxham, and the services of a motherly and appreciative local lady as cook, we felt we could cope well. We camped at Ettrick Church sleeping on palliasses in the church and using the vestry for meetings and other activities. The cook, Mrs Thomson, did not live such a great distance away so I took the boys over to her place for the meals. Despite the luxury of a home cooked meal every day, the camp itself offered few physical comforts but the boys seemed to enjoy themselves. Many of them had brothers and some had fathers serving in the war. For some boys the hardships of the camp seemed to feed their imaginations to bring them a closer understanding of what their absent relations just may be going through, no matter how distant the reality may actually be. I had been brought up all my life to wash in cold water. I still do this to this day and consider it absolutely normal. Indeed, I remain surprised that everyone doesn't do it, even now. My surprise therefore was even more marked in 1944 when the boys at the camp complained of having to wash in cold water. This was the one aspect of the camp that I had not even counted as a hardship. I was so non-plussed by this complaint that I found myself wondering whether washing in warm water was a characteristic of the peoples of Otago! It certainly could not have been entertained, I concluded, in Taranaki.

A few weeks later I took a small group of the older boys for a sleep out under the open sky away up in the hills at the back of Roxburgh. We travelled for fifty or sixty kilometres, climbing most of the way until we came to a lake among the hills where the vegetation was stunted because of the altitude. We put in a couple of chilly nights and we were hardly over fed with the meagre rations we managed to rustle up over an open air fire of twigs and dried sticks. We missed having the luxury of our cook, Mrs Thomson, this time and we suffered for it. I doubt I was much of a skilled scout leader and fear that the boys learned nothing much from the experience other than probably being put off camping for the rest of their lives! I gave up trying my hand at being a scout leader with the church youth and never did it again, although several adult camps in my parishes were to follow.

Isolation always tends to breed parochialism and conservatism. So a small community such as Roxburgh, cut off by many kilometres of hills from other populated areas, and located at the bottom end of New Zealand was a fairly certain candidate for conservatism in every aspect of life. Although it was after my time that the Roxburgh hydro electric power station was built, I can imagine that the invasion of workers from many overseas countries that it brought with it, must have been something of a culture shock. All the old residents had been there for two or three generations. They not only knew each other well but they also knew their forebears and the family histories. Suddenly they found in their midst people they knew nothing about, people who spoke with foreign accents, people who had different social customs, morals and values.

Roxburghians were traditionalists to the core which was evident even in the way funerals were expected to be conducted. The first funeral I conducted for a parishioner in Roxburgh was of an elderly man who was the local milkman. On Sunday morning, after finishing his rounds in the township, he drove out to Dumbarton about five kilometres away and called on his married daughter and family. On returning he drove at breakneck speed, hit the bank, crossed the road, tore through a fence and plummeted down a long paddock sloping towards the Clutha River. His light truck somersaulted one or two times and finally came to rest on its side. I passed by the very spot shortly afterwards on my way to my service at Ettrick. I saw a group of men gathered at the roadside. Sensing that something was wrong, I stopped and solemnly they told me that the driver was dead. At that time, however, I did not realise that it was one of my own parishioners. At the inquest later, the coroner ruled he had had a stroke.

In due course, I had to take his funeral. The funeral director was based at Lawrence about fifty kilometres away so I had had no previous contact with him. When the hearse turned up, I was surprised. It was an old vintage car which carried the casket on a raised open air platform in full view to the public and exposed to the elements. As I travelled next to the funeral director in the hearse on the way to the cemetery, I commented, "It's a long time since I saw a hearse of this vintage. I suppose in such a scattered and thinly populated area there would be little call for you to invest in a new hearse."

"As a matter of fact", he replied, "I have a new and modern hearse at home which I use regularly in Lawrence but I don't dare use it here. I brought it to Roxburgh once and I had a near riot on my hands. They objected most vigorously to having the coffin enclosed and more or less out of sight. So I never use it here. What is more, they object strongly if we drive at more than walking pace. They say, that has always been the pace for funerals and it is disrespectful to the deceased to go any faster."

I looked back and there, sure enough, were all the mourners, except the deceased's family, slowly plodding behind the hearse. Said the undertaker, "I am trying to educate them. When I get about a mile clear of the town and near the cemetery I speed up just a bit." Although I knew that traditional funeral services of one kind or another had survived centuries of ritual in many countries, New Zealand, on the whole, had kept pace with the thinking of current generations. This had certainly been my experience anyway – until now. Roxburgh clung to a ritual that I had not even come across as a child.

Our two years in Roxburgh years passed very quickly and very happily. Towards the end a letter came inviting us to take up an appointment in Wellington East Circuit. When I reported this to my officials they said they were disappointed and felt let down by my leaving them after only two years. I pointed out that I would be ordained at the forthcoming conference and as such my status in the church would be changed. The conference in its wisdom might feel disposed to move me with or without a direct invitation from another parish.

On 25th February 1945 at the conference of the Methodist Church of New Zealand, in Trinity Church, Dunedin, at long last, I was ordained. I was nearly thirty-three years old. The 1945 ordinands with me were Reverends Harold Kilford Brown, Gordon V Thomas, J Henry Woolford and Harold A Darvill. At the same conference, my appointment to Wellington East was confirmed.

In one way I was not sorry to be leaving Roxburgh. Throughout the two years I had the feeling of being isolated and cut off from the church. The nearest Methodist minister was nearly a hundred kilometres away at Milton and there was no other between Roxburgh and Queenstown. The main church offices were located in Auckland and Christchurch and to me in central Otago that seemed an interminable distance. I was always hungry for news of church activities and of my fellow ministers. For the previous appointment I had been in the middle of Christchurch and prior to that I had been in the middle of New Zealand's largest city of Auckland for three years with fellow students at Trinity College. Basically, I was professionally lonely. Conference often expressed its concern that there was serious lack of ministers willing to accept appointments in the south. Could this sense of isolation be a factor?

But isolated or not, there was no doubt that the southerners were a friendly people. Altogether they were a very warm hearted people and our time there was most enjoyable and rewarding. For my farewell service they did me the honour of crowding the church to overflowing. Chairs were added at the ends of pews and placed down the centre and side aisles, all available space in the foyer was used, the vestry behind me was then used, people then were seated on the pulpit steps and in the doorway behind me and then, as stewards frantically sought more ways of accommodating more people as they arrived at the church, many more stood on the steps outside. I had never seen that church, or any church since, so packed for me. I was deeply moved.

As we packed up to leave Roxburgh, our second son, Riley, was born on March 8th 1945. Rae did not come back to the parsonage again. From the Maternity Home she went directly for our last few remaining days to Mrs Weaver's place. Mrs Weaver was one of our "shared Presbyterian parishioners" and she cared for Rae, Weston and new baby Riley, lovingly in her home until it was time to leave.

On April 1st 1945, I preached my farewell sermon and almost immediately afterwards left Roxburgh for Christchurch where we were to take a short holiday staying with Rae's parents for a week or two before flying on to Wellington.

Unbeknown tragedy lay ahead of us. Although Rae's mother had visited us in Roxburgh and spent time with toddler Weston and taken him for walks, a happy and proud grandmother, it was now less than a year away before Rae would lose her mother, suddenly and tragically – an event which changed Rae's life – and consequently ours – forever.

THE METHODIST CHURCH OF NEW ZEALAND

Certificate of Ordination

This is to Certify that

Charles H Bell

having been admitted into Full Connexion with
the Conference of the Methodist Church of New Zealand
was on the 25th day of February 1945,
duly ordained by the imposition of hands
as a fully accredited Minister of the Christian Church.

[signed] ? ? Scrivin, President of the Conference
[signed] W? G? Slade, Secretary of the Conference

The New Zealand Methodist Times April 28th 1945

Seldom if ever, has our [Roxburgh] Church been attended by such numbers as gathered on April 1st to hear Rev C H Bell preach his farewell sermon. Chairs had to be placed in the aisles, while the overflow were seated in the vestry and porch. The whole service was most inspiring and the singing was worthy of the best Methodist tradition. After hearing Mr Bell's stirring address, those present adjourned to the Presbyterian Sunday School hall, where arrangements had been made to spend a social hour to say farewell to Mr and Mrs Bell. Speakers from various parts of the circuit, as well as representatives of the Presbyterian and Anglican Churches, paid a high tribute to Mr and Mrs Bell, and each speaker expressed sincere regret at their departure after a stay of only two years in the district. A gift in the form of a cheque was handed to Mr Bell who in reply, stated that his term in Roxburgh had been a most happy one. Being Easter time, a considerable number of visitors from various parts of Otago and Southland were present, and over an enjoyable cup of tea, many friendships and acquaintances were renewed. At the close, all joined in singing, "God be with you till we meet again", and Mr Bell pronounced the Benediction.

The Roxburgh Methodist Parsonage with the Ford V8 Coupe (c1934 model) parked outside. A figure outside the front door may be Rae.

Charles, Rae and Weston and the Ford V8 Coupe, Roxburgh, 1943.

Weston in his Durham Street Methodist Church christening gown (the first person to wear it was his cousin Graeme Barrell). Christened in Roxburgh (in the church below), 7th November 1943, by the President of the Methodist Conference Rev CH Olds.

Weston, c1944, Roxburgh

The old Roxburgh Methodist Church where Charles preached and where Weston was christened in 1943. Today it is a play centre. Photo 1995

A unique occasion and rare photograph: both sets of parents visiting Charles and Rae in Roxburgh for Charles's ordination February 1945. This is taken on a day's outing to Queenstown. It is not known who took the photograph, although it could have been Hilda Barrell. However, Ev vaguely recalls that Hilda was not well and stayed behind in Roxburgh so it may have been Rae although she herself was expecting Riley, due within a few weeks of this visit and may not have come either. L to R: Charles Weston Barrell, Evelyn Bell, Laura Bell, Tom Bell and Charles with Weston on his knee.

Weston (left) and Riley, Hawera, 1945

Charles's ordination in Dunedin with his parents, Thomas Edwin and Laura Florence. February 1945. Charles aged 32 years, Tom and Laura aged 68 years.

Weston with his grandmother Hilda Barrell in Roxburgh, February 1945, visiting with her husband and other family for Charles's ordination. Exactly a year later Hilda took her own life.

Chapter 15

IN THE CAPITAL

1945 - 1949

A fully ordained Minister of Religion
Miramar, Wellington

Wellington is a lively city and today it has established a reputation for being an arty place with four permanent and two touring theatre companies, a symphony orchestra, a dance company and international festival that brings the world's best to the capital of New Zealand. But even by New Zealanders, it is a much misunderstood place. By passing through it, one can get an altogether false impression of what type of city it really is. Hosts of people only pass through or stay for but a day or two as it is the cross-roads of travel between the North and South Islands (and hence the historical logical reason for the selection of the position as the capital of the country). Its reputation for extremely strong and boisterous wind has a lot of truth in it. "The windy city", as it is known dismissively by many, even has an unofficial emblem of an umbrella blown inside out. (Few Aucklanders like to be reminded that Auckland has more windy days per year than Wellington! But of course Wellington wins hands down when it comes to the *strongest* winds!) In contrast to Wellington's gale image, however, it can have gloriously sunny days and it is a most attractive city.

I would imagine there are few places in the world that can match the beauty of sailing into Wellington harbour in the early morning of a fine day on board the inter-island ferry. Wellington itself at the head of the harbour, spreads in a semicircle nestled amidst shore-hugging hills, all of them dotted with houses. As the ferry makes its way up the harbour bright sunshine sparkles on blue waters and streams down on the hilltop homes, calling the city people to rise. One gets the impression of a city washed clean and stirring with bursting energy, eager to apply itself to the challenge of a new day, renewed, refreshed, all senses alert with nothing it cannot meet and overcome.

Many a time have I come in to Wellington[1] by ferry and felt my heart warmed by the sight. But Wellington harbour can be serene as I have described but it can also be ferocious. Steered through the narrow confines created by the positions and proximity of the North and South Islands to each other, the wind is forced through a funnel and it creates a veritable vortex. Indeed, on 10th April 1968 the inter-island ferry the *Wahine* sank near the entrance of the Wellington harbour on Barrett's Reef only metres from the shore in full view of hundreds of Wellington's hilltop homes. The howling storm on that day was so terrible that rescuers could see the huge vessel but not reach it before it toppled over with the loss of fifty-one lives. Bodies were washed ashore all around the harbour.

It was just such a storm that greeted us most unkindly on the day of our move to our new home in mid April 1945. The wind was blowing from the south at one of its frightening forces, with rain beating down and lashing the city and hills. You would have thought we would have been thankful that we decided not to sail in that morning. But the alternative proved to be just as bad, if not worse. Air travel for the public was a fairly new innovation and we would not normally have chosen it in preference to the inter-island ferry, but with Weston, a toddler and Riley, a babe-in-arms, it seemed to be a more desirable mode

---

1 From Lyttelton, Christchurch. Today this service has ceased and ferries are between Picton and Wellington only.

of transport. Besides, the war was still in progress and ferry schedules were often upset at the last minute by reported sightings of Japanese submarines. So we opted for the skies. The DC3, the good reliable workhorse of the airways in those days, flew at low altitudes and when storms struck there was no way out but to fight its way through them. And fight it did on that fateful April day with the Bell family aboard.

Riley was barely six weeks old. The flight from Christchurch started reasonably quietly but every mile closer to Wellington the more it bucked and bounced, behaving at times like a frenzied rodeo horse. The time came for baby Riley's feed, so Mum undid her seat belt to oblige. The next thing she knew she was somewhere near the roof of the plane. It had hit a massive air pocket and dropped a sickening few hundred feet. From then on the bouncing and bucking continued with increasing ferocity, respite coming only with touch-down at Wellington airport, the landing itself not doing much to add to our delight to be on the ground at last. Eventually, and to our immense relief, the plane came to a final halt. Emerging from the aircraft and down the narrow steps did not see the end of our ordeal as we had yet to cross the tarmac to reach the safety, yes safety, of the terminal building. Amidst sweeping hurricane force winds and pelting rain, we clung desperately to our hand baggage, hats and children, as we made a hasty dash, heads down, bodies almost bent over double, to our refuge.

We were met by our new chief official, Mr Nathan R Seddon, and by a life long friend of Rae's, Gladys Wederell. Gladys was, like Rae, a Christchurch girl but she had recently moved to Wellington as her husband was training with the air force. She wanted to take us home where a good dinner was on and "cots are ready for the bairns". Rae explained that we could not do that as a welcoming committee was waiting for us at the church. Gladys insisted on taking the children off us, however. Weston and Riley were far too bewildered by their first, rather traumatic introduction to flying, to object to being "dumped" at that particular point. They were handed over with no tears, but probably they were more stunned than well behaved. That first, awful air trip for the stunned baby, however, must have made a deep impression, for when Riley grew up he had only one ambition – to be an airline pilot.

We were no sooner loaded into the car when Mr Seddon announced, "I might as well tell you the worst straight away. Your furniture and effects have not arrived yet." This was a real blow! There were many such hitches at the time because of war conditions, but we thought we had taken these into account. We had seen our belongings safely on their way from Roxburgh before motoring through to Christchurch in our Ford V8 Coupe where we had stayed with Rae's parents for a short holiday. We did not think of checking on the progress of our belongings, naively believing all was well. The situation was made worse by having such young children to be provided for. Mr Seddon went on, hastening to put our minds at rest. "Of course, there are tables and chairs and beds in the house as provided by the church and you will shortly be meeting a welcoming committee of the ladies from the church. They will discuss with you what you will further need and no doubt, knives, plates and such like will be forthcoming."

We arrived at the formal reception committee ill prepared for socialising. To start with we were feeling strange without our children, as if we had abandoned them at the port of entry and Rae, although relieved in one way, was still anxious about them. We were feeling ill from the effects of the dreadful flight. We were unimpressed with the relentless rain and winds. We were not refreshed or changed. And on top of all that, we were upset by the news that our furniture had not arrived and we would, at best, be camping in our new home for obviously some days (or even weeks?) to come.

In such a frame of mind, we greeted the committee representing our new parishioners and enjoyed a very acceptable cup of tea which was awaiting us. They expressed their concern for us and kindly offered to provide what we lacked. Rae tried to think out what would be needed but her mind was as much on her missing children and wondering how Gladys was coping as it was on what she might need immediately in the house. As a result (together with her reluctance to impose and ask for everything she needed anyway) her list of requirements was rather pathetic and camp we did for a good while. Such was our introduction to the windy city.

Our appointment was to another double-church parish, similar in many ways to my Richmond-Shirley appointment in Christchurch a few years earlier. This, too, was a four minister parish consisting of Wellington's eastern suburbs and I was to be responsible for Miramar and Worser Bay. Our home was the Miramar Methodist Parsonage, 39 Strathavon Road, Miramar, Wellington[1].

The Wellington Airport was in this area and the runway was not too far from the parsonage[2]. As Riley grew into a toddler and acquired a tricycle he determinedly found his own way to the airport and spent his time gazing at the planes as they came and went. To reach the airport perimeter fence, however, he had to negotiate the main road that carried Wellington's commuter and airport traffic. Despite our anxious moments and warnings and efforts to accompany him to the airport as often as we could to appease his enthusiasm, our enough was certainly not his enough. Not only did he want to go to the airport every day, he wanted to go for hours on end. On one occasion when Rae was going in the tram into the city, firmly believing the children were safe at home with me, she looked out of the tram window and to her horror, saw Riley on his tricycle, parked right up against the airport perimeter fence beside the busy road with trams and cars rushing past him. The little boy was spellbound by the planes and quite oblivious to everything else. At the next tram stop, which was, disturbingly, some way on, Rae got off and rang me at home to tell me where she had seen our son. Although I was supposed to be looking after him I was quite

---

1 See photos end of this chapter.

2 The present Wellington airport was not extended on to reclaimed land until the 1950s but the original airport on the same but smaller site was the one Riley visited.

unaware that he was even missing! On that occasion Riley was barely three years old but we knew from then on where we would find him whenever he went missing – on his tricycle, nose close to the wire netting perimeter fence of Wellington Airport. He ultimately became the pilot he dreamed to be and has now been flying for thirty years[1]. He joined the Royal New Zealand Air Force when he left school at the age of seventeen and started flying commercially at the age of twenty-seven[2].

One of my parishioners in Worser Bay was Norman Chisholm, a lay preacher. Today he lives in Pahiatua[3]. Norman recalls distinctly the tale I shared with him concerning the reading of one of the "Golden Books" to Weston and Riley. Both boys never tired of the story as they asked me to read it over and over again. I did tire of it, however, and to amuse myself more than them I think, I started to change the odd word or two. However, the boys knew the story so well they objected, "It doesn't say that, Daddy!!" and I was promptly and persistently corrected. Although I really forgot about this, it is interesting that Norman remembers that tale vividly!

Our first reception committee had included the leading ladies of the two churches that came under my care. Of course, we were working closely together over the next five years and we came to know them very well, some, indeed, are still friends to this day. But there was one lady who made an immediate and lasting impression from that very first meeting. A Mrs Smith. She was very short and although she sat on the lowest chair, her feet never touched the floor. As Secretary of the Worser Bay Ladies Guild she was all for getting my attention whenever she could and was full of what we had to do and not do. It was only about a fortnight after this that I heard mid-evening on a Saturday night that her much adored son had been killed in

---

1 Riley has since retired, 2005, after 43 years of flying.

2 In 1993 Riley was appointed Chief Pilot (responsible for standards), Air New Zealand

3 Norman spotted the death notice of Uncle Charlie in the local paper, May 1996, and contacted my cousin Graeme, to make the connection with Mum and Dad and to whom he related this story. - GB

action in Europe. What deepened the sadness was that her son was among the very last who died in the battlefields as the war was to be declared ended just a few weeks later. Her home was high up on the hills behind Worser Bay and in an area that I still did not know. I drove up and down the road looking for the lane that led to her house on the face of the steep hillside. I remember being anxious as I was initiated into the treachery of negotiating Wellington's steep streets in the dark.

In the usual course of events, Mrs Smith was not slow in demanding a good deal of her minister's attention. But on this one occasion she got it without demanding it and not in the happy way it might otherwise have been. Her personal tragedy apart, she was a real character. As the Guild Secretary she recorded for the minutes all the family events of the members. Mrs "A" had had a cold and Mrs "B" was absent because she was having a baby and Mrs "C" was having trouble with a leaking tap at the moment. Rae would come from the meeting having a good giggle about what Mrs Smith would faithfully, thoroughly, and of course most seriously, enter into the minutes.

Shortly after we settled at Miramar, on June 6th 1945, the war in Europe was declared over. There followed nation-wide celebrations and much jubilation although our own celebrations were much quieter. Rae's friends, Gladys and Arnold Wederell, came to the parsonage and spent the day with us. For Arnold celebrating at the Methodist parsonage must have been an anticlimax. He was in Air Force uniform and in training with the very real prospect of shortly going overseas. The relief of having the European theatre of war ended must have been tremendous for him, but there he was celebrating with teetotaller friends, with not so much as a beer in sight. I had to remain cold sober anyway as I had to prepare a sermon on that day. It had been pre-arranged that there would be a church service on the evening of the day the end of the war was announced.

Sober, quiet, busy or not, we all shared a great feeling of relief and celebrated the cessation of the tragic loss of life. We also were able to look forward to getting back to a more normal order of life – no more rationing of petrol, clothing, meat, butter, chocolate, silk stockings and a freer market for cars. Of course the war in the Pacific was still raging and all these apparent luxuries were slow in coming. In fact, when I bought my Ford Prefect to take to Nelson nearly five years later, it was possible only because of my parish steward, Nat Seddon, who dealt directly with the then Government Minister (later to become Prime Minister), Walter Nash. He persuaded him to help secure the easement of restrictions on the purchase of cars so that ministers of religion, amongst other specified professions, could do their work.

The parish covered the Miramar peninsular and along the waterfront from Scorching Bay to Worser Bay and Seatoun. It included Strathmore Park which was then a newly developing suburb, with hundreds of Government houses. All these areas came under my pastoral care. The Superintendent Minister, Reverend W A Burley[1], was based at Hataitai and two other ministers had Lyall Bay and Island Bay between them. Each church was required to raise a sum of money to contribute to the outgoings of the parish as a whole, the stronger ones being required to pledge more because of their larger membership and/or history of more generous giving. Apparently they expected donations to improve when I arrived as they raised my annual salary as the parish's second Minister to £300 and increased the Miramar contribution requirements to £4-10-00 a week.

This expectation put the congregation under pressure, but they coped and over the years they raised greater amounts. Many years later the congregation numbers at Hataitai declined and Miramar became the main contributor to the parish funds. It grew in other ways too.

When I first arrived in Wellington, Mr Seddon told me that the youth work was strong with the Sunday School roll standing around a hundred and the Bible Class about seventy or eighty.

---

1 Rev William A Burley 1885-1969

But the congregational attendance at church services was weak with the roll of regular attenders only about sixty. I was charged with the responsibility for seeking to increase this.

I took him at his word and gave visiting my top priority. Of course, one of the major aspects of a minister's work is "pastoral visiting". In addition to visiting the bereaved and the sick in hospital and in their homes, the minister has the task of calling on his parishioners in their homes for no other reason than demonstrating an interest (a genuine one) in their welfare and well-being. Today, with the increasingly typical phenomenon of both husband and wife being out at work, this is not so easy to do. But in my earlier ministry years this was far from typical and it was unusual not to find the housewife at home. So every afternoon was set aside for pastoral visiting. It is a most valuable way to get to know the members of one's church members – regular church attenders or not. Sometimes the visit would be no more than a social and pleasant discourse. But frequently, the minister would be expected to fulfil a role of nothing less than an untrained psychotherapist with the most intimate confidences and despair being revealed. On so many occasions throughout my ministry, a visit which began with the offer of a cup of tea, would end in breakdown. A mother with teapot in hand, apparently chatting idly, could suddenly burst into tears and subside into the armchair. The minister, after all, was present, and here was someone to talk to in confidence. Here was the minister's real work: outpourings of woes, concerns, anxieties, fears, disappointments, broken marriages, tense family lives, hopelessness, disillusionment, shattered dreams, boredom, anger, and plain, simple, but deeply painful, hurt. The offered cup of tea was often never served. I have always rated the task of preaching as unique: where one presents God to the people and the people to God – and although I struggled with the responsibility, surely, there is no higher calling in all the world[1]. But behind it is what one learns from

---

1 Dad left this sentiment to be expressed in his eulogy at his funeral.

people in their homes and in their lives. I did not always relish this afternoon work and would often set out with a little reluctance. But often I came home again, greatly uplifted and with a deep feeling of satisfaction and fulfilment that I had been able to play a small part in helping someone find a balance. I wonder with the decline of pastoral visits these days, if a valuable personal and social support mechanism in the community has been lost – quite apart from any accrued benefits to church membership.

As I visited and introduced myself to families in Miramar I discovered a lot of people who were new there, attracted to the developing suburb. Most had not become active in the local church since settling in, letting their membership lapse, or remained on the roll of the church they had first joined as young people in their original homes. Through regular visiting and getting these people involved from time to time in some undertaking or other, I encouraged them to become interested in the church again and regular attenders at worship. Converting "outsiders" to regular church attendance through home visiting was often a thankless task. Occasionally you succeeded in getting one member of the family to attend church just once or twice. But the attendance was not sustained. To get a regular attender was the greatest challenge of all and it was rarely achieved. Nonetheless, in Miramar, I succeeded in holding "Recognition of New Members" services two or three times a year for a small handful of new members each time. In my five years I managed to increase the small adult membership roll from sixty to nearly one hundred, mainly through visiting. I was only disappointed that I did not manage to double the roll but I contented myself with the two thirds increase.

Visiting was only one side of the coin, however. I had to ensure that the church services themselves were more attractive to attend. We introduced a special family service which became firmly established as a feature of church life at Miramar. The excellent attendance at Sunday School and Bible Class meant we had an "entree" into many homes with parents who rarely, if ever, attended church but who believed their children should do so (a common phenomenon). Family Service therefore developed as a call for all young people to bring their parents along and, to my delight, they responded with almost unexpected enthusiasm. Indeed, the small church was often filled to capacity and this had been unusual to see for many years. It was a case of "shoe-horning" everybody in and sometimes the officials, having done just that, found there was no room for themselves. Sometimes I would find they had gone for a stroll down the street until the service was over!

It was not until later in my life that I began to recognise the common human trait to be critical of another person's success or envious of their achievements. In Wellington East I experienced it (or perhaps just noticed it) for the first time: as one hurdle was overcome, its achievement would be lost amidst the cry that would immediately go up to fix something else. As the church began to fill up there was no shortage of suggestions as to how the attendance "could be increased further and more effectively if only the minister would see things my way". There was one group of parishioners whose suggestions I considered would not so much increase the congregation as deplete it, if not wipe it out altogether. But there was one member in Miramar who I felt made some worthwhile suggestions which arose from his experiences as a youth in Bible Classes. By and large his ideas centred on extending these activities into the adult church.

The man concerned was Cyrus Lovatt, a very loyal and devout member. He loved his church and was eager to see it prosper. Most of his life he had suffered from epilepsy and on my arrival at Miramar I was warned that he was liable to have an epileptic fit during a church service. Although Cyrus never did have a fit in church while I was there, I remember well how someone else did take ill to the point of collapse. A young woman who was a newcomer to our evening service had apparently taken a fancy to one of the church officials (indeed, was this why she had started attending?). On the occasion when she passed out during a service, not without a certain amount of drama, it fell to the same official, who no doubt saw it as part of his duty, to carry her bodily out of the church and to drive her home. To this day, many question the motivation behind her "attack"!

One of Cyrus's ideas was that the church should hold weekend retreats on the lines of Bible Class camps. It so happened that the ministers of the parish were shortly to attend a seminar at an Anglican Campsite at Otaki. As soon as I saw it, I realised that this was the very kind of setting that would be ideal for Cyrus's idea for the adult weekend retreats. It had facilities for cooking and eating as well as a hall for meetings. But it was the accommodation that was particularly good. The Anglican Church had procured ex-army huts and there was an abundance of them scattered over the area. It was possible to put up families and give them all the privacy they needed, those with teenage children taking a second hut. The idea caught on and the organisational machinery was set up with appropriate convenors in charge of different committees. I believed that it would weld the congregation together in a way that Sunday services alone could never do. This is exactly what happened. Some expressed concern that it might divide the congregation, making the non-attenders feel like outsiders, but it was felt that the unity it would create would outweigh any possible drawbacks. The weekend was a great success. Family camps such as these are no longer uncommon, but then they were a very new idea indeed.

The church anniversary was always regarded as the occasion when funds were raised for maintenance of the church property. The usual practice was for the trustees to request the Ladies Guild to organise some fundraising efforts. Although this had worked successfully for a number of years, I suggested that the trustees (all men) should do this themselves – or as well. My idea was greeted with horror. "What on earth can we do? The ladies do it well enough," the men chorused almost with disdain. Some felt decidedly uncomfortable at my suggestion and virtually indicated that I had broken the bounds of decency by coming up with such a suggestion. When I persevered and actually gave some suggestions of how they could raise money (galas, social evenings and concerts among them) one extremely stuffy gentlemen oozed "Don't be ridiculous!" and attempted to move the meeting on to another subject. In one sense I could understand their reaction. They were prominent people in the commercial world of the capital city and how could they disport themselves with childlike things which apparently my suggestions conjured up in their frightened minds. "It doesn't bear thinking about," echoed another trustee. I refused to let my idea go and concluded that we should at least put it to the gentlemen of the congregation.

The response was tardy at first, perhaps because of shock, but quite unwittingly, the idea of a revue of some kind took root with some members of the congregation. Some felt they had hidden talents that they were dying to exploit (and to expose!). Indeed, one of them, Gordon Shakes, had aspired to be a radio announcer and this idea appealed to him immensely. Two others, brothers Alan and Harold Johnson, had recently returned from the war where they had been in prisoner-of-war camps. There, many revues had been organised by the prisoners themselves and they were soon enthusiastic to share their experience in this way. Supported by others who could be said to have less talent but no less interest, an enthusiastic group emerged. I have to say there was indeed a notable lack of trustee participants, but nonetheless "the men's concert" soon became the talk of the congregation.

It was a resounding success – and not just in Miramar Church Hall. After that night, the Johnson brothers and Gordon Shakes formed themselves into a trio and were in demand all over Wellington. Their "piece de resistance" was the Andrews Sisters[1] sung in mime. For this they had their dresses specially made.

---

1 Three sisters born between 1911 and 1918 in Minnesota USA to a Greek immigrant father & Norwegian American mother. They formed a close harmony singing group that became world famous in the 1940s.

When we moved to Richmond several years later and built a new hall there, I invited the trio to perform their now almost famous Andrews Sisters act. Even though they had to cross the Cook Strait they gave up their weekend to do so. They flew to Blenheim and the Richmond men drove through to bring them the rest of the way. On the Sunday of their return the weather had closed in and the planes were grounded but the Blenheim Methodists came to the rescue and gave them accommodation for the night. The next morning the weather had cleared but back in Wellington they arrived late for work.

Included in the Miramar church concert party was a young talented pianist, Peter Averi. Peter, while still at school and hardly big enough to be seen behind a piano, had not only played the piano at Sunday School but also the organ at church. As an adult he became well known at a national level for his talent and work in music, as an organist, pianist, singer and conductor.

After that first and highly successful attempt at coercing the men to raise funds for the Miramar church, I suggested to the trustees that the church needed a Men's Fellowship. Although it seemed to some that I was going "just too far Mr Bell", it was wonderful to receive, in 1978, an invitation to join the Miramar Methodist Church Men's Fellowship in celebrating their 30th birthday.

Our predecessors in the parish, Ralph and Bertha Patchett[1], had started an Evening Women's Fellowship which, at the time, was a new move in church activities. It arose from the apparent reluctance of younger women and mothers to join the long established Women's Guilds which, traditionally, met in the afternoons. Perhaps it was because the current members had grown up with the group itself and now assumed a kind of propriety interest in it. As such they showed little inclination to share the leadership. Neither did they appear to have any patience

---

[1] Rev Ralph E Patchett 1910-1989

for the noise and interruptions that would, inevitably, come from having small children about were younger mothers to attend.

Whatever the explanation, the fact remained that "young mums" were being ignored in the life of the church. The setting up of the evening group was greeted enthusiastically. The Miramar-Worser Bay meetings were held monthly in different homes of the members and they became a source of great strength and support for the church.

When we moved to Richmond, Nelson, by coincidence, we again followed Ralph and Bertha Patchett and they had inaugurated a similar group there. In both Miramar and Richmond we were able to build on and expand a most creative and enthusiastic band of church workers. They kept the church in touch with groups who, with family commitments, had little time for church attendance and who, but for the work of the groups, may easily have remained remote from the church even when their family responsibilities had lessened.

While all this was going on among the adults, the youth work continued to expand and we were suffering from lack of room. So greatly daring, we launched on a building programme. I think we would have most liked to have a building dedicated to church worship as until now we had been using the building for meetings, social activities and church services. But a sole-use church building was not our greatest need. With the youth in such cramped conditions we decided to build Bible Class rooms and expand the church kitchen in our current Sunday School hall. In and through these improvements we envisaged the church could maximise the benefits of the investment through multiple uses. Following several fundraising initiatives, including a very big gala, we added three new rooms to our buildings.

It had been a while since I thought I was missing the farm but I knew I was certainly missing manual, practical work. I had always thought until I left home that any talent that I may have, lay in my feet and hands, not in my head. I was becoming too cerebral for comfort! I thought of buying a cow. I had another of those wonderful ideas of mine. The government houses in the area had been built in a kind of semicircle leaving some land vacant. *(Vacant land! What can I do with it?!)* It may have been intended to develop into a park or children's playground at some stage, but right now this was no man's land and it lay to waste. It was a perfect place, I concluded, for a house cow. I thought about it often, but on this occasion I did nothing about it. This was surprising for me, I suppose, because all my life I have persisted in coming up with ideas – most of them mad – but most of them I have at least turned into some form of reality. Naturally, always, but always, they were ideas which involved me in outdoor pursuits – where I wanted to be most – or in using my hands.

But an opportunity came up to do some practical work which I just could not ignore. The church needed painting. Why not do it ourselves?! One substantial local industry was paint manufacture and there were several thriving paint factories in and around the area. It occurred to me that being a local congregation one of these businesses might be willing to offer a significant discount on their paint to help us with our project. I persuaded the trustees to let me investigate the possibility (and that took some doing as usual – a singularly unenthusiastic bunch as I recall them today). I thought that over the quieter time in the summer school holidays in January, we might be able to get the painting of the church done with several voluntary working groups, rather quaintly and traditionally known as "working bees". The trustees didn't like the idea of working bees (of course). They were a good and capable group of men but they all had ideas of their own and all wanted to have their say. Even after the meeting when I made several more attempts to enlist the support of some parishioners I did not get far. The outcome for me was one of sheer frustration and nothing, but nothing, started.

I became fully involved, as I usually do with such projects, taking an enthusiastic interest in it. Refusing to sit back and see nothing done at all, I set to in getting the church painted myself. I did not have any particularly significant success in gathering in gallons of cheap paint but I did manage to secure some discounts here and there. Over the month of January I finished painting the church virtually entirely alone. I was absolutely thrilled with my efforts although I have to acknowledge the bit of help from two brothers Alan and Harold Johnson. Their homes were on a hillside, overlooking the church and they could not but help to see me working. Perhaps it was too much for their consciences and they did put in a hand!

It was with a certain amount of pride and indeed a little sense of triumph therefore, that I attended the first Trust meeting of the New Year. I was greeted by the trustees in rather sombre mood considering how well I had done and I thought that they might have expressed a little bit more appreciation. I was puzzled but my puzzlement did not last long. The minutes were read out and the one relating specifically to the painting of the church given an interesting emphasis – the pitch of the reader's voice dropped and the pace was measurably slower: *It was agreed that Reverend Bell should look into the matter of the painting of the church. He will report back to the Trustees at the next meeting when the Trustees will take the decision on how to proceed.* Apparently I had been the cause of embarrassment to some of the trustees who had been criticised by some of their business friends and associates for letting me do it without their help. The church was not painted again for another six or seven years and embarrassment or not, I remained very pleased with myself although the trustees never did thank me.

The Miramar Methodist Church building we used for our church activities was pretty basic albeit functional. It had an interesting history though as it was built in precisely one day, more than twenty years earlier on Saturday 26 April 1924. It was completed with the help of many volunteers and as night fell, work continued in the beams of car headlights. The first service in it was held the next morning, appropriately a Sunday. It was a multi-purpose hall, used for Sunday School, Bible Class, meetings of every description and social functions but when it came to the church services, I thought it was difficult to create a worshipful atmosphere. The idea came to me that it might help if we had drapes right across the back wall and extending around the corners a little way down the side walls. For this we chose a deep red colour and it certainly gave a warmth to the Sunday services.

A couple who had been very active in the church from the time of its inception, Mr and Mrs Tom Hinde, took the opportunity to add to the renovations in a most touching way. Tom himself had been Trust Secretary for fourteen years from 1928 to 1942 and in that final year of service he had received word that their son was missing on the war front, shortly afterwards to be confirmed that he had been killed in action. To honour their son's memory, they decided now to give a Communion Table to the church. This too did a lot to help generate the atmosphere of worship that we were keen to instil.

* * *

It was while we lived in Miramar that Rae suffered a tragedy that was to affect her deeply and markedly for the rest of her life. The personal shock was so great she was never ever to return fully to the person she was before it. During 1945, her mother had, unknown to us, suffered two severe depressions. This was all the more surprising as it was that very year when her mother's popularity and success and recognition in the community seemed to reach its peak with her being made a Justice of the Peace only at the end of July. But despite this, gradually the depressions deteriorated to the extent that she required medical treatment. It was astonishing for me to see my mother-in-law in this way as I had long been convinced that Rae's own sense of humour and love of laughter had come directly from her cheery mother. Indeed, when Hilda was well again, there was no sign that anything had ever been amiss and she carried on her church and public duties as eagerly and enthusiastically as before (as far as we could tell).

But the depression returned. In December 1945 a close friend of Rae's from Christchurch, Hilda Gribble, came to spend Christmas with us. On sharing with us the news of Rae's home town she let slip that Rae's mother was quite ill, not realising that the family had kept this from us. Rae immediately phoned her father and once confronted with the fact that she had heard the news, he admitted reluctantly that Hilda was not well. Rae wanted to go to Christchurch immediately and spent the rest of the day packing for herself and the two toddlers. That night they caught the inter-island ferry to Lyttelton and arrived at her home to have her worst fears confirmed. Hilda was indeed ill: her nerves were frayed and she was suffering bouts of depression. She was admitted to the Balmoral Private Hospital where she was seen on 8th January 1946 by Doctor Melville H Aiken who confirmed the diagnosis was one of "anxiety state" and, according to a later statement, "recently aggravated by her many public duties and obligations". Hilda returned home where Dr Aiken saw her again on 23rd January 1946. Another doctor, Donald Currie, also saw and treated Hilda in the last eight weeks.

The drugs she was prescribed were not helping. Indeed, we speculated that they were making her decidedly worse, intensifying rather than dissipating her expressions of despair. The concern was so great that my father-in-law and brother-in-law had severe disagreements with the doctor[1] about her treatment. The doctor was beginning to wonder whether Hilda would have to be admitted to Sunnyside Mental Hospital. This suggestion absolutely horrified Hilda, and her depression plummeted to new lows.

Nevertheless, Hilda's depressions fluctuated on a daily basis. About six weeks later I decided I would take a few days off and join Rae and my sons. I crossed on the ferry arriving in Lyttelton, as usual, early in the morning. It was February 12th 1946. The Barrell house was full. Not only were Rae and Weston and Riley staying, so too was May Fitzer[2] from Dunedin, Hilda's sister-in-law and widow of her brother Ray Fitzer[3] who had died five years earlier from heart trouble. At that time, Hilda, had spent a lot of

1 Although it is not clear, I believe the disagreements were with Dr Melville Aiken – the family doctor. It is likely that Dr Currie was a hospital doctor or specialist. - GB.

2 Now May Pile, widow for a second time from her second marriage. In May 1995, she was still in Dunedin in a Rest Home. She sent a sympathy card to the family when Mum died in March. - GB.

3 Sgt Raymond Edward Fitzer 1888 (Melbourne) – 1941 (Dunedin)

time in Dunedin helping May to care for Ray. Now May had also come to Christchurch to be with Hilda during her "low" weeks.

When I arrived that morning, Hilda was keen to talk to me. She asked "What do you think will happen to my family if anything happened to me, Charlie?" It was extraordinary to hear Hilda talk like this, but I took it as indicative of her depression. Keen to ease her mind of any such worries I made a point of saying that should such a sad thing happen her husband and children would surely cope. "You mustn't worry about such a thing, Mum. Dad would miss you dreadfully, but he would cope. And as for Girl and Boy, they have their own families now who need them. They must cope for them." Hilda gave a brief, soft reply, "Of course, Charlie, of course." She got up and walked away quietly. For the rest of that day Hilda pottered about the house dusting here, re-arranging bits of china there.

I gave my reply to her anxious question not another thought, I had surely set her mind at rest. But less than twenty-four hours later – and indeed for the rest of my life – those words were to burn into me with searing pain. I feared it was precisely the wrong thing to say. She was, I am sure, wanting to hear that she would be needed, not that her family could cope without her. I can still recall those moments with her with startling vividness. To this day, I choke with remorse at the missed opportunity to say something else which could well have been far more comforting and reassuring for her.

That night of February 12th, Rae and I went to the cinema. It was a good opportunity for us to go out together because Charles and Hilda and May were able to babysit Weston and Riley. After getting back we went to bed before the others. May had been sitting with Hilda for some time. Hilda had been unsettled and pacing the floor. Charles and Hilda had slept in separate bedrooms since she had been ill and "restless", but that night he noticed when Hilda changed for bed she still had some of her clothes on. He didn't question her about that odd behaviour and nor did he say anything to Rae or May or me – until the next day. May said that had she realised she would have continued to sit with her[1].

Hilda took her life on the morning of February 13th 1946. We were all there in the house, her husband, her daughter, her two grandsons, her son-in-law and her sister-in-law, when she left her home without a sound, long after we had all gone to bed. She left a family she was devoted to. But no message[2]. I have found the fact that she was not alone in the house, and indeed had rarely been surrounded by her family in such numbers – including her grandsons whom she adored – all the more bewildering for they were right there when she decided to leave them.

Just once in the night, I heard our young Riley, not yet a year old, whimper, but before I went downstairs to him, he stopped and appeared to have settled again. I have always been convinced that Hilda went in to see her grandson, picked him up and returned him to his bed before she left the house. To think that I may have heard her as she was saying some form of goodbye to her grandson and preparing to leave the house fuels a terrible memory for me.

Rae's father woke early on that awful morning. As usual he took her in a cup of tea shortly after six, but she was not there and her bed had not been slept in. In great consternation he searched the house and outside. Her bicycle was missing. He woke both Rae and I abruptly with the urgent, sharp words, "Do you know where your mother is?" They were as chilling as they were confusing in our broken sleep. He suggested she may have cycled to her favourite spot in Hagley Park, less than a mile down the road. I dressed hastily and we drove in his car to the park, leaving Rae behind me utterly bewildered and deeply anxious. Although Charles and I were worried about her absence, I am sure we were both optimistic that we would find her, perhaps acting strangely but maybe only sitting under a tree, day dreaming. The family had

---

[1] In a letter from May to Dad, written in 1992 after she had seen the announcement of their Golden Wedding in the Otago Daily Times which prompted her to recall her memories of that night.

[2] Charles, Hilda's husband, never admitted to one, if there ever was. But he was up first that morning and would have found it, if anything had been left for him.

noticed her vagueness for a day or two. Besides, my father-in-law said with great confidence that Hilda had this favourite spot in the park which she loved. She would surely be alright – even happy – there. Whatever else we may have been expecting in those moments, none of us at any point, then or in the weeks before, ever contemplated what she had apparently been contemplating. Even with that sudden and mysterious disappearance that morning, death, suicide, accident, never crossed my mind: I wondered only where she may be sitting and hoped that she would not be too distressed.

Meanwhile, May had walked around the corner to Rae's brother, Boy's, home. She knocked on the door and woke him up. Boy remembers going to the front door and May simply saying, "Hilda's gone." "Gone where?" Boy asked. "Hagley Park," May answered. My father-in-law and I had already left the house so Boy called Arthur Barrell[1], his uncle, and they went off together to look in North Hagley Park also. We later realised that each pair had been looking in the same area, around the lakes and the tennis courts and behind the hospital, but we had not seen each other.

My father-in-law and I walked into the park across the dewy grass in the misty, early morning light of a summer's day. Gracious English trees stood tall and willows bowed low with their branches dipping in the shallow, slow running waters of the Avon River. Our hunch proved to be correct. There, very near to the croquet lawn, was her bicycle leaning against a tree – and the lamp was still on. Why had she not switched it off when she dismounted? Our hearts lightened as we looked around for Hilda thinking she would be just here. It was a relief short-lived. From a bridge further down, near the old Nurses Home behind the hospital, I spotted her – before her husband did. In utter disbelief and with a chilling feeling that made my mouth go dry I saw her body lying face down in the river beneath me[2]. I did not want my

---

1 Arthur Frederick Barrell 1888 (Christchurch) – 1960

2 The choice of these words "beneath me" when Dad relayed this tale, makes me wonder, with hindsight, if he was standing on a bridge when he spotted her. I regret that I did not

father-in-law to see her, but if I did not say anything he would spot her himself in the next few seconds. He was only a yard or two from me looking into the park – away from the river. The moment when I had to draw my father-in-law's attention to what I had found is an experience too painful to describe. When he saw her, he made no move towards her. I went to rush into the river to reach her, but he stopped me and said simply that we must call the police. He just stood there and said absolutely nothing more. The next few minutes, while he and I were quite alone in that still, deserted, park in the first light of an insultingly beautiful day, were minutes where the entire world seemed not to speak or breathe.

It was Police Constable Francis Flanagan, who, according to his statement, retrieved the body "at 8.35am…several hundred yards upstream from the Christchurch Public Hospital". He "waded into the river…where the river is some twelve to eighteen inches deep and slow running…the body appeared to have been in the water for three or four hours."

This was puzzling. It meant that she drowned between 4.30 and 5.30am. Did she leave the house, as I had suspected when she may have picked up Riley, about midnight or just after? And if she did leave then, what did she do for the rest of the night? Maybe she was just sitting in the park? Or did she leave the house much later than that? But as my father-in-law said, her bed had not been slept in. The hours between when I last saw her at 11.30pm and her drowning in the early morning, will never be accounted for.

---

question him more closely at the time as I may have been able to pinpoint exactly where she was found.

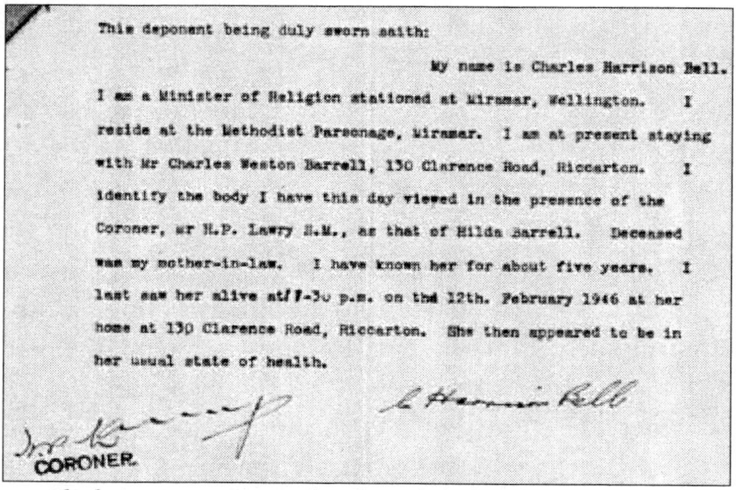

This deponent being duly sworn saith:

My name is Charles Harrison Bell.

I am a Minister of Religion stationed at Miramar, Wellington. I reside at the Methodist Parsonage, Miramar. I am at present staying with Mr Charles Weston Barrell, 130 Clarence Road, Riccarton. I identify the body I have this day viewed in the presence of the Coroner, Mr H.P. Lawry S.M., as that of Hilda Barrell. Deceased was my mother-in-law. I have known her for about five years. I last saw her alive at 11-30 p.m. on thd 12th. February 1946 at her home at 130 Clarence Road, Riccarton. She then appeared to be in her usual state of health.

C Harrison Bell

CORONER.

Charles's sworn statement identifying the body of his mother-in-law, Wednesday 13th February 1946. The time appears to have been changed by hand to read 11.30pm.

In my father-in-law's statement to the police he said: "I found her bicycle in Hagley Park about fifty yards from the River Avon and about two hundred yards from Victoria Lake. A search of my home failed to find any note left by the deceased."

Later reports concluded that Hilda had probably drowned in a deeper part of the river and that her body had floated downstream. However, it was never established with any confidence at exactly what point she may have entered the river.

It was my painful and unpleasant duty to identify the body in the presence of the coroner, Mr H P Lawry.

The experience for us all was numbing. Rae's father and twin were devastated. But Rae herself went into a state of shock where she was somehow, albeit unintentionally, cruelly unreachable. She shrunk and withdrew into a shell so complete and private that, very worryingly, she did not, could not, shed one tear. The shock was so severe that to this day I believe she still has not got over it. Every year she still pointedly marks her new diary with a personal, poignant, note. Even as recently as 1987[1] she had written for February 13th, "Mother died 41 years ago." There is a pain and

[1] Dad related this story to me about 1989. - GB

sensitivity in her regarding the loss of her mother that is almost beyond bearing.

Hilda's body was brought to her home but both Rae's father and twin brother, forbade Rae to go into the lounge to see her. They feared she could not cope with the sight or the grief. In fact, quietly and secretly Rae did go in to see her. She did not tell even me that she had done that until about fifteen years later. And I doubt if she ever told her father or brother.

Despite all the encouragement of her family, friends and doctors to entice Rae to cry and to feel her grief openly, she never did. That is, surprisingly, until a few months ago as I write these notes. She is now eighty-three years old and suffers from what we can only believe are the early stages of dementia. Completely out of the blue one night, she asked me how her mother had died. I looked at her, astonished. She looked at me directly and awaited my reply, openly and patiently. I was not sure whether to avoid the truth but I had read when dealing with dementia sufferers that often when misleading answers are given, ultimately confusion is greater as one day they will recall the facts correctly themselves as well as remembering your incorrect answer. Besides, Rae's signs of dementia then were only minor. As kindly and as gently as possible, I reminded her that her mother had drowned – although I did not mention the word suicide – and I did not need to as she asked no further. She replied, "How awful, how truly awful", and burst into tears. It was the first time in the forty-six years since her mother died that I had seen her grieve in this open, natural way. In all those years she not only refused to cry, she refused to discuss it. Rae internalised her suffering completely and a great silence descended on the subject for the rest of her days. Although her mother was regularly talked about and her memory kept alive with the greatest affection, no one was allowed to discuss the manner of her death beyond the simple explanation, that her "darling mother" had died "suddenly" at the age of sixty years.

Apart from bearing the natural sadness of losing her mother so young and so suddenly, the other appalling burden Rae took upon herself was the fact of suicide itself. Her parents as well as

Rae and her brother, were all deeply committed Christians. Suicide, in the church's viewpoint, was a sin and it was not acceptable in society. Although today suicide carries far less of a stigma (if any at all for many), in the mid 1940s it remained an abomination and condemned by nearly everyone in the church and in society. For someone like Rae who had always been so concerned about right and wrong, good and bad, kindness and cruelty, this was a bombshell. Rae's very faith, not only in Christianity, but in life itself, was completely and utterly rocked. Rae clung desperately to the fact that her mother had been under the doctor, that the pills had made her worse, that she was not herself when she took her life. It was a doctor's mistake. It was a mistake. It should not have happened. It was not her mother's wish to die. She was drugged. This, at all costs, had to be made clear. And it was all true. But in reality, Rae was crushed.

The period of denial and anguish has lasted beyond its normal course. The open grieving never came but the hidden grieving certainly did and the signs were there for all to see, every day thereafter. Not only did her hair prematurely turn pure white, but her dancing brown eyes never danced, I swear, quite the same way ever again. The carefree spirit vanished. She shudders when anyone, anyone, uses the word 'depressed'. As our own children grew up the word itself seemed to be in vogue. Our sons could come home from school announcing quite flippantly, "I'm depressed". But Rae could not accept it. She swooped on each occasion. "Don't use that word. You mean you are down. You have no idea what depressed really means." The boys may have been puzzled by this predictable and insistent response, but never got any explanation even when they retorted, "Don't be silly, Mum. I am depressed, I really am. Have you any idea how bad that exam was?"

Her refusal to share her tragedy with her sons as they grew up brought its own pain. A set of extraordinary circumstances combined to bring about a shattering reminder nearly eighteen years later. Her father, now an old man, was not well and we offered to stay in the same family home in Riccarton in January

1964, as his second wife, Madge, took a short break from nursing him. Godfrey had a school friend Charles Pollock with him for the school holidays and so we all stayed in Riccarton together. Christchurch offered both Godfrey and Charles a chance to explore the city and the sights and they filled their days in their own way. One morning they hired a canoe and paddled up the River Avon. Fooling around, as only teenagers can do, they eventually toppled the canoe and fell right in. Struggling with the canoe and splashing around in the Avon, they attempted to drag it up on the bank. They were totally soaked and in hysterics as they cycled back through the same Hagley Park, to Clarence Road. Godfrey ran into the kitchen where Rae was preparing a meal. "Mum!" he shouted with glee, "I nearly drowned in the Avon." Not only was it the same river. Not only was it near the same point in the river where they fell in, for Hilda had loved to watch the canoes go past as she regularly visited her favourite part of the park. But also it was here in the very same kitchen that Rae had received the news that her mother had drowned in the Avon, eighteen years earlier. And there was one other extraordinary fact that could not be ignored. This, her youngest son, although she had not wanted it to be, had been born on the 13th of February, the anniversary of her mother's death. In total innocence, Godfrey, in his joy of sharing his experience with his mother as he stood in front of her still soaked to the skin, could never understand why, if he had even noticed, Rae dropped her vegetable knife and hurriedly left the kitchen for the solace of some other room in her childhood home – that house full of so many very happy and yet so many very painful memories.

There was a dreadful, almost unforgivable, haste over Hilda's funeral. Rae's father insisted that it be a completely private funeral and refused to have it in Hilda's (and his) beloved Durham Street Methodist Church. It would be held at home, the following day, February 14th Valentine's Day, as quickly as possible, and no one but family would be allowed to attend. People had hardly heard of her death before she was buried. Refusing to allow the funeral to be in a church was, in my view, a dreadful, indeed cruel, error of judgement and compounded the grief – and the shock. But my father-in-law was adamant about all the arrangements. I shared in a distressing and emotional funeral service held in the lounge of their home. Throughout it all Rae sat tight-lipped and dry-eyed, finding apparent comfort and diversion in supporting her father whom she had to help out of the room when he could not sit through any more. Rae appeared remarkably strong and in control, but too much so, and my worries for her own health were only just beginning.

The Press, Thursday 14th February 1946

DEATHS
Barrell - On February 13th at Christchurch, Hilda, beloved wife of Charles Weston Barrell, 130 Clarence Street, Riccarton and loving mother of Charles Durham and Mrs C H Bell, Wellington. Make her to be numbered with Thy saints in glory everlasting. (Private interment Thursday afternoon.)

The Press, Thursday 14th February 1946

BODY FOUND IN RIVER
The body of Mrs C W Barrell of 130 Clarence Road was found in the Avon River yesterday. An inquest into her death was opened last evening before the Coroner (Mr H P Lawry). After identification had been established, the inquest was adjourned sine die. Mrs Barrell had been in ill health for some time and recently had been in hospital.[1]

The Press, Thursday 14th February 1946

OBITUARY Mrs C W Barrell
The death occurred yesterday of Mrs Hilda Barrell, wife of Mr C W Barrell. Born in Dunedin and educated at a private school in Melbourne, Mrs Barrell had lived in Christchurch since her marriage which took place in Christchurch at the Durham Street Methodist Church of which she was a staunch member.
Many years ago Mrs Barrell began to take an active part in the public life of Christchurch and proved herself an able administrator and a kind and generous friend to those in less fortunate circumstances. For two and a

1 Been in hospital? This is believed to be incorrect.

half years, until her death, she was president of the Christchurch branch of the National Council of Women after having held the office of vice-president for several terms. She was vitally interested in the Women's Christian Temperance Union, having been president of the Riccarton branch of the union for more than twenty-one years and she held the office of district president and Dominion president at the time of her death. During the depression years, Mrs Barrell did good work as chairwoman of the Girls' Employment Committee. She was a useful member of the Methodist Orphanage Board and was also a Justice of the Peace.

But Mrs Barrell will be longest and most gratefully remembered for her many personal kindnesses and for her practical sympathy with patients in the mental hospital. For years she visited every Sunday, patients who had few or no friends. She learnt the likes and dislikes of each patient and tried to cheer them by taking gifts that pleased them.

Mrs Barrell is survived by her husband, one son (Mr C D Barrell of Christchurch) and one daughter (Mrs Bell, wife of the Rev C H Bell, Wellington).

The Press, Friday 15th February 1946

WOMEN'S NEWS

At the monthly meeting of the North Canterbury Post and Telegraph Women's Association held on Wednesday evening, a motion of sympathy was passed to the relatives of Mrs C W Barrell. Members stood in silence as a mark of respect to her memory.

The Press, Saturday 16th February 1946

WOMEN'S NEWS

At the general meeting of the Christchurch branch of the Women's Christian Temperance Union (WCTU) , at which Miss C Henderson presided, a vote of sympathy to the relatives of the late Mrs C W Barrell was passed. Mrs Barrell had been president of the district committee and vice president of the Dominion executive.

(For several weeks later, there appeared in The Press *various reports similar to the above regarding the death of Mrs C W Barrell, as different women's and public groups met. However, no public announcement was found in that Christchurch paper regarding the result of the inquest.)*

Another published obituary: source unknown

OBITUARY Mrs C W Barrell

BARRELL: At Christchurch on February 13, 1946, Hilda, the beloved wife of Charles Weston Barrell and loved mother of Charles Durham and Hilda Rae. "Make her to be numbered with Thy saints in glory everlasting."

Mrs C W Barrell passed immediately from active service to higher service. It was most fitting for the great needs of the people would not permit her to rest or think of retirement.

Born in Dunedin in 1885 and educated at a private college in Melbourne, Hilda Fitzer came in early adolescence to Christchurch. Her first associations with Methodism came when she linked up with the Richmond Methodist Church (Christchurch). Later on she associated with the Durham Street Methodist Church, of which she became a member, being most actively associated until her passing. It was in the Christian Endeavour Society of that church that she came to know Christ as her Saviour – she loved Him truly and in this love was the secret of the great service she rendered the community in the following years. One of the pledges taken at that great decision was to read her bible twice daily and in spite of manifold activities, that vow was never broken. She entered fully into the activities of the church life, being a member of the choir and a talented elocutionist. The Bible Class movement had its beginnings about this time and Miss Fitzer was one of the foundation officers of the Canterbury Union.

In December 1907 she married Mr Charles W Barrell, a member of a prominent Durham Street family. They settled in Riccarton and it was in their home that the Clarence Road Methodist Church was fostered.

Her gifts were above the average and she was in demand by other than church organisations. For the last three years she was the President of the Christchurch branch of the National Council of Women, a task involving a tremendous amount of work, bringing her in contact with all manner of organisations, the chairing of many large public meetings and speaking at many civic functions. An indication is given of her ability and capacity when it is said that she filled this office with conspicuous success.

Keenly concerned about the welfare of women, she was a great protagonist for their rights. This involved her in active association with very many organisations. She worked hard in helping to establish a force of women police. In 1945 Mrs Barrell was made a Justice of the Peace.

The church gave her connexional recognition when in recent years she was made a member of the South Island Orphanage Board. But it was to the work of the Women's Christian Temperance Union that Hilda Barrell made her greatest contribution. For a period of twenty-three years she served it as President of the Riccarton Branch, as President for Canterbury District and Vice President of the Dominion[1]. She felt deeply about the evil of the drink traffic and in her work for its overthrow she showed outstanding gifts of statesmanship, vision, courage, judgement and faith.

For somewhere near twenty years, once a month, on a Sunday afternoon, she visited the mental hospital where she called on a number of women who had no friends to see them. She came to know their individual fancies and armed with cookies and gifts, she brought a ray of sunshine regularly into their drab lives. For these and all people who knew ill health and misfortune, Mrs Barrell had a sympathetic ear and heart. Her vivid imagination put herself in their places and "she sat where they sat" and the result was a very helpful sympathy, which in the long run took a heavy toll of her health and strength.

This practical sympathy was nowhere more seen than in the days of the depression when she not only helped on the organisation side of the Unemployment Committee but went personally to the homes and the people in need.

Although Hilda Barrell could move in the highest of circles with the ease, grace and dignity of a queen, she could enter the most humble home with equal ease and with no sense of condescension. Very many have been glad of her coming in times of sickness, sorrow and need, and in spite of a very busy public life, she always found time to help and visit such people.

Yet with all her public duties, Hilda Barrell was first and foremost a wife and a mother. Never in the multiplicity of her activities did the home suffer neglect. She dearly loved her husband and family and was loved by them. Always they came first and for them she always went the second mile. Cast in a humble genteel mould, she was a home lover. She did not seek public life and public honour, but they sought her and always she had a sense of call and vocation.... [transcription incomplete here][2]

On the following Sunday in the church she loved and served so long and faithfully, a memorial serviced was held, her own minister, the

---

[1] There is a conflict of evidence here. Some sources say Hilda Barrell was Dominion President of the WCTU, others say she was Vice President.

[2] This obituary was a copy in Mum's possession and it is suspected that Mum herself cut out this sentence or two which probably referred to her mother's suicide. - GB

Rev R Dudley presiding, assisted by the Rev C H Bell. A glowing tribute was paid to Hilda Barrell's sterling worth and her honoured memory.

The sympathy of a large circle of friends goes out to her husband, Mr C W Barrell, one of the best known figures in Christchurch Methodism, to her son Charles Durham who is a choir member and Trust Secretary of the Durham Street Church and to her daughter, Hilda Rae, the wife of the Rev C H Bell of Miramar, Wellington.

It is not often that we look upon the life of a Hilda Barrell and we thank God that she lived. She was a gift to our generation and her works will bless generations yet to come.

Hilda had been a wonderful and loved person in the community. She was well regarded for her leadership, community work, her appointment as one of the then very few Justices of the Peace, as an elocutionist and as a public speaker.

She was Vice President of the National Council of Women (Canterbury) for four years (1940 – 1943) and for two years President (1944 – 1945).

When the war finished in May 1945 there were VE Day celebrations across the world. Several organisations combined for a victory march in Christchurch on 10 May and along with several civic leaders, Hilda as President of the National Council of Women (Canterbury) was invited to speak. She spoke on a dais to a crowded Cathedral Square and the occasion was broadcast. Rae did not attend but listened with pride to her mother on the radio. Hilda considered her selection as one of the speakers as a great but wholly undeserved honour. There was a great deal of recognition, pride, celebration and joy – and also, surely, a sense of achievement – for Hilda that day. With that in mind, it is hard to credit that this confident, able and respected public speaker and community leader, within the year took her own life.

Not only had she spoken on this auspicious occasion only a few months earlier, but Hilda was also still President of the National Council of Women when she committed suicide.

> Mrs Lorrimer referred to the passing of our president Mrs Barrell and the loss sustained by the council both locally and nationally. The secretary read a number of letters received from various societies paying tribute to Mrs Barrell's memory and expressing sympathy with the branch. Many members paid personal tribute to their late president and the great work she had done for others. Members then stood in silence in memory of Mrs Barrell.

Minutes of the Christchurch branch of the NCW 7 March 1946 (Minutes 1944-47 MB126 item 5g). Acknowledgement: Macmillan Brown Library, University of Canterbury

> Correspondence has been received from Mr C W Barrell and family thanking NCW for its expressions of sympathy.

Minutes of the Christchurch branch of the NCW 26 Feb 1946 (Minutes 1944-49 MB126 item 4b). Acknowledgement: Macmillan Brown Library, University of Canterbury

Much of Hilda's community work focused on pure acts of kindness. For years on end, every Saturday she would bake or preserve all day and every Sunday afternoon take Madeira cakes and scones and jars of jam or fruit to the Sunnyside Mental Hospital and would seek out those residents who had been abandoned by friends and families when they could adequately care for them no longer. Occasionally, too, she would take cookies to the women's prison. She got a name for her generosity and kindness, and I suppose inevitably, it was not long before word spread around "the poor" that a visit to her home would result in a handout of cakes or biscuits. She never turned anyone away, ever. It was usually Boy's responsibility to drive his mother, in his father's car, to Sunnyside on Sunday afternoons. On one occasion, Boy says, as they went in the back way to Sunnyside (the Riccarton entrance) he swerved too suddenly, narrowly missed the gate, and plunged into and over the carpeted lawn, through rose beds and then through the tulips flattening them in their tracks. They were so embarrassed that as the car emerged on to another driveway on the other side of the lawn, Boy proceeded straight ahead to the main gate and exited calmly as if nothing had happened. They went straight home. In the back seat, the special stand erected by his father for his mother's weekly delivery of cakes and goodies, was bare. All were on the floor of the car.

These visits and kindnesses endeared Hilda to many. "She was a saint", they would recall. Despite the funeral being private a large number of people gathered outside the house, lining the path and standing on the street beyond the gate and by the waiting hearse. When Hilda was carried out, a slightly dishevelled character shuffled forward and threw rose petals onto the pathway in front of the pallbearers and onto the coffin as it passed. Rae approached him later to thank him and to apologise for not recognising him. "Nothing is too good for your mother," he said. "She has helped me and my family in the past. She was a real lady."

In 1992, May Pile (1st marriage: to Raymond Fitzer) (nee Scott) saw in the *Otago Daily Times,* the announcement of Charles & Rae's Golden Wedding. This sparked memories for her and out of the blue a letter arrived from May, aged 86, living in Dunedin.[1]
Extract:

> 8 June 1992
> Dear Rae and Charlie
> I have been sitting and thinking about the past. The past surely comes back to haunt us, all by a Golden Wedding notice in the paper: Rae Barrell and Rev Charles Bell. All these memories came flooding back.
> How well I remember that awful day, when my sister-in-law took her own life. Hilda was 21 years my senior, and so it was Rae and me who were more like sisters. I never ever really felt comfortable with Hilda because of the age difference but I did my best. I would hear her walking the floor at night so I would go and sit with her. Little did I think she would do what she did although she was very unsettled that night. She didn't want to go to bed. Rae and you had gone to the pictures. Finally she went to bed[2] but Charles (her husband) said the next day he had noticed she still had some of her clothes on. I wished he had told me that as I would have stayed with her. When it was all over he said, "I am

[1] I visited her in the Belhaven Rest Home, Dunedin, 1995: aged 90, but she was vaguer in her recollections. - GB

[2] This recollection is at odds with that of Rae's father who said that Hilda didn't sleep in her bed that night.

> finished with the Fitzers now thank goodness"[1]. He didn't seem to realise that my children were Fitzers. He also asked, "Why did this have to happen to me?" I said to him that it had as much right to happen to him as to anyone. His second wife didn't have it easy. I quite liked her. She died years ago.
> Little did I realise that tragedy was to touch my family also. Years later a policeman came to me to tell me my son [Keith] had been killed[2,3].
> Well, I have got this off my chest.
> My love, May

Rae refused to accept that Hilda's death was a "normal" suicide and understandably went out of her way to protect her mother's memory, defend her and dilute the pain of what "really happened". Rae would only say that her mother was not in her right mind and this was caused by an experimental drug – in short, a doctor's mistake. The strong drug and pre-existing heart condition are indeed facts but Rae somehow would not condone any other interpretation. It was as if Rae was grateful that there was something and perhaps someone she could blame. She clung to those reasons almost desperately all her life. Perhaps she was right, but Rae's life would have been an easier and happier one had she not held such a horror of the final outcome – that her mother took her own life.

For years, Rae did not share this story with her own family. It was a kind of watershed, but not for long, and not one that led to much of a greater acceptance, when in 1985 (nearly an astonishing forty years after her mother's death), she finally "opened up" and wrote a cathartic letter to our three sons about it. We were living in Tauranga at that time and I had long since retired. The story had already "leaked out" to the boys by then, much to Rae's sadness. I

---

1 This must be a reference to the alcoholism and/or the Roman Catholicism in the family which Charles W Barrell never accepted well and/or to the memory of Hilda's Uncle Harry, gambler and alcoholic, living with them for many years.

2 Keith Raymond Fitzer, died at the age of 21, 1934-1955 (Herbert, Otago)

3 Can her words "that tragedy" be interpreted as her own son having also committed suicide? He died in a "train accident" but no records of any train accident relating to his death in 1955 have been found.

think she had somehow clung to a forlorn hope that it would have been a secret she would have taken to the grave with her. She didn't want her sons to have to bear not only the sadness but what she considered to be the burden of a suicide in the family. But when she realised they already knew, and yet it had still not been discussed, she decided it was time to "put the record straight" and her words emphatically and purposefully do that. The letter made very clear how Rae dealt with the tragedy of that black day herself and how she wanted her sons to deal with it too.

Letter from Rae to her sons and daughters-in-law about her mother's death

Tauranga
6 February 1985
Dear Sons and Daughters [Weston & Prue, Riley & Anne, Godfrey]
For years I have tried to get a letter to you but I hesitated because I preferred that Godfrey be older. Until a couple of years ago I had no idea that you were aware of the nature of mother's passing and I was extremely upset because I looked on it as being extremely unfair to her – I wanted you to think of her and know of her from what *I* told you. However, that has passed and now Godfrey is with us it gives me the opportunity to give each of you a copy of the obituary – it has been tucked away in a box all these years, and being on very fine paper it is discoloured and the bugs have spoilt it. Dad [husband Charles] went through it and said it is all in one piece and that he could photocopy it for you, so here it is.

It was an experience which one could never forget – I was very bitter for quite a time. I felt we had forgotten her by going to sleep [that night of February 12th]. My brother [twin Charles], of course, was not there – lived two streets away. Mother's sister-in-law, Mrs Ray Fitzer [May] , from Dunedin, had come to help me so there were four adults in the house. Not one of us heard a sound and seeing she had to go down the stairs, it is always a wonder to us how we missed hearing her. Her heart was in such a bad condition that the doctor had told my father she wouldn't live another month[1], but there was a certain amount of strength there or she could not have got to the park [Hagley Park] and river – despite this being not far away. After what the doctor said I rang Dad

[1] Only another month? This was complete news to me. In no other account or recollection, even of Dad's, has this fact been referred to. - GB

[husband Charles] (we lived in Wellington) and he came the next night and this meant so much to me, especially with Riley being quite sick. He was eleven months – and a virus caused the trouble.

Mother's special friends came to talk with me some while after the funeral – pleading with me to realise Mother must have slipped and fallen into the river. They reminded me how she loved the river and the trees around.

The funeral was from the house as my father wished this because Mother was so fond of her home. I had to leave the room with Father as he was so upset. As I got outside folks who had been helped by Mother over the years with soup, food and so on, were putting flowers on the path. They also wanted to leave me their names in case I needed help.

I stayed with Father for a long time, trying to get a housekeeper, but he was hard to satisfy – wanted no one – quite natural. My brother and Ira did all they could to get one but it was slow going. I then felt I must get home to Dad [husband] and he came and got us. I was so relieved, but found it hard to leave my father alone.

When Mother first developed her illness, starting with severe flu and then frequent heart turns (I did not know this, of course) a friend came to see us [Hilda Gribble] at Christmas [in Wellington, Dec 1945] and told me how ill Mother was – they had not told me earlier because Mother said I had enough to do with the wee ones. Anyway I was on the boat [the overnight Wellington to Lyttelton ferry] the next night. Meanwhile Mother had been put in a private hospital. I went there immediately on my arrival home [Christchurch]. It was a beautiful place but Mother wanted me to take her home [Clarence Road]. The next day the doctor said OK and I was so pleased to be able to take her home.

The specialist came every day at first but I told him Mother seemed a bit better although not eating much at all. He said it would take a long time to pull her up as the heart condition was against her. This was the specialist. The family doctor had told Father she could not last much longer.

I decided to try her on fish and she quite enjoyed it so Father and I were delighted. There seemed quite an improvement during the next few days. She came downstairs to the table for food, nursed Riley and talked to him. She wanted to make quite sure Weston was not outside on the fence! However, the specialist returned and was pleased with Mother's slight improvement, but gave me a tablet (the latest and brand new drug) for her. He said only one other person had been given this – so new.

Well, it was just awful to see the difference in Mother – deteriorated quickly and told us that the drug was too much for her. Her eyes proved this too. We rang the specialist. He came and I said it was the drug, that she had been getting on so well without it. He went mad and said if I discontinued the drug he wouldn't continue as Mother's specialist. Father and I were at our wit's end as to what to do. We decided to ask her to take it one more night: she did and looked even worse – and the next night she was gone. The other lady who was given the drug wrote to us and said her husband had saved her by following her [presumably she means she went "wandering" as Hilda had done in the middle of the night?] and that drug was what killed my mother. In the paper a while afterwards I saw that this drug, name given, was to be written out completely. That speaks for itself.

So there is the history – yes I felt bitter, but one morning at a communion service – at the words "Do this in remembrance of me" I suddenly felt as if Christ spoke to *me* – as I sat there and took the elements I knew more fully what He Himself had experienced – had endured – and I also realised afresh what it meant to belong to a church – to be involved in the caring of lives – to remember the youth – and so on. It somehow came to me afresh. I owe to my much loved church life so much – with me in joy and sorrow. I am so grateful that you boys are followers of Christ. You Weston and Riley have married fine girls, from Christian homes as yours was, and those darling grandchildren are so precious.

We need not discuss this. It is all here for you to read. I know you will admire your grandmother – she so deserves this.

I must add that a proud moment for me was when I listened in over the radio on VE Day. She was a chosen speaker for Canterbury. She went up on the dais in Cathedral Square and spoke so beautifully and I was told that she looked gorgeous. She told me in a letter that she should never have accepted the honour, that she was not really fit. Next day she suffered a heart turn.

My love to you five
Mother

Rae's father somehow tried to distance himself and his children from the circumstances of Hilda's death. Perhaps the stigma was too great. When the headstone on her grave at Waimarie Cemetery was eventually erected, it did not bear the date of her death, nor the names of her adored twin children. The twins were so hurt by this that many years later they added their names to the grave themselves. At the time Rae's father bought a plot next to Hilda for his own grave. But, unusually, he did not buy the plot adjacent to her, but the one behind her, which would have put him head to head with his wife – where inevitably the headstones of the respective graves would have faced opposite directions. We wonder to this day why he did not buy adjacent plots and there is a suspicion that with the stigma of suicide he preferred his grave to be facing away from hers, but this is pure conjecture. The plot was never used[1] as Charles remarried and was buried on the other side of the same cemetery where his second wife, Madge, was later buried with him.

Eight months after burying his wife in such tragic circumstances, my father-in-law buried his mother, Ophelia, who died suddenly with cerebral thrombosis on October 11th[2] 1946 at the age of ninety-one years. She had lived in New Zealand for seventy-one years. Ophelia's last residence was 107 Merivale Lane, Christchurch.

For the second time in that year, Rae attended a family funeral, this time her grandmother's. It was on her 38th birthday, October 12th[3] and was conducted by Reverend Ray Dudley who had also conducted her mother's, but unlike Hilda, Ophelia was buried at Linwood Cemetery next to her husband George[4] whom she had outlived by twenty-five years. Rae lost her mother in devastating circumstances and then a few months later she lost her grandmother to whom she had been very close. 1946 was and remained forever, the hardest and saddest year of Rae's life.

But if it was a terrible year for Rae, it must have been intolerable for her father who lost his wife and his mother – both suddenly. His mother had had to attend her daughter-in-law's

---

1 Never used as intended by Hilda's husband, but Mum's ashes were buried in that plot, at her mother's head, on April 20th 1995, 49 years later.

2 That fateful date again: Dad died on the anniversary of her death 1993. As he also did on the anniversary of his own grandmother Eleanora Bell's death – 11th October 1924.

3 Rae's own grandson was to attend her funeral on his birthday 49 years later.

4 Linwood Cemetery Block 36 Plot 152

funeral and she was grief stricken for her son. Her own sudden death a few months later could well have been linked to the shock of Hilda's suicide.

Several Barrells are buried in Linwood Cemetery in Christchurch. George and Ophelia are there with their first two children and daughters Lucy[1] and Kate[2] who both pre-deceased their mother and died within a year of each at about the same age – fifty-seven and fifty-six. George and Ophelia had three daughters and none of them married. Evangeline (Eva) the third daughter, is also buried in Linwood, next to her parents.

Ruby Ellis Barrell[3] (nee Brown) is in a grave next to her parents-in-law and sisters-in-law, but in fact she died first. Ruby married Ernest Gladstone[4], George and Ophelia's 9th and youngest child but she died in childbirth at the age of twenty-three. Her baby daughter survived and took her mother's name Ruby Ellis Barrell. Ruby was brought up by her single aunt, Lucy.

It is interesting to note that it appears the three graves were bought together at the time of Ruby's death in 1920. However, when Charles Weston's wife Hilda died in 1946 he chose to bury her in another cemetery altogether – Waimarie. It is possible that the then stigma of suicide was so intense that he wanted to separate the family graves in this way because he even "anonymised" her headstone by omitting her age and years of her birth and death as well as the names of her children.

After Hilda's funeral, we returned to Miramar a more sober and different family. I was thirty-four years old, Rae was thirty-seven, Weston was three and Riley not yet one. But we were all much older. The children may not have registered it but they were being brought home – and to be brought up – by older parents.

I have always felt that no one is beautiful until they have been hurt, have failed or have suffered. It is through such experiences that the arrogant become humbled, that one's character

---

1 Lucy Viola Barrell 1875 (Christchurch) – 1932 (Christchurch)

2 Kate Ophelia Barrell 1877 (Leeston) – 1933 (Christchurch)

3 Ruby Ellis Brown married Ernest Gladstone Barrell, c1897 – 1920 (Christchurch)

4 Ernest Gladstone Barrell 1898 (Christchurch) – 1976 (Christchurch)

is deepened, that sensitivity is sharpened, that understanding of others is more complete and above all, that all human beings are equalled. From tragedy people grow, learn and trust.

In my pastoral role as a minister I was destined to listen to so many others in the years to come and to attempt to share and offer support in their bereavements, sadnesses, tragedies and disappointments. As I did so, to begin to understand, to begin to find the ability to offer true empathy, I found myself drawing on my own experience of finding a wife, mother and mother-in-law lying face down in a beautiful river in the middle of a garden park early on a summer's morning, and of supporting and cherishing a devastated wife over many years. It helped me understand and I am sure it helped me help: grief was not foreign to me. I can only reflect that God moves in mysterious ways. Over the years I have come to the clear conclusion that none has the so-called but ever elusive "perfect" life and none escapes without personal trials. But through suffering, beautiful people can be created and rounded characters can be formed, both of which give birth to joy.

* * *

Living in a university city again (after Christchurch) presented me with the opportunity to attempt to finish my Bachelor of Arts degree part-time. I had already completed four of the required nine units, Education I and II and Philosophy I in Christchurch and Philosophy II as a correspondence student in Roxburgh. I had taken the Greek paper in Roxburgh but failed it[1]. I was not exactly keen to take on the extra work but, after being posted to Roxburgh in the deep south and recalling my appointments in Home Mission days to far flung towns in the very outbacks of New Zealand's sheep and cattle farming communities, I feared that the chance may not present itself again. Here we were in Wellington with the Victoria College of the University of New Zealand on my doorstep. It was not an easy decision. The studies would add to my already

---

[1] Conflicting evidence suggests that he "pulled out" of Greek in Roxburgh, while another source says he failed it. - GB

very full life, a new church with its own challenges and a young family. I reminded myself that my job did not even offer me the normal weekend breaks which most laymen are able to enjoy or voluntarily devote to study. But in the end I decided to go for it despite having very little leisure time to sacrifice to the cause even if I had wanted to.

I tried to cut corners, but they were few and far between. New sermons had to be produced Sunday by Sunday and I felt that above all it was essential that nothing should interfere with my visiting programme. Many a time I would set out in the early afternoon to visit parishioners and then at the end of the afternoon, dash home to pick up my books and papers for University and catch the tram into the city centre (quickly checking, now as a matter of habit, that Riley was not poking his nose through the perimeter fence of the airport as I passed his favourite spot).

UNIVERSITY OF NEW ZEALAND

I have to inform you that as a result of the October-November Examinations, 1948, you have been credited with a section of the Degree.
You passed in:
Political Science (B) 56/68
To: C H Bell

After passing the airport (and not until) if I had been lucky enough to get a seat I would put my head against the window and doze off to sleep usually waking up in Manners Street in time to alight in Willis Street and clamber up the one hundred and seventy-six steps (note the precision there) to Victoria University. When lectures ended at seven o'clock I had time to catch the tram back again and get to my evening church meetings, but only if I went direct. Evening meetings at Worser Bay were particularly exhausting in my daily timetable if they followed lectures. The trams simply didn't get me near enough and after the ride I had a very long walk, always involving a brisk pace which only served to tire me out even more. Many an evening during this time, I would not get home until gone ten o'clock. Even eleven o'clock was not uncommon.

With only five pounds a year travel allowance I could not afford to run the car, the Ford V8 Coupe, so had to sell it. Then my only means of private transport was a bicycle. But this form of transport was unsuitable with Wellington's steep hills let alone its strong winds. University was nearly ten kilometres from home and no part of the route was level for much longer than a few yards at a time. And coping with the frequent and often severe winds made every cycling trip a major physical work out – and not a particularly attractive alternative to the trams, seat or no seat.

Tired as I used to be every day, it must have seemed worse for Rae, as she coped alone with our two young sons and the recent suicide of her mother. There were two people in our household then coping with their own stresses and distress. It is little wonder perhaps that I was about to succumb to many years of dreadful migraines.

It was on my return from one of my long, mentally busy and physically tiring days that I came home with a raging headache. The pain beat across my forehead like a hammer and I felt I would be sick at any moment. I could hardly stand up as I staggered home, holding my head and no doubt looking like some drunk. The pain was like nothing I had experienced before. I went straight to bed and fell asleep. It seemed that sleep was all that I was craving as I slept soundly, but as it transpired, for only a few hours. A little later the pain woke me again, but only briefly. Then another severe attack woke me up for a second time nearing dawn. I was rather worried about it because I could not see how this was a simple headache.

I don't know how anyone can imagine how awful migraine headaches are if they have never had one. That was the first of my migraine headaches which became so frequent that they went on to plague me for the rest of my ministry, the day arriving when they forced me into early retirement in 1967 at the age of only fifty-five.

Over the hill from my home in Miramar was the Worser Bay part of my responsibility. The church had been established before

Miramar and had a long history of effective ministry. At the time I came to it, it had weakened considerably. During the war the pacifist issue had led to a sharp and deep division of opinion in the community – quite simply those who supported the war and those who definitely did not. The congregation was small and inevitably the officers of the church comprised supporters of both camps. This called for considerable forbearance and Christian charity from everyone. The situation that existed was manifested particularly vividly in one family. One son, a church official, attended meetings in army uniform while one of his brothers, another key figure in church affairs, was a conscientious objector whose appeal had been allowed by the Objectors Board. A third brother was simultaneously "serving time" in an Objectors Camp.

In the church those young people who did not object to the war left New Zealand's shores in active support of it. Those young people who stayed behind were either unfit or were the war objectors and as such most felt that they did not want to be part of a church in which any official supported the war, let alone one in which an official openly wore an army uniform at church meetings. With congregation numbers in the Worser Bay church virtually slashed in half by the strong feelings over the pacifist issue, we struggled to keep the church functioning. In spite of it all, it was a warm hearted congregation and many ministers found pleasure in conducting worship with them.

Over the years several lay preachers preached their first sermon in the Worser Bay church, and the congregation there had many an amusing tale to tell of these first efforts. More than one lay preacher moved on from these humble beginnings to become prominent ministers in the Methodist Church of New Zealand. One of these preachers was very particular about his appearance in the pulpit. This included stiff starched false cuffs fixed with diamond or diamond-like cuff links. On one occasion, as he waved his arms about in grand gestures seeking to enthuse his congregation with a powerful address, one of his cuffs came off and flew high up into the air with all the force and direction of a ground to air missile. He paused and as the cuff came down he snatched it with the precision of a cricket fielder and stowed it under the pulpit. He carried on without a word but, needless to say, the congregation was in near hysterics.

The strongest work done in Worser Bay was among the children and youth. In my time the Sunday School was led by Reverend Alun Richards, a Presbyterian minister who was not engaged in parish work at the time. He was an exceptionally able man, later becoming editor of the national Presbyterian Church paper, *The Outlook* and then of the national Methodist Church paper, *The Methodist* (both papers today being merged, *The Cross Link*). He was exceptionally talented at drawing word pictures and he exploited this to the full when working with children. All the Sunday School staff were wide open to new ideas and new methods and the children benefited from the experiments their leaders put to the test with them.

One weekend we held a retreat for the Sunday School teachers of the parish. Alun Richards spoke on the use of illustrations in Sunday School teaching, I took a tutorial on devotions for Sunday School teachers, and others planned activities all centred on Sunday School teaching. Altogether it was a very useful exercise but it was not until some time later that I learned that the originator of the idea, June Morris, had worked the programme out in the back seat of the church while I was taking a service!

The Worser Bay church was situated on a narrow strip of land and nestled against a hill which rose abruptly and steeply behind it. Directly opposite the church over the road was the Worser Bay beach. When the District Youth Council ran a beach mission in the summer holidays, the Worser Bay Church was a natural place to choose for its base. Inevitably therefore I became involved in my first beach mission. I have always been conscious of the need for the church to make contact beyond its own members and to reach out to the public at large whenever it can. So I was interested to share in and support this venture. However, it was difficult to assess what impact, if any, the effort had and I must confess I did not altogether feel at home in the enterprise.

There was no evening service at Worser Bay so a Mr and Mrs Masters of the congregation gathered together young people in an evening Bible Class. Mr and Mrs Masters were as modern in their outlook as any in the church and they too experimented with new teaching techniques. At least they were successful to the extent that they gathered and held together some very lively teenagers who would normally have shied well away from anything too overtly to do with the church. Not surprisingly they were a tough bunch to handle and on more than one occasion reduced Mrs Masters to tears bringing her to the edge of despair. She did not give up on them however and beneath their apparent toughness they came later to appreciate what was being done for them.

Among the characters I worked with in the church were Mr and Mrs Beatty[1]. Mr Beatty was nowhere near as strong in character or as intellectual as his wife. Although he was overshadowed by his wife he was a very nice chap in himself and made a valiant effort to keep pace with her. It was probably this situation that led to a character hiatus in him and one day Mrs Beatty came to me in tears.

"My husband has got into trouble at work," she sobbed.

I was puzzled. "Whatever has happened Mrs Beatty?"

She did not look up. "He has been caught stealing. He has no need for anything he took. He says he doesn't know why he has done it. The company says that they will not be going to the police but of course he is to be sacked."

I was shocked. They had both been on several church boards at national level and they were devoted to the Worser Bay church. Of course I hid my shock as best I could. "Where does that put you Mrs Beatty?"

"We have talked it over and feel it would be best to leave Wellington. We have good friends in Mapua, Nelson, who will help us. They have a cottage on their orchard and they say we can stay there. They could also give us some work at fruit picking time."

---

1 Name has been changed. - GB

This is what they did but it was a tremendous wrench for them. All their married life, and much of it as single people, had been spent in Wellington. For the last service they were to attend I felt I should say a significant word and worked hard in preparing a special sermon. Their departure reduced still further the working strength of the already small congregation but it also took away a strong, dominant personality and with it some of the tension which had become familiar in the congregation at Worser Bay.

I remember how a most unusual situation evolved when one of the congregation got married. Her father had died and her fiancé's father was divorced. Through meeting at the wedding of their children, a romance started up between the bride's mother and the groom's father. Before long they too married. I could not help but be amused by recounting that the bride's father-in-law was also her stepfather and the groom's mother-in-law was also his stepmother.

It was normally accepted that church trustees were men. However, with the small membership at Worser Bay there were few men available for the positions and the church pioneered women trustees. In those days when the role and place of women in society were so very strongly housewife and mother orientated, this move was considered bold and revolutionary. Amidst a certain feeling of scepticism and not a little disapproval from some quarters, it was satisfying to find that the Worser Bay Trust Board with its unique mixture of the sexes was no less efficient than any other I had been on. Indeed if the men had wanted to admit it, it was probably more efficient. One of the trustees was a Mr Kellow and later his daughter also joined. Mr Kellow was financially well off and more than once he came to the rescue of his small church which had always struggled to survive. As a trustee it was natural he was close enough to learn of and understand all the financial difficulties of the church more than any ordinary member of the congregation. I remember, almost with embarrassment, one trust meeting when a vote of thanks was passed to him for preventing the church's gas supply being cut off due to an unpaid bill. He paid the entire bill of one shilling and eight pence himself and this notable act of Christian charity was duly minuted. This was not the only time he put his hand in his pocket to rescue the church from debt, and the other amounts required greater generosity than the gas bill.

On many occasions after the evening service I was invited to Mr Kellow's home and found respite in his good companionship and that of his family. From it sprang a life long and valued friendship that has lasted for nearly half a century. When a little while ago I was introduced to a new Kellow baby I was meeting the fifth generation of the family since those Worser Bay days.

Mr Kellow was Dominion Treasurer of the Ministers' Children Fund. When he despatched the allowances each quarter there was, as often as not, a personal note of cheer and good wishes and a kindly enquiry about the minister and his family's well being. He had an appreciation, not always found among the church's laymen, of the difficulties and particular problems faced by ministers. He recognised that it was important that they should be well read, but there was a difficulty in purchasing books on the salaries they were paid. On one or two occasions, he pushed some money into my hand, saying, "Buy yourself a book Charlie, buy yourself a book." I remember him with great affection.

Almost without exception, I found in the youth groups of my parishes that a clear leader would quickly emerge. They became leaders not only because of their undoubted leadership skills but also because of the keen interest they expressed in questions of faith and religious practice. From among them some would also show ability in public speaking. In each parish I made a practice of encouraging these leaders to allow me to tutor them for exams in lay preaching. Many of them did so and went on to become strong and reliable leaders in their respective congregations. In the case of Miramar, the two who showed most promise were Brian Wilton and Graham Shakes. Unfortunately, both of them left Wellington and the last I heard of them they were providing strong leadership in the churches in their new homes. One of them got actively involved in politics and became a Parliamentary candidate for one of the minor political parties.

I cannot recount my church days in Wellington without thinking on my duties as secretary for the Ministers' Fraternal where the ministers of a synodal area met from time to time to discuss common affairs or to organise combined services. The office of secretary always seemed to find me rather than me finding it, and secretarial positions in the church seemed to become a forte without me ever really knowing why. I certainly never set out to establish this as one of my areas of interest but in every one of my parishes, sooner or later, I became Synod secretary.

Indeed, even my first unwitting involvement in a secretarial ballot was rather embarrassing for me. It happened in this very Wellington synod where I had arrived directly following my ordination. The current secretary had taken ill and it was doubtful if he would return to a full working life again. The chairman of the Synod, Reverend W A Burley, thought a successor should be appointed without delay. The practice of the Methodist Church at the time was that these top positions should be filled by ballot without nomination. As a newcomer to ministerial status, I sat back fully relaxed. I was almost stunned to find my name near the top of the list. Further ballots followed, but my name remained there, ominously. In the final ballot it was still there, dead-heated with one of the more senior ministers of the synod. It was now the chairman's turn to be embarrassed. Finally, and most diplomatically I am grateful to recall, he cast his vote for the senior minister and I sighed with relief. But it was not very long after that I was made secretary for the Ministers' Fraternal, which was a monthly meeting of the ministers working in the Wellington district.

Around this time the annual Dominion Conference of the Methodist Church was switched from February to November. It was one of my Trinity college colleagues, Reverend H C Dixon[1][2], who was the prime mover for this change. It meant that in the year

---

1 Rev Haddon C Dixon 1913-1990

2 By pure chance my friend Beverley Keall (who Dad never knew or met) came across this name of Dixon as she proof read this book for me, only to realise that Dad was referring to Haddon Dixon, her husband's uncle. - GB

of the change no conference business could be done for eighteen months. There were legal repercussions to this, for the church was required by Act of Parliament to appoint its ministers to the parishes every twelve months. To answer this dilemma, an "Interim Conference" consisting of synod chairmen, president and secretary of conference, the heads of departments, college principal and staff, and a few others in key positions were called together to do all legally required business. It met in Wellington and as I was then stationed there, I was co-opted as an assistant to the conference secretary. A few years later the role became more permanent. I was enrolled for the conference staff and for six years was one of the Minute Secretaries. This meant that I could not enjoy conferences as much as I had done before. Conference was always a busy enough time for everyone, but before my imposed official conference duties I found I could always relax to a certain degree as I and my colleagues could leave the bulk of the grind to the appointed officers. As young ministers we enjoyed, perhaps more than others, the opportunity to get together to share each other's experiences. Once I was on the staff there were not so many chances to take things quite as easily as before and I missed this.

It was at the first conference after I had assumed official duties that I had one of the most embarrassing moments of my life. Usually the annual Dominion Conference was held in the main central church of one of the four main cities. The president and his retinue occupied the platform at the front of the church and the secretarial staff took over the choir seats behind, but in full view of the conference. Quite often we worked away *sotto voce* while the conference got on with its job, with the results filtering back to us through the conference secretary. On this memorable day of the conference, the staff were busy chatting to me about my new job. Unnoticed by us, a quietness had fallen over the conference as the president began addressing the new ordinands. Apparently our chatter, low in volume as we thought it had been, wafted down to the pews below and formed a disturbing background to the president's speech. Worst of all, the president himself noticed it and he was not amused. Instead of continuing, politely trying to ignore it as I think I certainly would have done, he stopped in mid-sentence, turned, and looked up to the choir stalls. There and then, before four hundred conference members, the President of the Methodist Conference of New Zealand, an esteemed office, gave us the sharp edge of his tongue as if to naughty school boys. I have never forgotten it and I can still recall the colour that burned from underneath my collar rising rapidly to my cheeks. Of course the rebuke was not aimed at me personally as there were several of us chatting, but I took it personally.

The secretary of the examination committee appointed me examiner of the lay preachers. This gave me a seat on the Examination Committee, a position I held until I retired from the ministry. It was an important committee dealing with all matters relating to the receiving, training and ordaining of all candidates for the ministry. I did not make any significant contribution to it but I valued the opportunity of sharing in this aspect of the church's life. It always meant an extra day at conference, for it met ahead of the main conference. Usually it involved listening to candidate and ordinand trial services. If you were the youngest "listener" (which I often was) you would present the report on the preacher to the examination committee. In light of my own tough selection process and the hurdles I had fallen at so frequently, learning the criteria for objective selection was of great interest to me. I feel I learned a lot – unfortunately all with hindsight.

In 1948, little more than two and a half years after Rae's mother had died, her father announced, quite abruptly, that he was going to marry again. The announcement was sudden, although he had apparently been seeing Madge Pengelly for some time. Their father rang each of the twins and said, "I am getting married this Saturday. If you want to come, you can." Neither Rae nor her twin brother Boy found the proposal easy to accept. Rae wanted to be happy for her father, but despite this found the idea hurtful – and the absence of her mother was a pain relived yet again. Their father, Charles Weston Barrell, was sixty-five years old when he married thirty-seven year old Madge Evelyn Pengelly, a book shop owner, on October 16th 1948 in the Baptist Church of the small

Canterbury town of Greendale. Madge was nearly thirty years his junior and only three years younger than his twin children. Rae did not attend the wedding but Boy did – but just the ceremony. "I will come," said Boy to his father, "but for Mum's sake. You know she will be there, don't you?" His father knew Boy did not have a car and so offered him a car from the business to take himself and the family to Greendale. "It was most appropriate", Boy commented to me later with a twinkle in his eye, "that we attended the wedding in a mourners' car." His six year old son Graeme, who thought the huge black car was absolutely wonderful, went off to school and announced to his teacher that they had gone to a wedding in a hearse! Graeme had wanted to stay on for "Grandad's party" after the church service, but Boy headed back for Christchurch the moment they got out of the church door.

A daughter, Annette Weston, was born of their father's second marriage on October 20th 1949, a half sister for Rae and Boy. It would have been wonderful for Rae if Annette and she had become close – the longed for sister. But the age gap proved too much. Annette was only four months older than Rae's youngest son and her father's second marriage reminded Rae so much of the loss of her own mother that she could not separate the two. Relations between Madge and Rae were always strained, and between Rae and Annette, regrettably distant. Today, Rae's twin who has lived in Christchurch all his life, as has Annette, has become close to his half sister[1]. Perhaps if Rae had still lived in Christchurch near Annette, the relationship could have had the opportunity to develop as the years moved on.

---

[1] Charles D Barrell since moved (1994) to live with his son and daughter-in-law, Graeme and Caroline, in Woodville. He died there 20 May 1996, fourteen months after his twin.

Obituary of Charles Weston Barrell

CHARLES WESTON BARRELL

Mr Charles Weston Barrell, born at Leeston, Canterbury, 17th April 1883, later moved to live in Christchurch, spending all his days in this city. Mr Barrell was Funeral Director with his father and two brothers – George Barrell & Sons. For Charles Barrell this was more than just a job – he made it his ministry and many many people found consolation and encouragement in their sorrow because of his kindly manner and gentlemanly approach to them, and supremely because of his own Christian faith.

Mr Barrell found a great joy in preaching and was a most acceptable preacher in all Christchurch and North Canterbury Methodist pulpits. He took a special delight in reading the dramatic portions of the Scriptures and in descriptive preaching, one of his favourite subjects being the God of Nature. People still recall sermons and texts that he preached from upwards of 50 years ago. It is 62 years since he began this service and he preached until ill health prevented him from doing more.

Mr Barrell was widely known for his work with New Zealand native timbers. He possessed a knack of recognising potential beauty in an unprepossessing log. When he had finished working on such a log it became to him a "thing of beauty and a joy for ever". His work in this connection was recognised when he was asked to make a jewel box and a wooden replica of the gavel used by the Queen at the foundation stone laying of the Wellington Cathedral. These gifts were presented to the Queen on her New Zealand visits.

Mr Barrell was a keen sportsman, playing rugby and being a Canterbury champion swimmer. He was no mean marksman and did a deal of hunting. On two occasions he was approached to stand for Parliament. He was a personal friend of the late Tommy Taylor[1] and had a great appreciation of the keen debaters of his generation as well as the great preachers. He had many opportunities to know them because he had, since a boy, been a member of the Durham Street Methodist Church, holding many offices – most notably that of Church Steward for 25 years and also that of Circuit Steward for a number of years. He had a deep and

---

[1] Thomas Edward Taylor 1862-1911: prohibition leader and reformer; a powerful propagandist, forceful speaker and known for his fervid eloquence; elected junior member for Christchurch in 1896 as a radical independent, he fearlessly attacked the Seddon administration. He was a brilliant political evangelist and by his powerful speaking could sway any audience. He became Mayor of Christchurch in 1911 but died three months later.

abiding love for the Durham Street Church. That, however, did not prevent him from helping to establish the [Clarence Road] Methodist Church in the suburb of Riccarton where he lived. Some of the first [Methodist] services held [in Riccarton] were conducted in the Barrell home and his first wife and he gave of time and substance to put up the first Methodist Church in Riccarton [Clarence Road].
Circumstances denied to him opportunity for advanced education that he had planned for himself, but when the WEA[1] came into being he seized the opportunity it presented and developed his understanding and appreciation of the poets in particular. Blessed with an excellent memory he could recite whole sections of Shakespeare right up to the end of his days.
Marriage in 1907 in Durham Street Church to Miss Hilda Fitzer began a most happy home life that was lived out for 39 years – a home noted for its warmth in hospitality. A few years after the passing of his wife, Mr Barrell married Miss Madge Pengelly. A severe illness[2] eleven years ago nearly lost him his life and he retired from his business but he kept his business acumen and maintained his interest in all the things that had filled his life. He suffered a serious accident[3] in October and was in hospital until last Christmas when he returned home. It was a happy thought that he died in the home he so much loved. He died on 18 April 1965, the day after his 82nd birthday. He was buried from his beloved Durham Street Church, full of years, good works and good character and is laid to rest at Waimarie Cemetery. He is survived by his second wife, his son Charles Durham Barrell (Riccarton), and daughters, Rae (Mrs C H Bell, The Parsonage, Rangiora) and Annette (Riccarton).

Rae's father died in 1965 and was buried in Waimarie Cemetery, Christchurch. However, he was not buried at the grave he bought for himself next to his first wife, Hilda. He was buried on the opposite side of the cemetery with the intention that his second

---

[1] Workers' Educational Association. WEAs came to NZ in 1915 with the goal of making learning opportunities available to those who missed out on such opportunities in earlier education.

[2] I have failed to establish what this "severe illness" was. - GB

[3] He was knocked off his bicycle by a car, but in his old age he took to riding in the middle of the road often absentmindedly. - GB

wife, Madge, would be buried with him. The grave next to his first wife (head to head location) lay unused and almost forgotten.[1]

In 1949, at the age of thirty-seven, at last I completed my degree. Since I left school to this point, I had sat nearly fifty exam papers. It had been a long drawn out saga, doing it all part time or by correspondence over many years but I feel this made the sense of accomplishment all the more complete. The long tiring days where lectures were squeezed in between church meetings and tram rides and long walks across Wellington were at an end. I remember that it was at this point in my career when I had a wonderful feeling of having "arrived". The long pilgrimage to get into the ministry was over, my degree was "in the bag". I was still very much in love with my wife, I had two bonny sons whom I adored and I was seeing work in my parish yielding rewarding results. What more could I ask for? Life was being good to me and I was deeply content. Rae was thrilled too that my degree was finished. She could now expect me to be home earlier in the evenings and less tired. I had hoped too that the migraine headaches may ease up, but this did not prove to be the case.

I had suffered a hernia for a long time while I was in Miramar and when I completed my degree I sought to have it fixed. I remember that it was almost with a sense of relief that I crawled into my hospital bed knowing that in so doing I was laying aside, for a while at least, the pressure that had been on me for the last four and a half years. Only when I was discharged did I come to realise that I had really been too exhausted to cope with the operation. I do not think I have ever felt quite so low as I did then. To say a simple "Yes" or "No" seemed almost too much for me. University work had worn me down. I had made a conscientious effort to be fully and actively involved with every aspect of work in my own and first parish as a fully ordained minister. Farming interests had, at last, begun to take a back seat in my mind – and

[1] Shortly before Mum died, we thought of the empty grave and asked Mum if she would like to be buried there. With uncharacteristic clarity and understanding, she said she "would love to be with her mother", and so her ashes were buried next to her mother in that grave. - GB

my lack of contact with the country or indeed, countryside, helped to distance those interests. In one sense this parish had been like my first job, the first rung on the career ladder, and I did not want to let anybody, anybody at all, down. And not least, I had also carried and supported Rae through her own tragedy. And in that tragedy, inevitably I shouldered a small part of the severe shock which took its silent toll even now as the years passed. My recuperation was very slow and I have never known such tiredness.

While I was still in hospital I received an invitation from the Richmond (now Waimea) Parish to be their new minister. In the state of mind I was in, a move was the last thing I felt like facing up to, but after some delay, I finally accepted. I did so with little enthusiasm. It was not that I had anything against the idea of Richmond, but I felt that the invitation simply came at a bad time for me personally. My acceptance signalled the slow curtain fall on my five busy and notable years in my first post-ordination parish.

Reverend R E Patchett, my predecessor, was the first ordained minister to be appointed in Miramar and for him they had purchased the first parsonage. It was not up to the standards that the church had set down, but the trustees were permitted to proceed with the purchase on condition that preparations were made to bring it up to minimum requirements. This is how we lived in it. During our years in Miramar, we had made a number of special fundraising efforts and funds had accumulated sufficiently to refurbish the parsonage completely but when we left it still had not been done. Although the situation was understandable, I always thought it was disappointing, for Rae in particular, that just after our departure the church completely refurbished the parsonage ready for the arrival of our successor, my friend and groomsman at my wedding, Reverend L V Willing. Well, at least it was for a friend, which lessened the disappointment!

We left Wellington on a sunny January day in 1950. Once again, with our two young sons we set off for a new home. Weston and Riley were now six and nearly five years old. Rae was eight months pregnant with our third child so we decided she should fly across Cook Strait to Nelson. She was delighted as she had always been a poor sailor anyway. Rae took Weston with her and I sailed with Riley on the inter-island ferry to Picton taking with me our new car, a Ford Prefect, which I had bought in readiness for the scattered churches and homes in the country parish to which I was heading. Farming was destined to raise its head again.

The crossing between Picton and Wellington is even more beautiful than that between Wellington and Lyttelton, the port for Christchurch, a journey I had made several times before. The Picton ferry first crosses Cook Strait then heads through the narrow entrance into the picturesque Marlborough Sounds. As the ferry follows every twist and turn of the bays it winds itself through to the head of the Sounds where Picton is the gateway to the South Island, and about a hundred and sixty kilometres east of our new home, Richmond.

As Rae flew and I sailed out of Wellington, back to the South Island once again, we left behind yet another set of friends and memories, seemingly fulfilling one's life as one reads a book, by closing one chapter and moving on to the next.

Rae with Weston (right) and Riley c1946

Rae and Charles in Auckland c1945

Rae and Charles, Weston (left) and Riley Wellington Wharf, April 1948, "Cliff Symon's departure for Australia"

Charles and Rae in Hawera, Christmas 1945 with Weston (left) and Riley

Miramar Methodist Church in the Wellington East Circuit, as it was when it was Charles's parish in 1945. The church was built in one day in April 1924 although an extension had been added since.

Worser Bay Methodist Church about 1947.

The Methodist Parsonage, 39 Strathavon Road, Miramar, c1947. It was due for refurbishment but it didn't happen until after Charles and family left the parish.

39 Strathavon Road, Miramar, today. Photo Beverley Keall 2006

Rae's uncle Tas Fitzer and his second wife Eileen 1950

Tas and Eileen Fitzer with Weston and Riley, Miramar, 1949

Riley (foreground middle) with his kindergarten class, Miramar 1949

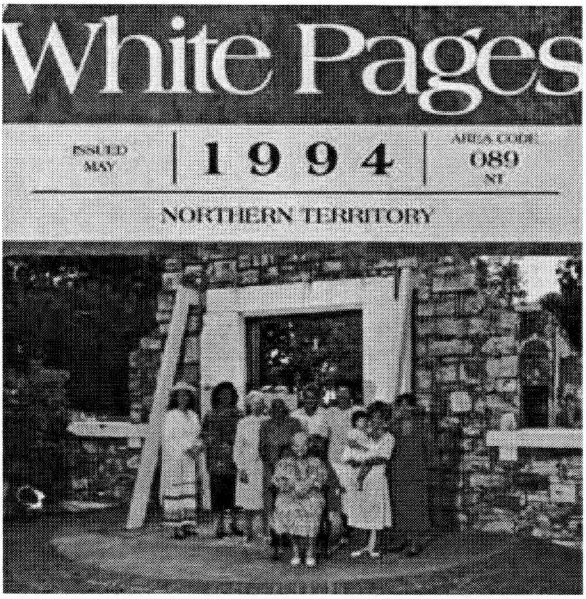

Eileen Fitzer became quite a celebrity in Australia's Northern Territory as one of the State's earliest pioneers. She took pride of place on the cover of the 1994 telephone directory, seen here seated.

Weston and Riley crawled away from their parents in the long grass. Convinced they were not observed and could not be spotted, this is the moment of their discovery! 1946

Baby Weston with his grandmother Laura. Grandfather Tom Bell, Charles and Rae, Hawera, 1944

Tom and Laura Bell's and Evelyn and Jean's Rimu St, Hawera home for many years after Tom retired from the farm (c1944). Photo 1982

Riley (left) and Weston, October 1947

Laura Bell (nee Riley) with her grandson, Riley, Hawera, 1947

Weston (left) and Riley Helensville, 1947

Riley (left) and Weston c1948

Charles with Riley, Christmas 1945 in Hawera

Weston with his decorated bike, 1948

Tom Bell with grandson Riley, 1946. Taken at Golden Wedding of Tom's sister Mary Elizabeth (married Albert James Orchard).

Rae's mother, Hilda Barrell

Hilda Fitzer, May 1886, aged 7 months, Dunedin

Hilda Barrell, about 1916, aged 30 years

Hilda Barrell at Molly McKeown's (m Scott) wedding 29 March 1939 at Woodbury (near Geraldine). Aged 53 years. Handwritten on back by Rae: "My lovely mother".

Hilda aged 57, with her grandson, Weston, outside her home in Christchurch, 130 Clarence Road, Riccarton, 1943.

Hilda's grave in 1946. Her husband refused to put the children's names on the stone or any dates. He did not want the facts of her death easily researched. After her father had died the twins added their names. After Rae was buried next to her mother in 1995, her sons re-did Hilda's stone and included the dates. Handwritten by Rae on the back of this photo: "Mother dear!".

The original headstone, above, reads:

HILDA

THE LOVING AND DEVOTED WIFE OF

C W BARRELL

MEMORY WILL BE MY HAPPINESS

FOR YOU ARE ENSHRINED THERE

VE Day celebrations in Cathedral Square, Christchurch, 10 May 1945
Hilda Barrell was one of the selected speakers and would have spoken from the same dais on the right where another speaker is photographed above. Perhaps Hilda is in the photograph too, standing quite nearby. We will never know. *Photo:* The Press *11 May 1945, page 8. Acknowledgement: Christchurch City Libraries, Aotearoa NZ Centre, Christchurch*

Hilda Barrell, 130 Clarence Road, Christchurch.
As always on her mother's photos, a note of affection handwritten on back by Rae, "Darling mother".

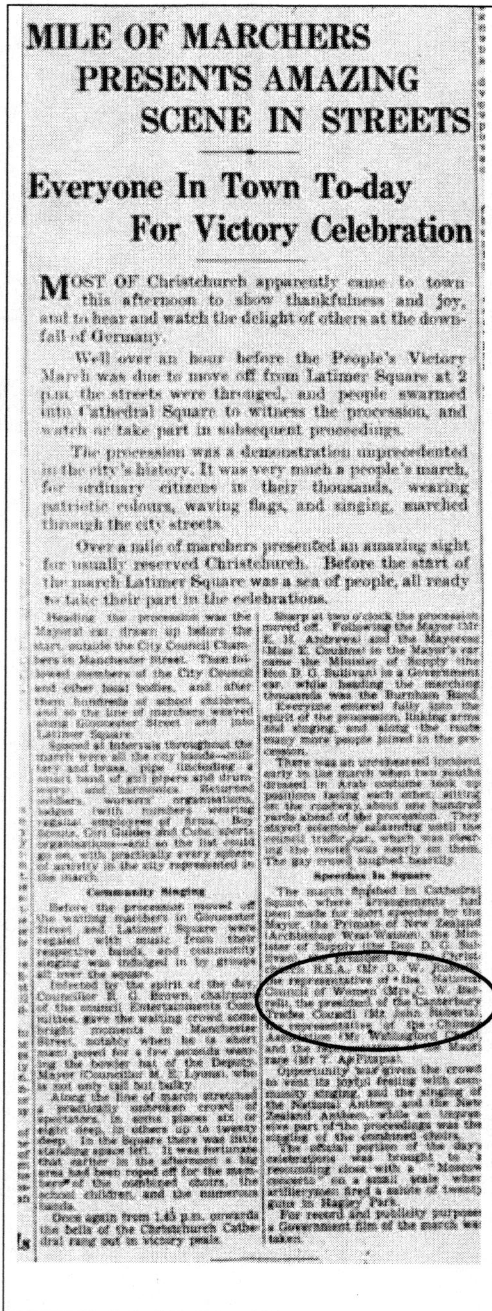

MILE OF MARCHERS PRESENTS AMAZING SCENE IN STREETS

Everyone In Town To-day For Victory Celebration

MOST OF Christchurch apparently came to town this afternoon to show thankfulness and joy, and to hear and watch the delight of others at the downfall of Germany.

Well over an hour before the People's Victory March was due to move off from Latimer Square at 2 p.m. the streets were thronged, and people swarmed into Cathedral Square to witness the procession, and watch or take part in subsequent proceedings.

The procession was a demonstration unprecedented in the city's history. It was very much a people's march, for ordinary citizens in their thousands, wearing patriotic colours, waving flags, and singing, marched through the city streets.

Over a mile of marchers presented an amazing sight for usually reserved Christchurch. Before the start of the march Latimer Square was a sea of people, all ready to take their part in the celebrations.

Heading the procession was the Mayoral car, drawn up before the start outside the City Council Chambers in Manchester Street. Then followed members of the City Council and other local bodies, and after them hundreds of school children, and so the line of marchers weaved along Gloucester Street and into Latimer Square.

Spaced at intervals throughout the march were all the city bands—military and brass, pipe (including a smart band of girl pipers and drummers) and harmonica. Returned soldiers, workers' organisations, lodges (with members wearing regalia), employees of firms, Boy Scouts, Girl Guides and Cubs, sports organisations—and so the list could go on, with practically every sphere of activity in the city represented in the march.

Community Singing

Before the procession moved off the waiting marchers in Gloucester Street and Latimer Square were regaled with music from their respective bands, and community singing was indulged in by groups all over the square.

Infected by the spirit of the day, Councillor R. G. Brown, chairman of the council Entertainments Committee, gave the waiting crowd some bright moments in Manchester Street, notably when he [illegible] posed for a few seconds wearing the bowler hat of the Deputy-Mayor (Councillor M. E. Lyons), who is not only tall but bulky.

Along the line of march stretched a practically unbroken crowd of spectators, in some places six or eight deep, in others up to twenty deep. In the Square there was little standing space left. It was fortunate that earlier in the afternoon a big area had been roped off for the members of the combined choirs, the school children, and the numerous bands.

Once again from 1.45 p.m. onwards the bells of the Christchurch Cathedral rang out in victory peals.

Sharp at two o'clock the procession moved off. Following the Mayor (Mr E. H. Andrews) and the Mayoress (Miss E. Couzins) in the Mayor's car came the Minister of Supply (the Hon D. G. Sullivan) in a Government car, while heading the marching thousands was the Burnham Band.

Everyone entered fully into the spirit of the procession, linking arms and singing, and along the route many more people joined in the procession.

There was an unrehearsed incident early in the march when two youths dressed in Arab costume took up positions facing each other, sitting on the roadway about one hundred yards ahead of the procession. They stayed solemnly salaaming until the council traffic car, which was clearing the route, was nearly on them. The gay crowd laughed heartily.

Speeches In Square

The march finished in Cathedral Square, where arrangements had been made for short speeches by the Mayor, the Primate of New Zealand (Archbishop West-Watson), the Minister of Supply (the Hon D. G. Sullivan), the president of the Christchurch R.S.A. (Mr D. W. [illegible]), the representative of the National Council of Women (Mrs C. W. [illegible]), the president of the Canterbury Trades Council (Mr John Roberts), the representative of the Chinese Association (Mr Wellington [illegible]) and the [illegible] Maori race (Mr T. [illegible]).

Opportunity was given the crowd to vent its joyful feeling with community singing, and the singing of the National Anthem and the New Zealand Anthem, while an impressive part of the proceedings was the singing of the combined choirs.

The official portion of the day's celebrations was brought to a resounding close with a "Moscow concerto" on a small scale when artillerymen fired a salute of twenty guns in Hagley Park.

For record and publicity purposes a Government film of the march was taken.

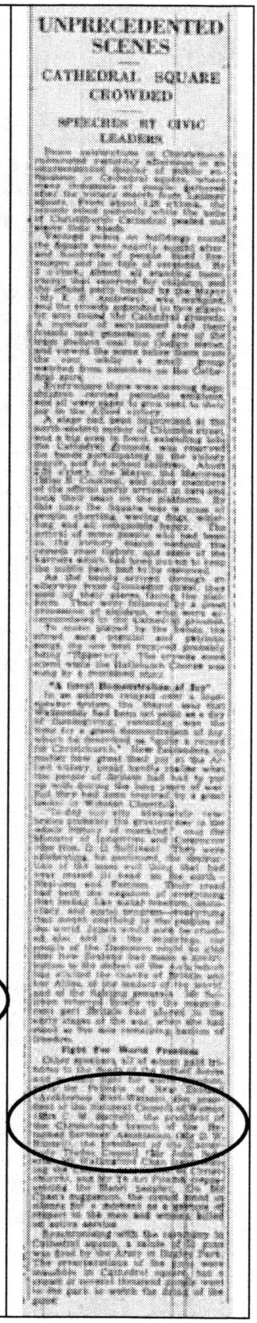

UNPRECEDENTED SCENES

CATHEDRAL SQUARE CROWDED

SPEECHES BY CIVIC LEADERS

[illegible]

Christchurch Star-Sun
Thu 10 May, 1945

The Press
Fri 11 May 1945

The monument and inscription at the graves of George and Ophelia Barrell and their first two of three daughters, both of whom died single, and within a year of each other and more or less at the same age. The inscription for Kate Ophelia which does not show above is on the left hand side of this same monument (see below right). Linwood Cemetery Christchurch Block 36 Plots 151/152 Area 4 Row 1 No 2017.

IN SACRED AND LOVING MEMORY OF RUBY ELLIS. DEARLY LOVED WIFE OF E.G. BARRELL. DIED JAN 12TH 1920 AGED 23 YEARS. THE MASTER COMETH AND CALLETH FOR THEE

The headstone inscription of Ruby Ellis Barrell (nee Brown) who died in childbirth. Linwood Cemetery.

KATE OPHELIA BARRELL
DIED 29TH DEC[1] 1933 AGED 56 YEARS.
AT REST

Photos Riley Bell.

---

1 This date is barely legible on the stone and there is some dispute as to whether it reads Apr or Dec. *The Barrells of Durham Street* booklet records her death as Dec.

The headstone inscription of the third and last daughter of George and Ophelia, died, like her sisters, unmarried, but outlived them by many years. She died at the age of 88 years.
Linwood Cemetery Area 4 Row 1 No 2016 Photo Riley Bell 2005

Annette Weston Barrell, aged 4 years
Rae's half sister. Christchurch 1953

Rae's father, Charles Weston Barrell was buried in Waimarie Cemetery Christchurch 1965, but not next to his first wife, Rae's mother, who was buried in the same cemetery but on the other side. Directly in front of his grave are the graves of his son, grandson and daughter-in-law.
Photo Hilary Donaldson (nee Bell) 2004

The last photo of Rae's twin Charles Durham Barrell with his nephew Riley Bell shortly after Rae had died in 1995. Taken in Woodville where he lived with his son Graeme and daughter-in-law Caroline. Charles Durham died the following year in May 1996 and was buried in Waimarie Cemetery with his first wife Ira and next to his son Ray and in front of his father Charles Weston Barrell.

Directly in front of Charles Weston Barrell's grave (which can just be made out above) lie his grandson Ray Durham Barrell who died at the age of 15 with leukaemia, and his son Charles Durham Barrell with his first wife Ira. Waimarie Cemetery, Christchurch. Photo Hilary Donaldson (nee Bell) 2004

Headstone on left:
IN GRATEFUL AND LOVING MEMORY OF
RAY DURHAM BARRELL
DEARLY LOVED SON OF CHARLES AND IRA
AND LOVED BROTHER OF GRAEME
CALLED HOME ON MARCH 15TH 1961
IN HIS SIXTEENTH YEAR
"IN THY PRESENCE IS FULNESS OF JOY"

Headstone on right:
FRAGRANT MEMORIES OF
IRA JEAN BARRELL
DEARLY LOVED WIFE OF CHARLES DURHAM BARRELL
AND MUCH LOVED MOTHER OF GRAEME AND THE LATE RAY
PASSED HOME 13 -8 -1973
ALSO HER BELOVED HUSBAND CHARLES DURHAM BARRELL
PASSED HOME 20- 5-1996

Chapter 16

LOUSY FLOCK

1950 – 1954

Richmond, Nelson

Blessed are the meek, for they shall inherit the earth.
— Matthew 5:5

Nelson district is a delightful place in which to holiday. The days are full of sunshine and there are beautiful beaches for swimming and dozens of gullies and bays and river banks on which to picnic. Fruit grows in plenty. It is not really a place where one should go to work, only retire or holiday. It is not called "Sleepy Hollow" for nothing. But, alas, we went there to work.

As we crossed Cook Strait I barely realised then that we were heading for an area with deep significance for me: my Riley roots. Of course I knew my mother had been born close by but other than that I showed little interest in my Riley ancestors. (Interestingly, another parish I was to be appointed to later on, Rangiora, was also closely connected with my past, this time the Bell ancestors.) Richmond was really a suburb of Nelson, a small town on Nelson's boundaries. We were to live only a few kilometres from the spot where my great grandparents John and Mary Riley landed off the *Thomas Harrison* in 1842, and where they settled. I had not even visited Nelson or Marlborough before so I was looking forward to getting to know the place. Pakawau in Golden Bay, where my mother was born, was not that far away and the thought crossed my mind that she might choose to come and stay and visit her childhood stomping grounds again. This was not to be.

The Richmond Methodist Parsonage was at 105 Queen Street[1], an imposing two storey house. Weston and Riley did most of their primary schooling in Richmond and our third and youngest son, Godfrey Durham (middle name after his uncle Charles Durham Barrell and in turn, Durham Street Methodist Church), was born here on the first Sunday after we arrived, 13th February 1950. Rae was forty-one and in 1950 it was not considered a very safe age to be pregnant, in fact some thought it alarming. Her anxiety was only increased when the doctor told her to expect her third child in the month of February.

Not only was it to be February, but the very date in February in which Rae had locked away a thousand painful memories. Rae's labour pains came on just after midnight: the thirteenth of February. The irony and the sadness of the timing was inescapable. The coincidence and significance of her having another baby at all let alone on the thirteenth of February had far from escaped Rae. She had actively and dearly been wishing for weeks that the baby would not arrive on what was for her the saddest of all days in the calendar year. I have often wondered if it was because of her anxiety of the date that she went into labour so soon after midnight. Godfrey arrived on the 13th at 6pm. Rae had been wishing for a girl, another aspect I concluded of her unexpressed and deeply silent grieving for her mother.

When Godfrey was born on the fourth anniversary of his grandmother's tragic death, the reality proved to be that Godfrey brought a joy to Rae she had not realised she had been deeply craving. We had wanted another child, but I think, initially, I was keener than she was. I was wanting Rae to renew her faith in life and become totally absorbed in her own living family. But initially the plan went wrong. She suffered her first miscarriage ever in 1948, another sign I feared of her inner turmoil as she had never

---

[1] The street has since been renumbered and today it is 205 Queen Street.

had a problem with or prior to the births of Weston and Riley. The miscarriage itself only added to the strain. Rae was now yet another year older before she became pregnant again in 1949 and a new worry started creeping in about the wisdom of it all. Eventually his birth was straightforward and when it was on that day of all days, I could not help pondering if God was moving yet again in mysterious ways. Perhaps Godfrey's birthday would shatter the most painful memories of Rae's private misery which the 13th of February held for her each year. As it transpired, his birthdays were celebrated as normal and Rae said nothing as the candles would be lit, her youngest son counting his age, his mother counting the long, relentless and unforgiving years which would never bring her own mother back or lessen the reality of the way she died. Godfrey was twenty-three years old before he discovered why his birthday was shared with such pain for his mother.

Weston and Riley also played their part in making that night memorable when Rae went into labour. Only being in Richmond a few days, there was no one we felt we could call on to mind Weston and Riley when the time came to take Rae to the hospital. We felt the best option was simply to explain to them what might happen and they were not to be alarmed if they awoke one night to find us missing. The Nelson hospital was only twelve kilometres away so we knew it would not be for long. When the time came we were not too concerned about leaving the two boys young as they were. At about one in the morning we crept out, left the house in total darkness, and quietly as possible took the car down the drive and headed for the hospital. I returned at about two in the morning. To my horror, as I drove down Queen Street, I was confronted by our house standing amidst a row of dark houses, a blaze of light. Every single light, upstairs and downstairs, was on. It looked as if there was someone in every room, that an entire household was in the middle of some all night party, but not quite. I could hear no loud music and no hubbub of any party filling the air. The large two storey parsonage just stood there, quiet and eerie, as if it were some strange lighthouse.

My blood ran cold as my imagination ran riot wondering what could have happened to our two sons at this time of night in this large house on their own. The confidence I had earlier of our wisdom at leaving them on their own now turned to guilt and shame at my stupidity. Burglars? Fire? Kidnapping? Murder? In my shock and disbelief, and in our newness to the district, I found myself quickly and pointlessly checking the position of our house in the street to reassure myself I was looking at the right one. It was ridiculous, our house was quite obvious – it was the only two storey one in the street. Still disbelieving, I hesitated momentarily and virtually stalled the car. This knocked some sense into me and recovering my composure almost simultaneously, I suddenly put my foot down and sped to the house, swinging the car into the drive furiously and dangerously, the gravel under the wheels of the car spitting to either side as I slammed on the brakes. Hardly thinking I even had time to switch the engine off, I threw open the car door, fell out of the car, and ran, almost in blind panic, into the house not knowing or preparing myself for what I may find – or not find.

I went through the back door into the kitchen. Not one sound. Lights on. Not a soul. Into the hall. Not one sound. Lights on. Not a soul. To the staircase. And there I met the first sign of abnormality. On every step was a sheet of newspaper. I rushed up the staircase. On the landing was more newspaper, laid out neatly, and leading a careful path to the boys' bedroom. I followed these newspapers stealthily, as one would follow a trail of blood. Still no sound. I carefully and quietly reached their bedroom door, bracing myself in case my sons were not there. They were sitting up, wide eyed, in their pyjamas on their beds. "Hello Daddy," said Riley.

"What's going on Riley? Why are all the lights in the house on? Why are all the newspapers on the floor? What are you doing up?"

"Weston is sick. He woke me up and I went to find you and Mummy but you were not here. He has to get to the toilet quickly. I put the newspapers down the stairs in case he didn't get to the toilet in time."

Indeed Weston suffered that night from diarrhoea and the newspapers were a sensible and logical precaution but hardly one I would have expected a four year old (nearly five) to take. The way Riley looked after his older brother in that emergency revealed that the boy was the father of the man. All his life he has shown himself to be unflappable[1].

In fact it showed itself again not very long after this. A Mardi Gras was being held at Stoke and I took the two boys. Late in the afternoon I lost them in the crowd and a search of the ground failed to find them. A few people started to help me look and after a while as the day drew to a close, the crowds started to thin out but Weston and Riley still did not turn up. Greatly concerned I decided to go back to the car and inform the police. I had not previously considered going to the car because it was deep in the middle of a large car park on the very edge of the fair grounds, a long way from the crowds and all the activity. Indeed a separate path led the way to the car park itself, but there the boys were sitting contentedly on the step of our Ford Prefect. Realising they were lost, Riley had taken Weston by the hand and led him to the car and waited patiently for me to show up. I thought this was pretty good for a five and a six year old, in what was at the time new territory for them. Riley has made his career as an airline pilot, so I guess this "homing instinct" attribute would be of real value in that role![2].

My hopes that Rae would find it easier to put the last four years behind her and that she would find a new emotional and physical stability and peace of mind when Godfrey was born, faded quickly, shortly afterwards. Far from gaining a new strength her health deteriorated. She developed severe stomach and bowel problems and lost a lot of weight throughout 1950 and 1951. Once

---

[1] This entire tale of Dad's is vehemently contradicted by Weston who says it was exactly the other way around! It was he, Weston says, who looked after Riley – who was ill. But Dad having checked the script I wrote above, made some alterations but none alluding to the incorrect identity of the players! Therefore, even if for posterity alone, the tale is as recorded by Dad, not by Weston. And history will remain correct or incorrect depending on whose memory time is playing tricks!

[2] This time, Weston does not recall the incident at all. So it may be exactly as Dad related!

or twice we briefly feared that she was pregnant again which would have been disastrous. She was under the constant and watchful eye of a doctor for months on end. Rae was, quite simply, "an ill woman" but she never let me acknowledge it and under no circumstances would she acknowledge it to anyone else. Being sick was not socially proper. Seeking sympathy was unacceptable and selfish and all her life she has been an appalling patient. Despite this outward claim to good health, she privately kept a suitcase ready packed in case she was rushed to hospital. That secret suitcase was the only indication that Rae knew deep down that she was indeed ill. It was awful seeing her like that and I was still convinced, even five long years later, that the death of her mother continued to take its toll with days of severe stress and internal grief. The upset stomachs and bowel problems which developed in those first years since her mother died, were never totally cured. To this day she gets the same, albeit infrequent, attacks, all in my view a physical response to that one major shock in her life.

My mother had never seen her youngest grandson when she became bedridden in Hawera from what seemed to be a series of minor strokes during 1950. Godfrey was little more than a year old and it was obvious to us all that if his grandmother did not see him now, she never would. I wanted Mum to see Godfrey.

We could not afford for both Rae and me to fly north. Rae's financially comfortable single days were now distant memories. She was getting used to bringing up a family on a minister's salary which was always little more than a basic liveable wage. In 1951 I was earning £500[1] a year and we had no private income to supplement it. Financially things were not, were never, easy, but Rae had adapted completely to her new circumstances and what we could not afford, we could not have. I have often noticed that those who have, adapt well to having not. Those who never had are the spendthrifts. And that surely includes me.

When we did want to buy something other than the weekly budgeted expenses for food and so on, something had to give.

---

[1] I could not make out from Dad's handwritten notes here whether this was $500 or £500. - GB

Weston and Riley started school while we were in Richmond and I decided that they needed to have some encyclopaedias at home to encourage them to enjoy learning. I noticed an advertisement in the paper one day that someone in Stoke was selling a set of Arthur Mee[1] encyclopaedias in their own small purpose-built wooden bookcase. They were for sale for £10. We could not afford that but I was sure the boys needed them, so I sold my bike which was not in so much use now that I had the Prefect and that I was no longer going to university lectures and seminars. When the books duly arrived Rae made sure that the boys knew that they were "to be treasured" because she was keenly aware that I would miss the bike despite having the car. It was not a big sacrifice but it was indicative of the way we managed to make any special purchases or manage to give any gifts to anyone[2].

So it was, in the interests of the purse and much to my disappointment, that I set off without my wife to take Godfrey to see my mother. Bundled up with piles of nappies and many more instructions, I took Godfrey in my arms and headed north on the dreaded windy Wellington DC3 flight before changing planes for Palmerston North. Evelyn met us in her brand new Ford V8. Hers, she always took great delight in recalling, was the first new car bought in Hawera after the war. Ev and Jean were running their florist shop as well as looking after Mum in Hawera, a two and a half hour run away. I was gladly relieved to hand Godfrey over to my sisters' care. But the short visit was worth every minute. He bounced around on his grandmother's bed to her obvious delight despite her having then lost much of the power of speech. I spent

---

1 Arthur Mee (1875-1943) British writer, journalist and educator, best known for his Children's Encyclopaedia.

2 These Arthur Mee encyclopaedias went on to be kept by Weston for his children and despite their increasing age and being out of date, were well used by the next generation. Eventually the bookcase itself collapsed and the encyclopaedias were the worse for wear for being homeless. In the end Weston threw them out. In 2006 Riley spotted a complete set of Arthur Mee encyclopaedias in tip top condition in a second-hand shop in the small "one horse town" of Omakau, when he was on the Otago Central Rail Trail bicycle ride. Although this set was a red set, in every other way they were the same and for pure nostalgic reasons he bought them for $16.

several hours at my mother's bedside in that short visit and when I left a few days later, I was to never see her again.

We had a dreadful journey home. I was nearly sick before we landed at Wellington, but I was relieved that I touched the ground without incident. But on the final leg of the journey, between Wellington and Nelson, the DC3 pitched and tossed in the clouds as if it were flying through giant ocean waves. Notorious Wellington, once again, I thought. I clung to Godfrey desperately but could not avoid being violently sick. A kindly man sitting across the aisle from me, quietly reached across and took Godfrey off me and nursed him for the rest of the journey while I sat there – still a deathly shade of pale. The modern man of the 90s, looking after babies, taking them for walks, changing their nappies, is hailed with much applause as the liberated man today I understand. I and my stranger friend in the DC3 in 1951, nappies and shawls being exchanged between us across the aisle would have given them a run for their money more than forty years ago!

My mother died on November 27th, 1951. Weston and Riley were eight and six years old and Godfrey only one, when they lost their last grandmother. Godfrey has told me since that he very much missed not knowing either of his grandmothers. I flew back for the funeral but Rae chose not to accompany me. Of course money as ever was a consideration, but it would not have stopped her if she had really wanted to come. It was the excuse though, together with the children – and a good and fair one at that. But I knew better. I did not insist because I understood. Since the funeral of her mother she found it immensely difficult to attend others. She never said so in so many words, but over the years if she possibly could she would find any excuse to avoid attending a funeral. The closer the person was to her, the more elaborate became the reason why she could not go. It was undoubtedly a safety mechanism to avoid confronting her inability to deal openly with the sadness of others without it rocking her finely balanced composure in dealing with her own.

Once again I had been appointed to a twin town parish, Richmond and Stoke. But the Richmond parish covered a much wider area than I had been used to (apart from my Home Mission days in Northland) and included some far flung places. We lived in Richmond and Stoke was about six kilometres to the north. To the south was Hope three kilometres away and Brightwater six kilometres beyond that. Then came Spring Grove and Wakefield, further on up the Waimea Valley. The farthest place was Dovedale, some sixty kilometres inland beyond the Waimea Valley and over the Moutere Hills.[1]

The Methodist Church of New Zealand
THE NELSON METHODIST
The Quarterly Magazine of the Nelson, Motueka and Richmond Circuits
No 13 April 30, 1951

Ministers of the Nelson District

Rev H G Brown[2], Superintendent of the Motueka Circuit and Chairman of the District, Pah Road, Motueka. 'Phone 66K
Rev Ashleigh K Petch, BA, Superintendent of the Nelson Circuit, 320 Hardy Street, Nelson. 'Phone 274
Rev C Harrison Bell, BA, "Epworth", Queen Street, Richmond. 'Phone 34
Supernumeraries:
Rev C Blair[3], "Noeldene", Main Road, Stoke. 'Phone 1961M
Rev C B Jordan, MA, BD, FRES, Maitland Road, Stoke
Rev F B Lawrence, Sadlier Road, Stoke.
Home Missionary Supply:
Mr H A Holdaway, Murchison

NB: Use of C Harrison Bell, not Charles, and the long tel number!

Spring Grove, Wakefield and Dovedale had once been a Home Mission station, but was in my time merged into the Richmond Circuit. It was intended that, combined together we would qualify for a second ministerial appointment. Although we applied to conference year after year for a minister to take over the Wakefield-Dovedale parish, there never was a spare minister to take the appointment. Meanwhile, a senior minister, Reverend Charles Blair had retired to Stoke and arrangements were made with him to

---

1 See map at end of this chapter.

2 Rev Hubert G Brown 1899-1979

3 Rev Charles Blair 1881-1972

supervise these three places, preaching at them on alternate Sundays and sharing some of the pastoral care with me. In the absence of an official second minister appointment the parish had to rely heavily on lay preachers to complete the roster. On the alternate Sundays when I was required to take the services at Spring Grove and in the Waimea Valley churches I had to follow a precision timetable. It meant being at Dovedale by eleven o'clock, lunching with a church family there, arriving at Wakefield by two, leaving for Spring Grove by three and returning home for the Richmond or Stoke evening service at seven.

Eventually I had success in getting full ministerial support, but not until my last year. This time I changed my tactics and asked conference for a second District minister but for Stoke, not Wakefield-Dovedale. Stoke was a new, large and rapidly developing suburban area. The request was granted at the very first conference. In 1954 the Stoke church had its own full time minister for the first time and it has not been without one since. Stoke was moved out of the Richmond Parish into the Nelson Parish. Today it is larger than the Nelson church itself.

The small Spring Grove church was interesting on several counts. It was struggling to keep open, having dropped to a congregation of four or five elderly people. But it had had a robust past. In the vestry I found a cupboard with a complete dinner service with the church's monogram on it, a relic of flourishing days when church dinners were a common occurrence. The church building itself went right back to the early settler days having been built of pressed earth. I had visions of having it preserved as a memorial to the pioneers, but the parish had enough money problems and they did not want to take this on board. Unfortunately the present Historical Places Trust which offers financial support for projects such as this did not exist then, and this was one time when my pleadings for fundraising were not heeded.

There was another good reason for it to be preserved. Ernest Rutherford, later Baron Rutherford of Nelson, the man who split the atom, had been baptised here and his mother had been the church organist. Since then a memorial has been erected to him, but it is only on a bare piece of land where it is reputed his home stood. I feel it was a loss to the whole nation when the parish turned away from the opportunity of saving that church from collapsing into ruin. The last time I saw it, cows were roaming through the building, a mournful sight.

Officially I was Superintendent Minister overseeing these places but the rest, Brightwater, Hope, Richmond and Stoke, were my direct responsibility. At all of them there was a full range of activities going on every week – Sunday Schools, Bible Classes, Ladies Guilds, Women's Missionary Auxiliaries – and they were all fully supported. At Stoke and Richmond we had to cover two services each Sunday as well as the weekly ones at the other places. The Stoke Sunday School was even too large to be housed in the Sunday School hall. The Sunday School stayed operational only because Nelson's salubrious climate allowed classes to be held outside regularly. Throughout my five years there we often debated building programmes but we could never hit on one that was totally acceptable. Part of the problem arose from the fact that the church buildings were on a triangular shaped piece of land with roads on all three sides, one of these being the main West Coast road which brought that road hard up against our building. One could almost have touched the passing vehicles. What is more, the road had been widened about that time and it carried an increasingly heavy flow of traffic. After I left there the trustees sold the whole area (today the public library stands on the site) and moved to a larger site where they built a whole new complex.

The family faced another crisis in November 1950, one, for Rae's sake in particular, I felt we could well have done without. Riley went into hospital to have his tonsils out in the Hillcrest Hospital in . I was away at conference in Dunedin but the operation, even then, was quite routine so I did not worry. After I had returned home and they were back from hospital it was evident that Riley was not recovering as well as he should have been. We think he caught a chill while in hospital. It developed into pneumonia, a particularly alarming illness in those days. His conditioned worsened and became critical. As the doctor left us late one night after another visit to Riley's bedside, he turned to us. "I have never yet lost a child with pneumonia – and I do not intend to lose yours. But I feel I must share with you that I consider tonight is critical. If we are going to lose him it will be tonight. You should know that. But if he pulls through this stage, we've saved him. He will recover completely." Surprisingly we were not shocked. We knew he may die. The doctor was right. It was the only time we had cause to think we could have lost one of our children. It was a numbing horror that left a feeling of revulsion in the pit of your stomach. As we sat by his bedside, watching Riley slide as the doctor rightly predicted to his lowest ebb, the night was very long, very dark and very quiet. But the heavy black lightened to grey. The sun rose the next morning and Riley saw it.

Even in my time, Richmond and Stoke towns were expanding at a rapid rate. Herein was the potential for expanding congregations and also a challenge to the minister to keep pace with the influx of new people. Many times I had to fit in two meetings in one evening, dashing sometimes the six kilometres between the towns to attend both of them. On one occasion I booked in a wedding at Stoke on a Saturday for four o'clock. It was not until close to the appointed day I discovered that I had double booked a wedding at Richmond for the same day and time. Arrangements with caterers and so on were all firmly in place and it was not convenient for either party to change them. Eventually a somewhat satisfactory compromise was reached but I always felt that one party never quite forgave me. Whether it was from this shambles or some other I might have unwittingly overlooked, I don't know, but I got the message loud and clear when I received through the post a diary and pencil!

My ministry was dotted with embarrassing moments and another for me happened shortly afterwards. Since I had recently completed my degree in Wellington I had taken to wearing the graduate hood with my pastoral gown but I felt that it was inappropriate to wear it at the communion service. One Sunday I had come out of the pulpit and approached the Communion Table, a particularly tiny space in the Richmond church. As I started the communion service I suddenly realised I was still wearing my graduate hood. Reaching up I slipped it over my head and removed it but in so doing it swept off a vase of flowers and sent them crashing to the floor. What was I to do? Stop in the middle of the service and gather them up – or ignore them and step over them for the rest of the service? I stared down at them for a stunned moment and decided to carry on, but either way the atmosphere of the service had been shattered.

It was customary in this area for all lay preachers to be called on to preach in all the churches from time to time, irrespective of what parish they belonged to. The ministers likewise often exchanged pulpits. It so happened that Reverend Ashleigh Petch took the Richmond service on this particular morning while I would probably be in the Nelson Methodist Church. I left the pulpit notices for him in the vestry. They contained one rather inconsequential item. An umbrella had been found in the church porch which had not been claimed after some weeks. Would the owner please contact Mr White. I had hesitated to bother putting this in but knowing Mr White who had asked me to include it I decided it was diplomatic to do so. But Ashleigh Petch didn't know Mr White as I did and left it out. At the end of the notices, suddenly Mr White stood up in the middle of the congregation and solemnly announced, "Mr Petch you have left out one of the notices. There is an umbrella. . . . "

It is not often that a preacher finds an urge to laugh in the pulpit. But one very cold day a girl with bright red hair was sitting in a pew when a boy in the seat behind her held up his hands above her head and rubbed them together as if they had really been warmed up. I could not help but notice it and I could not help but smile – although the congregation could not be told and the red haired girl continued to stare up at me solemnly and oblivious to my predicament. It took all my self discipline not to chuckle out loud. The young boy continued to catch my eye and winked as he warmed his hands up yet again. He was ready for a real laugh and the trouble was, so was I. Thankfully I pulled myself together before making a fool of myself.

Among the many duties that befall a minister is that of counselling and it brought me into contact with people in distress and in all sorts of troubles. On one occasion I had been counselling a middle aged woman and was opening the door for her to leave. As I did so, I sympathetically patted her on her back. She said, "There's nothing there. All the interesting parts are in front of me." And although she tried to pass it off as a joke comment, I could see it was only half a one. Alarm bells started ringing and I got her out of the door in record time.

On another occasion a young married woman was having matrimonial problems and had been to see me on a number of occasions. However, she could not get her husband to come with her. Finally she prevailed on him to let me call on him in his home. So a time was arranged and I set off to make the call. On my way there I met her coming away so that he would be free to speak to me. After I had knocked several times, the wife returned to the house having rightly suspected that he may not have answered the door. She went in and found he had locked himself in the bedroom. She tried to persuade him to come out but it was a difficult situation with them talking to each other through the door and me sitting in the lounge listening to it all. I remember she was one of those who blamed God "for everything": why had God led her into this terrible marriage? I asked her if she had asked God to save her from it. Had she prayed about it before she got married? Had she asked God to guide and direct her life? Had she asked God if this man was the one that God had directed her to and was she convinced that her marriage had God's blessing? How then, could she now blame God for anything at all? Of course my responses were more a technique to reverse negative thinking, than the promotion of a particular way of behaving. But over the years I have noted that many are quick to blame God when things go wrong and I have seen it help put things in perspective when I ask them if they had counted God "in" in the first place.

The Nelson Evening Mail used to run a weekly religious column and they called on me to take my turn at contributing. At the time I was reading a book on the churches in different countries around the world and I used this as a source of inspiration for my column. Apparently it impressed some of my fellow ministers. When the World Council of Churches held its 1954 meeting in Illinois, USA, the Methodist minister in Nelson, Reverend Charles Hailwood was selected to go as a delegate. To mark the occasion the Nelson churches united to hold a service to coincide with the opening of the conference. The Secretary of the Ministers' Association rang me to ask if I would be the preacher for the occasion. It was only when I was in the pulpit and the service was unfolding that it dawned on me, or in the very least I started imagining, that I had been invited to preach this sermon specifically because of what I had written in the *Nelson Evening Mail* and not simply as a gesture of goodwill. There was nothing in my sermon, even though it related to topical world church issues, that drew on my opinions which I had espoused through the newspaper. The sermon in my pocket got colder and my heart sank deeper with each passing minute. Somewhere, somehow, in that phone call I had missed the point or the Secretary had failed to stress the significance of my selection. It was one of the longest services I ever sat through and one of the sermons of my career that I still recall with anxiety.

The parish was dogged by a debt that they could not be rid of. Another challenge of the kind I enjoyed! I called a meeting and suggested that we host a fair and market day to raise enough money to wipe out the debt. As usual my apparently hairbrain idea was met with scepticism (I was getting used to that) but also as usual I persevered. Eventually, we hired the local sports ground for the day, hired a band and organised buses to run from Nelson. We bombarded the local homes with a mail drop seeking their support in the way of contributions to the stalls. We arranged entertainment to attract the crowds. There was a merry-go-round, children's races, nail driving, guessing the weight of a sheep and so forth. It was a success: the debt was more than cancelled and the sceptics predictably passed no comment at all or complained about *something* – which meant anything at all, but *something* – or overtly laid claim to a stake in the glory of its wonderful outcome.

When I first arrived in Nelson, I was thrown into the middle of a legal battle. One of the church members had been killed overseas in the war and his mother gave his estate to the church for the purpose of building a new Sunday School hall. The existing hall was totally inadequate and very old. But things were not going smoothly. The mother, perhaps understandably, felt that she had a right to direct the building project and she wanted the new hall to be used for a community kindergarten. It was accepted that the church would have full ownership of the proposed building and could run it as it wished so long as a kindergarten was incorporated. Having a public kindergarten in the new hall actually compromised the church's use and need of it. About this time the mother herself died and her lawyer took over her cause. He continued to insist that the building incorporate all her wishes for the kindergarten even demanding that the hall be built on the main street – if necessary overshadowing the church itself. Obviously, this was totally unacceptable to the church officials. But they argued the toss to the last ditch. A compromise seemed impossible and meetings ended without agreement. Eventually we established that there is no such thing as a lawyer to a dead person and that strictly speaking, this lawyer representing his dead client's simple wishes had no legal punch at all. At our last meeting with him we kept this card close to our chest and we reached agreement without resorting to the fact. We all breathed a sigh of relief. The hall would be built and both parties were content. But the next day, the lawyer phoned me. "I'm not satisfied." I was flabbergasted. "I'm sorry", I said, "This is where the road stops. We are going ahead as planned and as we agreed last night." The new Sunday School hall was built – and used as a kindergarten, it was.

The young people in this parish were a joy. Many were devoted to the church and many were or wanted to become lay preachers. Some went on to become fully ordained ministers. In the winter months I held a weekly evening class at the parsonage for any young people interested in becoming lay preachers. This was responded to by some very fine young people from the Richmond-Hope-Stoke areas. I remember in particular John Marshall, Bevan Smith and Murray Webby.

There was a small talented group in Stoke who formed a band. They gave up a lot of their leisure time and played regularly at church and at camps, youth councils and "working bee" groups. In the band were Joan Ching, Mary Corby and the Taylor family. This was a notable Methodist family. Barbara Taylor married a minister, Beverley Taylor became a Deaconess and then went into the ministry herself having two distinctions: one for being associated with the Pitt Street Methodist Church in Auckland longer than anybody else (except for the caretaker!), and the other for having been the minister at the church where one of New Zealand's Prime Ministers (Hon David Lange) worshipped. Finally, Philip Taylor went into the Methodist mission field as a carpenter. He too, however, entered the full time ministry and was later nominated for President of the Methodist Conference, although he missed out on the final vote.

During my time in Richmond a number of immigrant Dutch families settled in the area and joined the congregation. One of them, John Gerritsen, had a keen mind and a deep interest in theology. On Friday evenings he would go to the public library and load himself up with books for the next week's reading. Then he would call around at the parsonage to spend the evening discussing with me the theologians of the time, Barth, Brunner and others. He became a loyal and valued member of the Methodist Church. His preaching was deep, provocative and intellectually stimulating although some people, perhaps, felt that his services were too intellectual and beyond them. John's eldest son Hank had just finished his schooling when his family came to New Zealand. At first he appeared to be shy and quiet but surprised me when he said he felt a call to the ministry. The examination committee was a bit taken aback when it was reported he had studied four languages. In New Zealand this was virtually unheard of! He was duly accepted by the church and has been a parish minister in various parts of the country since. As I write, however, I hear he has been released from parish duties to write a thesis on religion and the earth.

* * *

While we were in Nelson an aunt (by marriage) of Rae's, Eileen Fitzer from Darwin in the Northern Territories, Australia, came to visit us. Eileen was the (second) wife of "Tas" (Tasman – so named because he was born at sea crossing the Tasman from New Zealand to Australia in 1896), the third younger brother of Rae's mother.

Rae's Uncle Tas first married Lawrie Jean Osborne (known as Jean) in October 1931 and by her he had his only child and son John Desmond (Des)[1]. The marriage did not work and Jean left Darwin in the World War II evacuation due to the threat of Japanese bombing and never returned. Des was sent to board at The King's School, North Parramatta in Sydney. He returned to live in Darwin but his career took him to Papua New Guinea where he lived from 1954 to 1990. Des started as a Patrol Officer employed by the Australian government and finished up as a District Commissioner. Finally he became an advisor to the PNG Prime Minister Sir Julius Chan. Today, Des's wife Vivien lives in Sydney[2].

Des's father Tas married again in April 1945 (less than a year before his sister took her life in New Zealand) at Tipperary Station on the Daly River. His new wife was widow Eileen Gribbons (nee Styles).

Tas was a most interesting and notable character who earned considerable recognition in his career. Tasman Charles Vivian Fitzer's birth at sea was registered in Melbourne as on 4 July 1896. Although he spent his first years in Albert Park, Melbourne, and went to school in Princes Hill, he came to New Zealand and

---

1 John DESmond Fitzer 1932 (Darwin) – 2006 (Sydney)

2 Des died 27 June 2006 – some time after Vivien had helped me with the Australian Fitzer research. Sadly, the book was not finished in time for him read it. - GB

completed his education in both Dunedin and Christchurch. After returning to Australia he went to Thursday Island in Queensland to work for the Army in 1918 and 1919. He joined the Northern Territory Police Force as a Mounted Constable in 1925 at the age of twenty-nine and was posted fairly early on in his career to outback stations. He went on to man the police stations at Daly River and Timber Creek.

Tas Fitzer was one of a handful of members of the Force who kept law and order in some of the loneliest regions of the sparsely settled Territory. Its 837,000 square kilometres was mainly frontier country in the twenties and thirties. He is remembered as one of the most popular men in the Force. He was a friend to bagman, stockman, drover, station folk and all and had a humane understanding of the problem of the Aborigines. Only the toughest of men were recruited into the Northern Territory Police Force and they usually considered themselves seasoned troopers after they had served a term at the isolated Timber Creek Police Station. Out from Timber Creek the country was known as "bad blackfellow country". Even up to the thirties the men of Timber Creek were having trouble with the natives. Nemarluk and his warriors from the Fitzmaurice River tribes were wanted for the murders of three Japanese, a Malay, whites and blacks, and for cattle spearing on the nearby pastoral runs. Jack Mahony, Ted Morey and Tas, with his intrepid Aborigine tracker, Bul Bul, finally caught Nemarluk.

The search for and capture of the notorious Nemarluk is well remembered in Northern Territory history. The story is documented in detail in the book *Man Tracks* by Ion L. Idriess which was first published in 1935 and re-printed many times. Tas is a central figure in the book.

Extracts from "Man Tracks"

Chapter XXXI
Mounted Constable Fitzer, in charge of Timber Creek police station, was worried. This Nemarluk, grown over confident by repeated escapes, was now a distinct menace. Probably his example would be emulated by bucks anxious for native hero worship. And the Fitzmaurice River country mothered material for a dozen Nemarluks. How to catch this elusive firebrand before he set the tribes alight?

> Fitzer walked out on to the police station veranda and gazed at the rocky hills. Close by was Timber Creek, meandering along to the Victoria River one and a half miles away. The river there was one quarter of a mile wide but shallow and tidal, and there was The Crossing. Three miles below The Crossing, and eighty miles from the river's mouth, is Victoria River Depot, where the *Maroubra* brings the stores for the cattle and police stations. . . .
>
> Timber Creek police station is one of the most isolated police outposts in the Northern Territory, and because of its geographical position one of the most important. This police outpost is merely of four rooms with a veranda all round, a detached kitchen, store, harness room and stockyard. Fitzer stood watching his baby toddler, as usual when apparently unobserved making on chubby legs to the nearest waterhole. Baby's inseparable companion "Beris" walked gravely beside him, his big shoulders gently urging the youngster to explore in some other direction. But the toddler was determined, so the big Alsatian, despite energetic protests, simply shouldered him right away from the danger.
>
> Fitzer smiled. Great dog that, the best nursemaid ever. Would not let a native go near the baby either, would tear a bush native to pieces if he dared to come within a hundred yards of the child. ...
>
> With his mind full of Nemarluk, Fitzer walked to the harness store. He unlocked the door and walked down between the big heavy rails with their neat arrays of riding and pack-saddles for horse and mule, their saddle-cloths and bridles and halters. The usual accoutrement store of any northern Australian mounted police station. Everything in place with military precision, all ready for immediate patrol.
>
> **Chapter XXXIX**
>
> By many a subterfuge known to the cunning among primitive men Nemarluk evaded capture for a long time. He probably would still be free, certainly would have cost the country thousands of pounds, had not Fitzer worked with his head.

Tas stayed on in the north during the Second World War years in a non-constabulary role in an Army Observers Unit to train and instruct troops in the elements of bushcraft. Where invasion by the Japanese was likely, defenders in Australia were taught about living off the land. For eighteen months, Tas taught groups of young soldiers how to find bush tucker and how to cook goanna, crocodile eggs and other things.

In 1952 Tas was asked by his friend Charles Chauvel to play a small role of a Northern Territory mounted policeman in his film called *Jedda*. Although professional actors play the major roles, much of the supporting cast is composed of social actors "playing themselves" (Tas, for example). It is the story of a teenage aboriginal girl torn between two cultures. Adopted and raised by white parents, Jedda is strangely drawn to and then unexpectedly taken captive by a tribal aborigine. A life and death chase follows, played out against the spectacular landscape of Australia's Northern Territory. Charles Chauvel's last feature film, *Jedda* was the first to star aborigines (giving top billing over the white players) and the first filmed in colour by an Australian company. Shot on locations around the Northern Territory, *Jedda* was, and still is, emotionally intense and very beautiful. The film raises issues that remain both powerful and painful today. At the time of its original release in 1955, it revealed a land and a people largely unknown to the world – and to most Australians. Although radical and courageous in its subject matter, *Jedda* proved a commercial and critical success and is now acknowledged as a great Australian classic. Today the film is part of *The Chauvel Collection* and also of the Australian National Film and Sound Archive in Canberra. It is often replayed on Australian television. Unfortunately, as was the custom in those days, the Australian voices were dubbed by British voices and thus Tas's voice has not been recorded for posterity.

Tas died on August 21st 1966 at Avalon, Sydney, in New South Wales. His efforts were later recognised when he was commemorated as an "unsung hero" in the Australian Stockman's Hall of Fame and Outback Heritage Centre at Longreach in Queensland (Honour Roll of Unsung Heroes, Certificate Number 285). Fitzer Drive in Darwin perpetuates his memory.

The Press, **22 August 1966**

Fitzer, Tasman Charles - On August 21, 1966, at Sydney, devoted brother of the late Hilda Barrell and dearly loved uncle of Rae (Mrs C H Bell) and Charles D Barrell.

Rae's aunt herself became a distinguished woman receiving the MBE for her services to nursing and the Territory community as a

Territory pioneer. Eileen Marjory Styles was born in Brock's Creek, Northern Territory in 1902 and, as I write, is still alive today living in Darwin.[1] Eileen's mother[2] had been born in Palmerston (the earlier name for Darwin) to parents who were amongst the very first European settlers in the Territory. Eileen's only brother, Walter, was killed on the battlefields of France in 1918. Between 1928 and 1932 Eileen studied nursing in Melbourne getting her "double certificate" in Queen Victoria Hospital. But Eileen missed the Territory and as soon as she had sat her exams she took the train to Alice Springs. She was appointed nursing sister at the Bungalow, a home for part Aboriginal children. While she was there a severe trachoma epidemic broke out in Alice Springs and she spent several weeks in isolation treating the sick. She and her two teenage assistants saw no outside people while they were administering the treatments.

In 1934 the Territory's chief medical officer transferred her to Pine Creek where she was Sister in charge of the hospital. It was during this time that she met Dr Fenton, the famed Territory flying doctor who was stationed at Katherine but visited Pine Creek at least once a week. He was a practical joker as well as highly skilled doctor and pilot, and Eileen, who often flew with him, experienced many of his stunts first hand.

In 1936 Eileen's sister Gertrude died in Perth . Eileen was distressed by her loss and decided she did not want to be single any longer. Within a few weeks she married a long time friend Harry Gribbons, whom she affectionately referred to as her "wild Irishman". They moved to Darwin for a while before trying their luck on the Wauchope Wolfram mining fields near Tennant Creek in 1939. For about eighteen months Eileen was the only European woman on the fields and was often called on to nurse sick miners. Following this, Eileen was asked to relieve the nursing sister for a few months at the quarantine station, the Channel Island

---

[1] Eileen Marjorie Fitzer (nee Styles) 1902 (Darwin) – 2001 (Darwin). For a long time she was the last surviving member (albeit by marriage) of grandma Fitzer's generation – Hilda Barrell's sister-in-law. - GB

[2] Eleanor Styles (nee Tuckwell) 1873-1910

Leprosarium in Darwin harbour. She looked after about one hundred and twenty lepers.

In 1941, Eileen and her husband who was then very ill, were evacuated from Darwin in fear of a Japanese invasion and went to Sydney. Shortly afterwards Darwin was bombed and evacuations continued in enormous number. She decided to go to Alice Springs to help out with newly arriving evacuees. Eventually she moved to Adelaide River and stayed at nearby Mount Bundy Station. She was the only civilian woman there at the time. During her four week stay in the region she heard aeroplanes and sirens almost daily as the Japanese continued their bombing raids on the "Top End".

After her husband Harry died in 1943, Eileen went to Tipperary which was still very much in the military zone and often visited by soldiers. It was while she was here that Eileen renewed her friendship with a man who was now one of the Territory's most famous policemen, Tas Fitzer. She had first met Tas in the early 1930s when he was in charge of the Pine Creek station and when he captured Nemarluk. But now he was officer in charge of the Daly River police station.

The Daly River police station, which was for many years the home of Tas and Eileen, is described in *Man Tracks* as it was in the 1930s:

> The little Daly River police station (one hundred miles south of Darwin) is about sixty miles up-river where it is barely two hundred yards wide. On rich level soil dotted with paper-bark trees, the police landing is on a high bank and backed by splendid trees. One magnificent banyan would easily shelter fifty people. To this landing the little forty-ton motor vessel *Maroubra* brings the stores, then returns to Darwin loaded with peanuts. The river up-stream is lined with jungle areas and thickets of giant bamboo. Down-stream towards the coast there are no whites. The river gradually widens through richly-grassed flats and plains with swamps and billabongs swarming with bird life. Mangroves line the muddy stream where, nearly a mile wide, it empties into the sea. From the western bank here, for a hundred and fifty miles south, right across to the Victoria River, Nemarluk reigned as king.

By 1943 the Daly River station had been taken over by the military and it was Tas's job to look for lost airmen by horse patrol and black trackers.

The circumstances under which Tas and Eileen renewed their acquaintance were potentially tragic. Tas had been badly injured when a wild colt kicked him and had remained in agony on his verandah for seventeen days. As it was the middle of "the Wet", Tas knew a flying doctor could not land but also knew he was becoming semi delirious. He scribbled a note which he gave to his faithful black tracker, Bul Bul, instructing him to take it to Sister Eileen at Tipperary. The tracker travelled by foot over forty-eight kilometres to reach her and returned three days later with a note from Eileen explaining that with the help of fourteen Aborigines she had penetrated bogs and creeks to get within eighteen kilometres of the police station. She sent instructions for the trackers to improvise a stretcher and carry Tas back to her, a feat they eventually accomplished after many gruelling hours.

The year after Tas and Eileen were married in 1945, Eileen herself was taken critically ill and with the help of the Aborigine trackers had to be evacuated through flooded Daly River country to Darwin, where her life was saved and her ordeal made headlines throughout Australia. She returned to Daly where she soon became known as the "White Queen of Daly River " and often, "the White Queen of the Aborigines".

In 1950 Tas visited Christchurch, his home town, with his wife Eileen. Their visit was picked up by the media and *The Press* wrote about Eileen's reputation as the White Queen along with a photograph of the couple.

The Press, Wednesday, January 18, 1950:

"WHITE QUEEN OF DALY RIVER"

Visit to Christchurch with husband

"The White Queen of Daly River," Mrs Tasman Fitzer, is on a holiday visit to Christchurch with her husband, who has been a mounted constable in the Northern Territory of Australia for 28 years. The only white woman on the Daly River, she is revered by the aborigines to whom her word is law.

Born in Darwin, Mrs Fitzer has spent many years nursing in the back block of "the Territory". Before she left for New Zealand the natives danced a corroboree in farewell – a rare compliment, particularly to a white woman. Before she married

> Constable Fitzer, Mrs Fitzer worked with Dr Clyde Fenton, the pioneer flying doctor of the Territory.
>
> Although she holds no nursing position now, she is often called on by both black and white people.
>
> Her nearest neighbour is 90 miles away, but she has many visitors from all over Australia during the dry part of the year, Daly River being recognised as one of the beauty spots of Northern Australia. She has spent two Christmases on the Daly River, and on each occasion has issued an open invitation to the men – black and white – in the district, to Christmas dinner. Most of the guests were working on peanut farms and came by canoe, on horseback and on foot.
>
> While the lighting is by kerosene lamps, life in her backblock home is by no means primitive. She has a pressure cooker, "which makes all the difference to kangaroo tails". Kangaroo tails, Mrs Fitzer said, were a very tasty delicacy. She also had a kerosene refrigerator and she wondered why these were not in use in New Zealand.
>
> During the war Major-General J J Murray, who was later Trade Commissioner for Australia in New Zealand, was a guest of hers for several days.

Eileen was a short, stocky woman[1]. She was round faced, grey haired, and a kind and most loving woman with a warm, wonderful outgoing personality. At dinner one evening, Riley had not started his meal as he had his eyes transfixed on this "enormous" woman across the table from him. When Rae prompted him to start eating, he broke into a trance-like chant quoting, to Rae's dismay, words from the *Too Fat Polka* which was popular at the time and which he must have picked up from the radio or at school: "I don't want her, you can have her, she's too fat for me."[2] Rather than being offended, thankfully Eileen responded with a huge, loud and gleeful bout of laughter.

Shortly before her arrival in Nelson, somehow the local papers got wind of her reputation in the Territory. They printed a story about her along with her photograph and it appeared something along the lines of "White Queen of Daly River to visit Nelson" (similar to *The Press* coverage above). One evening after Eileen had arrived we went to the cinema together. As she

---

[1] Eileen has since died, at the age of 99, on 27 August 2001, a few months short of her 100th birthday.

[2] *Too Fat Polka*, Words by Ross MacLean and Arthur Richardson, sung by both Arthur Godfrey and the Andrews Sisters in 1947 (and others since).

approached the ticket office, the young girl recognised her instantly and proudly announced, "Oh no, we wouldn't dream of charging you Your Royal Highness. "[1]

After Eileen died, she was honoured with a personal tribute delivered in Parliament.

Parliamentary Record (Australia): 16 Oct 2001:

Ms MARTIN (Fannie Bay): Mr Acting Deputy Speaker, as the Minister for Senior Territorians and member for Fannie Bay, I rise to pay tribute tonight to a woman who, until her death a few weeks ago, was perhaps our most senior Territorian, and certainly one of our most tenacious, optimistic and inspiring Territory pioneers. She was Eileen Marjorie Fitzer, whose remarkable life spanned a century and who died on 27 August, just seven months short of her 100th birthday. I was privileged to have had Eileen as my constituent and was always uplifted and inspired by my visits to her at her unit in Kurringal Flats, and more recently at the Salvation Army Nursing Home.

Ever alert and smiling, despite being quite physically restricted in recent years, she would say, "I'm never lonely; I live on my memories", and what amazing memories they were. I would like to take a few moments this evening to place on the public record my personal appreciation, and I am sure that of most Territorians, for the very substantial contribution Eileen Fitzer made to the Territory throughout the last century. Eileen played many roles during her lifetime: entertainer, political activist, pioneer nurse, policeman's wife and partner, remote outback hostess, faithful friend and mentor.

Conceived as Australia was forming itself as a nation, Eileen was born in Darwin on 30 March 1902, to Eleanor and Tom Styles. She was extremely proud of her pioneering stock, her Darwin-born mother was the daughter of Ned and Eliza Tuckwell, who are among the Territory's earliest European settlers, and from whom Eileen inherited her strong spirit. Ned, who had been part of the South Australian expedition to establish a settlement at Escape Cliffs from 1864 to 1866, arrived in Darwin with George Goyder's South Australian survey party in 1868.

Eliza, a cockney who had immigrated to Adelaide as a servant girl in 1855, arrived with their four children on the first ship to carry passengers to the Territory in January 1870. To help pay the bills, Eliza took in washing and acted as a midwife, while Ned worked on most of the city's early buildings, including the first Government Residence. Eileen's mother, Eleanor, was born at the camp in Darwin in 1873, and spent her childhood and teenage years here. In 1893, at

---

[1] I rang Eileen in Darwin, 29 April 1995 and spoke to her for the first time. She answered the phone herself. "Darling", she replied enthusiastically, "how wonderful!" She lived alone, was wheelchair bound, but sharp as a tack. "The Labour Party is making a fuss of me here. I am now the oldest Territory born person," she said with great delight. - GB

the age of 19, she married English-born Tom Styles, and moved with him to Brock's Creek, where he was the underground manager for the Zapopan mine. By the time Eileen arrived on the scene, her mother had given birth to five children, three of whom died in infancy. Following Eileen's birth, Eleanor had another son, who also died as an infant, and another daughter. Eileen was proud of the fact that her grandmother and her mother were among the first Australian women to vote after South Australia passed the necessary legislation in 1894, and she would have been pleased to see the percentage of women in parliament increase substantially in the last Territory election. She spoke enthusiastically and vividly of the rich cultural life she experienced with her family, of travelling through the exotic Chinatown on the edge of Brock's Creek, and of days filled with singing and dancing, led by her father's rich voice and her mother's lively concertina playing. She remembered an early birthday the community gave for her, when guests danced on antbed and ash floors, and of the following morning when Eileen and her sisters had to sweep up all the dust. School was in a tiny house at Brock's Creek, where the five students had a tin whistle band. Sometimes Eileen and her musical sister, Myrtle, used to entertain the others by putting dusters on their heads and singing "Two Little Girls in Blue". When Eileen was eight, her mother died of cancer, and Eileen and her sister, Gertrude, were sent to the Darwin convent school where Eileen earned top marks and became an accomplished seamstress. Her other two sisters, Lillian and Myrtle, lived with their grandmother who had run a boarding house called Resolution Villa ever since her husband's death in 1882. A staunch Methodist, Eliza lived across the street from the historic Wesleyan Church, which she attended regularly. Eileen had vivid memories of her grandmother as a little lady always wearing a black bonnet and shawl, sitting in a rocker on the veranda and singing hymns in the latter years of her life. She also recalled the adventure of being a child in Darwin, of playing cowboys and Indians down at Fort Hill and exploring Chinatown, then in the heart of Cavenagh Street. Eileen described it as the most fabulous place in the world and the Chinese New Year celebration as the most exciting time in a European child's life.

During the First World War, in which her brother, Walter, died on the battlefields of France, Eileen and her sisters moved to Pine Creek to be with their father who, Eileen claimed, probably greased every nut and bolt on the Pine Creek railway. When Eileen finished school at the age of 12, as there was no further schooling available in Pine Creek, she took a job as a nursemaid at 10 shillings a week. She remembered her devastation when the family got a letter from the Army informing them that her brother had been killed on the battlefields of France, the first Territory boy to die in the war[1]. The letter from

---

[1] There is the possibility of conflicting evidence here. This Walter John Styles died in France in 1918. However another Walter Styles (also Australian) died in 1915 in Gallipoli. It is odd that this is "the first Territory boy to die in the war" when it was as late as 1918.

the Army said he was engaged on a mission when, without warning, a machine gun opened fire and he was hit in two places. They said he was most heroic in the manner in which he bore great pain and was an example to many a hardened soldier.

After the war, the girls moved to a bachelor pad in Darwin where they were extremely popular and active in all areas of the community and served on the ANZAC Day committee when the community constructed a monument to the Territory boys who had lost their lives in the war. Eileen got a job as a salesgirl at the large European shop of Jolly's and earned herself a reputation as an entertainer of note. After one of her performances, the local paper said that, 'If Miss Eileen Styles went to America, she would be snapped up by an enterprising picture film man'.

Eileen, who used to described herself as a bit of a rebel and game for anything, became a political activist when she was 19. In 1921, Eileen, who had grown up in a strong Labour household, brought roast dinners to leading citizens who went to gaol in a successful 'no taxation without representation' fight. Then she drove a sulky all over Darwin campaigning for one of those citizens, union and Labour leader Harold Nelson, who became the Territory's first member of federal parliament in 1922. Eileen carried on the tradition and remained a staunch supporter of Labour all her life. It was very rewarding and satisfying to me personally, as her local member, that she lived just long enough to see Labour finally win government for the first time in the Territory.

Eileen's political interests eventually took second place to the profession she chose to follow. In 1927, Eileen's sister, Gertrude, financed her to do a nursing course in Melbourne where she initially had problems with her feet because she wasn't used to walking on the pavement. After nursing school, she did midwifery at the Queen Victoria. The week she got her successful results, she caught the train to Alice Springs, so anxious was she to return to the Territory. At Alice Springs she carried out pioneer work at The Bungalow, working with Stolen Generation children suffering from eye disease. In 1934, she was transferred to Pine Creek as Sister-in-Charge of the hospital where she said most of her cases were caused by mining accidents or pub fights. She was visited at least once a week by the famous flying doctor, Clyde Fenton, who was stationed in Katherine. A practical joker as well as an amazing pilot, Fenton often involved Eileen in his flying stunts.

In 1936, Eileen married a long time friend, World War I veteran Harry Gribbons whom she affectionately referred to as her 'wild Irishman'. In late 1938, they went to the Wauchope Wolfram mining fields near Tennant Creek. For the next 18 months, Eileen was the only European woman on the fields and was often called on to nurse sick miners, mostly with eye problems. Here she lived in what she whimsically referred to as 'The Mansion', which was in reality a tiny

---

However, as yet, I have been unable to verify the origins of the two Walter Styles (other than the fact they were both Australians). - GB shed with the floor made of shavings and filings from the mine. She always wore a pith helmet with a fly veil on it and served meals under a large mosquito net to keep the flies off.

Eileen was next asked to relieve the nursing sister at Channel Island leprosarium for a few months where she looked after about 120 lepers. This was followed by another job as the Matron at the then new Bagot Aboriginal compound in Darwin. Some time later, she and Harry bought the Adelaide River Hotel which they ran until late 1941 when Harry became extremely ill and they were evacuated to Sydney on the *USS Grant* with about 250 women and children. Once Eileen got her husband settled in Sydney, she successfully sought permission to return to Adelaide River to settle up the business affairs. She caught the train to Alice Springs and then travelled in a truck convoy to Adelaide River where she was the only civilian woman.

After handing over her hotel furniture to the nurses, Eileen returned to Sydney where she remained with her husband until he died in early 1943. A short time later, she got a telegram from the Byrne family at Tipperary Station inviting her to come and live with them as a nurse. She jumped at the chance to return to the Territory. It was while she was there that Eileen renewed her friendship with one of the Territory's most famous policemen, Tas Fitzer, then the Officer In Charge of the Daly River police station. A romance blossomed and in April 1945, Tas and Eileen were married at Tipperary Station in a ceremony which lasted for three days.

After the wedding the couple moved to their home on the Daly River where Tas was stationed as a policeman. Eileen soon became known as the 'white queen of the Daly' and she was hostess to many of the military serving in the area. She made headlines across Australia when she became desperately ill one Wet Season and was dramatically rescued by a boom defence vessel which battled raging floods to bring Father Frank Flynn to her aid.

Eileen's famous good nature and generosity continued later at Timber Creek, where the couple served until 1955 when Tas retired and they moved to Sydney for health reasons. When Tas died in 1966, Eileen returned to her beloved Territory where she lived for many years at Kurringal Flats, making several extended trips overseas. On one visit she had tea at Buckingham Palace after receiving an MBE for her services to nursing and the community.

Earlier this year she moved to the Salvation Army Nursing Home where she got a renewed lease of life and was fond of telling visitors that she was still fighting fit. In her typical spirited style, Eileen began planning for her historic exit more than 20 years ago when she sought and received permission from the Darwin City Council to be buried in the Goyder Road Cemetery with her grandfather Ned Tuckwell who died in 1882, her mother Eleanor Styles who died in 1910, and her grandmother who died in 1921. When the cemetery was placed on the NT Heritage Register in 1997, the then 95-year-old made sure she had the permission of the Lands, Planning and Environment Minister for her family to carry out her last wishes of being buried with her pioneering family.

She left instructions that when she died she wanted people to celebrate, not mourn, her life. She often used to say, 'I have had a wonderful life and I have no regrets. I want people to be happy'. Dutifully, on 3 September, a host of family and friends attended Eileen's funeral mass at St Mary's Catholic Cathedral, followed by her special burial at the old cemetery which was reopened for the occasion, and later a wake at the Sailing Club, celebrating that lucky life.

While we record our regret at the passing of her remarkable life, we can be grateful that her life story has been richly recorded in oral histories, books, and many feature articles. It is indeed fitting that a few weeks before her death, Eileen was guest of honour at a special function at the Museum and Art Gallery, which had been featuring the small but significant exhibition called Threads of History. It was a display of four delicate embroidered linen signature cloths created by women in the Top End between 1901 and 1940, including two made by Eileen in 1913 and 1923, the latter being the occasion of her 21st birthday.

It is worth repeating what the Northern Territory newspaper said about Eileen at the time, and I quote from the 7 April 1923 edition:

The 21st birthday of Miss Eileen Styles, one of the most popular girls in the Northern Territory, was celebrated with great elat [sic] *in the Soldiers' Memorial Hall on Saturday night last. The guests represented every wholesome section of the community, and Eileen was the recipient of tangible tokens of affection from all her youthful friends, and practical demonstrations of sincere regard from those who have known her since childhood. Buoyant good nature combined with conspicuous generosity and a considerable amount of ability has made Eileen a figure in local life and as a product of the soil, the people of the place are evidently proud of her.*

That pride still holds true today, nearly 80 years later. Ironically, Eileen died the day the exhibit was dismantled. There is no doubt that her family's very significant threads of history will live on in the fifth generation Territory-born descendants of the pioneering Tuckwell family such as the Rixons, the Lovegroves, the Fawcetts and the Eastons, and in the memories of the hundreds of people whose life Eileen Fitzer touched.

So, from this parliament, we say, 'Vale, Eileen'. May we all learn from your rich and rewarding life and your ever-optimistic and inspiring spirit. May your life and spirit serve to remind us of the very substantial resource our senior citizens are in building this better Territory.

I would like to give my thanks to historian, Barbara James, for that history. She has recorded a lot of the history of some of our pioneers, and certainly recorded Eileen's with a great passion. My thanks to Barbara, and farewell to Eileen.

* * *

Queen indeed Eileen Fitzer was – in so many ways. But she came nowhere close to the real thing. Six months after Queen Elizabeth II's coronation in London in 1953, the Queen toured New Zealand – the first of a reigning sovereign. The last coronation had been of George VI in 1937 when I was twenty-five, but this time the celebrations seemed to make much more impact on New Zealand. Everyone was buying coronation souvenirs especially of mugs and plates and I think if I were to dig around I'd still find one of the mugs we bought for the children. The coronation in Westminster Abbey was covered by newsreels shown in cinemas throughout the world, but here in New Zealand the attendances were so great that they were to rival those of *Ben Hur* and *The Ten Commandments* a few years later.

At the time of the coronation, New Zealander Sir Edmund Hillary and Sherpa Tenzing Norgay conquered Mount Everest: "higher than any man before" at 29,000 feet. Communications were then primitive. Although they reached the top on 29th May 1953, the news, relayed from Nepal to England to New Zealand, was not announced publicly until June 2nd – the day of the Queen's coronation. The timing of the announcement elevated Kiwi excitement and pride to a global level as it inevitably became part of the coronation news and celebrations. The feat reached an emotional plane that New Zealanders probably had not felt since VE Day in 1945. This "Raleigh-like"[1] message of "where no man had gone before" was considered an appropriate royal gift from the New Zealand people[2].

The celebrations peaked when Queen Elizabeth and Prince Philip arrived later that same year in December to begin the first visit of a reigning sovereign. And it was a lengthy visit – five weeks – in which she called on many cities, large and small. She

---

1 A reference to Sir Walter Raleigh's several plans and voyages in the 16th century to travel to, explore and colonise the New World, and to his expeditions to Orinoco in search of the elusive golden city of El Dorado (which he claimed to have found in today's Venezuela).

2 Although primitive communications from Nepal were blamed for the delayed announcement, that is now believed to have been a ruse: the announcement was deliberately delayed to coincide with the coronation.

even visited Nelson in January 1954 and we took the family to see her in Trafalgar Park. Godfrey recalls the crowds and the waving flags as his earliest memory. He was three years old (nearly four).

Late at night on Christmas Eve, two days after the Queen arrived in New Zealand, there was a terrible train accident with the loss of 151 lives. The northbound Wellington – Auckland express had plunged into the Whangaehu River at Tangiwai in the middle of the North Island. On that midsummer's night a barrier to Mount Ruapehu crater collapsed generating a lahar which devastated the Whangaehu valley. A torrential flow of water-saturated volcanic debris, a type of mudflow carrying a massive volume of water, ice and rocks, surged down the volcano's slopes into the river, demolishing both rail and road bridges in its path. The express, with its crowded Christmas travellers of 285 passengers, plunged off the bridge at nearly full speed and the carriages were hurled downstream. A lone car driver who had spotted that the bridge had been swept away had anticipated the danger and walked down the track waving a feeble torch frantically to warn the train which he knew was due in a few minutes. The train roared past him and he watched in horror as the tragedy unfolded in front of his eyes. Ironically, the name Tangiwai translated literally from the Maori, means *tangi* – to weep and *wai* – water.

> Tangiwai,
> Tangi,
> O Weeping Waters
> waters that once claimed so
> many lives.
> Raging fires beneath the
> Earth - whose wrath moves
> mountains - a gentle stream
> swollen in anger
> and a bridge washed away...
> Some drank and sang
> Mothers put children to sleep
> and the engine hurtled into
> the endless night.
> Next morning
> among the splintered wood

the twisted metal
and the blood -
Rescuers found a kerosene lamp,
still glowing.
A wreath floats on the stream
at Tangiwai
Flowers thrown from another train
now gone, speeding
into a new morning.
And the flowers flow,
flow on the quiet waters
Flow on to the waiting sea.

Moyae Kennedy © 2003[1]

Tangiwai as a geographical feature had barely been known before December 24th 1953 but a few hours later it was being broadcast around the world by the Queen herself. It was her first Christmas message as monarch and it was broadcast from Government House in Auckland to London and the Empire. "Last night," she said reading from the hastily added paragraph, "a most grievous railway accident took place at Tangiwai which will have brought tragedy into many homes and sorrow to all upon this Christmas Day."

The very next morning, the morning of Boxing Day 26th December 1953, Weston and Riley left Nelson to travel alone through an area skirting "the disaster zone". They were to stay with my sister Gwen in Taranaki for some of the school holidays. Weston was ten years old and Riley was eight. We put them on the plane (a Heron) to Wellington where they were to be met by our good family friend Norah Kellow[2] who was to drive them to the railway station and put them on the train to Stratford where they would be met by Gwen and Len. Although the news had come through of the Tangiwai disaster, the Railways had assured the public that safe alternative arrangements had been made and Rae

---

1 Despite several efforts to contact Moyae Kennedy re this copyright and to a NZ poet society seeking her correct address, no response has been received.

2 Might have been Mrs Meadows, WTB cannot remember.

and I had no undue concerns (although I look back now slightly aghast that we let them go). Riley and Weston were safely put on the train in Wellington and seen off about ten in the morning. The boys were to follow the same route of the disaster just two nights earlier. As the train approached Otaki it slowed almost to a crawl. The rivers had broken their banks and Weston and Riley viewed landscapes of flooded farm lands with only the tips of fence posts showing above the invading lakes which seemed to go on for miles.

At Otaki the train was stopped and everyone told to get off and board buses which would take the passengers to Levin. There they were to join the train again and go on to Foxton, then change to buses again which would take them to Marton. From Marton, they would catch the train again to take them to Stratford. But the message was not clear and it was complicated – especially for young boys. Some buses were going this way, and others were going that way. Some passengers would join this one, and others should join that one. And where was Foxton anyway? Weston was getting worried, almost sick with worry. He had not really heard the message, and what he had picked up he did not really understand.

The journey was broken and re-started in several places because of the flooded lines and the destroyed bridge. In short, the journey was doomed to be chaotic. To make matters worse for the two boys, while most passengers had had their luggage booked through to their destination and it was the firm responsibility of the Railways to transfer it between the intervening various modes of transport to follow its owners dutifully right through to the bitter end, Weston had told Mrs Kellow in Wellington that he would rather keep it with him to keep an eye on it. He understandably believed that this would be easier. But now the boys had their two huge suitcases on the train with them and they had to move their cases alone. In them was everything but the kitchen sink, as Rae, as she became renowned for doing, had packed everything she could think of. They were crammed, heavy and huge.

Weston who had been instructed in no uncertain terms to TAKE CHARGE, that is, to look after Riley, took his responsibilities very seriously indeed. It was peak holiday season and in those days trains were the prime public transport, quite apart from the chaos caused by the tragedy. Weston fussed over the suitcases as hundreds of passengers without any luggage to worry about at all, disembarked the train lightly and quickly. Dozens of buses, or so it seemed to Weston, lined up at the railway tracks and people darted off in all directions to catch the right one, dependent on where their ultimate destination was. Weston was much slower. He sought help from the guard at first but was roughly told that he would have to pick them up himself or leave them behind: "Now hurry along, lad!"

Weston was anxious and worried. He tried to keep an eye on Riley, telling him to stay with him. He struggled hard to get the suitcases down. He was not sure where he was meant to be going. He could see that he had to get the cases on to the bus, then off the bus, then on the train, then off the train, then on another bus and so it loomed large in his mind. He was not a happy boy. He struggled with the cases but eventually got them on to the right bus. He sat firmly while awaiting the arrival of his baby brother whom he believed was following him, as he had been firmly instructed to do. Riley did not appear. Baby brother had got on the wrong bus, and was shortly to be on his way to Auckland, not to New Plymouth. The ten year old heard the engine of his own bus start and impulsively panicked and shouted to the driver, "My brother isn't here." But where was he, and which bus was he on? Weston found Riley sitting tucked away right at the back of the Auckland bus showing no concern at all that 1) his brother wasn't with him and 2) he was about to go north east and Weston was about to go north west. Weston pulled him out, ran back to the other bus, which by now was also about to pull away. They scrambled aboard. Weston has always said they should never have set out on the trip and that it nearly killed him – quite apart from the fear of any Tangiwai accident! "It was nearly a disaster as one or both of us could have ended up in Auckland and who knows what would have happened then?" as Weston has asked me on more than one occasion since. Weston collapsed with the responsibility weighing him down to a point of sheer exhaustion and stress. Baby brother, on the other hand, was enthusiastically enjoying every minute of the adventure. Riley had after all been on his very first flight from Nelson to Wellington – nothing much else mattered to the eight year old.

The delays mounted through the day. Luggage was picked up and put down, and transferred between buses and trains time and again. Our young sons lost and found and followed each other between buses and trains time and again. Trains and platforms were changed. Timetables were changed. Directions and routes were changed. Instructions were changed. Ten hours later than they were expected two small boys emerged as if from some black hole, into the arms of Gwen and Len on a station platform late at night. It had been a day of anguish for us all, a day marked by an awful silence that wrapped around our sons from the moment they said goodbye to Mrs Kellow to the moment they said hello to my sister. I reflect now that that silence – and that anxiety – would have been dispelled instantly with a cell phone call but that luxury arrived forty years too late to give us any such comfort. Instead, Rae and I simply felt that we had lost both our sons for ten hours, despatched cruelly somewhere into the bowels of the distant North Island, a long way from home. We have had our own personal memories of Tangiwai and the aftermath – ever since.

It was during my Nelson years that my urge to return to farming became irresistible. With a certain degree of self-satisfaction I told myself that I had resisted the call to do a little farming of some nature, any nature, in Wellington. I didn't have the time or the opportunity and I felt conscience stricken to give every minute to the church or university or Rae. I had not even had the small but welcome diversion of being able to pick fruit as I had had in Roxburgh or having a house cow. I had, inevitably, had the passing thought of having a cow in Wellington, and I had at least painted the church which was something manual and refreshing for me. But that was hardly enough. Now my feet and hands were getting impertinently persistent to do something outdoors, begging me to come up with ideas which would have something, something please, to do with the soil, with animals, with my hands. My new parish was relentless in putting temptation in my path. I was now visiting farmer parishioners, not urban ones, and I was driving through lush, attractive farmlands, not residential streets.

I was getting restless. So it was no surprise to me, at least, when I thought of the idea of a fundraising effort which involved growing vegetables. The announcement that a full time minister was to be appointed to Stoke meant that a new parsonage was needed there. The Kirkpatrick company (later to be bought out by the famous "Watties") had launched a new canning operation in Nelson. I saw the opportunity to approach Kirkpatrick's and negotiate a contract with them for the planting of some beans which we would provide for canning. I then approached one or two landowners and sought their agreement to use some acreage for the purpose. We ended up with two acres on a hillside in Richmond and an acre in Brightwater. I was in my element! I concluded that this was a wonderful part of my job, even though Kirkpatrick's and the landowners had never before been approached by "a man of the cloth" to arrange a commercial deal. Having set up the agreement in principle I then prevailed on the Richmond and Brightwater congregations to raise some of their share of the money for the new parsonage by growing a paddock of beans. They agreed and throughout the next season I, with many of my parishioners, were in the paddocks around Nelson, planting, tending and harvesting row upon row of beans. I unhesitatingly claim, that of all my parishioners helping in this exercise, I enjoyed it the most! I was certainly there the most often. I had discovered a wonderful excuse for being out of doors and the parishioners could not complain. After all, was I not doing it all for the church? Notwithstanding my perhaps over zealous enthusiasm for the project, it did work very well and the common purpose of the parishioners working together in the paddocks was quite helpful in developing the bonds within each of these congregations.

So I was growing beans and harvesting them. It was a most enjoyable pastime, but it was not enough. Far from enough. What about a farm? Rae begged me to consider something else. We could not afford anything anyway and the parishioners would surely not approve. What about sports? Yes, sports would have been much easier, if only sports attracted me. But I could not shake off totally my father's view of sports – disdain for the laziness, for the non-productive use of time. It was not to be wondered at then, that time off for sports did not figure in my upbringing, and nor did it come to figure much in my later years although I did play some (a little) tennis and bowls – occasionally.

No, Rae. My spare energy had to be diverted into land (but if I was doing my job well, how come I had spare energy? – question unanswered). At the very least we must have another house cow. Cow?! I bought one. It lived with one of my parishioners, Miss Papps, a rather fierce old lady who kept stuffed birds which she used to show with much glee to Weston on his frequent visits into this extraordinary menagerie. Her house was two or three hundred metres from the parsonage in Queen Street Richmond, opposite the Post Office. She had inherited the old family home, and it sat slap bang in the middle of two or three acres. Such a waste of land, that she would, of course, agree to my most gracious offer of allowing her to keep my cow there. She also later let me keep some sheep there.

I used to milk the cow every day, often with the willing contribution of the tiny hands of my children. On the surplus milk from the cow, I raised a calf. Surprisingly, the calf became a cow. So I now had doubled my herd. To cope with the extra milk, I bought a small separator. To cope with the extra cream, the family ate gallons of it. Rae used to put enormous jugs of milk and cream on the table. It was coming out of our ears. To cope with the extra work I moved my enormous herd from Miss Papps garden to the Best's place, a small farm on the way to Hope. I made an arrangement with Mr Best that if he did the evening milking, in return for rent of his land he could keep the milk. I, the Reverend Bell, would do the early morning milking.

I took on more calves. They served as pets for the children who proudly displayed them on Agricultural and Pets days at their school. And of course, it was only natural that they would now want a pet lamb or two also. So I bought some – for the children of course. On several occasions the pet calves and lambs were kept in the back garden of the parsonage itself.

All my life I have thoroughly enjoyed scanning the classified pages of newspapers carrying such columns as Agricultural Implements for Sale, Properties for sale, Farms for Sale, Small Holdings, and so on. Every advertisement was a job offer to me, a dream, an opportunity, an escape, an idea to work with. So many nights I went to bed with plans in my head that no doubt would have disappointed the President of the Methodist Church of New Zealand. My fantasies could not have been further from my career in the church. I must have been a disappointing prospect for any higher position in the church. (All of this was to prove ominously close to the truth when a few years later an invitation to a city church in Auckland, Epsom, was withdrawn.) And yet I had fought so hard to get in. It made sense not even to me.

But the newspaper column scanning offered me my biggest venture yet as a Reverend Farmer. One hundred acres about twenty-four kilometres from home on the outskirts of my parish was for sale. Stubbornly and foolishly I determined that it was just what I wanted. It was for me. Rae protested, nervous of the reaction in the church, but I ignored her warnings: nothing was going to make me happier than having this farm. Surely, with such an interest and with such joy within my grasp, I would become a much better and more fulfilled minister? I could relate to ordinary people more closely. I had all the reasons up my sleeve which supported my plan. I simply pulled them out as appropriate in response to the objections, one after the other after the other.

In today's terms, the cost was trivial. Three hundred pounds for the farm and three hundred pounds for the stock, but even that was more than I could lay my hands on. My parish steward himself came to the rescue: he offered to be guarantor for me with the bank.

When news got out that I had actually purchased the farm (until then it had simply been a matter of uttering "Mad. . . a mad idea") the parishioners spread the news like wildfire and it did not take long for me to learn of all the reactions. "Have you heard that Reverend Bell has bought a farm?" "A what? A *farm*?" "Why, what can he do with a farm?" "He has no time to farm." "A minister cannot know how to farm?" "Is he about to leave the ministry?" "How extraordinary" and "Astonishing!"

The farm was in the Moutere Hills between Richmond and Motueka, a town about fifty kilometres from Nelson. The Moutere Hills were not high nor steep, but easy rolling land and quite manageable for farming. But the soil was poor for the growing of grass or crops mainly because of a lack of trace elements and it consisted mostly of inhospitable gorse. It was while I owned the farm that the discovery was made that one of the missing trace elements was molybdenum. It required only one dessert spoonful to the acre to make a significant productive difference. Meanwhile gorse flourished and this was one of the main sources of food for my sheep – not very nourishing for them, but it kept them alive in the absence of better grasses.

There were no fences. I had purchased the farm with its existing stock, one hundred and fifty ewes, but with two pine plantations on its boundaries, the sheep spent as much time in these plantations or on the neighbours' farms as they did on their own and proper (albeit gorse-infested) grazing land.

My proposed work plan was that I would farm it just one day a week – my official day off – Monday. But I underestimated the workload (or did I under-announce it?). This didn't bother me of course as much as it bothered THE OBSERVERS, some of my parishioner critics waiting in the wings no doubt to pounce should I neglect any of my pastoral duties. Of course, I chose to be oblivious of the consequences. I had not been so happy for years. Every Monday morning I donned my old working clothes and heavy boots, drove my Ford Prefect into the rough and untidy hills behind Nelson and worked on my own farm, quite alone and quite content. I would sit on the step of the Prefect for my tea and lunch breaks, drinking from the thermos and eating the fat sandwiches Rae had so loyally prepared for me. As the sun grew hotter in the day and I began to sweat with my physical exhaustion I would seek the shade of a tree or move into one of the pine plantations itself for an after lunch kip. I slept like a child for my forty winks. As the hours of the day passed and my intended tasks were not completed it was quite plain to me that I would have to return before the next Monday. I was far from shy in finding excuses to spend more time on the farm than I had intended (or promised Rae). I visited it at every chance I could grab – or, more truthfully – and here was the real problem – create.

With the work and considerable satisfaction came considerable flack from many in my congregation. Some were amused, some were bemused, but some were very angry indeed.

Before I bought the farm, things were very different. As my parish spread over some sixty kilometres north to south, I could be busy on some pastoral duties in one part of it, and the church leaders would show no interest at all in knowing where I was or what I was doing. But once I acquired the farm, the antennae were out. Where was I? Where had I been? What were you doing? "I rang you yesterday – you were not home." The church had a right to know. Every day I was not in the parsonage, the Richmond church itself, or with a church leader, the immediate assumption was that I had been on the farm ignoring my pastoral duties. I should have been pastoring the congregation, not the sheep. They did not seem to want to take into account that there were other parts of the parish where I could be – quite justifiably.

The sense of humour behind this droll escapade of their Reverend Farmer Bell was fast running out for some. One member raised the matter at an official meeting. He made various accusations that I had no business as minister to be involved in farming operations, that because of this I was neglecting my ministerial duties and various other things. A hush fell over the group. Here was the attack that had been imminent for some time. The trial had begun. The accused stood to his feet.

"Mr Roughton," I said, "I'm sorry you feel this way about it, but before I bought the farm, I wrote to the President of the Church and he gave me his permission."

Mr Marshall, my chief official, rose to his feet. "As far as I am concerned, if you have the President's permission, that is good enough for me. You don't need to make any further explanation."

"Thank you, sir," I replied, "but I would prefer to say something as I know there is more than one who is unhappy with the farm. For me, this is my recreation. My District Chairman plays bowls for his recreation every Saturday afternoon and all my fellow ministers have various recreational activities. When they forego these, their interests, I will give up mine."

I knew I was stretching a point with the comparison. I knew that most would not see my acres and my sheep as a substitute for bowls! But to me the point was valid. It was true. It was my recreation. I just had to watch the hours I spent on it.

One thing I did like about Reverend farming was coming into contact with a lot of folks who viewed parsons with suspicion and never believed that they could do a hard day of manual work. But many parishioners remained unconvinced: I was, they believed, compromising my pastoral duties at best and ignoring them at worst. The real problem was that I could never quite convince myself that they were wrong and I was right. I felt uncomfortable but I was loving my farm and I struggled with my conscience for a very long time even though outwardly I defended my corner in every way I could.

Although I had intended to confine myself to working on the parson's official day off, the truth is that a parson is never off duty. Even on Mondays, it rarely turned out that the parson was excused being interrupted by phone calls, funerals, desperate pleas for counselling, or urgent meetings. And if I was not there to be interrupted – Monday or not – this was "not cricket". On several occasions, including several Mondays, neighbouring farmers were asked if they could seek out the parson up there in his isolated acres in the hills to ask him to return to the parsonage. Once again the reflection of having cell phones in those days makes me realise how different things may have been: perhaps my farming days may not have offended my parishioners so much. They could have reached me quickly and easily and perhaps had any immediate anxieties or problems allayed or solved with a simple phone call. Of course, there were many Mondays that I never got to the farm at all: but these were not "counted". The fundamental issue I came to realise was not that I had chosen farming as a recreation. Or that I had chosen a recreation at all. It was that I had chosen the ministry which gave no single day off, let alone a weekend. There is no regular day off for parsons, I can assure you, none. None at least, that parishioners will grant you as an inalienable right.

On one occasion, even though it was, thankfully, a Monday, and I was at least "entitled" to have been on the farm, I did little to endear myself to even my strongest supporters. I had been away all day burning and cutting back gorse in the hot sun, persevering with my fight to make the land more attractive for stock or crops despite it being a thankless task for one man working without machines. It had been a tough, physically exhausting day, but, as usual, I returned home highly satisfied, looking forward to my long hot bath and having a good dinner with Rae. This was always the best bit of farming: the closing of the day. When I arrived home at seven o'clock, my illusion of the peaceful evening ahead was shattered (once again, oh for the luxury of the cell phone!). An anxious Rae asked me if I had forgotten that tonight (yes, Monday) the Brightwater Sunday School was having its breaking up ceremony – at seven o'clock. Of *course* I had forgotten. Utterly and completely. Why should I think of such trivialities up there with my sheep and amongst the gorse, working on the soil, under the sun, on my *farm*?! I dived into a bath, had a quick shave, pulled on my good clothes and drove to Brightwater at record speed. It was unfortunate for me that it was at Brightwater for it was from this congregation that no other than Mr Roughton was patiently waiting. I walked into the hall forty minutes late. I was greeted with a thundering silence. It was impossible to make any explanations as the day in the sun had left me with a glowing red face. The silly thing was that they had a programme of children's items and all I did was to announce the items as they came along, with prizes to be distributed at the end of the evening. There were a number of officials present who were quite capable of starting the evening off. They didn't. They waited for forty minutes for my arrival, no doubt, I am sure at the instigation of Mr Roughton, to make the point he had so longed to make. But I was not going to capitulate to such pressure. Sunburnt and embarrassed as I was with the incident, I resolved (once again) that all I needed to do was sharpen my diary keeping skills.

On the farm I always had a job to get a good muster of my sheep because there were no fences and because they could hide from me most effectively in the adjacent pine plantations. One night I attended a meeting at Motueka so I took the opportunity (of course) to drive past my farm on the way home – to do nothing other than look at it – my pride and joy. It was a moonlit night and as I was half expecting, the sheep had come out of the trees to graze on the grass. As they ran away at the sound of the approaching car and from the headlights, there was quite a din from the dags with which they were well loaded. This was proof to any sheep farmer that these sheep had kept well out of sight of any musterer for a long while. This demanded an interesting action plan and I worked out the strategy all the way home. The meeting I had been to earlier counted for nought compared with what I was planning now!

I had to wait for the next full moon and I organised with a neighbouring farmer and friend, Murray Holdaway and his dog, to be there before daybreak. So it was that the parson could have been spotted (by Mr Roughton) creeping out of the Richmond Methodist Parsonage at four-thirty in the morning, and heading south to The Farm. Dramatically I cut the lights as I approached our rendezvous so the sheep would not run. Neighbour, Dog and Parson, met under the silhouetted trees and moved about as stealthily as burglars. The errant sheep were exactly where we had been hoping they would be, enjoying the full moon and the wildly mistaken security of their undisturbed night home. It was a simple strategy: under the cover of darkness, together and with the element of surprise we would cut off their retreat to the plantations and herd them into the sheep pens. But the operation took longer to carry out than it took to plan. It took some hours to hound the contrary and frightened beasts out of the gorse. This was uncomfortable work, dog or no dog. It meant walking right into patches of burnt gorse as well as into the thick, prickly growing gorse, to tease the animals from their desperate retreats. The day wore on and the sun crept up. We had all the sheep penned and we dagged them all. It had been a good muster and a highly satisfying day although I was tired. My animals were respectable as they returned to their plantations, but it was getting on for dark once again before I was ready to leave for home.

I threw a few stragglers into the trailer and hurriedly got on the way. The trailer was a borrowed one and, unknown to me, was not licensed for night use. Into the bargain, I had a bulb in one of my car headlights burnt out and replacements were temporarily unavailable. My car was not fitted for towing a trailer in that it had no suitable light on the roof. In short I was a living but unwitting invitation for a visit from a Traffic Officer. And the invitation was surely accepted with pleasure.

As I came into Richmond I suddenly found I was being followed by a Traffic Officer. Dutifully he stopped me and officiously started to take down particulars. "Name!" he demanded. "Address!" "Occupation". "Minister of religion", I replied softly. He stopped with pencil poised in mid-air. He shone his torch at me and I was fairly blackened with pushing through burnt gorse, then he shone it on the trailer load of sheep and then back at me again. He was plainly nonplussed and unsure of how to respond. He was clearly torn between throwing off at me and asking "What do you take me for?" and crossing himself. Finally, but uneasily, he said, "You ought to know better." I said that I did but I was not going to throw away a heavy day's work just to get home an hour or two earlier. To top it off, I was unable to present him my licence, but he concluded (with a slight air of *righteousness* believing he had handled a *Minister of Religion* appropriately) that he would let me off if I presented my licence at the Traffic Office the next day. I breathed a sigh of relief for it would have only fuelled my critics' arguments if Reverend Farmer's name had appeared in the local papers for traffic infringements.

Regrettably I did not keep my farming contained to the farm. Foolishly, with hindsight, I had to bring the farm to the church's door – literally. I was moving a flock of sheep from beyond Richmond to my farm but I needed somewhere in Richmond to hold them overnight. In my natural enthusiasm I wondered what better place than in the grounds of the church itself. It was reasonably well fenced and all I had to do was to block up two or three entrances. So local observers would have enjoyed the curious sight of Reverend Bell in the middle of the main street and outside his own church, shepherding, not parishioners, but real live sheep into his church grounds. This was hardly a rural parish, but it was beginning to look that way. Oblivious to any such onlookers, I retired to the parsonage to bed. But scarcely an hour had passed when I had a call from neighbours at the rear of the church. "Have you got sheep in the church grounds?" "Yes", I said holding my breath for what was coming next. "Well you haven't any longer. They are in my section and relishing my lettuces and cabbages." A small stream ran through the sections which backed on to each other and some of the sheep had found a way across it. I was around there at top speed and drove them back, then went on a hunt for a roll of sheep netting to keep them in. That was OK. It was only midnight. What else would you expect a minister of religion to be doing at that time of night? I shrugged my shoulders and searched on. This was OK. This is what farming is all about.

But the more embarrassing moment came next day, when the sheep were loaded on to a truck and despatched to the farm. I had quite overlooked a sheep's instinct to seek the highest ground when they rest at night. The highest point in the church grounds was none other than the top of the church steps hard up against the church doors, and on a verandah across the doors leading into the Sunday School hall. As the sheep were carted off their droppings certainly were not: there they lay in abundance on the church steps and Sunday School verandah for all the world (but in particular my parishioners) to see. Scurrying around to the parsonage I took buckets and brooms to clean up the mess hoping that not too many of my parishioners would appear before it was done. But to add to my self-consciousness, my darling ever-loyal wife, whether she approved or disapproved, insisted that she must help. She decked herself out with apron and appropriate headgear and the two of us with buckets and mops, dropped to our knees on the church steps and scrubbed furiously. No parishioners saw us. But someone else did – my boss. In the midst of our efforts, the minister of the Nelson Church and my superintendent, Reverend Charlie Hailwood and his wife, the last people in the world I wanted to see at that moment. "Why hello Charles", he said as he clambered the church steps and, "Oh, hello, Rae. We thought we might find you here when you were not at home." Rae and I stood to our feet clutching bucket and mop and adjusting headgear and wiping brow. "Oh hello Charlie," I replied, "Nice day." The subject of the weather obviously did nothing to allay his curiosity so I added, rather feebly, "Oh, do mind where you step." My boss was taking the day off, he wondered if we might join them? Rae couldn't speak.

In 1952, shortly after my mother died, my father came to stay with us and was on hand to help me with the farm. I was anxious to put up a subdividing fence but to do so, I needed to burn off some head-high gorse. However, the district was under a fire ban at the time and I had to apply for a permit. I waited for a few weeks for it to come, every day expecting it to be in the mail. In the end my father said that he must get back to Taranaki but, desperate for his help, I assured him that we would go ahead with the burning the following day, genuinely convinced that the permit was, undoubtedly, already in the post. The next day, before the post arrived, we headed off for the farm and struck a match.

There was no question about the wisdom of burning off this enormous and thick gorse that was on the proposed fence line, but when we emerged from the gully where we had started the fire it was racing ahead of us and in all directions. Realising it was beyond our control I sent off for the District Fire Warden. He downed tools and came with his tractor. After an hour or so he admitted it was beyond his control and sent for all the hands from a nearby timber mill. The fight went on all day. Dried grass had only to get hot and it would burst into flames. In a nearby paddock, which I had ploughed, the fire ran along burning the grass under the furrows. It swept through the boundary fence on to the neighbour's farm and across that to the road. It even jumped the road and it was only by a mighty effort it was prevented from taking off for kilometres more.

The outcome was disastrous. Of course there was no permit in the post. I was a sitting duck, totally unprotected from the accusations and the claims for compensation that flowed in. One was a demand from the mill that the Reverend Farm pay for their employees' wages. Another was from a farming neighbour who demanded I supply a new road fence. This particularly aggrieved me. The one which had burnt down was old, broken and only three-wired, buried deeply in head-high gorse. It was the gorse rather than the fence which kept the stock in. But he saw a chance to get a good strong sheep proof replacement fence and grabbed it. Each day I went out to work on it he would not accept what I was proposing to do. So I would leave and come back the following week with new proposals. These would be refused in their turn and this went on for several weeks. In the end, I told him I was going to do it my way and that was the end of it. Somehow I enlisted the support of some of my very own Richmond parishioners to help me. ("Your nerve Charlie, your nerve, amazes me", said Rae). And so it was, one Saturday a team of the faithful from the Richmond congregation joined their minister, not to pray or hear preach, not to watch open a village fete or to have tea with, but to replace a fence which he had burnt down in a fire he lit without a fire permit, on his own farm twenty-four kilometres from their place of worship, in rough, hilly land. The fence was finished in a day. It was up and if it was not what my neighbour was hoping for he would be able to find me in church the following morning preaching a sermon on "Blessed are the meek for they shall inherit the earth". I had no guilty conscience. If it was not what he hoped for, it was far superior to the fence he had lost.

The drama was not quite concluded. The elusive permit which never turned up had never been issued and the County Council threatened to prosecute me. Once again I was afraid that my critics would have really had a field day if my name had appeared in the court news. With this threat hanging over my head I worked frantically to talk the Council out of pursuing the matter. I was not slow in making the most of my position either, I am ashamed to say. Every time I met them, I put on my collar. I thought it might make them a little uneasy, if nothing else, for it was a unique negotiation situation here, was it not? Something worked. They dropped the case.

Reverend Farmer Bell was stretching his luck. Even I began to admit that. Something had to go and it proved to be me – voluntarily and properly of course. The normal five year term for Methodist ministers in their parishes was coming up. Some parishioners undoubtedly sighed with relief, but I didn't really as I had enjoyed it all. The end of both farm and parish was in sight.

I tidied up my business as Synod Secretary and handed over to my successor. Parish responsibilities were fairly easily finalised too as I kept them pretty well up to date. Disposing of the farm, however, was not so easy. The problem was with the stock. Although I had worked hard to fix and improve existing fences and to erect new ones, I had not reached the stage I could be sure all the stock was always on the farm. So once again calling on my friend Murray Holdaway and his dog, we scoured the surrounding plantations and neighbouring gorse-infected paddocks and joined the strays to the main flock. I had to make arrangements for a holding paddock so that I could keep them together and handy for sale day. In due course we loaded them on to a fleet of trucks and they arrived at the saleyards. I spent the whole morning drafting them into ewes, hoggets, wethers and lambs and I went off to lunch. I came back ready for the sale and full of hope for good prices but I was dismayed to find all the pens empty. The inspector from the Department of Agriculture had been, and in my absence had decided that my sheep could not be sold because they had not been dipped. A by-law required that all sheep presented for sale after January 20th each year had to be dipped, but in practice it was not enforced before the February sales began. In that year, however, it had been decided to enforce the letter of the law and I was the first to feel it. It was January 21st 1955.

It was the final penalty for my follies I concluded. I had ignored my pastoral duties of the people in preference to the sheep. This episode was undoubtedly to drive the point home. In despair, I resorted to my fast talking once again. I pointed out that I was due to leave Richmond for the North Island in a week and that I had no farm on which to hold the sheep until the next sale day. He was sympathetic but the sheep had already been put out of the pens and were all mixed up and there was little he could do about it. My fast talking, this time, did not work.

A friend in Brightwater came to my rescue by providing a holding paddock and a dip. But my bad luck dogged me. By the time it came round for the next sale, the climate had changed and there was every sign a time of drought was setting in. Prices slumped. And to add to my woes, in the interim some of my sheep had disappeared and I could find no explanation. I wondered if they had been lost or stolen but given the brick wall I came up against, I concluded that it was just as likely that some had simply evaporated.

As if I had not already learned all my lessons, someone was not letting go now. They had me and they were going to make the most of it. A few months later, after I felt I was well and truly distanced from Nelson and my farm, and I was still licking my wounds, I was delivered a "bluey" to appear in Court "for exposing infected sheep for sale". On enquiry, I was told that there had been too many sales of this nature and they wanted to make an example of someone. I retorted that there was little point in making examples of anyone if all the sales for the season were over. But the summons had been served and could not be withdrawn.

The case proceeded and I was convicted but not fined. But a bright journalist in the court when he heard the charge immediately constructed an appropriate headline for his story. In the next edition of the *Nelson Evening Mail* appeared "Minister has lousy flock". That story has followed me round New Zealand for thirty-five years.

I enjoyed living in Nelson. It has lovely weather, beautiful countryside and glorious beaches. I had good congregations and took some pride in the young people I worked with and who became lay preachers and ministers with some support from me. But I was never too sure that I had "clicked" with the Richmond Circuit. After some services I would feel that things were going well. But after others I felt the opposite and wondered to myself whether I should ask to be moved on. I was never quite sure I was making much of an impact (of the kind I should have been making, that is).

I think I just had too much on my plate to get any great satisfaction from my parish work. Was my farm the cause or the symptom of this? I cannot even answer that myself. It did help when the relieving second minister was replaced with a full time one. John Mabon[1] was young and enthusiastic, a twenty-one year old pre-collegiate probationer when he was posted to Stoke and Hope in February 1954. It relieved a lot of the pressure for me and I felt I did a better job in the rest of the parish.

John Mabon left Stoke to go to theological college at the same time as I left at the beginning of 1955. My Richmond appointment to some extent came back to haunt me only a few years later in an ill-fated career move. Although I have fond memories of my years there, on the whole I think it proved to be an appointment of mixed blessings, even though my misgivings may have been largely of my own making.

---

[1] John Mabon is now minister of the Union Parish in Woodville. He was the local minister for my uncle Charles D Barrell, Mum's twin brother, who moved from Christchurch in his last years to live with his son in Woodville. Of course he knew Mum through the Richmond days and so there was a special family association when he conducted Uncle Charlie's funeral in May 1996. - GB.

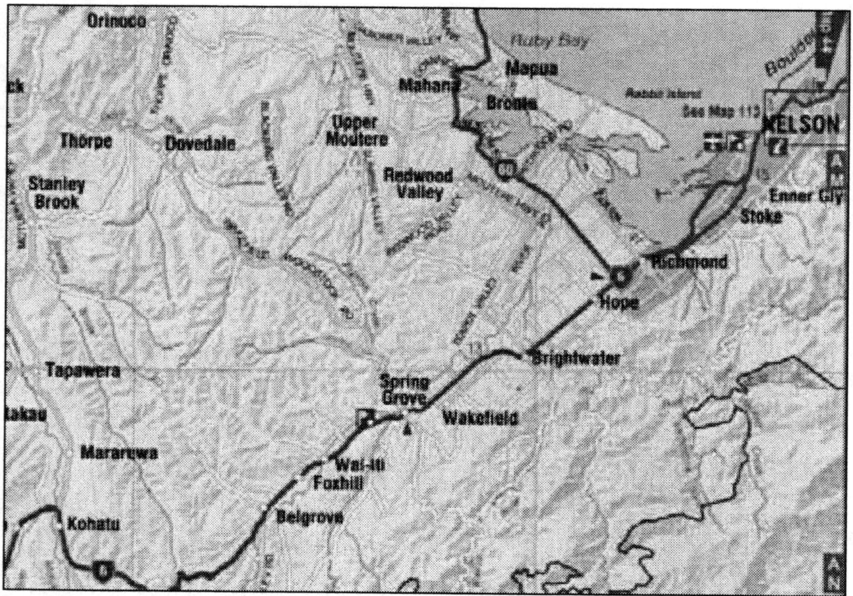

The Richmond parish showing the smaller localities where Charles preached.
Source: Wises New Zealand Travel Atlas 2005 edition

The earth-pressed Spring Grove church.
The boy at the gate may be Riley.

From baptism in Spring Grove church, (opp.) to burial in Westminster Abbey, London, Lord Rutherford 1871 - 1937

Charles with Weston & Riley

Riley, Godfrey, Weston c1952

Rae & Charles with Riley, Godfrey, Weston c1954

Rae with Godfrey, Weston & Riley 1950

Godfrey with Rev Ashleigh Petch on the day of his baptism

Charles's sister Jean with Godfrey
Tahuna Beach, 1951

Weston takes Godfrey for a ride on the merry-go-round but Godfrey is none too merry about it! Weston isn't that convinced either.

Three Bell generations: Riley (left) Godfrey and Weston with their father and grandfather Bell, 1951

Charles's youngest sister Jean married Don McDowall on 16 April 1952, in Hawera. Here with her father, Tom and sisters Gwen and Evelyn, just a few months after their wife and mother died.

Weston (left) and Riley with their grandfather Tom Bell

Riley, Godfrey, Weston, Richmond, October 1950.
A month later Riley became critically ill.

A studio photograph of Riley, Weston and Godfrey
Richmond, August 1954

One member of Rev Farmer's family greets another. Godfrey and the Methodist Parsonage calf in 1950.

The Parsonage farm – the lamb in the back garden. Godfrey feeding his lamb to Riley's accompaniment. 1951

Charles in his Ford Prefect with Godfrey. 1951

Was Godfrey brought up in a Methodist Parsonage or on a farm?

Richmond Methodist Church in 1950. The old Sunday School Hall behind the church was later demolished for the new building.

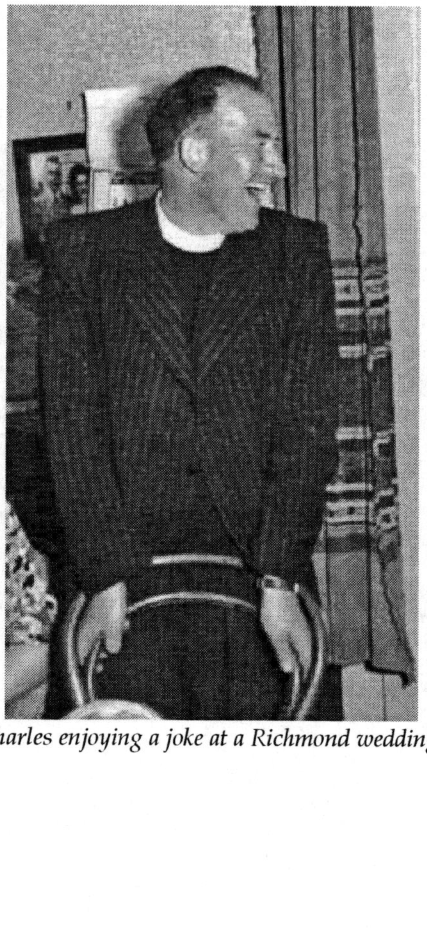

Charles enjoying a joke at a Richmond wedding.

Richmond Methodist Parsonage, 105 (now 205) Queen Street, 1950.

Virtually unrecognisable (apart from tracing the original roof lines) but in fact still there, the Richmond Nelson Methodist Parsonage of the 1950s is now a commercial property and the building has been extended right out to the street taking in the front garden. A car park behind it absorbs the old large back garden. The transformation is so dramatic it is surprising that the old parsonage wasn't simply demolished, but many parts of it have changed very little (see below). Then the parsonage was 105 Queen Street but today, after re-numbering, it is number 205. Photo Beverley Keall 2006

Charles and Riley, Godfrey and Weston, Richmond Parsonage 1954. Ford Prefect in background – along with the washing!

The 2006 photo above is taken very close to the spot where the photo on the left was taken in 1954. The features of the verandah can be seen very clearly. And where there is washing hanging and an old Ford Prefect in the back garden on the left, above is an empty public car park on a Sunday afternoon! Many family photos were taken on and in front of this porch. Photo Beverley Keall

The Parsonage farm – the calf in the back garden! Weston and Riley with their calf which won prizes at the Agricultural Show. October 1950. The boys had almost as much to do with animals as any of their friends off rural farms. In the background at the back door is a watchful parent with Godfrey in his pram.

Above: The porch and the back window of the old Richmond Methodist Parsonage taken in 2006. The same porch and window can be spotted in the 1950 photograph on the left. Photo Beverley Keall

Above: Riley , Godfrey and Weston at the gate of the Richmond Methodist Parsonage c1954.

Left: Riley, Godfrey and Weston date and location unknown

Charles and Rae at the Dickinson wedding, Richmond, 1953

Above, Charles (standing centre on verandah) opening the new Richmond Methodist Sunday School Hall that was funded by the estate of a young man killed in the war.

Below, the Richmond Methodist Hall as it is today. Photo Beverley Keall 2006

Tas and Eileen Fitzer (centre) standing in between Tas's film director friend Charles Chauvel (right) and wife (left). Tas appeared in one of Charles's films Jedda.

Margaret Fitzer (Ross Fitzer's daughter), Tas Fitzer, Billy (Ross Fitzer's son) and Des (Tas's son) at Manly Beach, Sydney. A day out of boarding school for Tas's son (The King's School, North Parramatta, Sydney) with his father and cousins. c1940 – 1941

Jedda, *the film in which Tas Fitzer acted the role of himself. Set in the Northern Territory of Australia.*

Constable Tas Fitzer

Wrecked carriages lie downstream from the bridge from which they tumbled into a since subsided raging torrent. Tangiwai rail disaster, Christmas Eve, 1953

Chapter 17

ROLLING GREEN PASTURES

1955 - 1962

Matamata, Waikato

My next appointment took us across the Cook Strait yet again, back to the North Island. This time we went to the Waikato, to a wealthy provincial town, Matamata, situated in the middle of one of the great dairying regions of New Zealand.

I had been invited to and accepted a call to our Cambridge Terrace Church in the heart of Christchurch – nothing could have been more different from Matamata. However, before conference had met and drawn up their stationing sheet, I was told that there was a move afoot to amalgamate Cambridge Terrace and Durham Street circuits with the intention of developing the former as a mission arm to the latter. This had some appeal for me, but I felt that with such a major step the conference should be free to look at the whole field of available ministers to make an appointment most suitable to the new development. So I withdrew my acceptance and left it to conference. Out of that came my appointment to Matamata, an appointment which proved to be the most rewarding and most happy years of all my years in the ministry.

However, perhaps there were drawbacks in coming to the Waikato. If Nelson's farmland had attracted me and I had enjoyed my own little farm despite its poor soil and gorse, then what on earth would the Waikato farms surrounding Matamata do for me? Everywhere I turned was farmland with lush pastures and neat fences and large herds of grazing cows, pictures of contentment and good treatment[1]. It all tugged at my heart strings and stirred the familiar old longings in me – to farm. I did not forget my Nelson lessons and I set out to avoid all temptation to repeat the Nelson experiment. I was a minister, wasn't I? Not a farmer? Nevertheless, here in Matamata I felt very much at home. Most of my parishioners were farmers, retired farmers or engaged in farm-related industries.

Matamata was to become a very special place for all the family. I particularly enjoyed my time there and the friendships made[2]. There were several major projects the church undertook, building a new Sunday School hall, buying new land for a future new church, building a new parsonage. I loved the farms surrounding the town and Rae loved the friends she made, the town, the weather and the shopping. Weston and Riley grew from young boys into young adults there and completed their schooling in Matamata, chose their respective careers and left home from Matamata to begin them. And Godfrey started school there and completed his primary schooling there.

Early in my appointment there was an influx of new members who had bought farms in the district. They were to provide a strong band of dedicated supporters. Such a couple were Mr and Mrs Mervyn Fernyhough who moved to Walton. For a while they were torn between coming to Matamata or going to Morrinsville, the neighbouring district. It was our gain when they decided to join the Matamata parish for in Mervyn we obtained a Bible Class leader and a circuit steward. Another couple, Bill and Ina Muckle came to Waharoa. Not only were they active, loyal members, but their son who took over the farm

---

1 In these green pastures, just a few kilometres far from Matamata, the village of Hobbiton was created and filmed in the late 1990s for the award-winning *Lord of the Rings*.- GB

2 It was Dad's wish that his ashes be scattered in Matamata, in the gardens surrounding his old church, now re-sited in Matamata Historic Village at the top of Tower Hill. - GB

later, along with his wife, followed their footsteps in the roles they played in the church.

Then there were Alan and Gwen Sing and their son John later on, who became a tower of strength in the church. Dick and Margaret Pickering took on a sharemilking job and Bob and Peggy McIntyre were farm managers on a Waharoa sheep farm. John and Ray Elliott bought a sheep farm at Waharoa. About the same time, a new postmaster was appointed to the Waharoa Post Office, Alan McNaughton and his wife Marion who were good Methodists. Bill and Vera Diprose were great farmers with a large family, all of whom were foundation members of the Matamata Methodist Church. Most of these people were of an age group which allowed Rae and me to relate easily to them. My natural love of farming helped me build firm friendships as I followed with keen interest developments and seasons and work on their farms. These friendships enhanced the leadership they provided to the church. Their ability and dedication in the church meant Matamata was a strong, healthy and wealthy parish[1].

Later on strength was to come from another source. It was in the days when Billy Graham was at the height of his fame and it did not seem strange when one day at a service I invited anyone who wished to become members of the church to come forward. To my delight, enough people came forward to form a line in front of the Communion Table from one side of the church to the other. From this initial statement of intention by coming forward, most became full new members of the church and one ultimately entered the Presbyterian ministry. Another one a while later rang me late one night and said he had been wrestling with a dilemna: he was sure that he had had "a calling" to the ministry. This was a problem not only for him to face up to its challenge but also to his family. He was a married man with young children and he was already in his thirties. The theological college training was not geared to a man in such

---

1 These friends stayed close. When Dad died in 1993, nearly all of them attended his funeral in Tauranga – 31 years after he left Matamata.

circumstance and he had to deal with the fact that there would be three years without an income. One by one these hurdles were overcome and he was given his appointment in due course. Unfortunately, at the final hurdle, he felt he could not accept what the ordination vows required and he withdrew from the ministry.

At one of my Te Poi services I felt led to make another appeal for new members and again I had a good response, this time from five or six people. This second positive response motivated me to do it yet again when the opportunity arose. Once a year the Walton Bible Class held a tea followed by an evening service. It was taken on alternate years by the Presbyterian and Methodist ministers. This particular year, it was the Methodist turn and the church was full of young people. The sermon I preached I had used once before in Nelson South Church. At the end I had a sudden impulse to make an appeal – although it was unplanned. "Any who want to accept Christ as their personal Saviour, please raise their hand while we pray." Some twenty-five hands went up. I was taken by surprise. I thought they might have misunderstood the significance of what I was asking so I asked them to leave the church during the next hymn to think about it before coming back to confirm what they felt. Nearly all came back to confirm their first commitment.

I have mixed feelings about evangelist services such as these. I can understand the response I got from one man who rarely came to church. He turned up at one of my services in my first year of ministry. During that service I made an appeal. He felt uncomfortable with the challenge and, to my knowledge, never went to church again. It is possible I did not handle the situation as well as I should have done and I believe the Methodist writer, A J Rattenbury, that we must `evangelise or perish'. However, in my preaching I always tried to keep myself aware of those in the congregation who were not committed Christians. Despite my successes with some of my evangelist services, in the end I was always more comfortable with my mission field being my visiting list: those who called themselves

Methodists but took no active part in the life of the church, rather than focusing mission drives on those who already attended church services – albeit infrequently perhaps. Apart from those active members who had a special need or sickness, I felt that it was important that I spent a lot of time regularly visiting those we called fringe members. My aim was to be interested in and to care for them. Through this I would hope that they may, one day, and entirely of their own volition, wish to attend church. So for me the meaning of evangelism is not so much the role of the emotive, moving preacher with large crowds and rousing appeals, as it is the role of the parish minister. It is part and parcel of the daily pastoral work and the Sunday by Sunday preaching of the regular minister in his own churches. I recall with pleasure that the membership in the Matamata parish grew steadily throughout my time there. On one notable occasion I held a special service for formally receiving into the Methodist Church no less than twenty-three people, an unusually high number for a small parish of a minority denomination.

Apart from anything else, these experiences alone made my Matamata appointment unique. But there were other things as well.

When we arrived, there was a move afoot to sell the valuable town centre property on which both the church and the parsonage stood and to re-site the church on new land on the boundaries of Matamata on a farm which had recently been sold for subdivision, and build a new Sunday School hall.

The church and parsonage were on a large plot of land on the corner of Tainui Street[1] and Broadway, the latter being Matamata's main shopping and commercial thoroughfare. Matamata was, effectively, growing up around the church's original position, making its central land an extremely valuable investment for industry or commerce. Vacant land lay between the church and the parsonage and this attracted several offers

[1] The Methodist Parsonage was at 2 Tainui Street, the house has since been demolished and a commercial building stands in its place today.

from buyers. Indeed, so central was the land that the Post Office was interested in it.

I opposed the plan to sell. If it was so valuable to commerce, it was certainly no less valuable to the church, but the church officials did not want to know. I stressed that if they followed their plan they would still not raise enough money to build a new church as well as a new Sunday School hall. This set them back a bit as they obviously had not realised it. I said, "If we are going to have to face up to a fundraising drive then, why not do so now, and see where we get?" But they were still not convinced.

We met time and time again. Each time a new objection was raised and they continued to resist my proposals. Each time I set out to find a solution before the next meeting as I was determined not to let the valuable land go. Finally, I came up with the idea of building on the site a Sunday School hall *and* a block of shops for letting. From the rents would come provision to meet any shortage in the initial building costs, and in the future, for building a new church.

The first objection was that the parishioners were unlikely to want to contribute to a commercial enterprise. So I suggested that we build a two storey building, with the Sunday School upstairs above the shops. Those that had any objections could stipulate that their donation must be used specifically to meet the cost of building the first floor for the Sunday School.

The next objection was that we would never be able to raise enough money for such a large scheme. By the next meeting, I had visited a number of people who I guessed were better off than most and who I knew would have no objection to the proposal. On the basis that there would be income from the rented shops, I was able to ask them for support in the form of either donations or interest free loans.

At the next meeting I reported that I had in sight £3,000 in donations or interest free loans. "That is not enough", said they. "No", said I, "but it is a pretty promising start and it comes from only a handful of people. After all, I can hardly carry out a full scale canvas without having any concrete decision from you to go ahead."

"Anyway", said a lawyer on the Trust Board, "you will never find a tenant. They come into my office asking for places to rent, but they never come back." By the time the next meeting was due, I had not solved that one. But that day Rae went to a furniture shop to buy a colonial couch and asked me to go along to see it. In passing I asked the manager if they would be interested in renting another shop. He looked at me and said, "What have you heard?" It appeared that he was having trouble with a leaking building and an uncooperative landlord and he went as far as saying that they "most certainly would be interested."

I reported this to the meeting that very night. "Well", they said, "we are not going to be able to manage without a mortgage and money is tight at the moment. We will never cope with that."

A week later I was able to report. "I raised the question of a mortgage with my bank and they will be happy to advance £5,000 on the basis of what I outlined." I waited to see if I had made any significant progress with my weary objectors. I felt a few red lights were turning to orange. The secretary of the Trust, Mr Val Anderson, was on the eve of leaving on an overseas trip. He rose to announce this and to give notice that he was resigning his position. Then he added, "I think Mr Bell is on the right lines. I, for one, support the idea and hope it will go forward." It was the first formal overt support I had received, and the first crack in the opposition. From then on, one by one, the Trustees fell in behind the scheme.

When all the lights down the track turned to green, I personally began the canvass for the necessary funds. I began with one who was strongly against it and suggested that if he would head the list with a handsome donation (say five hundred pounds) it would do a lot to overthrow the last vestiges of opposition and go a long way to heal any breaches that might otherwise arise.

He asked, "How much do you want to raise?"
"Five thousand pounds."
"You haven't got a hope."
With the knowledge of the earlier promises in my mind, I responded with an air of slightly dubious confidence. "I most certainly do have a hope and when I have raised that much I will come to you for another thousand."
Unimpressed and still cynical, he replied, "We will see."
I left without a penny.

We raised ten thousand pounds. A most impressive two-storey building was built on the corner site in the heart of the town and it became a landmark in Matamata. Iles and Burgess, the same retail furniture people with whom I had passed the chance remark a little more than a year earlier, moved into the ground floor and a large, multipurpose church hall, primarily used for the Sunday School, was built above. My cynic and chief objector, had, prior to the new building, always been a generous supporter of the church. Over the years he had more than once come to the rescue when there were arrears that were causing headaches. I think he did not believe the church could possibly find the necessary money without his backing. He was more than a bit miffed when the building was completed and opened, in 1957, without a penny from him.

One of the Matamata parishioners, Amy Smith, who became a great friend of Rae's, wrote and delivered this poem as part of the opening celebrations of the new building:

Our Building

The story that I am now about to tell -
At the back of it all, is our Parson Bell.
He came to this Circuit about two years ago,
Said, "Your need is a hall, you should jolly well know!"

So this proposal was put before Trust,
As you might well imagine, it stirred up a dust:
Some said a lot – some, they said nought:
Some quite a bit, that they shouldn't have ought!

However, somehow the hall scheme went through -
Now to raise finance was the next thing to do:
Yes, they agreed, we must always have <u>that</u>
So the Circuit we'll canvass, proposed Mr Wratt.

Then about four of them set up a team
And started in earnest to fulfil their dream:
Into the town and the country they went
To collect by the hundred was their intent.

One day out of BANK came George Simpson, so slow,
Held down by his side was a handful of dough:
Margaret said, "George, can I buy that new hat?"
Says George, "Can't afford it, the hall's getting that!"

Yes, they collected from members, from adherents as well,
And so the hall fund – it slowly did swell
And when the sought sum came into sight,
"Who'll be the builder?" was the next plight.

Tenders were called – the prices came in:
Some were colossal – some were a sin:
Though I haven't a clue where any came from
The builder succeeding - was Councillor TOM.

Then one Friday night, it was ever so dark:
I went with my Morris, as usual to park:
Just a terrible mess, was all I could see:
Our Methodist Park was no longer to be.

Bulldozers had come – with one mighty rush
They'd turned our good section to mud and to slush:
They'd turned out the hedge, they'd left it all bare
It just seems as if they couldn't less care.

But out of this mess – though at first 'twas quite slow
A two-storeyed building started to grow:
The butchers grew curious: they quizzed Mrs Bell,
Is it a Post Office, or a hotel?
She said, "No, it isn't – it's not that at all,
If you really must know – it's our Methodist Hall.

The months flew by fast – there was strain, there was stress:
'Cos they'd made a promise to Iles and Burgess
That into the showroom by Christmas they'd be
"That's out of the question", said Mr Jury.

But into the showroom, they have now got:
And seem content with their little spot.
And if into town you should come at night
Our once dark Methodist section is one blaze of light.

There's been Diprose, Anderson, Simpson and Wratt
To them and to others, we must raise our hat:
They've worked mighty hard and lost hours of sleep -
But don't worry boys, if you sow, you must reap.

Now the day's come, and all's finished at last:
The opening is over and the banquet just past.
Our hall is completed as you can well see
But then comes the thought: what's HIS NEXT SCHEME TO BE???

But please, Parson Bell, could you NOT? Possibly?
Let us, one and all, just R. I. P.

- Amy Smith (1957)

Hot on the heels of this major and magnificent effort, the Wells fundraising organisation appeared on the horizon[1]. After such a

[1] Modern fundraising has its origins in the 'Wells Organisation', established by Herbert G Wells. 'Wells' was predominantly a church fundraising programme, originally based in the USA. The US company launched a Canadian company, which in turn launched an Australian company in 1954. From there the Wells Organisation spread to South Africa, New Zealand and England.. The Wells Organisation revolutionised fundraising

tremendous effort in raising money for the new building, would one dare to suggest that Wells be invited in to lift the level of weekly giving to the church? The Quarterly Meeting was prepared to accept the idea that the organisation would make a survey and estimate the potential. The answer they came up with was a possible three hundred pounds a week. In the past, we had held an annual Bank Note and Silver Tree appeal, which usually netted us three hundred pounds and set the books in balance for another year. Here was a proposition that would give us the equivalent of our special annual appeal, each and every week.

With a certain amount of trepidation, we engaged Wells to advise us how weekly donations from parishioners could be raised. Some of the church officials thought that the proposed techniques for selling the idea of increased giving, were "sharp edged commercialism". But I could see that that was inevitable if we needed to change the perception of parishioners of what a "satisfactory" level of giving actually was. The Wells fundraising approach went ahead and the estimated commitment of three hundred pounds a week was achieved. It was a great accomplishment coming on top of the Sunday School project, but they said that it was because of the project that we succeeded so well. Anyway, there were no further financial worries. When the property next door to the parsonage came on the market, the church bought it[1], with a view to the future when we would be able to build a new church. With this in mind we knew that the existing parsonage would have to go. In due course, we bought a double section in Hohaia Crescent, a new cul de sac of subdivided land, half a mile from the church. A year later we built a new brick parsonage at a cost of £7,000. At that time this was by no means a cheap home. In comparison with the original parsonage, well over sixty years old, it was quite simply

particularly in relation to churches. It broke the 'two bob-in-the-plate" mentality of donors and Wells became very successful.

[1] 4 Tainui Street, the home of the Blue family

luxurious. All the rooms were exceptionally spacious and, relatively unusual for New Zealand and especially in 1962, it had central heating. We moved into the new parsonage in 1962 even though there were only five months remaining of our appointment in Matamata. After seven and a half years in the rather less than comfortable old parsonage, the short time in the new home gave Rae enormous pleasure, but I think it also made more acute the sorrow we both felt when we had to move on so soon afterwards. The old wooden, villa type parsonage, with the traditional front verandah remained where it was for several more years and was entrusted to the care of the church's young people.

My own children had been growing up while we were in Matamata, the two older ones becoming adolescents and young adults, and the youngest about to become a teenager as we set to leave. Weston left home in 1961 for Victoria University in Wellington to study commerce. Riley became Head Boy at Matamata College in his final year in 1962, before leaving both home and Matamata at the same time as we did, to join the Royal New Zealand Air Force. Godfrey was then to become our only son at home and we left Matamata, a much depleted family, in January 1963.

In Riley's last year in Matamata he led the Bible Class which converted the old parsonage into a coffee lounge and a centre for youth activities. One or two walls were removed and one painted with a mural. On Friday nights, the coffee lounge was a hive of activity. With the traditional late night shopping, the old parsonage coffee lounge was in the centre of the town and young people dropped in for coffee and chatter.

With all the building projects going on, I managed to divert my energies into fundraising and I was satisfied to the extent that I somehow always had a challenge to conquer in Matamata, in one form or another. I have always found that I need something "to do" to keep me content. Plainly, sitting still, reading, visiting parishioners, leading meetings, conducting funerals and marriages, preaching, on their own, were not enough. And so "the projects" were important to me. These projects did at least keep me from buying any farm!

Weston as an adolescent had started a number of hobbies. One was building radios. The other was far more interesting for me. He bought a small batch of day old chicks from Massey University. He nurtured them in boxes on a shelf above the coal range in our tiny kitchen. I am sure that the hygiene inspector today would not have been impressed! This interest in raising chicks grew and interested his close school friend, Neville Barlow, who lived on a farm on the outskirts of Matamata. It appeared that his father was keen to encourage this interest, perhaps as a way of establishing Neville's interest in the farm. Eventually Neville's father and I came to an agreement. We would raise chicks and Neville would take them over at six weeks of age to farm them as poultry. I was in my element!

Many years before we arrived in Matamata the old Sunday School Hall had been built behind the church and was taking up part of the parsonage back garden. What was left to us was a pretty small backyard, at least by New Zealand standards. But the old farming flame was still in me and I could not sit and look at any piece of land, garden size or not, and see it as a mere garden or back lawn. My hands were itching to do some manual work. The land must be put to use, without any doubt. I had the choice of being surrounded by animals or crops. No cows could live there, nor sheep (unfortunately) and what crop? No it was just too small. At last Weston and Neville presented me with the answer on a plate – I saw what to do with the small garden. To my wife's quiet despair, Weston's delight and Riley and Godfrey's indifference (for they had come to think that all ministers have cows or sheep somewhere around), the back garden of the Matamata Methodist Parsonage was about to become the Matamata Methodist Parsonage Chicken Farm.

Reverend Chicken Farmer Bell (acting, of course, on behalf of his son) ordered one thousand day old chicks to come in batches of two hundred and fifty over four weeks. Delivery address: Matamata Methodist Parsonage, 2 Tainui Street, Matamata. No, no mistake.

In one corner of the garden, just next to the old Sunday School Hall, Weston and I rigged up suitable pens with a heater cover to supply the necessary warmth for the chicks. With an eye to them growing bigger and needing more room, I then encroached further into the garden, against Rae's wishes and concern about the clothes line. We built a chicken house there taking due care that it would be warm and safe against rodent invaders even to the extent that I put a trench around the base and tacked wire netting on to the piles before replacing the earth. The backyard of the parsonage was beginning to look more like a farmyard again. It was wonderful.

The first batch of chicks arrived in boxes from which emanated an astonishingly shrill chorus of constant chirping – such a noise never before heard in the Matamata parsonage garden or, for that matter, probably in any parsonage garden. Weston and I put the cute chicks in the pens and they snuggled down into dry wood shavings, a large quantity of which had been delivered to the Matamata Methodist Parsonage door the day before - no doubt to the further bemusement of the local suppliers. The chicks bathed themselves under a glowing lamp and shade which spread enough warmth over them all as a very comfortable substitute for mother hen. We fed them with much care and affection. Even Rae thought they looked cute and we left them to sleep soundly for the night. I was well pleased with my (sorry, Weston's) new venture. After the sheep farm in Nelson, this was surely a pretty big peace offering for giving up farming altogether. It was, after all, only chickens, this time – and they were Weston's, not mine, were they not? At least I had not bought an actual farm.

As the chicks grew and flourished they soon outgrew their space and were moved (to make way for the new batch of chicks) into the fine new home I had been building for them – nearer Rae's clothes line.

This little farming project was going to be a great success! The next batch of chicks arrived and they snuggled down into the wood shavings for their first night at the Parsonage Chicken Farm. Early next morning I hurried out to feed them and to have a quiet gloat over my (sorry, Weston's) growing new family, before preparing for my day of pastoral duties. Whatever else happened, the chicks would not interfere with church life. How could they? They certainly did not need shearing, nor dogs for rounding them up, nor fences to keep them in, nor gorse to be burnt off. This time I would be a most successful Reverend Farmer.

As I surveyed our beautiful yellow chicks, still slumbering in the warm glow of the heater lamp, I could have sworn there were fewer than the night before. Indeed, as I looked closer still, there was nothing like two hundred and fifty chicks. It was impossible to get an accurate count but I did the best I could. I decided that there were one hundred, no more. More than a hundred, at least, were missing. I searched around the shed. Nothing. I looked in the garden. Around the garden. Around the shed. Nothing. Perplexed, I tried to count them again, but to no avail. There were definitely many missing, but I could not see how, why or where. I went inside and ate breakfast, sitting in silence, deeply puzzled.

I returned to the chicken house to count and look yet again. This time, I noticed in the very corner of the shed some marks of blood around a small hole where the hardboard lining was the merest fraction short of completely covering the stud wall. Instantly I realised what had happened. With a sinking heart, I ripped off the lining and there, sure enough, piled up one on top of another, stockpiled ironically so very neatly between the studs, as if some kind of insulation lining, were one hundred and twenty-eight dead chicks, the last two or three of which had not quite breathed their last. The job of a single rat.

The rat had clearly plunged into the two hundred and fifty chickens huddled together for warmth. As they slept the rat had crept up on them and silently picked them off one by one, perhaps while some slept on oblivious to the danger. It attacked each chick with a careful and swift nip in the back of the neck and dragged it across the shed floor to store in its lair. Where the rat had got in and where it went when I suddenly uncovered his haul, I had no idea. It must have taken hours for it to kill so many and stack them so carefully. I imagined that it must have started the gruesome battle on the defenceless chicks in the deep hours of the night, and judging by the fact that a pitiful few were still alive, it was still working on the project when I disturbed it that morning, and again, no doubt, as I had breakfasted. I felt sickened.

I moved the remaining, frightened chicks from the jaws of the ugly rodent, for ever, placing them high and safe in another shed. The terror they must have felt during the night can only be imagined. I then took a wheel barrow and filled it till it could carry no more, with the dead chicks which I picked from the layers in which they lay, one by one, as I would were I selecting tins of food off a shelf in a supermarket. The wheelbarrow hearse composed a pathetic and sad sight.

Determinedly I hunted down the rat and a few days later, with the help of poison I laid, I found it dead. It was quite the largest rat I had ever seen. It was enormous. I put it on a shovel and he was a weight to carry. It looked little short of a monster and I showed it to the boys before I buried it. Godfrey still remembers it to this day, although he was only eight at the time.

Despite this savage start to our little chicken farm, I continued undaunted, this time I am sure to the dismay of my wife. As the flock grew in number and in size, the parsonage section became fuller and fuller of poultry. Virtually every corner of the back garden succumbed to chicken housing of some kind. Rae drew the line at the front garden being taken over, but it was sorely attractive to me too.

Although I thought that this time my farming pursuits had escaped the censure of my parishioners, I was wrong. As the chicken flock increased, so did the smell. This did not impress the church officers, the visitors to the parsonage, the congregation on Sundays, or the neighbours, who were thankfully – as I had learned to become grateful for small mercies – only on one side, as the church was on the other. I never achieved popularity as a Reverend Farmer although I achieved notoriety.

I was delighted and relieved that during all this time Weston remained interested in the chickens. Ah, I was not alone in my hobby! Having a member of the family share my enjoyment meant I felt less isolated by the church and the neighbours who, as usual, looked on in disbelief. Weston was responsible for most of the daily care of the near thousand chicks which, to all intents and purposes if not literally certainly symbolically, now took over the parsonage. Neville had watched the back garden developments of his friend the parson's kid's father, in fascination, if not slight astonishment. He then started watching with more concern as the chicks rapidly approached full size, nearing the six week hand over date – to him. I have to admit now, although I certainly would not then, that I was watching with equal concern. The chicks were becoming very big indeed. And Rae, quite unreasonably of course, would not let me take over that front garden! The fact that the chickens in another week or so would soon be transferred to Neville's father's farm was the only thing which stopped Rae going absolutely up the wall. It was also the one relieving factor which becalmed the growing anxiety of the neighbours, the visitors to the parsonage, the Sunday congregations, and in particular the parishioners holding meetings in the old Sunday School hall which now backed directly on to the minister's chicken farm. And, yes, it came as a relief to me, too. Neville was only a young teenager at the time, but it is interesting to note that he became a professional poultry farmer.

In 1959 my father died and this meant that I now truly became a farm owner. The family farm, Coldstream, had been left to my three sisters and me jointly. This was a joy and total delight to me. Apart from the small, impoverished place I had had briefly in Richmond, this was the first time, I had a piece of real estate of some value and substance. Of course, being a minister and always living on a small salary subsidised by living in church parsonages, I did not even own my home and here I was at forty-seven years old. The farm had been leased out for quite some time but this was due to expire not long after my father's death and eagerly I looked forward to doing all sorts of things with it as soon as I could get on it. The end of the lease and the holidays could not come fast enough for me. Both of those events would unleash me from my parish duties to get on to my beloved Coldstream to work, work, work. I was extraordinarily excited by the idea. Disturbingly so. I had never felt the elation in the ministry that I now felt with the prospect of going back to my father's farm, *my* farm, our farm. Because I knew the farm so well from my childhood I could recall every feature of it, even to every undulation in every paddock. I had plodded over them all, driving horses with ploughs and harrows and topdressers and I had fed out hay and silage from the spring cart, on cold days, on wet days and on balmy days. I could remember every day I spent on that farm and I relished my memories. I dreamed and planned and I waited and waited for the first day I could take a break to drive to Taranaki, to drive home, and to start farming once again. Leaving the ministry to go back farming was a secret idea that I kept from Rae. I felt guilty that it even entered my head — surely it betrayed God and my commitment to the church? But cross my mind it did, and more than once. I could not admit to it – yet.

The farming of Coldstream went through several stages after my father died. There was the original leaseholder who finished off the lease before moving out, then David Jago, my sister's son, ran some dry stock on it with my visits there whenever I could make it.

One day amidst my growing excitement and secret anxiety over my real plans and dreams to farm Coldstream full time, my sister Gwen rang and asked if she could drive up to stay with us for a few days. She arrived with daughter Shirley. The point of their visit soon emerged.

"You can't really use the farm, can you, Charlie?" asked Gwen.

I was aghast. Had they read my mind? Had they some idea of my secret desire to return farming, of my battle of conscience with my ministry? I said nothing before they continued. "We would be happy to buy out your share."

My response was immediate, if not well considered, "No, thank you." The idea of being ousted from having a piece of land of my own after looking over fences for years, almost envious of the farmlands that edged the roads I travelled wherever my ministry had taken me to in New Zealand, the land of farms, was more than I could bear. That night, I could not prevent myself shedding a few tears. I had come to realise, nay, accept, that farming was in my blood and that my father's farm was my heritage, not only physically but also emotionally.

I knew in my heart that the farm would eventually have to go, but before doing so I cried out for one last opportunity to farm Coldstream by remote control. It was crazy, but I wanted to do it. I accepted that the farm must be sold, and would be sold, but before that day came I could surely farm the lot from here, Matamata, from here, the parsonage? What else would it do before a sale was finalised? Perhaps exasperated or at best bemused, my sisters agreed. My wife simply sighed.

I retained the farm and continued my dreams as best I could, contained as they were within my profession of active ministry. Occasionally, when parish duties permitted, I took trips to the farm, putting up fences, felling some stray trees, altering the old homestead. I worked on my father's land and I sweated all day long. And yet they were the most relaxing breaks I could ever wish for. Most of the time I worked quite alone and sometimes, when Rae and the boys did not come with me, I lived alone baching in my childhood home. I was happy, very happy.

When I had finally sold my Nelson property I finished up with a mere three hundred pounds in the bank. But after living on a minister's wage all my life, this was more money than I was accustomed to. I decided to use some of the money to buy a truck load of local Waikato cows and rail them back to the farm (my farm!) in Taranaki. My idea was to winter them there and sell them in the spring as cows near calving, which is normally when they are in greatest demand. My brothers-in-law, Len and Don, helped me as much as they could, but my remote control farming did not work. I saw nothing from my investment and eight months later, most of the three hundred pounds had gone as well. Farming was defeating me.

No matter how much I wanted to keep the farm, it could not go on like this: Gwen was right. I realised that a valuable farm could not sit there unfarmed. And of course (of course?) I could not give serious thought to the idea of leaving the ministry, it is not done, and I know in reality it would have felt like cutting an arm off. For although farming was definitely one arm my church was, no less definitely, the other.

In January 1963 as we shifted from Matamata to Rangiora, Godfrey and I went by car ahead of Mum and spent a week at Coldstream, where I enjoyed myself thoroughly working on the house, doing the odd repair and painting the new extension. All Godfrey remembers was the opossum which caused havoc every night with its incessant cry and clambering over the roof. Eventually I shot it although Godfrey was not too impressed with the solution.

This was the last time I would live in my childhood home. My sisters and I agreed to put a sharemilker on the farm. Mr N C Coxhead, his wife and two small children moved on to the land and into the homestead, and my role diminished to that of caring landlord. I missed the farm, but I still had it. There was some pleasure in that. Only a year or two later on October 30th 1965, the house was burnt to the ground. On that Saturday morning Mr Coxhead had summoned his wife to assist him fighting bloat at the rear of the farm. Fortunately they took with them their children. Returning home later, the couple were horrified to see their home engulfed in flames. They were safe, but symbolically it seemed my childhood itself had gone up in flames. The loss of the house and the memories that belonged to it, saddened me greatly.

But now there was a new question: to build again or not? The crisis presented us with a crossroads and a new pressure to sell. By now the sentiments I had of taking over my father's farm immediately following his death, were, perhaps, mellowing. Indeed, the dreamlike opportunity of changing my career, of owning land, of being a farmer again, had long gone and I now viewed the world with a more rational and pragmatic view but perhaps with no less emotion. This time we were of one mind. Sell the farm, divide the proceeds, and go our separate ways. No further idea of a joint farm in any shape or form was entertained. After the fire, Coldstream was sold and the Bell family association died with the sale[1].

I used my share of the money (about £3,000) from the sale of my father's farm to buy a tenanted house and dairy business at 62 Haumai Street, Johnsonville, Wellington, for £8,000. Even with a £5,000 mortgage it proved to be a good investment and I kept it for more than ten years, which provided me with a good, steady little bit of extra income. I sold it for $30,000 when I was in Wanganui and wanted the money to put into – a farm, naturally.

No fewer than five buildings which feature in the Bell family history have been burnt down, three of which are referred to in "Boots".

Boots
If boots could talk as well as walk
They would have a story to tell
They would take you first to Raetihi
The Nursing home[2] *of Grandma Bell*
Where I was born.
But it was burnt down.

---

[1] Except that we scattered some of Dad's ashes right there on the site of his old childhood home. - GB.

[2] "Cora Lynn"

They took me down to "Merleswood" home
Where from two to seven I did roam
They walked me up to Stanley School
From 5 to 12 and walked me back again
That moulded me and shaped me
As into books and knowledge I did delve
Then it, too, was burnt down[1].
They walked me up to "Coldstream"
From seven to twenty-one
They walked me into happy years
They walked me into fun
With cows and pastures green
Where I could jump and run.
Then it, too, WAS BURNT DOWN.

And now they have walked me from yesteryear
They have walked us into joys and sorrows
They have walked us into sunshine
And will walk us into "Tomorrow".

Gwen Jago, August 1996[2]

(Almost unbelievably, there were two other fires in this catalogue of disasters that were omitted in Auntie Gwen's poem. Dad's first home at the Raetihi farm was burnt down and Osborne House where Dad's grandmother lived and ran her private boarding house business, and where two of Dad's aunts were married, was ALSO burnt down! - GB)

In visiting parishioners around the Walton area, I became aware of a need for young wives and mothers to have an opportunity to gather together. Every year there was an influx of new people coming in to do sharemilking. There was little opportunity to meet each other or the local residents so I called a meeting of the young women of my Walton congregation, with the idea of creating a Young Wives group in the church. Out of the discussions grew the idea that it become a joint Presbyterian-Methodist fellowship. This raised the problem of those who had

---

1 Stanley School was burnt down twice, in 1916 and again in 1984
2 Gwen's poem was read at her funeral by her grandson Neil Fenwick, 25 Nov 2006

no real church ties and so one young lady put forward the idea of a Walton Young Wives Fireside Club, not affiliated to any church. This was received with great enthusiasm and the ladies started talking enthusiastically amongst themselves. I sat staring at a sea of bright faces, happy in that they were now absorbed with the idea and not only was the church being ignored, but far more humiliating, the minister (me, unfortunately in this case), was being ignored. I decided that I seemed to be shooting myself in the foot. I brought the meeting to strict order and expressed my concern by reminding them of the whole point of this meeting and why I (that is, I, representing the church) not they, had called it in the first place. Eventually however I agreed that the Fireside Club idea could be seen as a community service and that the church should therefore be happy to support it. "But", I insisted, "there should be some link with the church to recognise that support." This was accepted and into the constitution we wrote that there should be an annual church parade and also that church members should see in it a duty of service, through leadership.

The club took off with a bang! Every month it grew in membership, soaring to nearly one hundred until it involved practically every young wife in the small district. Husbands were soon made aware that the monthly Fireside Club meeting was sacrosanct and their lives, meals and own commitments had to revolve around their wives' Fireside night. Once a month the Walton husbands became babysitters, no questions asked, no excuses accepted. It soon became universally accepted in the district that if you chose the right night, every husband was alone with children and babes-in-arms in every farm homestead across the Waikato paddocks in and around Walton. *The Walton wives had gathered!*

It was inspiring to see how many of the young wives who were initially shy and quiet grew in self confidence and developed gifts of leadership. No one could hold office for more than two years so more and more people were called on to lead and they thrived and blossomed under its responsibility. But let it be whispered only, that not one, but all of the original executives of President, Vice President, Secretary and Treasurer, were pregnant at the end of their first year of office. None of them had been so when the club started.[1]

Anzac Day was always a busy occasion. All ministers of all denominations were involved in the special services. Each Anzac Day, Walton held its memorial service at eleven in the morning and I always felt there was something special about that Walton service which every member of the Walton Young Wives Fireside Club attended. In the afternoon Matamata celebrated its own memorial service at the Community Hall, but this was the second one of the day for the town. Matamata always began Anzac Day with a moving dawn service around the town's cenotaph. Although the sun might begin to rise by the end of the service, it was held mostly in the dark with the aid of torches. A lone bugler would stand some distance away from the crowd and when given the signal, for he was too far away to hear the service to follow it, he would play the traditional Last Post and Reveille. On one such occasion, the bugler started at utterly the wrong moment in the middle of the service, indeed in the middle of one of the prayers, drowning out the minister's voice. Someone had to race across to stop him, which he did, but so abruptly and inappropriately, that the embarrassment of the moment was intensified not lessened. The point of the message to the bugler was surely that he would fade out, not cut out! Apparently, the bugler had arranged with someone to signal to him with a torch, but this man stood listening to the service with the torch in his hand behind his back and absent-mindedly started flicking it on and off.

Following my usual practice, I formed a group of young men into a study group and prepared them for lay preacher's examinations. They were a dedicated group and persevered with the studies, resulting in a useful source of lay readers. Ian Diprose and Ron Vosper have continued lay preaching to this

---

[1] A proof reader's added comment in the column read: "Interesting what a little respect and self confidence can do!"

day. Ian McKenzie went on into the full ministry and completed more than thirty years of service in the church. He died recently with cancer.[1].

One young man, an Anglican, asked if could attend the class as he was thinking about entering the ministry, but was far from sure. This he followed through and is now an Archdeacon in the Waikato Diocese. My special delight in all these classes in all my parishes was not so much in helping them to become lay preachers, rewarding as that was, but in giving them a theology, an ordered systematic, reasoned grasp of the faith that was already in them. I wished I could have done this for all the members of all my congregations, for I knew only too well what a bulwark it was for them against ever changing winds of theological fashions.

Once again, I found myself elected as Secretary of the Methodist Synod. During my term of office the synod observed its 50th birthday in 1962. I pointed out that I too was fifty years old, so the Lord must have been making sure all those years ago that the synod would have a secretary lined up at its fiftieth celebrations. I was also on the secretarial staff of the national conference which meant that there was no relaxation for me on the annual visit to these gatherings. Also I was still on the Conference Examination Committee which stemmed from my work as the Theology Examiner of Lay Preachers.

There came a growing demand for study groups and we formed one in Matamata and one in Te Poi. We also formed a Men's Fellowship group. It never became large but provided a niche in the life of the church for some men. Particularly satisfying was the readiness of the group to be understanding and patient with men of lesser ability including one, I recall, who had a speech difficulty. He was offered and accepted an official position in the church.

It was while I was in Matamata that I bought the Armstrong Siddeley the story of which I have related in an

---

1 Rev Ian McKenzie 1932 - died 27 November 1990

earlier chapter. I seemed to enjoy looking at fine cars almost as much as I enjoyed scanning the newspaper for farms for sale (which I *still* did right through my days in Matamata). It was 1959 when I sold my Ford Consul, which I had bought brand new for £400, and replaced it with my 1954 Armstrong Siddeley which had done 60,000 miles, for £450. But it wasn't the purchase price that was so outrageous, it was the running costs and what it represented as a status symbol. Even though it was so much older than my Ford Consul the sight of the Methodist Minister in such a grand car did not do much to endear myself to the poor and the humble. It was not appropriate to my station in life (I was reminded more than once) and far more to the point, I could not really afford to run it. But I loved that car! The children remember it fondly. Both Weston and Riley got their licences in it and Weston in particular drove it frequently, including to Taranaki when my father died later that year. But perhaps the most incongruous and probably humiliating occasion we imposed on "the Siddeley" was when we took the majestic vehicle to nothing less than a campsite. In the summer school holidays of January 1962 we went to Kawakawa Bay and had our – and undoubtedly the Siddeley's – first experience of camping. Fellow campers were surprised on two counts: 1) that a minister of religion was in their midst and 2) an Armstrong Siddeley was in their midst – and what's more it was parked outside the minister's tent. The Armstrong had to suffer the indignity of being surrounded by tents and boiling billies instead of diplomatic residences and champagne corks, but I delighted in the trip with my pride and joy, which proved to be its swan song. The car that caused so much controversy in its short life with a man of the cloth, was sold a few weeks later.

In my fourth year in Matamata in 1959, I was approached by the Circuit Steward of Auckland East District, Frank Paine, to consider an invitation to be appointed to our Epsom Church in Auckland in 1960. In those days five years was the typical appointment term to Methodist parishes and so such an invitation was not untimely. I was delighted as it appeared to represent a very good career move for me. Rae was delighted not least because it was a university city and with the boys fast approaching school leaving age, it seemed a good move for the whole family. At my parish's Quarterly Meeting I informed them of the Epsom invitation and told them that I would like to accept. Only the national Methodist Conference later that year in November could sanction ministerial appointments but, despite this, the news got as far as the church newsletters and into various church notices around the parish.

But the whole thing turned sour and it was a dark and deeply disappointing setback for me in my life in the church. The Circuit Steward had approached me as my name was "on the list" but he issued the invitation in the absence of the Chairman of the District, Reverend Eric Hames, who was away at the time. Reverend Hames knew me from Trinity College days, but that did not help me now. When he returned and learned that Charlie Bell from Matamata had been invited to be appointed to Epsom in 1960, he and a number of senior church officials in Auckland, including Reverend Everill Orr[1], were not at all happy with the invitation. I believe to this day that it was my love for farming and particularly my farming interests so overtly displayed in my Nelson days, that cost me a move to a *city* church. Such appointments were coveted by young, ambitious and "high flyer" ministers: they were parishes that were known for opening doors for future promotions. It seemed that I had earned a reputation amongst some in the higher ranks of the church that I was not suitable for such an appointment. I believed that they felt I would "not fit in".

---

[1] Rev Everill A Orr MBE 1904-1971

The Methodist Church of New Zealand
Te Hāhi Weteriana O Aotearoa

Administration Division

Our Ref. Hist./FGP
Your Ref.

24th May 1996

Mr. Godfrey Bell
P.O. Box 31 333
Milford
AUCKLAND 1309

Dear Godfrey

re Rev. Charles Harrison Bell

I have read through your text on the Epsom "episode", and would not want to alter anything except the spelling of my name (Paine). You have helped me to understand the great distress that this caused your parents.

This is something that still haunts me, as it was probably the most difficult thing I have had to handle as a Circuit Steward. Through it I learnt of the power politics exercised by the Chairman and officials of the District. They had the power to see that ministers that fitted in with their thinking, were appointed.

I am still sure that your father's name was next on the list, otherwise I would never had written to him. The next thing I knew was Eric Hames ordering me to withdraw the invitation. That was a most difficult letter to write.

If you have a spare copy of your book you may wish to lodge one with us to put in your father's file.

Yours sincerely

Frank

Frank Paine
Associate Archivist

Morley House, 25 Latimer Square, Christchurch. Ph. 366 6049, Fax. 366 6009
P O Box 931, Christchurch. Please address letters to THE GENERAL SECRETARY

When I was rewriting Dad's story, I wanted to check on some facts about "the Epsom affair" and got in touch with the archivist of the Methodist Church. Little did I realise that the person whom I contacted was, by an extraordinary coincidence, the very Circuit Steward who was instructed to write to Dad and withdraw the invitation. He subsequently read what I wrote and checked the details for me. – GB

There was a terrible, embarrassing, and for me hurtful, hiatus amongst the powers that be. A small minority of "hard core" ministers felt that I had betrayed the profession: that my farming had come before my duty to my parish and parishioners. It forced me into a time of intense soul searching. Of course I had my supporters too. But amidst expressed "great regret" the invitation was withdrawn. Everill Orr later said that when the objections were lodged, he had not realised the situation had gone so far (that is, that I had understood that the invitation was official and that I had accepted it). Over those weeks there were many telephone calls, letters, and meetings, and hopes were raised and dashed. Rae and I discussed it for hours on end, in bed, over meal tables in front of the family who as children, sat largely in silence not fully realising the predicament that I had found myself in, nor perhaps the significance that any outcome would hold for them. My forever faithful, loyal and supportive wife and I together constructed carefully planned letters which I dictated to her as I had done for years on end using her shorthand typist skills. In my study, she typed and re-typed those letters for me, and we studied each phrase carefully so as to cause no offence to anyone. Amidst the apologies and the withdrawals were claims of misunderstanding on my part. Perhaps there were misunderstandings on my part, but it was a messy business and it was the first time that I had become entangled, well and truly, in the politics of the church as an organisation. And those politics appeared to me to have precious little to do with Christianity as a faith.

It was a time of trial. The outcome was plain enough, but I was left wounded, not least of which was my pride. The invitation was duly withdrawn (by Circuit Steward Frank Paine, under instruction) and I had to announce the same to my Matamata parish officials. This was a terrible personal experience as I felt embarrassed, foolish, and worst of all, inadequate. They were totally supportive and promptly issued an invitation for me to stay thereby saving the last ounce of self-confidence I had left in me as a minister. But I nearly lost it completely and my self esteem had never been so low. In the end I can truly say I was glad and happy to stay in Matamata and I did so for another three years. Although we were not in a university city, Weston was to leave home and go to Victoria University in Wellington, not Auckland anyway, and Riley left home to go to Christchurch with the Royal New Zealand Air Force. When we left Matamata eventually, the timing was quite perfect from the point of view of the children's schooling: Riley finished off his secondary schooling there as Head Boy of Matamata College and Godfrey completed his primary schooling there at Matamata Intermediate. The timing worked well for me too. I continued to love the Matamata folk and, as always, I was happy there but the Epsom "episode" left my career from an ambitious point of view (if I ever did consider myself ambitious), well and truly over. I was marked for good as a "small town" minister and when we left Matamata in 1962 the conference appointed me to Rangiora in North Canterbury, a town of exactly the same size as Matamata. Career planners in today's business world would have said with a great degree of accuracy, I was "moved sideways". I felt very keenly that I was never going to be forgiven by the church for my continued interest in farming and for carrying my childhood passion, indeed my father's heritage of love for the land, so strongly within – and about – me.

With hindsight, it was perhaps fortuitous that I was never appointed to Epsom. My health started to decline only a year or two later, and as it transpired I was to take early retirement from the ministry on health grounds not many years after that. But of course this did nothing to dispel the hurt and the inner doubting of my self-worth at the time.

In fact, I think Matamata would have let me continue a further year or two even beyond 1962, but by this time I was feeling that I had really given all I could to my parish, as much as I loved it. They needed fresh blood and I needed a new challenge, and so it was that I gave notice of my intention to ask Conference for another appointment.

And so back to the South Island we were to go. Rangiora was not unlike Matamata in several ways. Both towns had a population of about 3,000. Both Methodist parishes were of a similar size. Both towns were flat. Both towns were surrounded by rich farmlands, Matamata by Waikato's rolling green pastures and dairy farms, Rangiora by Canterbury's golden flat plains and crop farms. But there were differences too. Rangiora was not as wealthy as Matamata and the average of Rangiora's population was distinctly older than Matamata's. One good thing for me was that the appointment delighted Rae. Rangiora was only half an hour north of Christchurch, her home town, and where her ageing father and her adored twin brother Boy lived.

I left Matamata behind me with a new Sunday School hall and commercially let development, a new section added to the church property and a new parsonage. I enjoyed leading the changes and leaving my mark in this way and I looked back on my appointment with some satisfaction. My love for Matamata was never to leave me. I returned to my old church which had since been re-sited on the top of Tower Hill as part of an historic village[1] and took the weddings there of two family members. One was for the brother of my daughter-in-law, Richard Bearne who was out from England with his new wife to be, Sarah, in 1990. I returned to my old church almost a year to the day later to marry my granddaughter, Nicky, to Jim Costello in December 1991[2]. I was then only a few months short of eighty years old.

As we started to pack up the house ready to leave Matamata I pulled out all my filed sermons. I spent some moments alone in my study fingering through them. Sermons. Hundreds, if not thousands of them. No sheep, or chickens, or cows in sight – just sermons. This was my real work in front of me. I stared out the window of my relatively grand and spacious

---

1 Where, at his own wish, Dad's ashes are now scattered.

2 The last wedding service Dad ever conducted.

study in this our short lived, new and beautiful home[1]. After our previous home, a fifty year old parsonage, this home was bright and brand spanking new. The garden was new. The grass was new. Across the street another new house was being built which would almost be the last to fill all the sections and complete the development in this quiet cul de sac. I could see the edge of the vegetable garden that I had worked on and the flowers and shrubs I had planted. But I saw no paddocks out the window. No invitation to go milk the cows. And here I was facing a trip to the South Island to another parsonage, in another town, and a new flock of parishioners. I pondered on my future in the church as I faced my sideways move and looked back on the withdrawn invitation to Epsom. As I day dreamed, I spotted a reflection of the bust of John Wesley that was still sitting on one of the study book shelves, waiting to be packed. John Wesley – founder of the Methodist Church. It stopped me day dreaming and reminded me of who I was. My fingers rested on my boxes of sermons, all of them written in long hand over all these years. Week after week, I wrote my sermons, always in ink, always on the blank backs of used paper which I cut down to approximately five by eight inches, small note pad size. When I had preached each sermon, I folded my notes in half and put them in an envelope marked with the date and place where I had used it. The envelope went into a shoe box.

I had twenty shoe boxes sitting in front of me now. Some on the floor, some on my study desk. Quite needlessly, I decided to count my sermons and see where I had preached them[2]. As I sifted through them, I kept on thinking. I was leaving Matamata. My gorse ridden farm in Nelson had been a disaster. My father had died. My childhood home had burnt down. I had lost my money with those cows I railed to Taranaki. We had sold the one farm I did or ever could own. I had a rather grand car, but

---

[1] 4 Hohaia Crescent, Matamata. The house is still owned by the church, but ministers tend to have their own homes now and it is currently (1995) not the parsonage, but a rented out home.

[2] A couple of later sermons are reproduced in the Appendix.

briefly. The chickens had died or been taken away to someone else's farm. Epsom had rejected me. Weston had left home for university to qualify in commerce and as an accountant. Riley had left home to join the Air Force. Godfrey was still at school and would, according to him, no doubt become a school teacher. None of my sons was interested in farming – or in the church. Why was I?

I finished counting. I had written one thousand one hundred and fifty-two sermons. I had preached altogether more than two thousand five hundred times, from pulpits in the north of the North Island to the south of the South Island[1].

Reverend Charles Harrison Bell, BA. I was a minister.

---

[1] By the time he died, he would have preached another five or six hundred times and probably written another one or two hundred sermons. - GB

Matamata County Mail, December 1962

CHURCHES FAREWELL REV C H BELL

Representatives of district churches, members of Matamata Methodist Church congregation and other guests recently paid public tribute to eight years of ministering by Rev C H Bell and Mrs Bell.

During Rev Bell's ministry, church membership increased, Wesley Hall in Broadway has been built and a new parsonage built.

Rev Bell and family will take up a new appointment at Rangiora, North Canterbury, early in January.

Canon M N Richards, in paying tribute said he had worked side by side with Rev and Mrs Bell for six years and at all times there had been wonderful cooperation in interdenominational matters.

Father E Derrick said he had, for some years, shared with Rev Bell, the task of organising Corso work of the district and he regretted that this happy partnership was to end.

Presbyterian greetings were conveyed by Rev I Grant.

Rev R S Marshall of the Church of Christ had many treasured memories of a close association of seven years standing.

A fine tribute to the sterling quality of Riley, the second son of Rev and Mrs Bell, who has served his College as head boy for the past year, was paid by Rev Marshall.

Rev W Laws, Morrinsville, chairman of the South Auckland District, thanked Rev and Mrs Bell for their contributions to the work of the Methodist Church in his district.

One who throughout many years had attended the Matamata Primary School with Rev Bell to give scripture lessons, Mr A G Findlater referred to Rev Bell as a true friend and counsellor.

Mr J H Dalton, senior, a trustee of the Te Poi Church Committee, spoke of the fine qualities of Rev and Mrs Bell and from all Te Poi friends he made a presentation.

The Matamata Girls' Brigade showed their appreciation of the chaplain by making him a small presentation. Assistant-leader, Iris Wilbore, spoke on the girls' behalf.

Maori friends, too, took the opportunity to say "thank you Rev Bell for your friendship and interest".

Mr G Bellamy, deputising for Mr J Pate, made a presentation of an appropriate farewell gift.

Mr W J Diprose, circuit steward, spoke for all fellow Methodists in the district when he told the large audience of the accomplishments of Rev and Mrs Bell in the eight short years they had been resident in Matamata. Activities, both spiritual and social, associated with the church had grown in number and strength.

Youth, encouraged by the three Bell boys, were taking a more active part in Wesleyan affairs. Bible classes and Brigade were strong youth movements and the popular new venture "The Coffee Lounge" (in the old Methodist Parsonage at 2 Tainui Street) had surpassed all earlier expectations.

Weston, Riley and Godfrey were all complimented by Mr Diprose on their contributions to the work of their church and schools. All three were the recipients of book tokens.

Rev and Mrs Bell received a monetary gift from Matamata Methodist friends and Mrs Diprose presented Mrs Bell with a sheaf of pastel toned gladioli.

"A Great Reward"

Rev Bell in reply thanked the many speakers for their compliments to Mrs Bell, the boys and himself. With reference to the forward steps that the church had made during his years in Matamata, he could only say that it was the grand response of the people that made these achievements possible. "To work with the Maori people has been a special pleasure. Our relationship has at all times been most harmonious. Even though one five-year-old at a Maori school did inform me once that my singing was out of tune. To see the members of the youth organisations going into adulthood proud of their association with these groups was a great reward for the chaplain", he said.

For the younger members, Riley replied.

All had so many strong ties in Matamata, he said, that they did not feel they would be at home anywhere but Matamata and their many friends could expect to see them whenever time would permit.

For the earlier portion of the evening the ladies of the Women's Group entertained with some instrumental and vocal numbers, sketches and competitions which Canon Richards commented upon very favourably.

The chairman for the evening was Mr M Fernyhough and at the close of the programme Rev W Laws pronounced the Benediction.

Coldstream, Beaconsfield Road, Wharehuia, Charles's childhood home as it was when he was a boy.

Coldstream in January 1963 after Charles added the new extension. Unfortunately the figures have been cut off. One person (in the corner) may be Godfrey aged 12.

Coldstream on fire, 30 October 1965, two years after Charles had renovated his childhood family home.
Photo Stratford Press *4 Nov 1965*

Charles, elected secretary of the Methodist Synod, speaking at the South Auckland Synod's 50th anniversary meeting in 1962 – the same year as Charles himself turned 50.

Matamata Methodist Church on Broadway c 1958. In the 1980s the building was moved to the Historic Village in Tower Road.

The new Sunday School Hall and retail unit, Wesley Buildings, built in 1957 next to the church (which can just be seen behind it on the left) on the corner of Broadway and Tainui St. The retail unit was let to Iles and Burgess, a furniture store.

The interior of the new hall on the first floor.

The Methodist Church as Rae & Charles first knew it before the new hall was built. 1955

Godfrey (standing left) with neighbour friends, Neil Bibby[1] and in the apple cart Wendy Blue. The sport of racing apple carts on wheels up and down Tainui Street was a favourite pastime. c1956

Weston with one of his chickens from the infamous Matamata Methodist Parsonage chicken farm. c1959

Tainui Street, Matamata, taken outside no 2, the Methodist Parsonage. Its garage is seen on the left. Next door at no 4 was the Blue family. The garage further along at 6 Tainui Street belonged to the Bibby family. c1956. Today with old houses replaced by commercial buildings, it is no longer a quiet residential street.

---

1 Neil Bibby 1951-2002

The incongruous Armstrong Siddeley sitting outside a tent! It was in fact its swan song as it joined the family on their first ever camping holiday. Kawakawa Bay January 1962. The car was sold a few days afterwards.

Weston and Rae with Charles's pride and joy.

Rae, Matamata, Dec 1962

Riley and Weston on a family holiday in Northland with an earlier, more sober, minister's car, a Consul. 1958. The long trousers mark adulthood! It seems that Rae is sitting in the car.

Mittens and Matamata cannot be separated. The parsonage cat for all the years there.

Rae and Charles outside their bedroom window of the old parsonage, 2 Tainui Street Matamata, July 1962, just before moving into the new parsonage at Hohaia Crescent.

Riley, Godfrey and Weston.
2 Tainui Street, Matamata, 1959

Charles and Rae at Elaine Diprose's wedding Matamata 1956

Weston, Rae, Godfrey, Charles
2 Tainui St, Matamata

Riley, Wendy Blue, Godfrey in the Blue garden next door to the parsonage, 4 Tainui St. The top of the back of the Methodist Church looking beyond the Bell back garden can be seen. Godfrey just off to school?

Weston, Godfrey and Riley c1957

Weston, Rae, Godfrey, Riley, Charles, at the Jago homestead, Merleswood, Taranaki, on the occasion of Betty Jago's wedding, 21 May 1960

The last Christmas in Matamata before moving to the South Island was spent in the new Methodist Parsonage, 2 Hohaia Crescent. Rae with Weston on terrace Dec 1962. The garden had been planted with potatoes prior to being grassed.

Rae and Charles, on holiday at Paihia Bay 1958

Weston, Godfrey, Riley
2 Hohaia Cres Matamata 1962

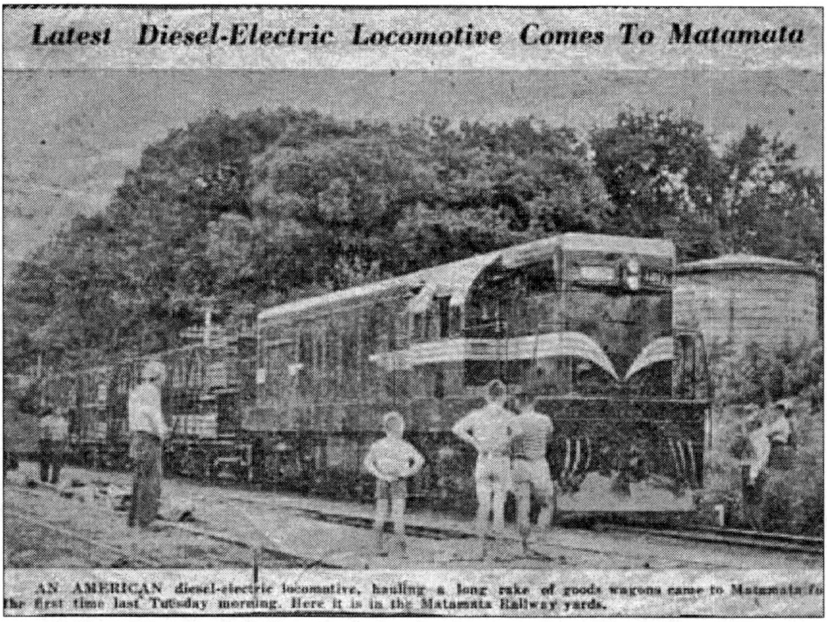

Latest Diesel-Electric Locomotive Comes To Matamata

AN AMERICAN diesel-electric locomotive, hauling a long rake of goods wagons came to Matamata for the first time last Tuesday morning. Here it is in the Matamata Railway yards.

Godfrey, Weston and Riley caught by the photographer of the local newspaper Matamata County Mail *as they watched the first diesel locomotive come into Matamata Railway Station. c1957*

The Bell family, Rae, Weston, Riley, Godfrey, Charles, Matamata c1958 taken by Huia Beaumont, a family friend from Christchurch

Chapter 18

THE LAST PARISH

1963 - 1966

Rangiora, North Canterbury

Rangiora is thirty-two kilometres north of Christchurch in the North Canterbury plains. The Canterbury Plains are New Zealand on a grand scale. Across them run dead straight roads and wide, meandering streams lost in wide riverbeds. Your eye can see forever, right across the plains to the spectacular backdrop of the Southern Alps, the mighty backbone which runs the entire length of the South Island. The roads travel over long bridges (some crossing rivers up to a kilometre wide), through crop fields and pasture land where lambs are fattened, the fields marked out by the dark green of pine shelter belts. As you head west from the coast the plains turn into the gold brown tussock-covered foothills of the Alps. Here are the sheep stations much larger than most other New Zealand farms and often isolated with a self-contained way of life.

The towns of Canterbury plains are essentially market towns, serving the outlying farming districts. Characteristic of the Canterbury towns are the English trees, elms, oak and planes, planted last century.

The Waimakariri River ran nearby Rangiora, just one of the plains' forceful rivers that plunge down from the Alps often through dramatic gorges, such as the Waimakariri Gorge, and then fan out across the alluvial plains in wide, shingle river beds. By the time the river nears the end of its journey crossing the plains often it is reduced to a number of narrow ribbons of water that navigate the shallow river beds not unlike veins on the palm of a hand.

In some senses, both Rae and I were returning to our roots. For Rae, Christchurch was her much loved home town and her father and brother were close by. Even closer to Rangiora than Christchurch was nearby Ashley where my grandfather had bought some land almost one hundred years earlier and had his blacksmith business, where my grandmother's family had lived and where my father had been born nearly ninety years earlier.

The Methodist Parsonage was at 162[1] King Street, Rangiora. It was a large two storey house and it seemed strange not having my two older sons at home. I missed having my three sons together. Since Roxburgh our family had grown, and now, it was depleting in front of our eyes. It was hard to credit that we had only one child left at home and in just a few more years he would be off too. Life was moving on and it was not all that nice seeing the family move out – and away.

Unknown to us when we arrived in this small town, it was to prove to be my last ministerial appointment. Before leaving Matamata my health had started to deteriorate in slight, minor ways. Nothing was serious, only an increasing weariness and more frequent and more severe migraine headaches. The days on my father's farm after he died were not only symptomatic, as always, of my love for farming, they also made clear to me that I actually *needed* breaks from parish duties. As a minister I was deeply tired and/or deeply unsettled. Looking back, was I unconsciously objecting to the discipline of constantly denying my longing to be a farmer? Whatever it was, it eventually manifested in my health.

---

1 The street has since been re-numbered and the property is now 204 King Street

The move to Rangiora brought refreshment as I faced up to a new parish in new surroundings. But it was not long before I was under the caring eye of the local doctor and before I continued to seek breaks by visiting my sisters in Taranaki for rests. The migraine headaches increased both in frequency and in intensity. They were unbearable. There seemed to be nothing specifically wrong but I rarely felt on top of the world. I had hoped Rangiora would have changed all that. It did not. Eventually I was sent to a specialist in Christchurch and his report recommended a change of occupation. To Rae it was a terrible shock but to me it was a great relief. It was only then I realised just how much I had been feeling under a burden of nervous tension. If we had taken longer to discuss it and consider it, we might have asked for leave of absence for a year, but I was all for the complete change and so the church authorities were notified.

When we went to Rangiora there were fourteen years to go to my normal retirement age. The parish paid us the compliment of suggesting that we stayed the whole of those years with them. However, it was to be four years, not fourteen.

Rangiora was an extensive parish with eight preaching places. There was no other Methodist parish minister between Rangiora and Blenheim (although there was a second minister in my parish). I went to Hawarden, sixty-four kilometres inland from Rangiora towards the Alps, every Sunday afternoon. Beyond here were a number of Methodist families and once or twice a year I would pick up Horace Hansen, a dedicated parishioner, and we would visit these families. Horace was one of those valuable laymen who had a pastoral heart and took a keen interest in the members of the church family. Three of the preaching places were under the direct care of the second minister, so in those places I was involved only as the parish superintendent.

One of the tensest meetings I ever attended concerned the second minister. A complaint had been laid against him at an official level and it had to be dealt with. Complaints about and criticisms of ministers are common enough and I suspect no minister gets through their career unmarked by them, but complaints rarely reach official levels. In this case however we had to sit through the discipline hearings of charge and counter charge. Fortunately for me, the Chairman of the District attended and took the chair. It is an experience that holds no joy for anyone and where each of us felt "there but for the Grace of God go I". It was a case where, not always rightly, the shortcomings of the local church are laid at the door of the minister and he is made the scapegoat for the congregation.

As usual we found some devoted people in Rangiora whose loyalty to and support of the church was wonderful. The Ayers family, Mr and Mrs Ayers Snr and Colin and Ken and their families were among them and their names were well known beyond the local church. There were, too, Ron and Ada Carpenter who became firm friends. So too did the Spark family. Bob Spark, at a young age, took on Circuit Steward duties and we developed a particular friendship. We still keep in touch with many of these friends more than twenty-five years later.

During my term in Rangiora, the church celebrated its centennial anniversary and it was observed in a way worthy of such an occasion. At the banquet we gave Mr Ayers Snr, then eighty years old, the main toast of the evening: "To the founders of the church" – which included his own parents. He gave the speech of the evening. He said, "In my young days, the church was full of old people and now I can find none!"

Rangiora proved to have a number of significant milestones for the family. Rae lost her father while we lived there. We were only a half hour's drive from Christchurch and it was good that we were handy to the hospital and to his home where Rae offered to help his second wife share the caring for him as he aged. He died at home on April 18th 1965, a day after his 82nd birthday. Rae was with him when he passed away in his home, in exactly the same room where her mother's funeral had been held nineteen years earlier.

Another notable milestone that happened while we were in Rangiora was when the first of our children married. I could hardly believe it. It was not our oldest son either, but Riley, then only twenty-one years old. Regrettably we could not afford to attend his wedding for it was in England. He married Anne, second daughter of Air Vice Marshal and Mrs Guy Bearne of the Royal Air Force, on September 6th 1966 in Goring-on-Thames, Oxfordshire. Riley had travelled to England on several occasions with the RNZAF and it was on one of these trips that he met Anne.

Riley brought his new wife out to New Zealand and we met them off the early morning inter-island ferry as it berthed in Lyttelton. We gave a small wedding party for them of our own in the parsonage and invited several of our parishioner friends. It was a happy occasion and Rae positively glowed with pride.

That same week as they stayed with us, Riley invited a young air force friend of his, Ralph Jones, with his new fiancée, to come to dinner with us to meet his new wife. They lived in Christchurch and the journey was only a half hour or so. I remember that night as we waited for them to arrive. But they never did. On the way to us they had been involved in an horrific car accident. They were both seriously injured, Ralph critically. He was unconscious for several weeks. I will always remember the sickening feeling as we realised that something was very wrong as we waited and waited and waited for them to arrive.

It was while we were in Rangiora that Godfrey began to show an interest in a variety of hobbies. None of them, sadly, included chickens but he did want to have a dog. We had always had a cat (it was "Mittens" in Matamata) but never a dog. Here in Rangiora, as yet, we were "pet-less". He chose to have a pug and I still do not understand why, but he was convinced that this was the type of dog he wanted. My sister Ev had a pug (in fact three or four over the years) and perhaps he picked up the attachment from there, but it was not apparent at the time. Most people think pugs are ugly – it is futile to deny. Godfrey however could see only cuteness where others saw ugliness. In fact, as Godfrey was soon to teach us, pugs have been the favourites of the English ruling classes since 1688. Give or take the odd corgi, pugs have long been the darlings of royalty. George III and George IV, Empress Josephine, Queen Victoria (who had thirty six) and the Duke and Duchess of Windsor were all devotees. When William of Orange crossed to Britain to become king in 1688, the Dutch pugs arrived as part of the royal retinue. The pug's bad points which the critics readily point out are its breathing, gluttony, stubbornness and lethargy. It walks in its sleep, snores and suffers nightmares and crying fits. But the strong points are its sunny disposition, good with children and the double twist in their tails which can be used to carry messages around the house!

And so it was amidst such fine history and comment that we helped Godfrey buy a pedigree pug, which was wonderfully named as "Lucky Turk of somewhere", somewhere – which I cannot now recall. Godfrey took to showing Turk in quite a serious way and became devoted to it. Although Turk was officially his dog, it was Rae who actually fell in love with the ugly bundle (and certainly I did too for that matter). Turk used to follow her out to the clothes line every day, to the back of the garden with the rubbish, to the front gate to collect the milk and to the front gate again to collect the mail. It followed her every where – outside and around the house and inside the house from room to room. Rae never thought she would enjoy having a dog, but she found she had a friend.

Turk was only two years old when he was killed by running out at a passing car and being struck by its front wheels and then again by its back wheels. This happened right in front of the parsonage and right in front of Godfrey's eyes on one balmy summer's evening before Christmas 1965. I was in a meeting in the church hall along the road and Godfrey interrupted it. "Can you come home?" he asked, "Mum's very upset. Turk's been killed." We were all upset, surprisingly upset. Mum was in tears and so was I. However, fifteen year old

Godfrey appeared not to be upset at all and was stoically calm. But he was in shock, a state he did not understand and had not experienced before. He did not shed a tear for a week but finally, when the shock eased off and the pain set in, he sobbed uncontrollably. I think it was his first experience of real sadness. He said to me later how awful he felt to realise that he shed more tears over his dog than he did over his grandfather who had died earlier in the year. He was ashamed as well as surprised by that.

Aside from Turk, and aside from his music (he was in the choir and he played the piano, the organ, the cello and even for a while the euphonium) Godfrey developed some new hobbies in Rangiora. He joined the town's amateur dramatic society and one production I recall him being in was Agatha Christie's *Ten Little Niggers*, since re-named *And Then There Were None*. He also became interested in photography and he joined the town's photographic society and converted the coal shed out in the garage into a dark room. He spent many hours developing photographs and enlarging his prints. But that must have been a passing phase, as he has never done it since. When he was thirteen he became a regular writer for the then *Junior Digest* magazine. His interest in writing, unlike his photography, has continued. He wrote an article on the Antarctic crash of Air New Zealand's DC10 which was published in the London *Times*. I have often wondered whether Godfrey developed this range of absorbing hobbies (including his interest in and time with Turk) because in Rangiora for the first time in his life, he was on his own.

Being on his own didn't help when he completely flunked his new secondary school entrance tests. It came as a shock to both him and us when he was placed in Form 3E. His primary schooling in Matamata had always seen him in A or top stream classes. There was obviously something wrong as when he left Intermediate School at Matamata he was in the running for Dux (although he did not get it). Godfrey was shattered, and his pride took a big fall as he could not understand how he could have done so appallingly. We felt for him and wondered if it was because of the move to Rangiora and feeling alone and totally unsettled. We did not seek to interfere with the school's decision and so we waited. Perhaps the standard at Rangiora was much higher than Matamata? Perhaps this was a reality check for Godfrey? Immediately it became apparent that either his tests were inaccurately marked or Godfrey had really and truly had a bad bout of nerves in taking them. He came first, by a long shot, in his 3E class. So at the beginning of the second term he was moved to 3D, where he repeated the process and the next term he was moved again this time to 3C. By the middle of the next year he was back to where I guess he should have been all along, in the top classes (although the streaming system changed right in the middle of his progression) and now he was back in familiar territory – having to struggle to hold his own, because he was by no means "a natural scholar". But the whole experience was not good for him. As he had arrived at Rangiora from Matamata, he had no friends to start school with. He was also for the first time brotherless in the family which I do not believe he liked. Each time he began to establish friends in his new class he was moved on to yet another new class – to start the process of belonging all over again. And of course, human nature being what it is, the boys he had just got to know in the previous class were hardly going to befriend the "nerd". Godfrey told me that starting a new class each term was not rewarding, he hated it. He recognised it for what it was, an adjustment for something that he mucked up on day one, not a promotion. And every time he moved up a class he felt it was like starting a new school – with the same stresses and anxieties. I think he found his adolescent years in Rangiora tough. Eventually, he sat with a new boy to the school (*he* was the "new one" in the class this time, not Godfrey!), whose birthday was only three days before his and from then on they did everything together. Michael King had just started at Rangiora arriving from Invercargill Boys High. Today, some twenty-eight years later, they are the closest of friends, both living in London and still doing things together, cycling weekends in France and such like. Michael, who was always, Godfrey says, top of the class and the brightest kid in the school, is now an eminent psychiatrist in London[1].

Godfrey was not particularly in love with his schooldays. He chose to leave as soon as he could, with his University Entrance accredited. Although today he has his own business, he had always said he wanted to be a school teacher (but we doubt he had even given time to think of anything else). When we left Rangiora for Wanganui, he left home for Palmerston North to start at Massey University and the Teachers' College there.

The church's "Boys' Brigade", similar in many ways to the Scout movement, on a much smaller scale but still worldwide, was strong here. The Brigade's leader was Dutch and he was rather militaristic in his approach. A roar or two and a stiff telling off he regarded as the only technique for achieving discipline, and he didn't shy from putting it into action. New Zealanders do not tend to take kindly to such methods, and in time tensions mounted. A meeting of the management committee was called and the leadership was put under scrutiny. At the end the leader asked if we wanted him to resign, which of course, was just what we did want. Then I muffed it. To let him down kindly, I suggested that he carried on until he completed his ten year term which he had set his heart on, but was two years off. He jumped at it, but was still there at least two years beyond that.

Rangiora was a particularly attractive place to country folk for retirement. As a result my congregation was rather elderly. There was much sick visiting to do and funerals were frequent, about one a week. I found it exhausting on the nerves and emotions. At the same time there was quite a strong Sunday School of about one hundred, and a regular Bible Class attendance of about forty. Space in the church was at a premium at morning services. To alleviate the problem, it was arranged that the children left the service after the second hymn and the Bible Class took their place at that juncture. The congregation

---

1 Now a Professor. April 2004. - GB

would get quite a lift out of seeing the sight of so many young people joining in worship. It was at this time we moved the morning service to ten o'clock.

The church was strong musically. The choirmaster and organist was Alex Lane, a talented musician who worked hard with his choir. The Junior Choir was under the direction of Margaret Spark which was of good size and made a good contribution to the services. Altogether, I felt that Rangiora Methodist Church was a church in very good heart.

It is always a cause for satisfaction when one can build a new church or erect an extension to the church buildings: it is a visible sign of growth, strength and stability for the parish. As usual I relished projects such as these and I was always keen to pursue every opportunity. The Rangiora opportunity was clear enough: the Sunday School hall there was very inadequate and well over one hundred years old. The Bible Class organised a function and invited Bible Class members from other churches around the District. It seemed as if they all came. They packed in like bees in a hive. It was totally impossible to seat them all, so they stood around completely filling the body of the hall. Modern dancing fortunately does not require much floor space per person – I noticed! – but I was mighty relieved[1] when the evening came to an end. Throughout it I held my breath half expecting the floor would literally collapse beneath the stamping feet. It was obvious that a new hall was urgently needed, so at the next meeting of Trustees I made this the top priority on the agenda – with a certain amount of glee. Contact was made with a firm of architects in Christchurch and it must be said they treated us grandly in all our dealings with them. It meant that the wheels had begun to turn and I was delighted. Unfortunately for me, my foreshortened appointment meant that I was not there when the new building ultimately went up. But, as always, I had pursued what one might well call my "parish hobby" of identifying, fund-raising for, starting, and completing a building

---

1 "mighty relieved" – these are Dad's own words and they make me smile as I read them, as it was a phrase which he used "mighty frequently"! - GB

project. Sometimes the parish circumstances did not allow me to complete the whole process, but every parish I served as an ordained minister, I pursued this hobby as faithfully as I pursued any farming one.

But buildings are born and buildings die. At Amberley it was well nigh impossible to get enough support to hold even a monthly service, so in time services were totally withdrawn. No one was happy with the prospect that the empty church would just stand there and inevitably fall into disrepair. It was felt that it was better to have just an empty section provided it did not become a jungle of weeds. So a team of men from Rangiora fell upon it with hammers, wrecking bars and chain saws. It was a sad ovation especially as in earlier times it had once been the centre of a very vigorous church life and had established a proud record. But the face of Methodism in Canterbury was going through vast changes. Preaching places throughout the Plains had been disappearing over a number of years, significantly influenced by the changes in agricultural methods, the increasing number of personally owned motor cars and the groomed, macadamised roads.

All my life I always felt there was something more to do: I could never feel that I caught up on everything. It was my father's good old work ethic. I even felt guilty reading any book or newspaper for pure pleasure (I am sure I can count the number of novels I have read on one hand). The pressure I put on myself to perform and to improve and to do more was good for me in many ways and I enjoyed it. But at the same time it was bad for me for I could not relax. Occasionally I would play tennis or bowls or go on a picnic or attend a concert. When I did it was usually done as a duty, a feeling that I ought to be associated with someone or other, or some group or other, because they were members of my congregation, or friends or relations who had some claim on my loyalty or support. Invariably when I was out supposedly enjoying myself, at the back of my mind I would be thinking that there was some task back home that I should be doing or that I should not really be here or that I should leave very soon and do some *work*. When I later took up school teaching I found it helpful to have my teaching duties regulated by a timetable, and the term breaks were determined for me by powers outside my control.

In the ministry all these kind of regulatory forces were practically absent and so I let the pressure of unfinished tasks drive me along. Towards the end of my ministry I found myself waking up in the early hours of the morning to write down ideas for next Sunday's sermon: I was sleeping poorly. When I suffered from my increasingly frequent and increasingly severe migraines I would come home to rest for a large part of the day. I required the house to be darkened and quiet. Godfrey recalls arriving home from school to be told on so many days that I was upstairs asleep and acutely sensitive to light and noise.

So it was not altogether surprising when the doctor said I should leave the ministry and take on a less stressful job. I was then fifty-five years old, a difficult age to be changing horses. I had by that time put in thirty-four years of active ministry. It was ending. For one year, 1967, I was officially "resting". In 1968, I left the church formally and became a supernumerary.

It was over.

W R Young BA, MB, ChB, Dip Obst, Rangiora

TO WHOM IT MAY CONCERN

This is to certify that Rev C H Bell has been a patient of mine for 3 years. During this time he has been treated for recurring migraine, nervous dyspepsia, tension headaches, insomnia and other related psychosomatic disorders. These arise from the stressful demands of his work which I think is not entirely suited to a man of over-conscientious temperament.

I think it is advisable that alternative employment be considered, free from such strain, to correct his present symptoms and ensure his maintained good health in the future.

W R Young, 3.2.1966

W R Young BA, MB, ChB, Dip Obst Rangiora

TO WHOM IT MAY CONCERN

Further to my certificate of 3.2.1966, I was requested to arrange a second opinion for Rev C H Bell. On 5.4.66 he saw Dr M H Aiken[1], a psychiatric physician of Christchurch. In a letter to me of that date, Dr Aiken said he agreed that Mr Bell's symptoms —

"are largely due to occupational stresses, and it would be regrettable if he had to retire at this stage. On the other hand, should he continue, or attempt to do so, he will almost certainly break down with what might be a crippling illness. It might be sound economy to retire him now. In fact, I am sure of this. No amount of medication can enable him to carry on efficiently and safely when this type of warning appears and you would be justified in insisting on a change of occupation to one more suited to his personality structure."

W R Young, 18.4.1966

1 This is the same doctor who attended Charles's mother-in-law Hilda Barrell 20 years earlier.

Retirement Tribute from *Methodist Conference Journal* 1967

As a church we deeply regret that strains on his health have compelled Charles Harrison Bell to retire from the active ministry at the comparatively early age of 55. At the same time we are grateful that he gave himself with such complete devotion to the Gospel over these last 34 years.

Just as the young fisherman, Peter, was called from the sea of Galilee to fish among men in Palestine, so the young farmer Charles was called to become a pastor of men. He never got farming right out of his blood. Indeed, only the strength of his continuing call to the Ministry prevented him from going back to the land. The only break in rural life had come when his mother, in spite of straitened finances, had the foresight and wisdom to send him for two years to New Plymouth Boys High School. As a young man working on the family farm in Wharehuia and attending the vital little church about half a mile away, he first heard the call. His parents and sisters have given very much to the life of our Church, and it is particularly appropriate that the only son should have become a Minister of the Word and Sacraments. At the age of 21 he was sent by the Home Mission Department to North Auckland - first Kaikohe - Kawakawa and then North Hokianga - from 1933-38, including four months as a colporteur, introducing books and sound films to Methodists in the North Island. Since then he has always had an eye for a good book.

Accepted as a candidate, he was trained at Trinity Theological College for the three years of 1938-40 and was ordained in 1945. As a Probationer he went to Christchurch East and Roxburgh, afterwards serving at Wellington East (5 years), Richmond, Nelson now Waimea (5 years), Matamata (8 years) and Rangiora (4 years). At the same time that he became a Probationer he decided to study for an Arts degree. With an iron determination he continued this special study while he had a young family around him, and amid all the demands of a Circuit ministry. It was a great day for his friends as well as himself when in 1949 he gained his BA cap at Victoria University College.

He has never been detached from his work. Identifying himself closely with people, he has given everything he had to the many sided tasks of ministry. He has read widely and deeply, preached strongly and thoughtfully, cared for people with singular devotion, shared camps, leadership schools, ecumenical encounters. He has taken his share of Connexional duties as District Secretary and at the Conference table. In every Circuit he has engaged in building projects, perhaps the most notable and strategic being in Matamata, initiated by him and supported generously by his people there.

Most men in the Ministry would probably prefer a tribute that speaks, not so much of their service to the Church, but of the way the Church has served them. This is the case with Charles Bell. When the Church confirmed his call, he would describe himself as a rather raw and rugged youth from a farm – but the Church opened up for him a world of education and scholarship, contributed greatly to his family life, led him into many situations of privilege, and enabled him to concentrate his energies on a full time service of God and of people. In the course of doing it he has made friends all over New Zealand, and in his person radiates friendliness. By his words and his life he has helped make Christian discipleship real and relevant to many. It is because of the intensity with which he pursued his ministry that those threats to his health have come.

Charles Bell and Rae Barrell of Riccarton were married in 1942. This brought into being a rich partnership in friendship and hospitality and outgoing service that has given happiness to many people and has proved a unique standard of life and vocation for their three sons. Now that the load of responsibility is lightened, he and his wife will be a rare asset to the local church and District in Wanganui where they have made their home. They have the gratitude and good wishes of the whole Church.

Godfrey (14), Riley (19), Weston (21), Charles (52), Rae (56)
Studio photo taken in Christchurch, Dec 1964

Riley (21) marries Anne Bearne,
Goring-on-Thames, England
6th September 1966

Rangiora Methodist Women's Fellowship October 1965. Front row from left: Jean Rands, Rae, Charles, Shirley Ayers

Rae and Charles in the much loved rose garden of Rae's twin Charles Barrell's home, 12 Rotherham Street, Riccarton, Christchurch about 1964

Rae at the gate of the Methodist Parsonage ready for church in her "Sunday best" Rangiora 1964

Charles and Rae, Rangiora, about 1964

Riley, Godfrey and Weston with their grandfather Charles Weston Barrell, Rangiora 1963

Charles & Rae's last Methodist Parsonage. Rangiora 162 King Street. Godfrey's pug dog, "Turk", is the small blob sitting at the gate. Dec 1963

Rangiora Methodist Church, King Street, 1963

Chapter 19

KIDS, PIGS and GLADIOLI

1967 – 1983

Wanganui

I don't quite know why we chose to live in Wanganui. I had no job and Godfrey had left home. We did not need to consider the children, or my career, but we settled for Wanganui.

The city was a thriving area of Maori settlement before the pakeha arrival. It has the largest regional museum in New Zealand and a famous Maori Court holds a seventy-five foot Maori war canoe and an extensive collection of rare greenstone artefacts. Wanganui is also well known as the exit point for the wild beauty of the Whanganui River which flows from the Volcanic Plateau. In the upper reaches a rapid churning mass of water twists through steep, bush covered gorges, the lower reaches gliding gently between willow-fringed banks. The river is navigable to Taumarunui and has more than two hundred and forty rapids attracting summer canoeing and jet boat safaris. Many places around Wanganui have biblical names, for example Jerusalem, and others are translated as near as possible to Maori, like Atene (Athens) and Korinti (Corinth).

This was the place we chose or which chose us. It was near to Palmerston North where Godfrey could go to both university and teachers' college as he was planning to do. And it was not far from my sisters. When I took the decision to heed the doctor's advice and end my active ministry, the big question was what was I to do. I was only fifty-five, too young and too poor to retire, but first I rationalised, above all we must find a home (I think others may have said I must first find a job). When I was staying with my sister at Stratford during one of my sick spells in that last year in Rangiora, I joined her family on a trip to Wanganui two or three hours south of Stratford. To fill in time while they did their business I contacted a land agent and looked at some houses. I found one that had some appeal to me so I sent an urgent message to Rae in Rangiora to join me in Wanganui the following day. She flew up and I was delighted when she too loved it. So somewhat fortuitously, Wanganui became our next home – and the first one we had ever owned in our lives.

At the end of the year we moved in to "Hillcrest", 196 Great North Road, St Johns Hill, Wanganui. It was right on the very northern edge of Wanganui, amongst the last houses before the main road broke free of the urban sprawl into the countryside. It was a small but lovely home. It looked out onto farmland and sheep (to my particular delight) and the view could not be built out. There was a farm to the left of the perimeter fence which was lined with tall poplar trees that framed our rural view quite perfectly.

When we first arrived in Wanganui we did not even have a table to eat from nor a bed to sleep in. The ministry involved us in living in "tied" houses, hence when we retired we had next to nothing in the way of furniture. Because our earlier retirement superannuation was not as large as it would have been had I completed my career in the church, it took all of it to pay the deposit on the house. It was not very long before we were scraping the bottom of the barrel[1]. I was fifty-five and it had come to this. We were starting from scratch as a newly married couple would thirty years our junior. I felt disappointed. I felt bad. I felt for Rae: had I let her down? I felt bad for my children.

---

[1] I have learned since that the money situation was critical but Mum and Dad never once let on, to me anyway, how desperate it really was for quite a while. - GB

Here I was at the end of my career and I had nothing for them. Nothing. I could not bear the thought. Rae was deeply anxious about this change of lifestyle but as usual and as always, she was totally and utterly supportive.

The first and urgent requirement was to get a job. Because of my age, this was not easy. However, my degree did open up possibilities in the professional world. One of the things I did not want to do was school teaching. I felt that my continuing migraine headaches would put me under tensions not unlike the ones I had had in the ministry and which were partly the cause of my early retirement. But school teaching was the one job which found me, rather than me find it. The principal of the Wanganui High School was a member of the local Methodist congregation. He offered me a position at his school and at first I hesitated saying I had one or two other opportunities in the pipe line and, grateful as I was, I could not accept immediately. But other opportunities there were not, or at least, they all drew blanks. I reported to school for a part time job.

Wanganui Central Circuit Trinity Methodist Church
TO WHOM IT MAY CONCERN

This is to certify that I have known the bearer of this letter, Rev Charles H Bell, for many years, and know him to be of excellent character. Mr Bell is conscientious in all that he undertakes and gives himself freely to his work.

He is of good standing in the ministry of the Methodist Church of New Zealand and is held in the highest esteem by his brother ministers.

I very gladly supply this reference in support of his application.

(Rev) Alan O Jones, October 16th 1967

Wanganui High School
TO WHOM IT MAY CONCERN

Rev C H Bell has been a friend of mine for a number of years and this year he has been a relieving assistant for two terms on my staff. I have pleasure in writing on his behalf.

In previous years I knew Mr Bell's father and his sisters, actively concerned with the Methodist Church, Hawera. I had a great respect

for them and I know Mr Bell comes from a family of integrity and character. I have found him to possess these qualities.
He is the kind of person in whom one instinctively places confidence. His manner is genial and gentlemanly and on acquaintance it is soon obvious that it is the outward portrayal of a natural unselfishness and concern for others. His religious convictions govern his life and translate into a philosophy and conduct of assistance to others.
I found him a man of intellect. He has read and studied deeply and in discussion his statements are closely reasoned and concerned with things important. He is interested in social and world trends.
As an assistant Mr Bell fitted in well with school requirements. To attempt another occupation at his age requires adaptability. Mr Bell had a genuine interest in young people and he set about his new work conscientiously.
I am grateful to him for the work he did on this staff.
A T (?) Gibson MA DipEd, Principal
12th October 1967

My first year teaching was not good. I did not enjoy it and I found keeping discipline hard, very tiring and unfulfilling. But it offered me a good salary, defined hours, weekends off, and some peace of mind for Rae and me as we started out alone and in debt with the new house. The second and subsequent years proved to be better, but only slightly. I reminded myself all the time that I had to be grateful that a job had turned up for me at all, and at the right time.

The principal was mindful of my health condition and initiated me gently by giving me supervision of classes doing study periods. After a term of this I was given a couple of classes of slow learners. On paper that sounds all right but in reality it is probably harder than dealing with bright children. My patience was put to the test as it never had been before. Now and again the pupils would get excited as they came to understand something in maths and all they wanted to do was more and more exercises of the same thing because it was satisfying for them. The following week, however, they would have forgotten entirely how it was done. I came to have a great admiration for teachers of slow learners. Their patience with them and understanding of them was incredible.

The third term saw me move on to the Wanganui Boys College because of the arrival of some overseas teachers that the principal of the High School had contracted for employment in the previous year. I was now treated as a normal full time teacher and was expected to pull my full weight. The migraine headaches were still dogging me and most weeks saw me go down with one, but they were beginning to a get a little less frequent. Having the classes finish at 3:20 each day was a boon to me after having no such time parameters in my ministry days. By hanging on grimly, I generally could get through a day and then hurry home to lie down and pass into the glorious oblivion of sleep. The days after such occasions were often heavy going because I was left exhausted and often went to school unprepared for my lessons. However, the work-free weekends followed by the long holidays helped tremendously, and in the course of two or three years the migraine attacks became more rare.

In that first year of teaching I had taught at two schools and at the end of it both principals separately announced their resignations. It became a staff room joke that it was teacher Reverend Bell who had finished off two principals in his first year on the staff.

It took me some time to find the clue to class discipline (if I ever did). On this score children presented a different challenge from that of my parishioners. I tended at first to treat them as young adults but soon learned that they did not respond as adults. I had always regarded myself as even tempered, but at that late stage in my life, as a school teacher I learned that I was not. I was shocked to discover my weakness and disappointed that I could not contain it. I found myself raising my voice in anger – or, more truthfully, in frustration. And I had the right lungs for the job. In my Theological College days I had taken voice production lessons and I could emit a good roar if the occasion demanded. Sometimes the class would fairly jump as I erupted. At the same time I knew that that was by no means any form of an admirable technique for keeping control. Against my better judgement I even resorted to caning from time to time. I have always believed that schools can and should be run without resorting to corporal punishment. But, I figured, if corporal punishment is to be avoided, the school must gear itself to the fact and provide for alternative forms of discipline.

On one occasion, a boy came to the school who had been pushed around from home to home as a foster child and this meant being pushed around to almost every school in the area. The result was a very unsettled, disturbed boy, who was difficult to handle and a disruptive influence in every classroom. As I was taking the class one day I noticed that I had opened my cupboard and left the keys in the door. I made a mental note to collect the keys and went on with the lesson. The bell rang for the end of the period and the boys tumbled out to go to the classroom for roll call by their form master just before lunch break. I went to collect my keys and they were missing. Immediately I suspected our troublemaker, so I hurried to his class's form room to investigate. Nobody was forthcoming with any keys or any information. By this time my anger was beginning to rise as my car keys were on the ring and I was unable to go home for lunch and the lunch hour was melting away. I asked the suspect to show me his bag and his locker. At his locker he brought out his gear but left some things in the back. When I demanded that he bring out the rest, he said that it belonged to his friend who shared the locker with him. The corridors had filled up with boys on their way to lunch. Under this cover, one of his friends had cleared the locker of the rest of the articles in it. By this time my temper was fully aroused when suddenly I found my heart racing and pains shooting through my chest. I knew immediately that I was putting myself at risk, so had to drop the matter. Later on one of the boys in the class confided in me that he had seen the boy I suspected take the keys.

It was only a matter of a few weeks later I was again in confrontation with the same boy, and I told the principal that either the boy was moved from my class or I would leave. (I was acting only as a relieving teacher at this stage, so was under no obligatory contract to stay.) I was taken aback when some time later they told me the boy was expelled. I did not really want that as I felt it was only going to add to his problems.

In my second year I stepped into the shoes of the departing teacher of Commercial Practice and I found this more to my liking. One lad did particularly well at it and in due course took up teaching in the same subject as a career. A term or two later, the teacher of bookkeeping moved away on promotion and I was asked to pick it up as being a related subject to commercial practice. In my high school days I had a smattering of the subject taught me, so building on that I kept myself a lesson ahead of my pupils. But it was in commercial practice I was first entrusted with a School Certificate class and in my second year had a higher than average pass rate. The next year I was given, in addition, a 5th Form English class. It was a low stream which had never had a School Certificate pass in the previous years, so I had an uphill fight. My year of tuition was no more successful than my predecessors but at least one pupil came within two marks of a pass[1].

Among my extra-curricular activities was the coaching of a rugby team. They called themselves "Bell's Angels".

Once a year the secondary schools of Wanganui supplied collectors for the Corso appeal, Corso being one of New Zealand's largest charities for the hungry and poorly clothed. This cause was close to my heart so I took responsibility for organising the Boys' College group. It was always held across

---

[1] It has always been my own view, having been a teacher myself both here in NZ and in London for a short while, that teachers whose main strength lies in their subject knowledge should take the top streams, but teachers whose main strength lies in their SKILL as teachers, should take the lower streams and slow learners. It was very tough on Dad, an untrained and inexperienced teacher, to be given some of the most difficult and certainly the most challenging classes in the school. What those classes needed were top SKILLED teachers, not simply "intelligent" graduates! - GB

the country in the heart of winter in mid-June and more than once we had to contend with cold and wet weather. The worst moment though came when we discovered that some of the boys had been helping themselves from the collecting tins. All collectors were called to the assembly hall, told what it was all about, and it was then explained that several of the staff would be waiting outside the doors until the culprits owned up, or others who knew who the culprits were came out and gave in names. It was a long wait, but in the end one boy after another came out to the teachers. A few days later there was a line up of teachers, culprits and canes and quite a session resulted. It was all over before I heard about it, the teachers explaining that they did not think I should be involved. I don't know whether they didn't think I could cane hard enough or whether it was in deference to my being a clergyman.

One Friday lunch time the deputy principal asked to see me. The bell had gone for starting the afternoon classes and I hesitated to go, suggesting I came at the end of the day. But he insisted it would not take long. All the other classes had started, however, by the time I walked down the corridor approaching my own room. I was expecting to be greeted by an unholy din but instead there was an eerie silence. Puzzled as to why it was, I walked in and there in the seat was the principal. It was the first and only time he had visited my class and he was there to observe my teaching. Completely bowled, I tried to gather my thoughts and blundered on, but I had been so taken aback and ill prepared for The Visit that I made some ridiculous mistakes and on each one my confidence evaporated further. In the end I stopped trying to teach and gave the class some writing work to do. It was a murderous hour for me and the principal never referred to it, so I guess he was pretty unimpressed. Frankly, nor was I.

I hated teaching to tell you the truth and I resented having to do it. I began to hate Monday mornings and dread the week ahead – a feeling I never had as a minister. I concluded that I had gone out of the frying pan into the fire. My health had improved slightly and my income was better than the ministry. But I was not enjoying myself. What I still wanted to do more than anything else in the world was farm but there was little I could do about my predicament. Even if I had been a young and healthy man (which I wasn't) I still had no money to set myself up on a farm. Adding to my problems was the fact that in the last few years I had developed an arthritic hip. It seemed clear that there were no more chances of ever getting on to the land again.

As usual though I always read the agricultural columns and news in the newspaper. I spied land for sale night after night for years on end. I could well have become the local commentator on Wanganui's farm estate business, without ever being a farmer or an estate agent. One evening as I sat in front of the fire and read the paper, I spotted that there was a piggery up for lease. I thought I just might be able to afford a lease, so I followed it up. It was the third largest piggery in the Wanganui area, so I was faced with an outlay of thousands of dollars which I did not have. As was typical of me I felt in those situations I was not to be defeated at the first hurdle so I approached a stock firm with an idea. This concluded in an arrangement with them that made it possible to take on the lease.

The piggery was called Kaitoke Piggeries but I set up a company, Coldstream Ventures Limited for the business, and an advertisement in the paper produced an experienced manager. Soon I found myself in business producing pork and bacon. Reverend Pig Farmer! Indeed I used my title and my hardly relevant arts degree (with Greek!) on the piggery company letterhead. The Reverend as Managing Director of a piggery must surely have been unique and caused a wry smile or two, of disbelief or at the very least intrigue. It was July 1969. My eyes and heart lifted once more and I found some renewed enthusiasm in my days. I became greatly absorbed in the piggery and working out balances of nitrogen and carbohydrates and trace elements was quite a challenge – and enjoyable. And so was the relationship of food intake with weight increase. The merits of marketing porkers as against baconers was another call for intensive study.

Letterhead:

Coldstream Ventures Ltd	Managing Director
Section: Kaitoke Piggeries	Rev C H Bell BA
Registered office	196 Great North Road
McDonald and Bell	Wanganui
Maria Place	Phone 30 368
Wanganui	
Phone 4140	

Newspaper advertisement:

Coldstream Ventures Ltd: Capital $3,000 Subscribers C H Bell 1600 shares, H R Bell 1100, and W T Bell 300. Farmers and studmasters.

Advances:

Wellington property[1]	$2,000
Insurance	$1,000
Shares WTB	$300
3rd mortgage Wellington property	$700
Freeman R Jackson	$5,445

All of this was not conducive for keeping my mind on teaching. I often found myself gazing from the school in the direction of Kaitoke and the piggery just on the southern outskirts of Wanganui, in eager anticipation of the end of the school day so I could go and visit it.

When the piggery manager R Bennett left after four years I felt ready to tackle it on my own. It was 1973 and I was sixty years old. At long, long last I resigned from school teaching and an enormous heavy burden lifted from my shoulders[2]. It felt absolutely wonderful to be doing my own thing. I felt a sense of freedom, an excitement and a sense of hope that had escaped me for many years.

---

[1] 62 Haumai Street, Wellington

[2] But he appears to have returned to teaching (presumably part time or on a relief basis) at some time: he was teaching while he had Whangaehu farm in 1979. Strangely though Dad doesn't make any formal reference to returning to teaching in any of his notes or diaries although he refers to being offered a temporary Senior Teacher position which he turned down. Despite this in a 1979 diary he writes that he "went out [to farm] after school" (2nd April 1979). - GB

Purchases:

11 July 1969	322 pigs	$7,475
	Truck	$600
	Tractor	$120
	Milk tank	$150
27 January 1970	1 boar (Eric) born Aug 1967	$46
	4 sows	$194
28 January 1970	4 sows	$355
29 January 1970	8 weaners	$90
1 April 1973	Take over from R Bennett, 1 truck, pigs . etc	$8,152

[Dad wrote up his accounts by hand with little notes to himself in exercise books. Last of his own records were dated 1974-75. The care with which he wrote up the detail is, somehow, a manifestation of his deep delight in farming. - GB]

Some of my pig food came from wastage at the local biscuit factory and I collected about two tonnes of this every Saturday morning. A local dairy factory produced whey in season so I carted this to the piggery in a fifteen hundred gallon tanker each day. This required me to have a Heavy Vehicle Licence and I was rather thrilled with myself when I got it – at my age. But it was not easy to get used to. Driving the tanker was rather tricky when loaded up with whey, especially going downhill when it seemed the load was more in control than I was. It was particularly tricky coming down St Johns Hill the main road into Wanganui. Even with the brakes hard on, I always wondered if I could bring it to a complete halt at the railway line which crossed the road at the bottom of the hill.

One Sunday afternoon, on the way to the piggery in my truck, I was coasting down the gentle hill of the main road which swept past Virginia Lake on St Johns Hill, a beautiful lake with a park at the side of the road. Today the park was full of Sunday picnickers. Suddenly I heard some squeaks coming from the wheel and within seconds I saw racing down the hill ahead of me, a front wheel of the truck. I was horrified. I slammed on my brakes and eased the laden truck to a stop, miraculously without tipping it. At the same time I was holding my breath watching the wheel careering down the road on the edge of the crowd. Just there, there was a slight bend in the kerbing. It hit the kerb, hurtled into the air, sailed over the heads of the crowd at about three metres, and plunged dramatically into the lake. If it had not been for the shock and real danger of the situation it would have made a terrific action-packed movie scene. There followed all kinds of complications in getting the truck towed away and other things, but nothing seemed too much trouble after my relief at the wheel not hitting anybody.

I preached occasionally in Wanganui. I helped out with services in the local churches and sometimes the Presbyterians also called on me. When the Turakina Parish fell vacant I was engaged by them for Sunday services and half a day a week for visiting. This continued for eight months until a new minister was appointed. When the minister of my own church, Trinity Methodist, needed to go on an overseas trip, I took over his services for three months. It was good to keep my hand in. One service however was quite unscheduled. As the minister started his sermon he stumbled over the first sentence or two, announced he had come over ill and could not continue whereupon he disappeared into the vestry. Several officials rushed to his aid and so I went to the pulpit. In spite of all my years of experience, my mind went blank and I could think of nothing to say. As a matter of fact I thought of several things to say but felt I could not enlarge on any one of them in any sensible fashion. I discarded each idea as quickly as it came to me, panicking all the more with each passing moment. In the end I decided to close the service and announced a hymn. From the choir came a voice telling me we had just sung the hymn I had announced. But he did me the kindness of suggesting an alternative. I was embarrassed and surprised at my inability to cope with the situation. Had I been out of the ministry for too long? Had my confidence eluded me in the intervening years? Had my ease with pouring out whey usurped my ease with pouring out words?

My piggery days came and went. The six year lease on the piggery ended. Rae was not sorry to see the end of the smelly clothes which I dumped in the laundry and which she so faithfully and uncomplainingly washed day after day. But I was sorry. I had enjoyed my pigs very much and I found myself with nothing to do. The school had asked me to do some teaching but it amounted to only a few hours a week. And I was not in a hurry to go back to that anyway.

In 1976 a dream came true. We went on a wonderful trip to Europe. It was the first time I had ever left New Zealand's shores (I was sixty-four) and it was Rae's second, but for both of us, Europe itself was a very big first. Having Godfrey in London was the draw card: an opportunity not to be missed. On Tuesday 2nd March 1976 we left Wanganui to spend our first night with my sister Evelyn in Taranaki. Then we went on to Auckland and stayed with Riley and family. We flew to Sydney with Air New Zealand with Riley on board and spent the weekend at Travel Lodge Motel in King's Cross. On Riley's birthday, Monday March 8th, we left Sydney on a Lufthansa flight to Frankfurt and then on to London. All the way, neither Rae nor I really believed that at our age we were heading away on our big "OE"[1] approximately forty-five years later than most who set off on theirs.

Godfrey lived at 41a Porchester Terrace in Bayswater, London, at that time and the apartment was too small for us to stay with him. But for our first few nights we stayed in a hotel just around the corner. We visited our daughter-in-law's parents, Guy and Aileen Bearne at their home "Fagus" in Goring-on-Thames, near Reading. It was a beautiful village and the biggest thrill for us was to see the church where Riley was married.

Before the end of March we had bought a 1970 Volkswagen, with a mileage of 66,000, for £675. Rae and I and our little car set off to see our big new world of the United Kingdom together. We hired cottages, farmhouses and flats at strategically selected points from where we could do one or two day trips to form a spider's web of travel and visits across the country. One cottage we took at Evesham we liked so much we

---

1 "Overseas Experience" - which most young New Zealanders do as a matter of routine before settling down to their "serious lives".

returned there three times. In so doing, we became good friends of the Stows who owned the place. We also set up temporary homes at Flint, Flintshire (North Wales), Honiton, Devon, Sandy, Bedfordshire, Cambridge, Ruthin, Denbighshire (North Wales), and Sennybridge, Powys (Wales). Unless I relate every day of our trip[1], I can only recall names and places at random. For the next few months, we toured and visited Cornwall, Wales, the Lake District, Scotland, Scarborough, Colchester, Cambridge, Ely Cathedral, Carlisle, Gretna Green, Dumfries and Galloway and Dumfries itself – as well, of course, as spending a lot of time in London. In London I went to the Oval (to see the end of the West Indies test) and Rae and I dropped in on the British Government busily working in the House of Commons. Rae was keen to complete a kind of shopping pilgrimage and this included a seemingly unending list of shops including Heals, Habitat, Harrods, Selfridges, John Lewis and Peter Jones. Of course we also "ticked off" all the major tourist attractions such as the Tower of London, Westminster Abbey, St Pauls, Kew Gardens, Greenwich and so on. On 11th July we went to the International Eisteddfod at Llangollen in North Wales with Godfrey. A few days later Riley and Anne and family visited us too during their own trip to the UK. That was wonderful.

An extract from Dad's diary which he started to fill in daily from the moment he departed Wanganui. It is symbolic of his excitement at the first trip he made out of New Zealand. It also provokes one to reflect that he was experiencing something that his children and grandchildren had already experienced – international travel – and were already becoming somewhat blasé about it. But to Dad, it was a dream come true and an enormous adventure. — GB

Tuesday 2nd March 1976

We got away at 2.10pm to the waves and good-byes of Weston, Dolly, Eric and Madeline [Buchendale][2]. An hour or two earlier it looked hopeless and Madeline declared it couldn't be done. Rae said it would be within 30 minutes of specified time. Had morning tea with Dolly (scones) and lunch with Buchendale's (macaroni cheese). Eric loaded

[1] Every single day is carefully written up in great detail in Dad's trip diary.

[2] Next door neighbours

suitcases in the car and the VW carrier for Riley. Landed a ticket for overrun meter. Bank took longer than expected but finally ironed out after travel manager came to house and got Rae to sign travel cheques at home. Met Jean, Don and Alison at Stratford (3.40pm) had cup of tea and enjoyable chat and final goodbyes. Ev Bell's for tea at 6pm and a restful evening.

Wednesday 3rd March 1976

A quiet day. Len and Gwen in for dinner and spent a few hours chatting. Tom and Jim McDowall for dinner at night. Jim brought his hot rod. A nice job, with its chrome parts sparkling.

Thursday 4th March 1976

Away at 9.10am Morning tea (80c) at Mokau. Lunch 1pm at Te Awamutu. Petrol ($5) at Hamilton and on to Riley's. Warmly greeted by all the family. A nice dinner and a good chat about tripping in general.

Friday 5th March 1976

A morning in town fixing up about purchase of BMW. Riley advised against air conditioning. Looks as if 300 line could be quite good. Worth investigating. Britrail gone up and haven't left enough money in account to meet it. Left cheque ($142) with Riley and $50 to pay by Weston. Petch coming to tea tonight.

A most enjoyable evening with the Petch's. Anne served a tasty meal which we all enjoyed and so to bed for our last night in New Zealand. Hard to realise that things have really arrived at this.

Saturday 6th March 1976

A good start and left on scheduled time as calculated by Riley (8.35), Charles and Frances [Pollock] met us at airport and we had morning tea together. Anne kept reminding us that announcements were being made about our flight. We just didn't hear them! Not a good omen for launching babes into a foreign world and a new experience!

Said goodbye to the children and we were ushered aboard. Found ourselves in middle row. Not a good position for seeing out, but later at 35,000 feet, it didn't make any difference. Modern travel is fast and efficient but not attractive. It's a matter of sitting and waiting for the time to pass. (Not promising for the 20 hour leg to London later on!) However, the excellent meal was an occasion and helped pass the time. The crew certainly earn their wages, coping with all they do in the time available. A visit to the cockpit was of most interest. A bit awe-inspiring to a novice. Pilot most friendly and full of good advice for holidaying in the UK. Co-pilot an old boy of Wanganui Boys College from the 1950s.

Had a small fright when what we thought was our case disappeared. However, the real one turned up later.

Driving in from airport we were taken on a Cook's tour of Sydney. Driver delivered passengers to their various destinations. By this time we had seen a lot of Sydney and were utterly confused. Riley knew all about it and helped us to get orientated haling taxis as required.

Traffic is mad. Taxi engines are so rough one expects they will stop altogether. Interested to find so few long haired louts about. People often scantily dressed and few with bras, but all clean and tidy. Riley shouted us to a ferry trip and a visit to the Opera House – a tremendous achievement. Also next shout was dinner at a Chinese restaurant. Had a great meal, duck, beef, chicken – each one in a delicious gravy with rice and vegetables. Visited Riley's hotel – a fabulous place ($45 for a bed). Looked out over Sydney from top of hotel – 26 storeys up. Sheer luxury. Sydney is a strange place – a mixture of super modern and really old. Restaurants, motels, churches, houses, flats, shops of all kinds in a complete mix-up. Seems to have no centre. (Although a bus trip on Sunday showed us that there is a commercial centre up from Circular Quay).

Interesting to discover that the famous King's Cross, which is a real centre of Sydney's life (commercially and in every other way) is a landmark. Several properties in the area were once owned by Edward Riley[1], one of the family ancestors[2] who came to Australia in the early 1800s[3]. Riley's hotel and where we are staying (Motel Lodge) are actually in this area that Edward Riley owned. There is a street (Riley Street) named after him; also Sophia Street after one his daughters.

Riley left us after 8pm and we went to bed soon after. Plenty tired by this time.

In August we did an even more daring and exciting trip. We left on a European guided tour – to Germany, Austria, Italy and

---

1 Edward Riley 1784-1825 (and his brother Alexander Riley 1778-1833)

2 The link to our Rileys has yet to be established, although it has long been suspected that there is a connection. - GB

3 When Edward Riley died in 1925 he owned "several large freehold estates" of considerable value, including "farms and lands, and buildings and houses in Sydney, a windmill, and a mansion house at Woolloomooloo". [Ref *Sydney Morning Herald* 16 April 1832 re Supreme Court hearing over Edward's estate]

Switzerland! On August 11th we flew from Heathrow to Munich from where we began our tour. After a beautiful drive through mountains and villages, lit up only by the bright moonlight, we arrived at Mutters in Austria where we spent our first night. We were awakened at 6am by a chorus of church bells. On Monday 13th September we visited Innsbruck. It was thirty-three years to the day since we rejoiced in the arrival of our first born. I could not help reflecting what a long way removed in time, place, experience and situation this day was from then. We went on to Venice, driving through the Dolomites which were awe-inspiring. From Venice we went on to Cabenabbia (Lake Como), then Verona, Lugano, Beleggio, St Moritz and Innsbruck. In Switzerland we stayed in the Hotel Albana (St Moritz) which for us was quite luxurious and we enjoyed our stay there immensely. On our last day when we were returning to Mutters, our coach ran into the back of another. It was not really a bad smash but it was surprising how shaken up some people were. Some were shaking, one was in tears and another was vomiting. There were a few minor injuries such as bruised knees, bitten tongues, bumped foreheads. We had to wait for more than an hour for a new coach to come and pick us up. Rhona, the courier, was great and sprang to everyone's help, but we feared the driver would lose his licence so we all signed a letter to protect him. It seemed to work and later we heard he had been fined, but kept his job. On Saturday 26th September we returned to Munich and caught our flight back to London.

We stayed with Godfrey in London only a week, with a day trip to Brighton, before we left for Italy again. This time to Rome. On Wednesday 6th October there we were in Rome – quite unbelievable. A city of many centuries of history – known to us by name all our lives but little dreaming that we would one day walk its streets ourselves. We spent five days in Rome visiting all the sights, struggling with the language, eating unusual food. And this time we did it all alone, with no help of a courier in an organised tour. We were quite proud of ourselves.

After seven months in the UK and 13,000 miles we sold our VW car in London for £200. We left London for home on 6 November. We had a stopover night in Munich before flying on to Sydney. We arrived in Sydney at 7.30am and stayed at the motel we stayed at on the way through. We slept the rest of the day. Rae was ill the next day and slept all that day away too. We arrived back in New Zealand to be met by Riley and Hilary and then to their home to a warm welcome. It was a lovely feeling to be back in our native country. It was 10 November 1976.

Our wonderful trip was over. I was home and had no more pigs to occupy me. So what could I do now? I could not just sit there. Surely I could still do something out on the land. But what? At my age? And what may not send Rae into resigned, quiet, despair with her ever restless husband? (How she longed for me to stay at home and read a book![1])

I spotted an opportunity when Weston sold off a small part of his hundred acre farm in Whangaehu. A road ran through a corner of Weston's farm separating off six acres with a house on it. In 1977 I bought this from Weston although he let me have it while I still owed him money for it. I decided to use the six acres for market gardening. It was exciting to have some land again and I was thrilled.

Lo and behold, what better thing to follow pigs, than gladioli! Staggered yet again at my new hobby as she was, Rae at least thought flowers were much more congenial than pigs: my work clothes would certainly smell more pleasant anyway. I established quite a sizeable trade as a gladioli farmer and at one time had fifteen thousand gladioli corms planted. Each year after gathering and selling the blooms I had to lift the corms, clean them, spray them and put them away for the winter. By the time I replanted them the following season I found myself pretty fully occupied. The balance of the area not required for the gladioli I used for market gardening. One year I had a contract to supply a local pickle factory with ten tonnes of gherkins. Among other

[1] So did his sons! - GB

things I grew were potatoes, pumpkins, spring onions, broad beans, kume kume, rhubarb and dwarf beans. On the whole, I concluded that if I was going to make a career out of it, I would not get rich.

It was while I was busy market and gladioli gardening that my old school approached me to stand in as Senior Teacher[1] for a short time. Because of the seasonal requirements of the gardening I felt I could not do it, but I always wished since that I had done it, even for the transitory satisfaction of holding a really good teaching position at last.

Working from an old 1964 Whitcombe's NZ Diary, Dad recorded his market gardening days in great detail. A few excerpts, all in his own handwriting, follow. He monitored the weather, the frosts included, very carefully. [Extracts only. When Dad visited the Whangaehu farm, which was almost every day he carefully recorded what he did and the weather conditions.] — GB

Front pages

Gladioli Varieties:

Green Woodpecker	Green with red blotches
Brigitte	Apricot orange
Angel Eyes	Milky white with blue blotches
Bridal Wreath	Ruffled white
Pink Dawn	Pink with white throat
Isobel	Salmon red
Antique Gold	Ruffled golden apricot
Nearly Perfect	Ruffled pink
Impromptu	White wine with red blotch
Green Ice	

(The "A" rows - 280 - 290 in double row. Yellow bucket holds 90.)

Pumpkins:

Triamble

Warren Squash

1978

Last fire: 14th September

Cold day: 26th Sept. Lit fire

Cold day: 22nd & 23rd October. Lit fire (after trip to Rarotonga; Godfrey & Leon here)

[1] Not sure from Dad's notes whether "old school" was Wanganui Boys College or Wanganui High School.

1979
Missed fires most of Sept 7th - 15th Started again. Finally finished 6th October.

1978 (extracts only)

Sept 13th	Weston's birthday. Had tea with them tonight. Spent afternoon at farm. Collected draw bar for harrows from garage. Planted Row 11:- Green Ice (creekside and some on roadside). Planted Isobel on roadside from Alabaster's to peg. Planted Row 12. Creekside to water pipe (Alabaster's end): Christine. Roadside: Angel Eyes.
Sept 14th	Spent afternoon at farm. Planted balance of Row 12. From water pipe to shed, creekside: Limelight. From water pipe to roadside: Brigitte. Row 13: creekside: Green Woodpecker.
Sept 16th	Row 1A (on slope) Brigette, Finished with Woodpecker on Alabaster side from peg to end (about 130). Dillon looked at farm, but did not offer more than $85,000 so turned it down. Suggested they might sell gladioli on their roadside stall. Anne and girls down for weekend. Gave Anne samples of several varieties of gladioli.
Sept 18th	Planted Row 2A: Melody Row 3A: Frolic Row 4A: Gold Ruff Row 5A: Impromptu
Sept 21st	Planted by garage at home (from road end) Christine, Angel Eyes, Brigette. Past workshed door a mixture, but mainly Brigette. The first shoots are showing from the shallow ones. Erected the windbreak. The one roll just enough for the fence from Alabaster's to cow yard. At a cost of $50 "Netlon", it is very promising. Tried discing the Karatau paddock. Gave up after an hour. Needs a little more drying out. Peter Whitton finished ploughing Weston's front paddock. Planted baby corms by garage. I they would be Angel Eyes.
Oct 2	Morning at farm. Disced, harrowed and rolled the house paddock. Used both discs first but too drastic. Finished with small discs and harrows. Ground reasonably soft after some rain after a dry month. Still have the area around the shed to be done. Order beet seed and pumpkin seed.
Oct 3	Planted seeds most of day. Little Finger Baby Carrots, 2 rows, covered ¾ of the rows (creek end) lightly with dirt from home. The rest was covered with dirt from paddock. Other seeds were cabbage (*Jubilee hybrid*), leeks (Musselburgh), Silver Beet (*New Green semi dwarf*), brussels sprouts (Fillbasket) and cauliflower (*Phenomenal Main Crop*)

Oct 4	At the farm until midday. Spent the whole time clearing rubbish from paddock behind the house.
Oct 5	A day at the farm. Planted fodder beet by hand a row (middle paddock) and a half row on Karatau side. Purpose to check out the herbicide residue. For some reason also planted pumpkins (*Whangaparaoa Crown*) by the river. Pottered around. Gathered some more rubbish from back paddock and did some preparation of wind breaks. Planted lettuce in seed box.
Dec 30	Got to the farm after a lot of messing about. Prepared ground and planted the last of the corms for Easter. Row E9: Antique Gold. Row E10: Blendette. The Blendette looked as if they might have died. The shoots had shrunk. Finished the day by weeding the vegetable section. Mrs Wilkie called and bought 2½ dozen ($4). Sold 90c worth at the garage. Picked 86 for garage tomorrow. 1st flowers on last 2 rows (A4 & A5 blooming).
Dec 31	Fitted up the glads at the garage. All sold except last dozen. Netted $9. 80

1979 (extracts only)

Jan 1	Went to the farm early and collected enough flowers to stock stall for 2 days. 300-400. Went back this afternoon and weeded pumpkins. Weeds are getting away and it looks like a formidable task. Should have been quite reasonable if I did not have to leave them for other urgent work.
Jan 2	Put flowers out again and collected $13. Got started at the farm by 10.30 and worked until 5.30. Whole time on pumpkin weeding. Beginning to make some impression. Probably take the week to do the first 4 rows (*Triamble*).
Jan 3	Picked 300 intending buds for Wellington. 1-2 flowers open for Ngan Kee[1] and fuller out for stall. Ngan Kee took 80 of buds and 1-2 blooms so decided ship WGN despatch. Ngan Kee $16. Replaced old stock at stall. Bundled rest up for tomorrow's auction. Took all day, so no pumpkins weeded. Stall $4.70.
Jan 4	Flowers to auction – 28 bundles. Stall $6.40. Sold all but 10. Mowed behind house for Weston. 2 hours. Weeded pumpkins until 5.30 (i.e. the whole afternoon).
5 Jan	E4 and E5 showing through. Put price up to 20c & 25c because put out buds & 1st flowers. Notably sales down. Will revert to 15c tomorrow.

[1] Greengrocers in Ingestre Street, Wanganui

6 Jan	Don and Jean came for the day. Had a picnic lunch by the river. After they returned I picked flowers for tomorrow's stall and then weeded pumpkins until rain intervened. Had a puncture on way home. Stall took $6 today.
Jan 18	Took 38 bundles to mart and returned Prue's car. Mine not quite finished so borrowed Weston's to collect flowers for Mrs Bolt - 6 dozen ($7). Was scratching to get the required number. The majority have flowered and they are now falling off in number – as well as blooms. It now looks as if they were at their peak about 2-3 weeks ago – i.e. about 5 Jan.
Jan 22	Weeded the melons.
Mar 8	Short afternoon all used up with returning the cultivator to Vic Dillon. Went with Rae to auction and bought cake mixer ($39)
April 1	Prue & boys came out, helped me gather in red squash. Brought home 200, spent eve bagging up. 2 boxes rock melon, 1 bg squash, 7 bgs buttercups, 1 bg triambles , 3 watermelons
April 2	Went out after school[1]. Found the glads battered by last week's storm. Brought home some bags of squash. Did some odd jobs.
April 8	Tried selling at gate. No interest in pumpkins but sold 6 watermelons in an hour.
June	*NEWSPAPER CUTTING glued in Dad's diary: [There was a similar cutting, reporting on the weather, every month]* Headline: *"MAY WET, WINDY" If you thought May was unusually rainy, you're right! Figures released by the City Council's meteorological officer today show rain fell on 18 days in May compared with a May average of only eight.*
August 22	Have had a week in Christchurch and first day back to the farm. Weston has made a firm decision to sell, so I am a bit frustrated as to what to do. [Weston selling his farm across the road meant Dad would have to pay Weston the money he still owed him for the farmlet. If he couldn't Weston would have liked to include the farmlet in the sale of the farm. – GB] Picked up rotary hoe from Whangaehu garage and went on to bring big discs up from pumpkin patch and use them to cut up paddock across the road. This meant discing out the balance of the turnips. Rang Robert & Althea McLean as prospective buyer of the farm and they were happy to let me plant my corms where I originally intended, so that clears the way ahead. Nevertheless, have lost so much time. Am only a week ahead of last year at this stage.

[1] This diary note suggests that Dad must have done some relief teaching. He resigned from full time teaching in 1973. - GB

August 27	Expected help did not materialise so Rae went out with me for the afternoon. Ground pretty well soaked and rained again while we were there. Planted 3 rows starting on Alabaster side, Row 1 Limelight and 2 & 3 Pink Dawn.
August 30	Advertised house on farmlet to sell off or let with idea it would help me settle my debt with Weston and be able to keep my six acres. Overwhelmed with rings. *Advert cutting glued in diary: "Gracious country living 2-3 bedroom house with ½ acre to let with possibility of purchase. $22 weekly. Ph 50-368 evenings"* [Dad eventually did sell the house which allowed him to pay off Weston and keep the farmlet. However, once the house had gone, the farmlet was bare of any farm buildings at all and Dad had nowhere to keep his implements particularly when Weston's farm and farm buildings across the road had also been sold. He had to leave them in the paddock on full view to the passing traffic. Although he did not suffer any theft, it was not a good situation and prompted Dad to sell the farmlet too a few months later. – GB]
Dec 21	Picked flowers all the afternoon with Rae's help. Decided at 6pm to take another trip to New Plymouth to avoid too much handling of the flowers. Delivered 80 to Patel (Patea) and 120 to Lovell's (Hawera). On to New Plymouth where I stayed with Len and Gwen with them helping me in the morning bundling the glads up. Left them 500 plus 15 bonus there for Bluebird to pick up. Called on Ev briefly and then home with the van again giving trouble at Midhirst. Got home 4.30 and after tea Rae and I both went out and picked more flowers until 8.30. Took them home and Rae and I sat up until late into the night bundling them.
Dec 26	A very very wet day. Went out with Rae after tea to find hundreds in bloom – a very pretty sight but not an economical one! Rae and I picked about 200 blooms and prepared them later for Thursday's auction. Noted that a very attractive row is called Jester.

1980 (extracts only)

Jan 9	Took Riley to see the farmlet.
Jan 11	With Nicola, went out and picked until dinner time with Nicky bundling up. This has made a pretty clear sweep of picking. Buds still to open, but numbers are decidedly going to fall off from now on.

April 7 [1980 contd]	First call to farm after Easter. Meanwhile I have sold the farm to Trevor Granville ($19,500). Also grader blade ($375). So concern now is to get equipment moved and wood cut up.
April 12	Spent morning shifting gear from paddock to Wilkie's and the afternoon sawing up the tree and bringing home a load for fires.
April 30 **[LAST ENTRY]**	Dipped, dried and bagged corms ready for storing. But on Thursday had to rush them into shed with help from Eric and Madeline [Buchendale - neighbours] and Rae because of onset of rain. Set them out again on Friday and got them in in late afternoon.

My granddaughters Nicola and Hilary occasionally came to stay with us in Wanganui and sometimes helped me out in my acres of gladioli, mostly playing in the blooms and in the pumpkins, but also giving some serious help. I would drive the tractor down the rows of pumpkins and they would place the pumpkins on the trailer. On one occasion, at the end of the day, I let Hilary drive the tractor a wee way – when there were no pumpkins to run over! She was ten[1] and today recalls the vivid impression of the acres of different coloured blooms which seemed to her to stretch as far as the eye could see. She also recalls how much she liked the house at "Hillcrest"[2], its tiered section of lawns and its view out to the farm and sheep. On that holiday, which she seems to have enjoyed, she remembers seeing the film *Sword in the Stone* and that one evening when she went to bed early not feeling too well, Rae left her Kentucky Fried Chicken meal in the oven for her all night to keep it warm in case she woke up hungry. She ate the KFC next morning gleefully, although it was no doubt completely dried out.

I had baptised baby Hilary in Wanganui in the house on the very morning of the day Riley and family left for Fiji when Riley joined Air Pacific. It was 1st July 1972. Hilary delightedly relates that she was baptised from a bowl of water which I had placed on top of the television set in our lounge. But she was

---

1 Date not verified

2 196 Great North Road, Wanganui

baptised there in front of the view which she came to know so well when she visited us later on as a young girl.

October 12th 1978 was Rae's 70th birthday. Godfrey came home for it with a friend of his Leon Screene who had not been to New Zealand before. We had a celebratory dinner at the Red Pepper Motor Inn in Wanganui and all the family were together for it. Leon was very good to us, for when we returned to England in 1981 he let us make use of his country cottage there. Rae's 70th birthday present from the family was a week's holiday in Rarotonga. Riley flew the plane – which was a special thrill in itself – and Rae and I, and Godfrey and Leon, spent a lovely relaxing week in the South Pacific paradise.

Our first trip to Europe in 1976 was a thrilling experience and a dream come true: one that enriched our lives. But then I never would have believed we would ever do it again. We did. Out of the hardships and struggles and shortages of early childhood and youth and even adulthood, such a thing seemed impossible. But there we were on Thursday 30th April 1981, sitting in Godfrey's flat, this time in Fulham[1], in London! This time the trip was marred to a certain extent by my immobility as I was dependent on my walking stick and my leg gave me frequent pain. It was a very different trip this time and more relaxing in some ways as we seemed to stay put in Godfrey's flat rather than travelling around the country. We went to see some shows, including *My Fair Lady* in very good front seats which Godfrey got for us. We went to the Chelsea Flower Show which was a truly great sight, but oh!, the crowds! Mavis and Harold Brown visited England around the same time and one Sunday we met them at Central Mission church and on another occasion at John Wesley's Memorial Church in City Road. We visited the Bearne's again, of course, this time in their new home in the Deverills in Wiltshire. Leon offered us the use of his cottage in Bearsted Green in Kent and we spent some time there. On the 6th of June we were lucky enough to have tickets for the

---

[1] 12 Arundel Mansions, Kelvedon Road, Fulham, London SW6

Trooping of the Colour. We had good seats and sat next to an employee of the New Zealand Consulate, an RNZAF engineer, Shaun Robertson, who knew Riley.

In June we set off for another wonderful European tour. This time we left by train from Victoria Station and crossed the English Channel from Dover. We joined a coach to cross Belgium and The Netherlands and we spent our first night at Arnhem. The next day we went into Germany, to Berlin and into East Germany (as it was then) to Dresden, the home of fine china. Dresden is the capital city of the state of Saxony, Germany and this area including the nearby mountains is known as Saxon Switzerland. We drove into Czechoslovakia (now the Czech Republic), through the countryside of Bohemia to Prague. We crossed Austria and followed the Danube on the way to Vienna. We spent a day or so in that beautiful city walking amongst fountains and gardens and then we went to Budapest in Hungary. Our tour continued to Salzburg and back through West Germany, following the Rhine, through the Black Forest foothills, and we visited Heidelburg and Frankfurt. It was two weeks later when we approached England again, through Brussels, Ostend, Dover and back to Victoria Station. Godfrey was almost astonished at our trip. He was much travelled himself but he had not gone behind the "Iron Curtain". I do not think he could believe that it was his "New Zealand bound" parents telling him of new adventures and experiences, this time of visits to places that he, as well travelled as he was, hadn't been to himself. To tell you the truth, we could hardly believe it ourselves!

Postcard to Rae's twin "Boy & Madge" from "Girl & Charl"

> Vienna, 21 June 1981. Hello there! Can't believe we are here! Weather OK now. Rather strenuous tour but easing now, more leisure time from now on. Beautiful cities. Prague amazing with its massive buildings. Talk about producing passports and visas! We sit for an hour to 2 hours to be inspected on their borders! The hotels are good but we don't think we get treated as first class really! Love Girl & Charl.

A month later we returned home to New Zealand. We were back in Wanganui on 31 July 1981 putting an end to our mad international travels, although, had I not been so immobile, there have been many times since when the idea of travel once again appealed to me. I continue to read my diaries of both our overseas trips and look at all the photographs and postcards I collected: they bring me much joy. I still find it hard to credit that we achieved either of them!

In March 1982 Rae and I celebrated forty years of married life with our Ruby Wedding and my seventieth birthday. We visited Auckland and along with cakes and presents the occasion was a joy with my family and grandchildren around me. Godfrey came from London especially for it. On the night of the 19th March, we went to the Hobson House restaurant. Around the table with Rae and me, were Weston and Prue, Riley and Anne, Godfrey, Ashleigh and Gwen Petch and Henry and Rene Woolford. As Henry was one of my groomsmen exactly forty years earlier it was fitting he was there. I also went to Taranaki to share the occasion with my sisters.

We stayed in Wanganui for nearly seventeen years, the longest Rae and I had lived anywhere[1]. As I reminisce about our Wanganui days, I realise they were momentous years. By most people's standards it must have been odd that we bought our very first home when the children were no longer living with us. Rae was looking for furniture and I was looking for a job. Money was tight and life was not without its hardships – and disillusionments. It was as if Rae and I were starting all over again and yet in our first year in Wanganui we celebrated our Silver Wedding. Weston came to live in Wanganui with a teaching job at Wanganui Collegiate. In December 1968 he married Prue Thornley in Auckland. They lived in Wanganui and Weston started his first accountancy practice there. All our grandchildren from both Weston's and Riley's marriages were born during the years we lived in Wanganui too. In the first

[1] And, it proved, the longest ever. - GB

couple of years, Godfrey used to come home for most weekends on his motorbike and then in his old Ford Prefect from Palmerston North, but we saw him less often when he went to teach in Christchurch and then in Auckland. Eventually he left for England but did not return "in a couple of years" – as he had planned and flippantly promised. He still lives in London now, nearly twenty years later[1]. In Wanganui I had no parish and no ministerial or pastoral duties (apart from the occasional relieving work). And no parsonage. In Wanganui, I taught and hated it. In Wanganui I had a piggery and a market garden and loved it. From Wanganui we left not once but twice for trips to Europe and once to Rarotonga. The Wanganui days were crammed with firsts – and lasts – and onlys.

The years were rolling by and I began to wonder what must have happened to my life which was ending before I had hardly begun doing what I wanted to do with it. It is a sad day when one realises that there really and truly is no more time left to do something else. Dreams start to contract. Instead of thinking how I would meet the challenges of a life that was starting, I had to start thinking how I would meet the challenges of a life that was ending.

I had left the ministry behind me and I had left teaching behind me. Now my age was at last telling me it was time to leave farming behind too. However, I was not about to give up. I was still reasonably well, and as long as I was working for myself and could go at my own pace, I did not feel that I would need to stop *just* yet. What sort of sickness or weakness would catch up on me and force me to stop? Or would it just be tiredness pure and simple? Apart from this overtaking me, I could see myself going along for a while yet. Yes indeed. I convinced myself that there was still time.

A friend of mine who had given up a transport business had found relaxation working on the land so we had quite a bit in common. In the course of our conversations he often

---

[1] I returned to live in New Zealand for 10½ years 1991 to 2002. - GB

expressed a desire to retire to Tauranga, extolling its climate as well as the small farm development opportunities that were there.

One wet and cold day in June 1983 I was inspired, probably by the weather, to buy Auckland's paper the *New Zealand Herald*, and quickly turned, quite typically, to the property and the small farmholdings pages. I spotted a house for sale in Tauranga. I was already predisposed to the place through my friend's advocacy, and Rae's great friend Eileen Armit lived there, so it was quite easy to take the next step and ring the given phone number.

As was typical of us, it seemed, we just bought it. And just like that we moved. It was July 1983. The family was surprised and so, in our way, were we. I wondered vaguely if this would be the last move of our lives, but I really envisaged even then that Auckland would probably be the last – when we would finally move to live in the same city as our family and grandchildren. At least with this move we would be significantly closer to them than we were in Wanganui.

"Hillcrest" 196 Great North Road, Wanganui where Rae and Charles lived for 16 years – the longest they stayed in the same home in their married lives and the first house they, and not the church, owned.

View from the dining room, 196 Great North Road, Wanganui

Rae helps Charles cut his 70th birthday cake (and their Ruby Wedding cake) March 1982, Auckland

Godfrey (17), Weston (23), Riley (22) Wanganui 1967

The grandchildren: L to R: Michael, Simon, Hilary, Bryan, Nicky, Andrew. Wanganui, January 1980

Silver Wedding March 1967 Wanganui. Weston, Godfrey, Rae, Charles, Riley, Prue, Anne (pregnant with Andrew)

Rae in Auckland with grandson Andrew, August 1967.

Rae and Charles with Simon and Bryan. Wanganui 1974

No longer the minister's wife. Rae in her new role as market gardener's wife. Happily helping her husband "pick the glads". Whangaehu, Wanganui

Riley, Anne, Bryan, Charles, Nicola, Rae, Andrew, Simon, Hilary, Prue with Michael. Wanganui 1979

"Cindy of Christchurch" the angry Wanganui cat who loved only Rae. Godfrey bought her as a kitten and flew her up to Wanganui for Rae's Christmas present 1969

Godfrey (28) flew back from London for Rae's 70th birthday, October 1978. Typical of her joyous laughter here as the cake candles are lit. Red Pepper Motor Inn, Wanganui

Charles with Bryan and Weston with Simon, Wanganui, 1973

Prue with Simon, Wanganui, 1974

Charles's market garden. Some of his happiest days were here in Wanganui.

"A picture no artist could paint!" (as written by Charles on the back of this photo). Charles contentedly cleaning gladioli corms under the clothes line. Wanganui

Selling pumpkins off Charles's tractor and trailer outside his leased farmlet. Springvale, Wanganui

Rev Pig Farmer! Charles's much loved pig farm at Kaitoke Wanganui 1970

Charles with his sisters (from L Gwen, Jean and Evelyn) celebrating his 70th birthday. New Plymouth 1982

Charles and Rae with grandchildren Andrew and Nicky, May 1972, Wanganui

Rae and Godfrey on the day he sailed for England, 2 May 1972

Weston, Prue, Rae, Simon, Bryan, Michael Wanganui, Dec 1979

Charles with his grandchildren on his 70th birthday March 1982, Auckland L to R Michael, Hilary, Bryan, Andrew, Nicky, Simon

Rae and Charles on steps of Coventry Cathedral, England 1976

The Stow's cottage at Evesham, England, which Charles and Rae rented on 3 separate occasions, and their VW, 1976

Charles and Rae in Stratford-upon-Avon, England 1976

Charles and Rae in Italy. Written on back: "On way to Venice."

Charles and Rae, Christchurch, May 1970 "At Hilda & Ron's wedding." (Charles married them in Clarence Road Methodist Church.)

Rae at front door of 18th c. Eden Cottage, The Street, Bearsted Green, Kent. 1981

Charles's sisters Jean McDowall (L) and Evelyn Hickling (R) with their first cousin Mavis Pope (centre). Wanganui, Feb 1971

Rae with grandson Andrew, Anne, Riley, Charles. Wanganui, Christmas Day 1967

Rae's 70th birthday present from the family: a holiday in Rarotonga, flown there by Riley. Arriving at Rarotonga Airport. Godfrey, Charles, Riley, Rae. October 1978

Rae and Charles at Diana Rae's (nee Thornley) in London 1981 on their second trip to Europe.

Chapter 20

BEEHIVES and TOYS

July 1983 – October 1993

Tauranga

Sensibly we bought a house in Tauranga (52 Paine Street), not, as much as I would have loved to, a farmlet. It really did look as if my farming activities were at an end. Godfrey was not so sure I was wise to give it all up and sensing, I suppose, my frustration at having "nothing" to do, when he visited us for the first time in Tauranga he spent some time looking around for a section that I could perhaps utilise as a small gardening unit. But he found nothing which was somehow in between suburbia and a proper farmlet. So I settled down to content myself with developing my quarter acre section. This did not stop me keeping an eye open for other opportunities – just in case.

At the time, there was much talk of increasing areas being planted in kiwifruit. A side line to that was an increasing demand for bees for fertilising the plants. (Of course I read it in the newspaper – all my ideas came from newspapers[1].) And so another, ("Yet another, Charlie?" Rae would say), idea was born. It occurred to me that more bees would mean more beehives. This, I thought, is something I can do. So, of course, I did –

[1] Throughout his life, if Dad possibly could he would read every inch of the newspaper every day. - GB

nothing ever stopped me leaping in before and the fact that I knew nothing about bees or beehives was quite irrelevant. Had I ever known anything about pigs? Gladioli? Gherkins? Fortunately the shed in the garden of our new home had a good power supply laid on. All I needed were power tools and some timber. Without ever making one beehive and with a list of beekeepers before me, I sent out a circular, "Bell's Bees", telling them I was in business. It worked! Before long orders were rolling in. And I didn't know what I was doing. The cheek of it – but, I figured without pause, nothing ventured nothing gained. Sometimes in life you just have to go for it and not just sit there thinking about it. I realised that if in my lifetime I had done too much planning and fearing "What if?", I would have done nothing.

So with orders in front of me obviously I saw the wisdom in getting on to learn something about darn bees. I knew nothing about them other than the fact that they produced honey and they stung. I found I really enjoyed learning about them – and their homes. I learned for example that if there was the slightest gap where the beehive sat on its base then wasps or foreigner bees would enter and rob the hive of its honey. To get my measurements right and to standardise my hives, I took myself off to a commercial firm and bought one of their hives. Little did they realise when they sold it to me they were helping me set up a rival business.

I think I surprised Rae only a little more than I surprised myself when I found I could both build and sell beehives. A year or two passed and I was busy and happy out in the shed, as ever in my old work clothes, but this time pottering around a workbench instead of in the soil or around animals. Bell's Bees boomed! But yet again, not quite enough to make me rich and nor, frustratingly, satisfied. So I found I wanted to try something else as well.

Before I gave up my pottering around in the shed once and for all, putting off the dreaded day when I would have to face up to the fact that I could do nothing outdoors or with my hands any longer, for some strange reason I decided to try making some wooden toys. I still do not know what prompted this interest, but I built half a dozen or so wooden trucks. Without any of the right tools for the job (I did not even have a lathe), and of course no expertise whatsoever, I knocked together with saw, hammer and nails some rather crude kids' trucks and wheelbarrows. I painted them in bright colours – which no doubt helped to detract, momentarily at least, from the workmanship. Riley and Godfrey both thought they were pretty horrific as works of art and were astounded that I sold one or two for a few dollars each at the local market[1]. But someone liked them obviously and it amused me for a while longer.

So kids' trucks and barrows, and beehives, was the Bell business and intriguing production line in the shed at the bottom of the garden at 52 Paine Street Tauranga, for some time. But almost without noticing it at first, my right leg was aching more and more. I blamed it on standing for long hours on a concrete floor in the shed. To counter this I began leaving the shavings from the boards on the floor to act as a cushion for my leg. Soon I started to lose interest in the business and found myself putting in less and less time at it and I even began to turn down beehive orders. I was beginning to feel unwell. Trips to the doctor brought no relief, nor elucidated a name for my condition. I felt lethargic and almost constantly nauseous. So it went on until one day a lump very much like a boil appeared on my right thigh. It was an infection that had settled in my hip replacement of five years before. There followed many trips to Tauranga General Hospital as an outpatient in an attempt to clear it up, but it was to no avail. By this time the poison from it had worked itself through my whole body. One morning I woke gasping for air. I had had a heart attack. Fortunately it was only mild but I knew that I was ill. I felt it and my despair with each visit to the doctor

---

[1] I actually think the toys broke every health and safety guideline in the book, what with nails and rough edges and so on! But either Dad didn't even think about this or it simply didn't worry him and I was somewhat relieved that he only made a few and sold even fewer. - GB

increased as an answer could not be found. For days I sat in my lazyboy armchair and hours drifted by as I slept through much of every afternoon, slept, but not peacefully. I was drained of energy and of interest in everything and everyone. All I could think about was my feeling of sickness.

As each effort to clear up the lump failed, the doctor eventually admitted me into hospital in June 1987 to try to flush out the infection. I was put on some sort of irrigation system. This was done by inserting a tube in the affected part and pumping water through, first in one direction and then in the other.

Tauranga General Hospital was about six kilometres from home, on the other side of Tauranga to us. This as always posed a difficulty for Rae in visiting me as she could not drive and there was no direct bus route. Thankfully our good friends Eileen and Jack Armit who lived nearby were kind and generous with their time and Jack drove Mum in to visit me nearly every day. But it was undeniable that we had to rely on their generosity too much and I would have been much happier if I could have been in a hospital nearer Rae. This was not possible however because I had to depend on the national health system and the General was Tauranga's only public hospital.

I did not respond to the treatment. The pain increased and I felt that I was a very old man indeed with life ebbing away from me. My sons became concerned. Godfrey in London spoke to Riley on the phone and then phoned the family doctor himself. "He is a very sick man, Mr Bell", he was told.

"How sick? I must know, I live in London, I must know what you mean by that."

"I cannot say. We are trying to clear up the infection which seems now to be throughout his body. At the moment he is not responding well."

Riley had visited me a day or two earlier. I remember that the pain was particularly great and I was tired of it all. I was tired of the pain. I was tired of the constant experimenting. I was tired of the inconvenience. I lay still and quietly, keeping my eyes closed. He took my hand before he left and I said to him, "I can't take much more of this Riley. I don't want to take much more."

This news from Riley decided Godfrey. The doubt for him was more than he could bear and he flew out of London the next day. After his twenty-six hour journey, he hired a car on his arrival early in the morning at Auckland International Airport and drove straight home to Tauranga, two and a half hours south. That afternoon he was at my bedside.

I had lost weight he thought and I looked ill. I knew he was upset. He wanted to know more about what was going on. For the next few days he spent time on the phone ringing the family doctor and trying to have meetings with the specialist. It was confirmed that the infection came from the hip replacement and that the blood throughout my whole body was now being poisoned. They believed they could clear it up without taking the hip out which they were very reluctant to do because it would mean having two crutches for the rest of my life. For me as an energetic man this in any other situation would have seemed a totally unacceptable idea. But I was past caring about my levels of energy. I was only interested in stopping the pain.

After three weeks they sent me home as they could do nothing more for me in hospital. I was slightly better but each improvement was short-lived. Godfrey returned to London when he saw me back at home with a nurse visiting every day. She came to dress the lump which by now had become an open weeping wound. The theory was that it would heal of its own accord, "in due course", but it didn't.

By the end of 1987 I was still feeling very ill and I was desperate. I rang the specialist and pleaded that they remove the hip replacement. He said that he would be on holiday himself until the middle of January but a colleague could do it if I did not want to wait. I told him firmly that I had no doubt about that at all.

"Mr Bell", the specialist said carefully. "You do realise that this will mean that you will be on crutches for the rest of your life?"

"Yes I know, but I feel that I will soon be dead if I don't get it done. As far as I see it, there is no choice."

I was due to go into hospital in a few weeks time, but one night early in January 1988 I took a turn for the worse and I was rushed into hospital by ambulance. A surgeon whom I had not met before examined me. "Mr Bell, this operation should have been done months ago. We will operate immediately." The next day I underwent a six hour operation to remove the hip. I spent four days in intensive care and then six weeks in traction. Bit by bit, life returned to normal and I felt much better. But life was never to be the same for me again: I had to learn to walk relying on two crutches.

At the end of January 1988, a few weeks after my operation, Godfrey returned home (the second trip in seven months). I was still in hospital but the real purpose of his visit this time was to help Mum at home and to drive her around and in to visit me. It was more difficult for Weston and Riley to get down from Auckland for several weeks at a time, but Godfrey by the very fact that he had come from London was away from work for a few weeks on end and could stay with Mum and give her some continuing support.

Although I was in traction, I could tell the operation was a success. The poison gradually cleared up with the source of the infection removed. I felt life flowing back into me and each day was better for me than the previous one. The whole family could see the improvement in my colouring but most noticeably in my interest in living at all.

Meanwhile, during 1987 and markedly in 1988, Rae's eyesight was failing and her memory was deteriorating. Undoubtedly blindness was creeping up on her and equally undoubtedly she suffered from losses of memory which were as insidious as they were devastating. Even before this latest visit of mine to hospital, our sons had been getting concerned and had made several pleas for us to move to Auckland where we would be near to Weston and Riley. We resisted, even after one occasion when we went as far as putting a deposit on an apartment in a new residential village for the elderly (in South Auckland), but then withdrew it.

But now, despite it appearing that the worst for me was definitely over, Godfrey remained concerned about the future. He spent much of February 1988 going around the Bay of Plenty visiting "sheltered housing" homes for the elderly, undeterred by the fact that he knew we would continue to resist the idea. He had his eye on Rae as well as me and he knew that waiting lists were long and one often had to wait for years to get in to the home of your choice. At the very least he wanted our names to be on a list so that our options were kept open.

This made good sense to everyone except Rae and me. We both enjoyed our home. It was a four bedroom house surrounded by a lovely large garden. It was very much one of the nicest homes we had lived in and I thought that once I was home, now I was feeling well again, I could get back to my beehives.

The closest sheltered housing estate to where we lived was Melrose Home and Hospital, run by the Presbyterian church, but supported by the Methodist church as well. Indeed, coincidentally, it was only a few hundred metres from our front door and it had a very good name nationally. Without informing us, Godfrey arranged to meet Diane Connell, the Accommodation Officer of Melrose. The Home was on several acres of park-like gardens with a tree lined avenue drive. On the outskirts of Tauranga, it was positioned on a hill overlooking the city and the harbour beyond. In the grounds were some small cottage bungalows with their own garages, front and back doors, balconies, some with one bedroom, others with two. They were connected by a path to the Community Centre, a nursing home and a hospital, each cottage being only a few metres away at most. In addition there were a couple of terraces of some smaller motel-like "units" with their own kitchen and bathrooms. They were self contained but not detached with each surrounded by gardens and lawns as the cottages were.

Godfrey was shown over the grounds and cottages and saw one cottage that he immediately set his heart on: Number One. It was occupied so he could not be shown in it, but it was nearest to the Community Centre, had a wonderful view of the harbour and Mount Maunganui, was sunny and was slightly more private than the other cottages. There was a long waiting list and some had been waiting for years. However, he was told that who got in next depended on need as much as on the length of time they may have been waiting. Moreover, sometimes when a cottage did become available, the "next on the list" changed their mind, didn't like the space on offer, had moved away, even died, or their family circumstances had changed in the interim. Some simply were not prepared to act fast enough to take up the availability.

Enthusiastic about Melrose and not put off by the long waiting list, Godfrey persuaded Rae and me to visit Melrose and at least have an initial interview. Rae was especially reluctant but Godfrey, characteristically, totally ignored the objections and dragged her along. He came to pick me up from the hospital and drove us both to Melrose for the interview which he had strategically and carefully pre-arranged – without our agreement.

I was still very unsteady on my two crutches but I had to practise using them. The visit to Melrose put me through my paces, but with arms and hands ready to support me and a good number of rest breaks, I managed to walk around Melrose enough to see what I needed to see and for the Melrose staff to see how I could cope with the paths in and around the complex. We were shown one unit which was vacant. It was one of the terraced units. I had suspected that Godfrey had wanted us to move into Melrose in any event, so I was surprised when he was shown the unit that was available immediately that he rejected it out of hand. "I don't want you in there", he said. "It is too much like an institution. You are not ready for that. We must wait for the cottages to become available." Rae spent her entire time pretending that her eyesight was quite all right (even though by now she was registered partially blind) and that she could see far more than she actually could. Repeatedly, and to Godfrey's obvious frustration, Rae assured Diane and the Head Nurse that Godfrey must surely have exaggerated the need for his parents to move into Melrose. As we left, Rae turned to Diane and said, "You know we have only come for interest and really just to please our son who is going back to London soon. We are not nearly ready yet to move here, not nearly. Perhaps one day when we are older. Thank you so much for showing us around. Goodbye!" With an air of confidence which meant that she was convinced that she had satisfied Godfrey as well as Melrose that there was no way she or I would be moving into Melrose, she promptly turned around to walk out of the hotel-like reception area. She took two paces and suddenly grabbed Godfrey's arm to steer her down the hall, being completely unsure of her step in unfamiliar surroundings. "What's that, dear?" Rae asked Godfrey, pointing to an armchair and coffee table just to her left. Not nearly ready – indeed! Godfrey's efforts had been justified!

Godfrey talked confidentially to Diane Connell the next day concerned that she had fallen for Rae's claim that she was still "hale and hearty" and that there was "no need to go on any waiting list". He discovered, on the contrary. First of all, Diane told him, that it was rare for anyone to come to see over the complex who actually thought they were *ready* to move in. But more interestingly and somewhat alarmingly to Godfrey, Diane actually thought that Rae and I were not only ready to move into Melrose but should not go into a cottage (which Godfrey wanted for us), but straight into a unit. The units offered less independence than the cottages but more independence than the nursing home itself. "Your parents are almost too old for the cottages," Diane told Godfrey. "The people we put in there are much younger usually. In their early seventies. As they are more like private homes albeit just down the path, we like to put people in there who are totally independent. I don't think your parents are that independent anymore. The units are smaller and nearer the nursing centre. Having met your mother and father now and seen how they are, I think they would be much better in a unit."

Godfrey knew that if the units were the only option, we would not budge. "But they are in a four bedroom house now, Diane, on a large section," Godfrey protested. "I don't want them in a unit Diane. It is hard enough for Mum and Dad to accept the idea of moving at all. The cottages are, as you say, almost like private homes in themselves. The transition would be much easier for them if they didn't feel they were losing so much of their independence – and their pride – overnight." Diane could only agree to put them on the waiting list and see how Rae and I were coping when a cottage actually became available. But as yet we had not agreed to go on the official waiting list. Godfrey saw this as the next big hurdle.

That evening Godfrey visited me in hospital alone, leaving Rae at home. He wanted to talk sense to me. "You may think it is OK not to move Dad, but your children don't. Mum is much more blind than she admits to and here you are in hospital. Apart from depending on friends, and for the moment me, she is stranded up there not being able to drive. What is more, she is not safe alone. Even though you are getting better, what happens next time? Mum can hardly use the phone. We want you to find a place where you both can be looked after if things get worse."

"Yes, I know Godfrey, you are right. But not just yet. We will be fine for a few more years. We know the time must come, but it is not now."

"Dad, when you were in the ministry, years ago you told me that you found in your parishes as people got older they became more unreasonable – not consciously, but they became stubborn. You said you saw it yourself, time after time, people who could not see what was good for them as their situations and their health deteriorated around them. And more significantly, you said that when the time comes, you don't want the same stubbornness to set in with you. You even said that you didn't want to become a burden to your children. Well, you certainly are not that. But we are worried about you. We can't help worrying. You know that we have even got Mum an emergency bleeper in case she falls while you are in hospital. When I've gone back to London she will have to rely on that alarm totally. She is virtually blind Dad, she could slip on steps or trip over anything in the house. She refuses to believe she is blind. She won't have a white stick which would at least tell people to be careful of her as she crosses the road. If you were in Melrose you will still retain your independence but you would have nurses on call and if you had to go in hospital again it is just up the path. . . . . "

Godfrey did not give up. He had detected a note of acceptance by the very fact that we had agreed, albeit under some protest, to visit Melrose the day before. The waiting list was years long so he revisited Melrose home alone and asked for a registration form. He needed our signatures for the form and it was duly signed, under the most gentle pressure at my hospital bedside. Rae, sitting beside me, signed it too, but concluded with the remark, "We may be on the waiting list Godfrey, but we won't be moving for years yet," but she found herself turning to me for reassurance. She leaned across the bed and looked into my eyes and added, "Will we Charlie?"

Godfrey liked Diane Connell a lot. He rang her from London once or twice and wrote, making sure that Melrose would not forget that we were on the waiting list. He wanted to keep an eye on that waiting list and to monitor what was becoming available. Diane assured him that she had not forgotten us and following receipt of our doctors' reports and calling in on us at home, she was staying fully informed of our progress. Diane knew that Godfrey had his heart set on Cottage Number One, but she had told him that this was virtually impossible as the residents who buy the cottages live there till they move into the units or the nursing home when they are no longer capable of living alone, or until they die.

In February 1989, Godfrey returned to New Zealand for another holiday, always his favourite time of year for visiting home. He arranged to meet Diane again and to his total surprise she greeted him with good news. "The residents of Number One have just given us notice that they are moving out. Their son in Blenheim has contracted cancer and as he is a single man, they want to move there to care for him. The cottage you want is available, but we must have your firm answer immediately otherwise it will be offered to others on the list."

Godfrey was astonished at the turn of events and could hardly believe the news and nor could we really. We accepted it with less delight than he did, but with the gentle but equally determined influence of our very persuasive baby son, we overcame our reluctance and said we would take it. The die was cast. It seemed that circumstances were closing in around us. It looked like a one way road and the end was racing up to meet us. Yet there was the stark reality staring us in the face. This was where life had brought us. There was no real alternative. Our hearts might cry out against it, but the truth had to be faced. Rae accepted the decision, but found it particularly hard. She turned to Godfrey and said, almost accusingly, "Well, there goes my home. That's it then." Godfrey was plainly hurt by the rebuff and taken aback but wisely held his ground. It was clear that he wanted so much for us to enjoy the idea of moving into a very lovely cottage in Melrose. "That's not "it then", Mum. The cottage is a beautiful home. It is sunny and bright and there is a balcony with fabulous views over Tauranga and to the Mount. I know you will be happy there. Believe me, Weston and Riley and I would never want you to move if we thought you were going to be unhappy. I am so sure you will be happy there, and you will have peace of mind. If Dad is ill again, he won't be in hospital in town, he will be in hospital just up the path[1]. I promise you, you will like it Mum, I know it."

1 In fact this did not transpire. Dad's hospital visits were always to the main public hospital in Tauranga.

I knew Godfrey was right. The other two boys had been exerting as much pressure, gentle as it always was. Indeed for years there had been the cry for us to go to Auckland. I always thought that we might move nearer Weston and Riley, but if we took Melrose, our feet would be cemented in Tauranga[1]. Our days of independence were over. On crutches, I could not maintain a section. For Rae with her increasing blindness, cooking and house keeping were fast becoming impossible. Already the hospital was supplying us with our midday meal with the "Meals on Wheels" service. The future held no promise of getting better and this was decision time.

There was undoubted (albeit understandable) pressure from all our sons and not inconsiderable strategies in place on their part to get us to move. Nevertheless we liked to think we did have a choice and so we had dallied with the ideas put forward to us as long as we had dared. In the end, I know it was our own decision to move into Melrose even though it comforted us sometimes to think that the pressure was slightly unfair as we were not really that old at all!

Godfrey returned to London as we put our house at Paine Street on the market. We had to sell it in order to raise the finance to buy the cottage at Melrose. In truth, we wondered if we might be let off by having to do this. If the house was not sold, Melrose could not hold on to the cottage for us indefinitely and we would have to release it. Despite our decision, we did not really want to sell Paine Street. All our lives in the ministry we had lived in "tied" houses. This one was only the second that we had owned ourselves – only the second one where we did not have to wait on one committee or another to decide whether or not we could have a bit of concrete laid, or this or that alteration done to our own home, or a chair bought, a door hung or a cupboard repaired. It had been a lovely experience to know our

---

[1] Shortly before he died in Melrose, Dad did seriously consider moving again, this time, finally, to Auckland. We even looked at homes there together. But his sudden death pre-empted the move. With hindsight I very much wish they had moved to Auckland together and, given that he was destined to go first, that Dad had died in Auckland and then Mum would already have been in situ and not have had to face quite such a dramatic move.

home was really our own. In my pig farming days in Wanganui (1969 – 1975) I had had a bigger cash flow than at any other time in my life so we had indulged ourselves in expenditure on our home, a new carpet, new kitchen appliances, landscaped driveway, and so on. So normal for most couples. So unusual and such a joy for us a couple married then for more than twenty-five years. Were we giving away this freedom, once again, by moving into Melrose? Even though we would be in a "private" cottage, it would still be subject to institutional rules and regulations and guidelines[1].

But reality was relentless. However slowly and reluctantly it was, we eventually let go when we accepted an offer for our house. One day in May 1989, Riley and Anne came down from Auckland and with Eileen and Jack Armit and some other local friends and neighbours, we moved in several trips backwards and forwards with cars and trailers, across and down the road, into Cottage Number One, Melrose Home and Hospital for the Elderly, Waihi Road, Tauranga. As the cottage was so much smaller than the house, much furniture had to be sold or given to Weston and Riley in Auckland but the final moving day took only a few hours.

As Melrose was so close to Paine Street the move was hardly a big deal for us physically and our shops, banks, doctors, friends and our church did not change. All the same it was hugely significant for us emotionally. Apart from boarding in various homes in my single days, since being married Rae and I lived in eight different homes. *This one was to be the ninth – and the last.* That recognition really got to me, as I somehow found great comfort in clinging to immortality by believing that there were still moves ahead of us. We had got used to moving. It was the kind of life we led. And we changed homes easily and contentedly, sometimes completely spontaneously (as in the case of the move to Wanganui and here to Tauranga). We have been happy in all the places where we lived. We played host to a

---

[1] I never knew this was one of their anxieties about moving to Melrose until Dad told me of it years later. - GB

multitude of friends and parishioners. Strong and enduring bonds have developed between us and them and our lives have been greatly enriched because of it. And now, *this is to be our last home*[1]. Now we have a place with only one spare single bedroom and Melrose provides our main meal of the day. Entertaining and having people to stay no longer is as easy for us, but many friends still drop in for a cuppa and a chat. Others, further afield, write regularly and often.

I have noticed too, that we are appreciating more and more the ties we have with our children and their families. And, I confess, we are enjoying living here. Godfrey was right. Cottage Number One is a lovely home and it is sunny and warm. In the summer Rae sits out on the balcony every day in her chair staring out to the wide view across the Tauranga Harbour to Mount Maunganui. I have noticed that she is calmer now and more peaceful. She is happy to sit quietly listening to her taped book. All her life Rae never stopped working or cooking. I look around me. Every week a cleaner, Wynne Kerr, comes in – although Rae protested and continues to protest, perhaps because it indicated some sort of defeat and invasion into her life-long domain: but the reality of the need (her blindness) could not be denied. Every day we walk up the path together to the Melrose dining room for our midday meal. I myself cook a light evening supper[2]. All in all, Rae is unbothered and unworried[3]. For the first time in so many years of entertaining parishioners and baking for church meetings, it is delightful for me to see her take life so very quietly.

---

[1] It transpired to be true for Dad, but not for Mum. - GB

[2] This changed a couple of months before Dad died, when he could no longer cope cooking even a light supper because of his immobility. Help was hired, Beverley Shearer, who came in every evening about 5 to leave something which Dad or Mum could serve up quickly and easily. This upset Mum as she refused to recognise the need for any help in the house (as she had resisted for several years the need for the cleaner). Nevertheless, it proved to be a blessing. Even though Beverley had been doing this for only a few weeks, she arrived as usual, but on this evening at a critical time, just before 5pm on the evening Dad died. She found Dad on the floor and a distressful situation which she was able to take over and help both Dad and Mum in Dad's last minutes.

[3] Sadly, this peace of mind was tested by her increasing dementia as the years passed by.

Despite the long resistance to moving to Melrose, Rae has settled in very quickly and easily. She always comments as we drive in the main gate and up the avenue of trees, "There is no doubt about it, this is a very lovely place." One balmy evening when Godfrey took her for a walk along the drive, across the lawns and to the front gate and back again (with the occasional rest en route on benches under the trees), she said, once again, "Oh, yes, this is a very lovely place. We are lucky to be here." She paused and with her typical twinkle and smile, turned to Godfrey and added, "On the other hand, they are very lucky to have us!"

Life therefore remains rich for us and still full of interest with our families and friends. In recent days two men on two separate occasions, quite astonishingly, out of the blue shared with me that they thought of me as their "father in God"[1]. That was an enormous, personal and unexpected compliment for me, one that surely crowns the efforts of the years. Whatever I had to sacrifice by turning my back on farming for most of my life was hardly any sacrifice in the light of such an accolade.

The front wall of our lounge is all glass and a ranch slider opens out on to a balcony. Whether I sit on a deck-chair on our balcony or here in my arm-chair in the lounge, my vista is large. On my horizon is an estuary and the upper reaches of the Tauranga Harbour where I can watch the tides come in and go out each day and I can see the extraordinary extinct volcano of Mount Maunganui. Draped around the harbour and the Mount are Tauranga city's homes, roads, gardens and orchards. It is a picturesque mix of man and nature's handiwork. At night, with a mere glance away from the television, I can see a myriad of lights that twinkle like stars through the trees, a veritable fairyland. And I can see the stars themselves without moving from my chair.

As I write these words I am looking at the setting sun. It is casting its soft light over hill and vale and over homes and trees.

---

[1] I have found no diary note or reference as to who these two men were. - GB

On a road across the estuary I can make out the cars that are no doubt heading toward the homes of their drivers who are hurrying along as their day's work comes to an end.

So my day's work, too, is done and I face the last leg of my journey home, this time to one which needs no packing boxes or removal van. As the dying day smoothes out the harsher lines and merges all in a kindly mellowness, so I trust the sun may go down on my life, blotting out the memories of blunders made. And I trust that hurts to other people will be generously forgiven, wrong judgements under the providence of God turned to good account, and the good memories shed a glow as the mind and body give way to the weakness of old age.

I remember my small pig farm in Wanganui and how much I enjoyed working on it after I retired, but it was the end of the day which was always the highlight. As the westering sun came to sit on the horizon, I would head for home. My wife, as she has done every day of our married lives, greeted me warmly. Without exception she always welcomed me home with "Hello, dear" whether I walked in the door once or twenty times a day. These two simple words, for all their ordinariness, were as a fanfare of trumpets to me. For me they signified, above all else, my home. As a matter of routine, in the winter months, I would quickly kindle the fire in the open fireplace before taking a bath to wash away the grime of the day's toils. I dressed and put on my slippers. Back in the lounge I drew the curtains and in that moment my day ended. With the world shut out, I turned to the comfort of my "lazy boy" armchair, the daily newspaper and the cosiness of the glowing fire. Dinner with my wife and an evening of casual chat, reading and television, lay ahead. Since church days we rarely went out or entertained. After a life time of church meetings and socialising, and the "open door" policy twenty-four hours a day of the Methodist parsonage, aloneness in the evenings – with my wife – was blissful. Each evening together was so simple, uneventful and routine, but the anticipation of it was always very special for me. Indeed I have often wondered whether it is the evenings that are special to every farmer. The soaking bath and the warmth of the home fires at night, the meal and the company – and companionship – of those you love, often stand in stark contrast to the dirt, smell, roughness and physical exhaustion of work of the day out on the farm. The atmosphere of the traditional farm homestead in an evening is a very different one from the day. I've sought to recapture it so often since I was a boy.

Now, here in the lounge of our cottage in this park of sheltered housing for the elderly, Melrose is my home. As the sun today sets behind Mount Maunganui which I can see so clearly from here, I draw the curtains, not across the windows, but on my life. I know now and accept that this will be my final home. After a life time of moves every few years, so characteristic of those in the ministry, we will not move again. I know now, what I did not know for the last eighty years but I surely wondered on so many occasions as years came and went, where I would end my days.

And so it is to be here. Tauranga. Long sunsets wash over an attractive quiet city on the edge of the Pacific Ocean and a harbour edged with market gardens of oranges and lemons and kiwi fruit orchards. The wide open views from our home remind one of the beauty of New Zealand and I enjoy reflecting on that each day. We look over the red roof tops of houses sprawling in the hills between here and the harbour shore. The expansive skies and the views make this place. They give a great sense of openness and freedom and encourage us to look out even as we are old and could so easily look in. We can enjoy the beauty from our chairs and we can delight in our reminiscences knowing we are secure and warm here as we get slower and more frail. Yes, moving to Melrose has brought us much happiness and peace of mind.

I have no regrets. I wallow, almost as a spoilt child, in the solid love of my wife's affection and in her love for joyfulness and optimism over and above all other emotions. She is so willing and ready to smile and to laugh before she is ready to cry or complain, even as her sight fails and her memory goes. I am comforted too by the care and concern of loving and attentive sons and their families and the kindliness of more friends than I ever hoped to have at this time of my life.

These are the fires that burn warmly for me now and life is good. What I wanted to do and what I wanted to become in the days of heady, youthful dreams and ambitions, no longer matter to me. All the time, what I already had was all I ever wanted: love.

I think about dying. I wish I could watch over my sons forever and be around to see how life unfolds for each of my grandchildren. Denying me this pleasure is death's cruellest sting, but death in itself I do not fear.

I give thanks to God that I have lived at all.

I'll bless the hand that guided
I'll bless the heart that planned
When throned in glory
In Immanuel's land

— January 1992*

* *Dad died suddenly on Monday October 11th 1993, at home in Cottage No. 1, Melrose, less than two years after penning these final words. – GB.*

52 Paine Street, Tauranga, Feb 1988. Rae standing on terrace. Rae and Charles lived here for six years 1983 – 1989

Rae at Charles's bedside, Tauranga Hospital, February 1988, one of several spells he had in hospital while in Tauranga.

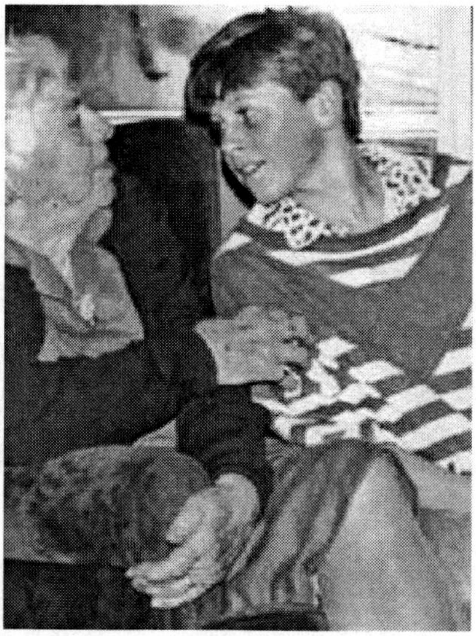

A special moment between grandmother and grandson. Rae (79) with Simon (15), Weston's second son, at Andrew's, Riley's son, 21st birthday. Auckland July 1988

Rae and Charles's Sapphire Wedding (45th) and Charles's 75th birthday Tauranga. March 1987.
L to R: Charles, Rae, Vera Diprose, Jack Armit, Bill Diprose, Eileen Armit.
Also present: Riley & Anne.

Reverend Toy Maker! Charles still up to his tricks. This time he turned to making wooden barrows for toddlers. His handiwork on the back steps of 52 Paine Street Tauranga 1984

Cottage 1, Melrose Home and Hospital, Waihi Road, Tauranga The sunny deck on the right looked out on a marvellous view towards Tauranga Harbour and Mt Maunganui

Cottage 1, Melrose, Tauranga, front entrance and car port. Rae and Charles's last home May 1989 – Oct 1993 (4 ½ years) and where Charles died.

Melrose Cottage 1, taken from the neighbour's garden. Charles standing on the path to back door. c1991

Rae (83), Tauranga, 1992 with Tauranga Harbour behind her, part of the view she and Charles shared from Cottage 1, Melrose

Charles's last trip to Auckland, and indeed out of Tauranga, was to Weston and Kathy's wedding in September 1993. He died suddenly a few weeks later.

Godfrey (28) and Rae (79) on front terrace of 52 Paine Street, Tauranga 1988

His love and compassion will endure

Dad's old Matamata Methodist Church moved from Broadway to Tower Hill and re-sited in the gardens of the Historic Village. Here Dad's ashes are scattered.

Inside the church (opposite), a Memorial Plaque for Dad has been placed at the Communion Rail from which he served communion and conducted baptisms, weddings and funerals for so many years.

IN LOVING MEMORY OF
REVEREND CHARLES HARRISON BELL
1912-1993
WHO PREACHED IN THIS CHURCH ON ITS ORIGINAL SITE
IN BROADWAY 1955-1962
AND WHO CONDUCTED HIS LAST MARRIAGE CEREMONY HERE
FOR HIS GRANDDAUGHTER 1991
HIS MINISTRY WITH THE MATAMATA METHODIST PARISH
WAS ONE OF HIS HAPPIEST
IT WAS HIS WISH THAT HIS ASHES BE SCATTERED
HERE IN THE GARDENS OF HIS OLD CHURCH
HIS LOVE AND COMPASSION WILL ENDURE

A tree of remembrance for the life of
Charles Harrison Bell

A copper beech tree planted soon after Charles died on Merleswood farm, Beaconsfield Road, Stratford. On this farm Charles lived and played as a young boy from the ages of 4 to 9 years (1916 – 1921) until his family moved further down Beaconsfield Road to Coldstream farm. Even after he left Merleswood, it was destined to contribute to a lifetime of memories for him. His sister Gwen lived there after she married Len Jago who owned and farmed it. All his life, Charles continued to visit – and to love – Merleswood.

Photo Betty Fenwick (nee Jago) July 2005

EPILOGUES

EPILOGUE I: DAD'S LAST DAYS

I want to be quiet now

Dad died suddenly on Monday, 11 October 1993 at 5pm at his home Cottage No. 1, in the Melrose Village, Tauranga.

But I think Dad knew months earlier, that things were "changing". He started telling me on my weekend visits where things were. He walked me to the hall one day, opened the cupboard door by the bedroom, and with one of his sticks, pointed to a box on a shelf, "There, that box there, I've left a few notes for my funeral." On another weekend he asked me if I would take a book he had *The History of Methodism in New Zealand* to Auckland to get it re-bound. He suggested that someone in the Church might want it. "I gave it to someone here in Tauranga at first," he said. "They thought they might be able to get it done, but in the end they couldn't. I forgot about it really and they hung on to it. I have now got it back and I would like to get that job done. There are a few things like that, that need sorting out. If anything happened to me, you wouldn't have even known I had that book had I not got it back. It might be valuable to someone some day." All quite apart from him chasing me regularly to finish this book.

A few days before he died he did not feel well and spent much of the weekend in bed. Unusually, none of his children visited him that weekend. It was Mum's birthday on the following Tuesday and it would have been normal for us to do so. Riley was in Canada, Weston had planned to go on the Tuesday itself and I took the opportunity to visit my nephew Andrew and his wife in Nelson to tie in with a convenient business trip there. I rang Mum and Dad from Nelson on Sunday afternoon, 10th October. I handed the phone over to Andrew for him to say hello to his grandmother but he did not speak to his grandfather. Dad said he was "OK".

On Sunday night, after I had arrived back in Auckland, I was in my car just leaving the airport car park when Dad rang me on my cellphone and, quite uncharacteristically, asked if I had clients the following day, Monday. I had, but asked him why he asked me that on a Sunday night – it was a most unusual question for him. He said he would like to see me and thought if I didn't have clients I might like to drive down. He said he knew that I must have just arrived back at the airport after my weekend in Nelson. Indeed, he timed his call very well and it was just a matter for me to choose to turn north to drive home or turn south to go down to Tauranga. "I don't feel up to much", he said. Those were his exact words, they are etched on my memory for ever. I told him I was sorry that I could not go down as on the Monday I did have important client commitments. Dad, as always, never insisted and nor did he express any real disappointment. I did reflect momentarily that it was unusual of him to ask anything of me at all, but the moment moved on. Dad went on to say that he had been in bed all day but he told me that the highlight of his day had been a visit from his sister Jean. He was really delighted with her visit. And I turned the car north, and went home. A wrong decision and for me an extremely sad mistake that I re-live and sorely regret to this day.

After I arrived home and settled in front of the television for an hour or so before going to bed, I rang him to suggest that there was something on television right then that he may enjoy. "Why don't you go and watch it Dad? It's very funny. You'll like it." He said that he did not have the energy or the interest to get out of bed. This was odd. I knew what made Dad laugh. This time he didn't seem to care.

The next morning I rang him from my car as I sat in an early morning traffic jam on the way to my client. He told me he still did not feel well and that he had fallen out of bed during the night. I was worried and said that things could not go on like this, as it was not his first fall in these recent months. The family had been encouraging him to come to Auckland to a rest home nearer us. He had started to come around to the idea and we had started looking. This morning, he said to me, "I know it can't go on like this. Have you heard from that rest home yet? Is that room available now?" This was not like Dad at all. I considered that he really must be very sick.

I was quite worried and when I had a break I rang him from the client Fisher and Paykel. I never rang Dad from a client's but I had decided that if he still felt ill I would tell him that I would try and re-arrange my business week and come down. It was 3pm. He was still in bed and he said, "I'm OK". I had to cut him short as someone came back into the room. I said, "I'll ring you later Dad. I might be able to get down." That was the last time I spoke to him.

Just before 5pm he sat up on his bed, leaned forward, and with Mum in the bedroom with him, fell heavily onto the floor, with a heart attack. He tried to instruct Mum, with her limited sight, how to use the phone to ring for help. In the end he managed to get her to dial 111. The telephonist was on the phone trying to establish her location when, fortuitously, Beverley Shearer arrived with the evening meal. She rushed to help Dad and Mum. She rang the doctor to ask him to come urgently. She offered Dad a glass of water and then he said he would like to be alone. He died a few minutes later.

Beverley had taken Mum through to the lounge, sat her down and given her a cup of tea. As she did this the doctor, nurses from Melrose, and ambulance arrived – all too late. While all the activity was going on around her husband in the bedroom, Mum did not move from her chair in the lounge. It was strange. They came and told her Dad had passed away, but, although clearly distressed, she made no move to see him.

I received the call on my cellphone at 5.20pm in a hotel in Greenlane where I had just arrived to meet a colleague for a drink after work. I left for Tauranga straight away not returning home even to pick up some overnight things. I was due to go to Weston and Kathy's for tea that evening. I rang them immediately and called in there, in Remuera, for a few minutes on the way south, but did not stay to eat anything. My one concern was to be with Mum as quickly as possible. From the car phone I also traced Riley's number in Canada where he and Anne were staying with Anne's sister and brother-in-law, Jill & Sebastian, at the beginning of a holiday and rang them with the news. Riley had just gone to bed there and was faced with a sudden and long trip back to New Zealand.

I arrived in Tauranga about 8pm. The cottage was a blaze of light except for Mum and Dad's bedroom where Dad had been lain on the bed: this room was ominously dark. It is strange I thought how intensely you notice these things in the fearful moments of your life when the whole world seems to close in on you like some sort of tolerable suffocation. There were several cars parked outside but a space had been left for me and I parked right behind Dad's car in the carport at the front door. "His car," I thought. What a strange thing to think. What an odd thing to notice. But I took it in. Dad's car, but no Dad.

I was met by Ruth McKinnon, the Melrose manager of the cottages, who had become a particular friend of Dad's and who had been especially kind and supportive to them both in all the years they had been in Melrose. She threw her arms around me. The doctor met me on the doorstep too. He asked if I wanted the funeral directors to come and take Dad away. "No," I said firmly and without hesitation, "I do not. I want him to stay with us tonight. I want him to rest. I want him to sleep. I want him to be there. I want to be with him." I don't know why I said all that to the doctor, but I just did as if no one was listening. But the doctor did listen as if he had all the time in the world and he seemed to be watching me think.

I walked inside, past the one darkened bedroom, straight to Mum who was still sitting in the lounge with a room full of friends, in particular Eileen and Jack Armit, whom had been called. Ruth was there, Wynne Kerr was there and Beverley was there too. I was offered the tea which Dad never ate. I could not quite believe it, but I was hungry and I sat at the table and ate some of it. The whole situation was unreal and I felt quite in control but at the same time feeling little. Shock, I guess.

When Mum and I were left alone, it was almost time for bed. I made Mum a final cup of tea and then, for the first time all evening, went in, alone, to see my Dad. It was quite quite awful. Not that he looked so bad. But he just was not there for me. Then I felt a hurtful, wretched, emptiness. I thought I should be crying. But for some reason I did not. Odd.

I had things to do. To look after Mum. She was not distressed, but she was quiet. I asked if she would like to sleep in my room that night and suggested we would make up the spare bed. She helped me do that and once or twice asked where Dad was, somehow knowing, but not quite knowing, asking as if she had to be sure this was all real.

Finally, I asked Mum if she wanted to go in and see Dad. We walked in quietly and sat on Mum's bed next to Dad's. I picked up Dad's book of daily devotions which lay on the bedside table next to him, awaiting his normal consultation around that time. I turned to the Bible reading and prayer designated for that very day, and read it aloud to Mum – Dad's job, not mine. On countless occasions earlier, as I had gone to bed in the next room, I had heard him read the devotions to Mum as they settled for the night. But tonight I had to read it for him. I was surprised to find as I read out loud that the words were strangely appropriate for that very day and for that very moment. Dad had been dead only a few hours and yet these words, designed to be read that night, could not have been more apt, so much so Weston read them at his funeral service. I was glad that I had told the doctor that I didn't want the undertakers to remove his body straight away. Dad was there for the final reading from his devotions book on his final day:

The reading for Oct 11th 1993, James I, v 12

James assures us that God rewards those who endure. The crown is a symbol of eternal life which no one or nothing can destroy or take from us. The crown is often associated with the cross by which Jesus triumphed. Our outward circumstances may change dramatically, our moods and feelings fluctuate, yet God wills only our well-being and is constant in showing love and goodness. God remains the source of all that is good in our lives.

The prayer for Oct 11th 1993

> *And now O Father we commit our struggles and sufferings into your Son's wounded hands, our hopes and aspirations into his praying hands, our poor and exploited into his just hands and our living and departed into his hands that hold the key of the world of death. Blessed be the Lord for ever. Amen*

We kissed Dad and said goodnight to that dear old chap whom Mum and I loved so very much.

As long as I live, I will sadly and bitterly regret turning down my Dad's request to visit him on what was to prove to be the last night of his life. He knew what was happening. I am sure he knew. I am sure he knew. Why oh why did he not elaborate? Why didn't he impress on me how much it would have meant to him for me to go down? But he went as far as asking – which he had never done before – and I ignored the significance of that.

During the night I was worried when Mum got up to go to the toilet or to get a drink, that she would, by habit alone, go back into her own room where Dad lay. Had she found him in there, she may have got very upset because she may well have momentarily forgotten that he had died. With Mum's blindness and worsening confusion due to dementia, she always depended on the familiarity of Dad's voice to guide her back to bed and to comfort her. Mum moved around the cottage confidently only by the familiarity of her routine and at night, by Dad's voice. Tonight there would be no Dad's voice. I slept poorly, lightly, keeping an ear open for Mum getting up, which she did several times. Each time she woke, I woke – instantly. I waited and listened to her movements, and by calling out, carefully guided her back to my room, not hers and Dad's: "Here I am Mum, in here." I offered the voice of reassurance like some kind of pulsing beacon, the voice that right up to the night before was Dad's. I lay awake wondering where Mum would find that guiding voice in the dark in the future. Her eyesight was so poor (she was registered partially blind), how would she manage now? She got so easily confused and her amnesia had been deteriorating markedly in recent months. I could not think properly. My mind was racing with too many things. All of them awful.

The next morning I got out a dress for Mum to put on: she was in a different room, she would not have found the wardrobe. She navigated her home only by familiarity and routine. When she was dressed I took her in to say goodbye to Dad for a final time just before the funeral directors arrived very early to take him away.

Then Mum and I sat down alone to have breakfast together. It was a sunny day but the house felt very empty. As I had my cup of tea, I looked at my Mum carefully holding her piece of toast as she buttered it slowly and cautiously as blind people are apt to do. I watched her for a moment, looking at this beautiful mother of mine, now a widow, so very dependent on Dad, and now on me. I did not know what we were going to do.

I stretched my arm across the table and touched her hand. I said to her quietly, "Happy Birthday, Mum". Then she cried.

Just after ten o'clock the door bell went and some beautiful flowers were delivered. Momentarily I pondered on how fast the news had travelled. But the card said, "Happy Birthday Mum. Love Riley and Anne." Ten minutes later more flowers arrived. "Happy Birthday dearest Girl, Love Boy". Twenty minutes later more flowers arrived, "Happy Birthday Mum, Love Godfrey". I, too, had ordered them twenty-four hours earlier. Then an hour later more flowers arrived. This time: "With deepest sympathy".

It was Dad's wish that his ashes be scattered in the gardens of the church he loved so much, Matamata Methodist. This has now been moved to Tower Hill in Matamata and is lovingly restored and cared for as an historic church amidst peaceful lawns and under New Zealand native trees. A memorial plaque has been fixed above the old communion rail inside the church, the rail at which he stood for so many years and served communion and conducted weddings and funerals. The last time he stood at that rail was when he conducted his granddaughter's wedding.

Some of Mum's ashes have been scattered with his around the same church. It is a peaceful resting place which holds deep significance for the family because Dad loved it so much. On August 13th 1995, the family returned there for the Christening of Dad's youngest great granddaughter, Catherine Anne Bell. With his memorial plaque at the end of the communion rail where Catherine was baptised, and their ashes in the gardens outside, Mum and Dad were both there.

Death Notices in all the main national newspapers

DEATHS

BELL, Charles Harrison Rev. On October 11, 1993 (suddenly) at his home, Melrose, Tauranga. Aged 81 years. Dearly loved husband of Rae and much loved father of Weston, Riley and Godfrey. Loved father-in-law of Anne and Kathy and grandfather of Andrew, Nicky, Bryan, Hilary, Simon and Michael and great-grandfather of Victoria. His love and compassion will endure. A funeral service will be held at Wesley Methodist Church, 13th Avenue, Tauranga on Saturday, October 16, 1993 at 10am followed by a private cremation.

BELL, Charles Harrison Rev. On October 11, 1993 (suddenly) at home (Melrose, Tauranga). Much loved brother of Gwen (Jago) (New Plymouth), Evelyn Hickling (Hamilton) and Jean McDowall (New Plymouth). Loved brother-in-law of Len, Don and Charles Barrell (Christchurch) and the late Bill. Loved uncle of all their children.

Dad's Funeral Order of Service

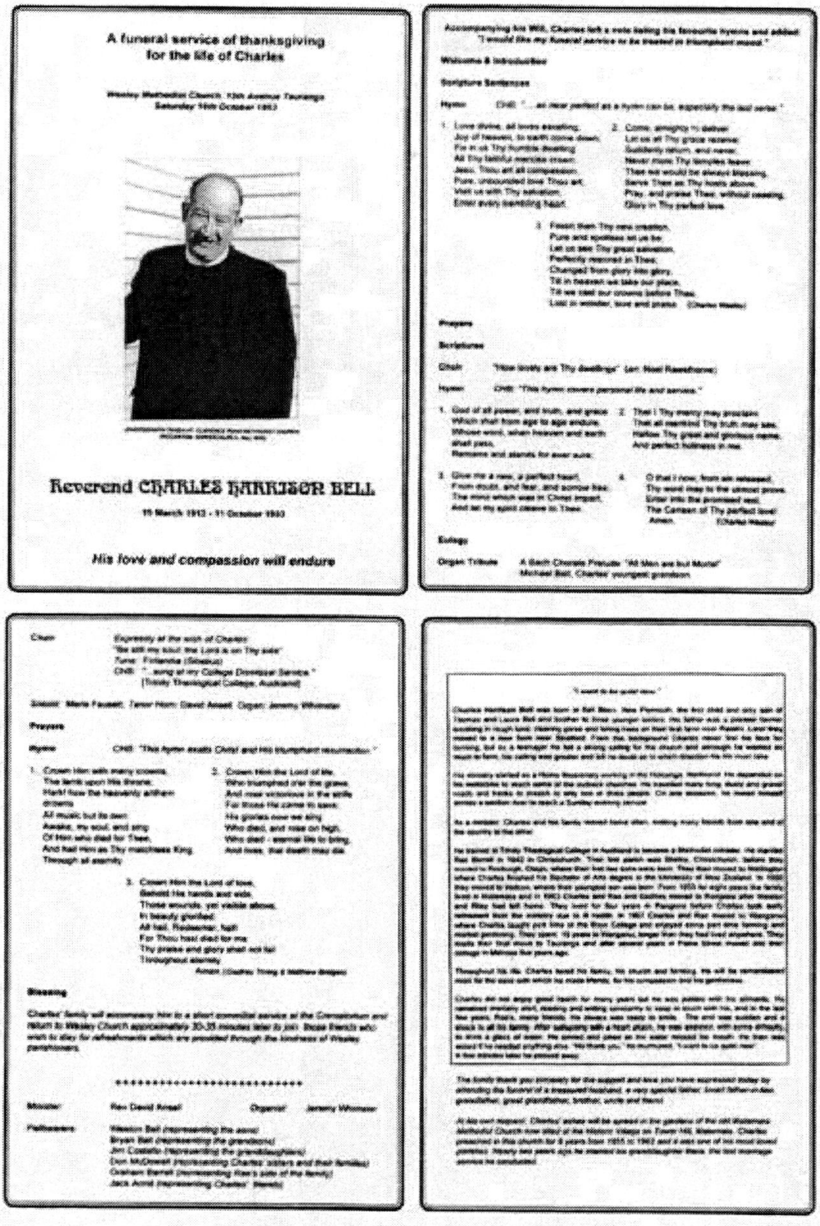

A funeral service of thanksgiving
for the life of Charles

Reverend CHARLES HARRISON BELL

His love and compassion will endure

Extract from Dad's Funeral Order of Service

"I want to be quiet now"

Charles Harrison Bell was born at Bell Block, New Plymouth, the first child and only son of Thomas and Laura Bell and brother to three younger sisters. His father was a pioneer farmer breaking in rough land, clearing gorse and felling trees on their first farm near Raetihi. Later they moved to a new farm near Stratford. From this background, Charles never lost his love for farming, but as a teenager he felt a strong calling for the church and although he wanted so much to farm, his calling was greater and left no doubt as to which direction his life must take.

His ministry started as a Home Missionary working in the Hokianga, Northland. He depended on his motorbike to reach some of the outback churches. He travelled many long, dusty and gravel roads and tracks to preach to only two or three people. On one occasion, he rowed himself across a swollen river to reach a Sunday evening service. As a minister, Charles and his family moved home often, making many friends from one end of the country to the other.

He trained at Trinity Theological College in Auckland to become a Methodist minister. He married Rae Barrell in 1942 in Christchurch. Their first parish was Shirley, Christchurch, before they moved to Roxburgh, Otago, where their first two sons were born. They then moved to Wellington, where Charles finished his Bachelor of Arts degree at the University of New Zealand. In 1950 they moved to Nelson, where their youngest son was born. From 1955 for eight years the family lived in Matamata and in 1963 Charles and Rae and Godfrey moved to Rangiora after Weston and Riley had left home. They lived for four years in Rangiora before Charles took early retirement from the ministry due to ill health. In 1967 Charles and Rae moved to Wanganui where Charles taught part time at the Boys College and enjoyed some part time farming and market gardening. They spent 15 years in Wanganui, longer than they had lived anywhere. They made their final move to Tauranga and after several years in Paine Street moved into their cottage in Melrose five years ago.

Throughout his life, Charles loved his family, his church and farming. He will be remembered most for the ease with which he made friends, for his compassion and his gentleness.

Charles did not enjoy good health for many years but he was patient with his ailments. He remained mentally alert, reading and writing

constantly to keep in touch with his, and in the last few years, Rae's, many friends. he always was ready to smile. The end was sudden and a shock to all his family. After collapsing with a heart attack, he was assisted with some difficulty to drink a glass of water. He smiled and joked as the water missed his mouth. He then was asked if he needed anything else. "No thank you", he murmured. "I want to be quiet now."
A few minutes later he passed away.

The pallbearers at Dad's funeral were:
Weston Bell (representing the sons)
Bryan Bell (representing the grandsons)
Jim Costello (representing the granddaughters)
Don McDowall (representing Charles's sisters and their families)
Graeme Barrell (representing Rae's side of the family)
Jack Armit (representing Charles's friends)

Transcript of Dad's Funeral Service
Wesley Methodist Church, Tauranga, Saturday October 16th 1993

Rev David Ansell:

Welcome to each one of you as we come together this morning to give thanks to God for the life of Charlie Bell. A man of God, a man of the Church, a man known to each one of us.

We are here because we remember the many ways in which his life touched and intertwined with ours, in friendship and in love. We come to celebrate his life, to give thanks to God for all that Charlie meant to us, as husband, father, brother, minister and friend; and we come for ourselves to seek help and strength as we touch the sadness that is in us and we feel the reality of his absence from amongst us.

Hear these words:

Blessed are those that mourn for they shall be comforted. Jesus said, I am the resurrection, and I am life: if a man has faith in me even though he die he shall come to life and no one who is alive and has faith shall ever die. There is nothing in death or life, in the world as it is or the world as it shall be, nothing in all creation that can separate us from the love of God in Christ Jesus our Lord.

You will see from the sheet that the hymns for the day were chosen by Charlie himself, "Love Divine all loves excelling", the perfect hymn of faith for him.

[Hymn: Love divine, all loves excelling]

Let us pray.

Ever-loving and ever gracious God, you have watched over all your people from the beginning of creation. You have given your gifts of life and creativity. You have given strength, and encouragement, hope and new beginnings. Hear us as we sing these words of faith and love. Words which remind us that in Jesus Christ who came into the world to share our life and to call us to be your people, words which remind us that through the power of your spirit and the reality of your love, you are always ready to change and renew our lives so that we may always know what is to be your new creation and one day to come before you, lost in wonder, love and praise. Loving God, we come to you as a community of faith, praising you for your goodness, knowing the love with which you draw us together and seeking the comfort that we also need at this time. And so we pray that as we celebrate Charlie's life, each one of us may be encouraged, that each one of us will know our own faith renewed. So help us to worship you, to know the reassurance

of faith and the peace which comes from you alone, We ask it in the name of Christ who taught us when we pray together to say
[Lord's Prayer]
Now we have the scriptures for today, chosen and read by Weston and Riley

Weston:
Dad left quite specific instructions about the hymns he would like at his funeral. He didn't, unfortunately, make our job any easier by not specifying the passages of scriptures he would like read. However, consistent with his enduring faith, each night he read to my mother from a special book of Bible readings and notes. When we looked at the one which was set down for the day he died, we thought it was a suitable passage of scripture to be read at this service. Godfrey actually read this to his mother, that evening.
[Reading] The reading was from James I, v 12.
The notes for that day say:
James assures us that God rewards those who endure. The crown is a symbol of eternal life which no one or nothing can destroy or take from us. The crown is often associated with the cross by which Jesus triumphed. Our outward circumstances may change dramatically, our moods and feelings fluctuate, yet God wills only our well-being and is constant in showing love and goodness. God remains the source of all that is good in our lives.
And the prayer for the day that followed this:
And now O Father we commit our struggles and sufferings into your Son's wounded hands, our hopes and aspirations into his praying hands, our poor and exploited into his just hands and our living and departed into his hands that hold the key of the world of death. Blessed be the Lord for ever. Amen

Riley:
The other scripture we chose was from Chapter 14 of John's Gospel.
[Reading]

[Choir: "How Lovely are Thy Dwellings. "]

[Hymn: God of all power, and truth, and grace]

Rev David Ansell:
It is my privilege to share with you today some thoughts, messages and memories as we remember and celebrate the life of Charlie Bell with whom we shared our life as husband, father, family man, as brother, minister, and good friend.
I want to begin by expressing a word of appreciation from the wider church, from our President, the Rev Keith Rowe, who asked me to say on behalf of the Methodist Church of New Zealand, that Charlie's contribution to ministry was known and appreciated in many parts of the Church, especially in the circuits and parishes where he worked as parish minister. He was known as a hardworking and competent minister of the Gospel, totally dependable in the life of our Methodist Connexion. And Keith also wanted to acknowledge the contribution made by you Rae, as you gave your own support and encouragement and offered your energy and gifts to the life of the Church.
From my own perspective, I want to affirm Keith's message on behalf of the Waikato Bay of Plenty Synod District. It is clear that Charlie's ministry in Matamata in the mid 1950s was a very satisfying time for him, and in recent months it has also been made plain that there are still many people from the Matamata parish who still remember him with deep love and affection.
You will see from your Order of Service, that Charles Harrison Bell, Charlie to all of us, was born in 1912 at Bell Block, New Plymouth, elder brother to three sisters. He was born into a farming family, into the pioneering days of farm development in Taranaki, growing up on a farm near Stratford. For two years he boarded in New Plymouth and attended the New Plymouth Boys High School leaving at the end of the fourth form to work on the family farm. And it is interesting to sense the change of expectation for education between that day and this. For the word, I gather, is that two years of secondary school in those days was considered to be almost excessive. Mind you, there are one or two today who think that now.
So for several years Charlie worked on the farm: a life that he loved and to which he was strongly attracted, a love that never left him. He grew up in a committed church family, knowing his own commitment to Jesus Christ, he was very active in the life of the church. So it was at the young age of 21 he was accepted by the Methodist Home Mission department to work as Home Missionary in the wilds of the far north. In 1933 he moved to the Hokianga. He and his motorbike became

familiar with the rough metal roads and names like Rawene and Kohukohu. They were not easy years and I think that most would-be ministers of today would probably have wilted under the pressures. It is hard for us to imagine what it was like; this is referred to in the text you have, to row himself across a swollen river, challenging enough in itself, only to find on arrival at the church that most of the congregation had gone home (presumably believing that he wasn't going to get there), to lead the service for the two or three who remained, and then back into the boat to row himself home. He must have been very fit, very determined and very committed. Charlie was involved with the Home Mission work for something like five years and became a fully accredited Home Missionary in 1936. And then for one year he carried the glorious title of Colporteur in Northland, distributing religious books and films and so on around the area.

The day came when with considerable trepidation he entered the hallowed halls of Trinity College to begin training for ordination as a Methodist Minister. We know that in those days there was a sort of class distinction between what was virtually seen as two orders of ministry in the church, categorised by different standards of training and the smaller, poorer circuits that were so often the domain of the Home Missionary. However, Charlie found that for him College opened up a whole new world. He thrived on the study programme and that, along with his other personal strengths, saw him made Senior Student in his final year. That commitment to study and learning, in order to understand and share the faith, was to stay with him and motivate him for the rest of his life. It was during his parish years in Wellington that he was able to complete his Bachelor of Arts degree from the then University of New Zealand. And not only was that a significant achievement but it was only possible because of the determination which saw him involved in a day of parish work, riding his bicycle up and down the Wellington hills, then biking to his lectures at university, then back home to tea, then out to a parish meeting in the evening. It would seem that the spirit of Bell Block and Northland was still present with him. And that same commitment to sharing the gospel, to sharing the message, was seen in a tape recording that Charlie made only something like two years ago for our Church library: still sharing the faith.

In 1942 the Methodist authorities graciously gave approval for Charlie and Rae Barrell to be married. And local Tauranga scandal has it, that the marriage broker for the Bells was one local Eileen Armit nee Ryan who introduced them in a National Youth Conference in Auckland[1] and has been held responsible ever since.

So Charlie and Rae were thrust in to the thick of parish ministry, Shirley in Christchurch, Roxburgh Otago, Miramar in Wellington, to Nelson, to Matamata, to Rangiora. In all of those places he offered vigorous and positive ministry expressed through careful and dedicated preaching and warm pastoral care. He was a man of energy and vision for the church and in those expansion days in our church, he was responsible for a number of building programmes.

After four years in Rangiora, he moved to take early retirement, finding that he was badly affected by migraine headaches, probably rising out of pressure and stress, reminding us that though he offered strong and acceptable ministry in many places and loved the opportunity to be a minister, it was always at considerable personal cost.

So Charlie and Rae moved to Wanganui, where for a while he was involved as a part time teacher, as well as running a market garden and a pig farm on the side.

Ten years ago they moved again, this time to Tauranga, and they have been much loved members of the church family in this place. During the years I have been in Tauranga I have valued Charlie's interest and support and his thoughtful responses that were appreciative of a particular service or event. From time to time he would phone me up, whatever the hour of day or night, and his opening words were likely to be, "I've been thinking". And he would proceed to tell me an idea that he had had, a thought for worship, something for the parish magazine, or whatever.

So as we pause to reflect on the life of this man, there are some key words that emerge, family, farming and faith.

And Godfrey is now going to share a family tribute to his father:

Godfrey:

You thought you would get away without hearing from me. I'm sorry.

When David said just now how Dad would ring up and start with "I've been thinking", in fact I remember he often began with "It's me here." And if the person he was calling did not know him well, they were left to puzzle for a few seconds, because he never added his name.

---

[1] Not quite correct.

For the last couple of years, Dad wanted to come and hear me speak at conferences. I always dismissed the idea with, "Don't be silly Dad." "But", he would reply, "maybe you will be a preacher one day." And I said, "That's a long way off."

When Dad was born in 1912, the *Titanic* had just sunk, and news was just beginning to reach New Zealand that the Scott party in the Antarctica was missing. That, I think, helps us realise just how long a life Dad has lived. And throughout his 81 years he loved and was loved.

For him, his whole life focused on his church and the love of his farming. Indeed, he was the most interesting minister of religion any pig or sheep must have met. Good heavens, this Reverend Pig Farmer even had a most useful degree, a Bachelor of Arts in Education and Philosophy.

A day or so after Dad died, we found in his drawer, amongst his many jottings (which I think is consistent with Dad ringing up people like David saying "I've been thinking"), a note in which he wrote of himself: "I was not a natural student, but I always felt a tremendous need to bring to my faith a mental understanding of what it was all about. Because of that, I greatly valued my days at Theological College, for the insights they gave me and for the friendships. For me, ministry meant the offering of my whole self in service. While other ministers outshone me in various ways, I felt whatever gifts I had for friendship, whatever personal traits I possessed, these were part and parcel of who I am and therefore, of my ministry. For me, preaching was the high mark of the minister's endeavour, to present God to the people and the people to God, was for me the highest activity in which any man could engage. So the weekly round of pulpit work required of me the best I could give. And to this end, I tried to give everything in my power not sparing myself. But in the end, with my preaching, my prayer was always that God would take my effort and my words and would speak his own message to meet every hearer's need."

Methodism was embedded deeply in Dad's life. His great great grandfather Reverend Calverley Riley, born in 1779 in Yorkshire was a Wesleyan minister and missionary. Calverley Riley was ordained by a personal friend of John Wesley himself. Now Riley has been carried down as a special family name for more than 200 years.

But Dad's decision to enter the ministry was at the cost of being a farmer. As much as Methodism figured in his heritage, so too did farming. From shearing sheep in Somerset, to breaking in virgin bush in New Zealand, his ancestors farmed as well as preached. Dad was at his most content working on the land. Anything else required dedication and effort. And for his church, he gave that willingly.

I will remember my Dad as a friend. I will remember him for his frequent phone calls, "It's me here", for his chats, for his extreme patience, his amazing kindness and his understanding, for his deep interest in all his family and all his friends. A more genuine fellow you could not meet. And I say sincerely, I never heard my father speak ill of anyone, ever.

But I remember him too as a most devoted husband. He told me once, "I do not want to die first: I cannot bear the thought of leaving Mum behind. But I do not want her to die before me either: I cannot imagine how I could ever say goodbye to her. "

Just a day or so ago in this sad week, an elderly gentleman said to me, "I did not know your father very well, nor for very long for that matter. But I am the richer for having known him."

Aren't we all?

Rev David Ansell:

Thank you Godfrey. Farming was always in Charlie's blood, Wherever he went it was important to give expression to that, so Nelson people are still wondering about the focus of his comment when he referred to having to deal with his lousy flock. They are still not sure whether it was the parishioners or the sheep. And I gather that Matamata'ians still have images of the Parsonage backyard filled with chickens everywhere. I also hear that some of them still lie awake at night wondering about a certain Methodist minister's Armstrong Siddeley pride and joy and a certain speed record between Matamata and Taupo.

Today then, we acknowledge that the undergirding of all that Charlie did and was, was a life of faith. A man committed to God from an early age, who felt the call to ministry and who committed all his gifts to Christ and his church, the gifts of study and learning, the gifts of administration, energy and determination, gifts of compassion and pastoral care, his love of music, his sense of worship, the importance of preaching the word. It seems to me, too, that he had an inbuilt confidence in the life of the church, and that he was a parish builder, not only of buildings, but with people, relationships and faith.

Today, then, we celebrate this life committed to God and we are glad for all these memories. Today we are glad to come and to support Rae and all her family and to encourage them with our sharing and our prayers. We know, too, that the last few years have not been easy, either for Charlie or for Rae, that health limitations have made day to day living difficult and in this situation we have seen the strength of faith and Charlie's steadfastness over this time.
It is important today again that we affirm the reality of faith. The words of Jesus assuring us that he has gone before us to prepare a place, that we may be with him. In every generation those words are the assurance that life continues beyond death, that to leave this life is to be in the greater presence of God. This is our faith, this is the confidence that enables us to know even now that Charlie has moved to the place where he hears that gracious word, "Well done, good and faithful servant. Come in and receive the blessing prepared for you, from the beginning" .
Amen.

We have talked about Charlie's love of music, we know that he delighted in Michael's ability on the organ, and so Michael offers this tribute on behalf of the family.

[Organ Tribute by Charles's youngest grandson, Michael Bell, playing a Bach Chorale Prelude, "All Men are but Mortal"]

Thank you Michael.
When Charlie graduated from Theological College that was a proud moment for him. And especially important the words of their dismissal hymn "Be still my soul", and he asked that we share those words today.
[Choir anthem]

Let us pray
Loving God from whom all life comes and to whom it returns, we thank you again for the word of faith and the hope that you give, for the life of Jesus Christ who came to share our life and to call each one of us to follow him. We thank you today for the life of Charlie Bell, husband, father, minister and friend. We thank you for his life and love, for his deep commitment to Christ and his church, for faithful preaching and sensitive pastoral care; we thank you for his gifts of intellect and vision

and for the determination which enabled him to use and develop those gifts in the service of your kingdom. We thank you especially for all that he meant in his family circle, for his vital interest in every member, for his sense of humour and for every thing in his life that reflects your goodness and love.
Give us grace O God to release him into your care, to release his spirit to you knowing that he is free at last, that in your keeping he is safe, happy and complete. Be with his family, with Rae, with Weston and Kathy, with Riley and Anne, and Godfrey, and their families. Encourage and strengthen them even as we ask that you will bless and encourage each one of us. Hear these our prayers, We offer them in Christ's name.
[Hymn: Crown Him with many crowns]
And now may grace mercy and peace be with each one of us, now and always. Go in the name of Christ himself.
Amen.

Obituary, Minutes of Methodist Conference, 1993

CHARLES HARRISON BELL 1912 - 1993

Charlie Bell, appropriately enough, was born at Bell Block, New Plymouth in 1912, the first child and only son of Thomas and Laura Bell, and brother to three sisters. His father was a pioneer farmer breaking in rough land near Raetihi and later moving to a new farm near Stratford. From this background Charlie never lost his love for farming. However, as a teenager, he felt a strong calling to ministry and made his decision accordingly.
At the age of 21 years he was accepted for Home Mission work and for six years worked in Northland, in the Hokianga. During those years he completed his training as a Home Missionary travelled the back roads on his motorbike and, at times, rowed a boat to reach the next service. For one year he worked as a colporteur.
He entered Trinity Theological College in 1939 and revelled in the study opportunities provided. In 1942 he married Rae Barrell in Christchurch

and in due course their family grew to include Weston, Riley and Godfrey.

Throughout his life, Charlie loved his family, his Church and his farming. He will be remembered most for the ease with which he made friends, for his compassion and his gentleness - for his smile and his sense of humour.

Charlie offered ministry in the parishes of Shirley, Roxburgh, Miramar (Wellington East) (where he completed his BA at the University of New Zealand), Nelson, Matamata and Rangiora. After four years in Rangiora, Charlie retired early on health grounds, but continued to be active in the Church both at Wanganui and Tauranga.

In some personal notes, Charles assessed ministry highlights as including six years on the Conference Secretarial Staff, and twenty years on the Examination Committee. He was responsible for a variety of building projects which still serve the Church today. "For me, Ministry was the offering of my whole self in service. While other outshone me in various ways, I felt that what gift I had for friendship, what personality traits I possessed, were part and parcel of my ministry and they must all be used in my ministering. Above all, while recognising that many people could outpreach me, preaching was for me the high mark of the ministerial endeavour. To present God to the people, and the people to God, was for me the highest activity in which a human could engage, so the weekly round of pulpit work required of me the best I could give, and to this end, I tried to give everything in my power, not sparing myself."

Charlie was a faithful minister of the Gospel. We will miss him.

The thank you card after Dad's funeral

†

Reverend Charles Harrison Bell

19 March 1912 - 11 October 1993

His love and compassion will endure

"Be still my soul: the Lord is on thy side"
[illegible]

Rae, Weston & Kathy, Riley & Anne, and Godfrey, and their families, were deeply touched and comforted by the many expressions of sympathy, love and support offered to them on the loss of a much loved husband, father and grandfather.

We gained strength from the beautiful flowers and the loving words expressed in telephone calls, cards and letters. We were particularly touched by the large number of friends who attended Charles' funeral.

Your thoughtfulness and kindness will always mean a lot to us.

Thank you.

Do not stand at my grave and weep.
I am not there: I do not sleep.
I am the thousand winds that blow
I am diamond glints on snow
I am sunlight on ripened grain
I am gentle autumnal rain.
When you waken in the morning hush
I am the soft uplifting rush
of quiet birds in circled flight.
I am the soft stars that shine at night.
Do not stand at my grave and cry
I am not there. I did not die.

Change of Address

Rae has now moved into a Methodist Mission Rest Home in Auckland near her family. She has a private telephone next to her bed.

Mrs Rae Bell
Orongo
60 Park Rise
Campbells Bay
Auckland 1310

Rae's telephone: (09) 478 2164
Orongo Main Switchboard: (09) 479 5211

In recent years Charles alone kept in touch with family and friends. Rae is unable to use the telephone by herself and can no longer read or write. However, she gains much pleasure in having letters and cards read to her and these will always be much appreciated.

EPILOGUE II: MUM'S LAST DAYS

Home at Last

There was something very unfair about the fact that Dad died before Mum. Although it is not ours to reason why, had I had any say at all in all this I would have dearly wished that Mum had never had to face the fear and loneliness of her dark, confusing world which she was plunged into with Dad's sudden death. Dad would have missed Mum very much but he would have mourned and understood. He would have, he could have, continued to live in the cottage in Tauranga alone, and come to Auckland when, and if, he was ready to come. He would have read the newspaper, and continued to write, he would have, he could have, watched television in the evenings. He would have, he could have rung the family and spoken to us every day, chatting and showing an interest, and being interested. He would have been a lonely widower. But not a distressed one.

Mum was denied a reflective sunset of widowhood. Rather, her final chapter was a tempestuous, frightening storm. Mum suffered dreadfully and her life without Dad was harrowing. She could not be left alone. The abhorrent, sad disease of dementia, most pitifully of all meant she could not understand and we, her children, simply could not reason with her. She was too blind to read or to watch the television. Her dementia did not allow her to understand and follow what she heard.

No one wants me to write about Mum's last seventeen months because her suffering was awful. But I do want to write about it. I had never been involved so closely with someone who had Alzheimer's. I knew what it was, but I had not *felt* it. I did not know how hard it was to witness and to bear. I did not *know* what it felt like to try to reach someone who at times, simply was not there. I did not know what it meant to feel so helpless. I did not know what to do to bring back a smile to the face of someone we all loved so much. And yet, every now and again, Mum was there. And there were moments, brief, shining moments, when she smiled again. Only to be abandoned to hours and nights and days of tears, of pain and of despair.

Mum was not a full sufferer of Alzheimer's Disease. She suffered from a related dementia. Part of the pain, perhaps, was that she was not always, completely confused. If she did not re-live Dad's death once, she re-lived it a hundred times, each as though she had realised for the first time that he would not be coming back. Perhaps nearer the end of her life, in the last weeks, she understood far more than she had for the last eighteen months. That was as long as she could last without her "Charl".

Before the week was up after Dad died, the family was faced with an urgent and drastic decision. Mum could not stay in the cottage alone. There were some alternatives. Uncle Charlie, who was recently widowed for the second time, may like to come and live with her. Mum could go into Melrose Nursing Home and go into full time care. She could come to an Auckland Nursing Home or she could live with one of the children. It was a painful decision. We wanted only that she would be happy but no option offered that neatly, simply or clearly. For one moment it crossed my mind that I could somehow go and live in Tauranga with her. This was by far the most desirable. Mum needed her familiar surroundings and needed time to get used to the fact that Dad had gone. Desirable, but unrealistic.

What made matters much, much worse, was that Mum could not appreciate that she could not be left alone. She did not remember her distress at being left alone for just an hour or two when Dad went to visit the doctor. She did not remember this, so she did not understand what we were talking about, and therefore thought we were cruel in insisting that her circumstances had to change at all.

In the end, we wanted her near us. We discussed her living with one of us, not once but a thousand times. But each time we came back to the fact that Mum could not be left alone at all, not at any time through the day or the night. She would sleep, but she would call out. She could walk, but she could fall. She could make a cup of tea but she could burn herself. She could not shop, read, or follow the television. We brought her to Auckland and she stayed with me in my apartment on Milford Beach for a few days while we hunted quickly for a suitable Rest Home. Even those few days were harrowing. But by the time we found a truly lovely place for her at Orongo Methodist Mission Rest Home in Campbells Bay, just five minutes from my apartment, the harrowing days had only just begun.

As we left her at Orongo the sense of betrayal for both her and us, bored deep. Barely a few hours had passed on her very first night there, when at 8pm a nurse rang asking me to go to help settle her. My sadness for Mum was soon to turn to a personal hell. When I arrived at her room, I paused momentarily at her door looking at her. She was sitting bolt upright on the side of her bed staring straight ahead of her. She held nothing in her hands. She was waiting. Just waiting for some kind of salvation from this. Of course she could not see me. She was in her blind, dark, lonely world. "Mum," I said softly as I approached her, "Mum it is Godfrey." When she heard my voice she suddenly threw out her arms into the emptiness in front of her but towards the sound where my voice had come from. She searched for me to take her arms but it was a frantic search for touch as if she knew that here was the one thing to stop her drowning. "Godfrey, oh Godfrey," she cried out quite loudly in stark contrast to my soft greeting. "Have you come to take me home?" It was a devastating question to ask me. She clung to me so tightly I could not pull away from her. I remember thinking that she was almost hurting me with her tight grip and I had never known her grab at me like that ever before. It was almost violent. She did not let go. She clung in a desolation that my mother should never ever have had to experience in her life time let alone at the end of it. She cried. And she pleaded, begged, to be taken home. Home to me. Home to Tauranga. Home to Dad. She did not know herself, but she knew that *this* was not her home. Somehow, I left her alone again after an hour. It was the worst hour and the worst parting of my life – and I do not say that lightly. And it was plainly hers too as it dawned on her that I would not be taking her home. That I could not bring Dad back. That I could not hand her back her life.

Quite frankly, her world had collapsed. In the space of two weeks, she had lost her partner of fifty years, latterly her carer, her home, her familiar surroundings, her sense of security, her life – and, perhaps most difficult of all for a blind old lady – her routine. I could not have coped with this, even with my full sight and mind. What it must have been like for her, not to be able to see where she was, not to be able to put her hand out and pick up the teapot where she knew she had last placed it, not to know where her bedroom was, let alone her bed, not to be able to call out to her husband and hear the familiar and reassuring answer "I'm here, dear", not to understand anything at all apart from the fact that she was alone, I just cannot imagine.

Time did not help: the future gave little relief. As much as we would like to believe otherwise, the truth is that her last seventeen months on this earth were by far her most unhappy. She was desperately lonely, confused, bewildered, lost. Why it needed or had to be like this after such a rich, full, loving life was a cruel blow to her family. The futility of seeking a reason was recognised yet keenly felt and resented. I detested, passionately, being helpless.

But something strange did happen in the very last week of her life. The confusion was not so total. The fog of mind cleared, I am convinced. She knew exactly what was going on. She knew she was dying. She knew enough to stop eating: until the communion. And to say goodbye to each of us.

I had understood for some time that dying people want – perhaps need – to talk about it. That it was harder for us to mention than it was for them. One evening at her bedside I decided to refer to it directly. "Mum," I said, "do you know what's going on here?"

"Yes," she replied. "Yes, I do."

"Are you comfortable, Mum? Are you sure you do not want anything to eat? You are not eating anything. You know that don't you?"
"No, I don't want anything."
"I'll miss you, you know Mum."
"I'll miss you too darling. But my time has come."

That was a week before she died. On the day before she died she took communion with her family in the hospital chapel. And she said goodbye to each of us. Later that night I sat with her, holding her hand and brushing her hair. She managed one or two words but I could not distinguish them. She was not in pain, as the morphine helped her but prevented her speaking clearly, even had she wanted to. I left the hospital about 11 o'clock, intending to return in the morning. But she decided not to hang on any more and died a few minutes before any of us arrived, just before nine o'clock on Thursday the 16th of March. I was sad and angry with myself. I should have been with her all night, her last night. The irony did not escape me either that none of Mum and Dad's children were with either of them as they died. When I hear of others who hold the hands of their parents as they take their last breath, I realise again what we missed. Where was I? Where were we? Twice I saw the signs, twice I ignored them: I did not go and see Dad when he asked me to, and when Mum was plainly dying, a nurse asked if I wanted to spend the night in her room, I said no. ("Would you like me to make up a bed for you next to her, Mr Bell?" "No thank you, I will come back first thing in the morning." The nurse couldn't have made it plainer, but I didn't heed it.)

Simon Bell, a pallbearer at Mum's funeral, buried his grandmother on his birthday, Monday 20th March 1995. A final coincidence was that Mum herself buried her own grandmother on her birthday, 12th October 1946.

We had kept some of Dad's ashes back and these were placed in the coffin with Mum along with her mother's Bible. Some of her ashes were scattered with Dad's at the Matamata Historic Village Church. The rest, with her loving agreement and delight, and to her twin brother's joy, were buried in Waimarie Cemetery in Christchurch, with her "darling mother" on April 20th 1995, 49 years after the tragic death of her mother and just one day short of exactly 30 years after her father was buried in the same cemetery. Mum's (and some of Dad's) ashes were placed in a beautiful fuchsia box – perhaps her favourite box made by her father. Mum had loved it and used it all her life. The Reverend Norman Olds conducted the short interment ceremony at the grave side. Weston, Riley and Anne, Mum's half sister Annette and Uncle Charlie's great friend and life long Barrell family friend, Ras Price, and I were there to say our final goodbyes. As we stood amongst fallen golden autumn leaves in the old part of the cemetery, Norman Olds said he was reminded of Thomas Gray's famous, plangently melancholic, *Elegy Written in a Country Churchyard*. Weston, Riley and I, together, placed her box in the shallow grave dug neatly at the head of our grandmother's grave.

For us all, it was very, very special that Mum was buried there. Somehow, the significance was far greater than it being Mum's final resting place. After nearly 50 years, we stood at our grandmother's grave, that of a woman who had died a tragic, sad and lonely death. As we prayed for Mum, we also prayed for Grandma, and we could truly say, "We are all here. We are back. Not forgotten, Grandma."

Mum is at peace. Her ashes are intermingled with those of her adored husband and her treasured mother's Bible. They lay in a box made by her father's own hands and she rests at the head of her mother in an old, quiet, grave under the branches of a gracious oak tree of her loved home town of Christchurch. We could think of nothing else which our precious mother could ever have wanted for her final farewell to this life. She is, indeed, home at last, both here on earth and in that far greater place.

I am reminded of the words of my great great grandfather John Riley in Nelson in a letter dated 20th April 1853 to my great

great great grandmother in Liverpool: *"It is very likely that I shall see my dear mother no more in this world. . .but shall strive to meet you in heaven where we shall part no more."*

Letters circulated to Mum's friends written for Mum by Godfrey after Dad died:

Godfrey Bell
PO Box 31-333 Milford Auckland 1309 New Zealand
Tel (09) 486 0811 Fax (09) 486 0776 Cellphone 025 978000

15 January 1994

Dear friend(s) of Mum's
The idea occurred to me of sending an occasional newsletter from the family to keep Mum's friends up to date with her news. This comes in response to the many kind cards and letters and phone calls she receives. As you know, Mum is unable to read or write now, or to make phone calls by herself. This letter I hope, therefore, meets a need. Mum often asks if we have thanked this person or that (a "healthy" sign of "planning"), and it is of comfort to her when she believes the job that Dad undertook so sincerely and thoroughly in recent years, "continues to be done".

Mum's Christmas cards and gifts poured in. She was thoroughly spoilt and the family were delighted for her sake: it was comforting to her as well as to us to know that in Mum's loneliness for Dad, she could smile over the number of friends who have remained loyal and thoughtful.

I must explain, however, that if you do not get a personal acknowledgement please bear with us. Often the Orongo staff open the mail for Mum and when one of the family arrive, cards are separated from envelopes or from gifts and it has been difficult for us to keep an accurate record although we do try!

All the cards and letters were read to her, often more than once. Mum's short term memory has gone (she sometimes cannot remember something just a few minutes later). Often she will not remember who, if anyone, visited her that day. And when one of the family take her home for tea, the next day she is apt to say that she has "not seen them for ages". This will help you understand how stressful it is for all of us. Nevertheless, the joy and comfort OF THE MOMENT is the most important thing we can wish for her and we all strive to achieve. If we did not believe that those individual moments were cherished – even if it is only to pass the time of day – I am sure we would be deeply disheartened. That is why your letters are often read and re-read to her, and as they are read, she smiles and often remarks with surprising clarity about the memories they evoke. As with the Christmas cards, simply the sender's name also brings a smile of recognition to her. These moments are happy and treasured ones.

You may have tried to phone Mum once or twice (09 478 2164). The telephone is next to her bed but she spends most of the day in the lounge further along the corridor. She often has a short sleep on her bed after lunch, but this can vary from five minutes to half an hour. It is therefore often more by chance than design if you manage to get hold of her. I know the staff sometimes pick up the ringing phone as they pass her room, so it is not always a wasted effort! Mum goes to bed anytime from 9pm on so you might be lucky.

There are often periods when Mum is not confused. Then she understands that Dad has gone and she grieves for him quite normally. But I think it is only fair to explain, in case you visit or talk with her, that sometimes she forgets that Dad has died and she lives in a world that was real to her a couple of decades ago. Her long term memory is as markedly good as her short term memory is markedly poor.

Since Mum has been at Orongo, her health has improved a little and her mental reasoning is a little better – that is, relatively speaking. The latest professional view is that she is not suffering from Alzheimer's itself (although Alzheimer's is still a "mysterious" disease), but an Alzheimer's *Related* Disease - multi infarct dementia. This perhaps gives us a little hope that she *may* not deteriorate to an "advanced stage" which is so dreadful. Mum knew it was Christmas, for example, and was able to talk about the need to send cards and buy presents. This, apparently, is not typical "reasoning" of a "pure" Alzheimer's sufferer who would not make any association with Christmas and the need to plan anything for it.

Mum had Christmas dinner with Weston and Kathy and their family in Remuera and then came to me here in Milford for Christmas tea. I had friends with me from England and Anne and Riley and their family spent the day with us. Anne, I hasten to add, was the cook! Mum enjoyed the day.

One of the family visits her almost every day and we take it in turns to take her to Takapuna Methodist Church on Sundays although this is proving a strain as she never misses Dad more than when she is in church, which is quite understandable.

Although I would like to report that Mum is settling in, the truth is that she is finding it difficult to come to terms with her new life. She is still far from happy. Each one of the family still finds the visits stressful. But we want you to know that she is being looked after and cared for as best we know how. Your letters and prayers may go unanswered, but never unappreciated.

With every best wish from all the Bell family for a very happy New Year. If we have missed anyone who should or would like to get this letter, or if we have omitted thanking anyone who attended Dad's funeral or sent a card, do please let us know.

Sincerely

Godfrey

[and: Weston & Kathy, 9B Garden Road, Remuera, Auckland 5 (09 522 0306), and Riley & Anne, 6 Birchwood Grove, Greenhithe, Auckland 10 (09 413 8169)]

(PS Most of the mailing list for this letter has been compiled from Christmas cards and gifts we know Mum received. We will try to extend it to a wider circle of family and friends as we continue to add names.)

Godfrey Bell
PO Box 31-333 Milford Auckland 1309 New Zealand
Tel (09) 486 0811 Fax (09) 486 0776 Cellphone 025 978000
On behalf of:
Mrs Rae Bell, Orongo, 60 Park Rise, Campbells Bay, Auckland
Tel: (by bed) 09 478 2164 Orongo switchboard: 09 479 5211)

24 July 1994

Dear friend(s) of Mum's

I promised that I would try and keep in touch with the friends who faithfully help to make Mum's life a little happier by writing, ringing or calling in to see her when they can.

I have not been very successful at keeping in touch frequently, but here, at least, is a mid year letter to say hello from Mum and to send you her love. She always adds at the end of every card or letter read out to her, "Now I must write to them." Occasionally, she realises that this is impossible and makes an impassioned plea that we write a reply for her. She cares very much that a "reply is written" - as always, polite and "right", and as always, devoted to her friends.

The family are always grateful for the contact you make with Mum and we often pick up the letters that have arrived in recent days and take them with us to read to her when we bring her to our homes or take her for a drive and sit for a while, in the car, at the beach or at some good vantage point. Mum always enjoys the drives, and in my own flat at Milford Beach which overlooks the sea, she sits quietly and is calm as she looks out over the water. Sometimes she picks out a figure walking along the beach although, disappointingly, she cannot make out the yachts or the ships that slowly cross the horizon in the distance past Rangitoto Island.

Mum changed rooms in Orongo earlier in the year (taking her own phone number with her however) to a more highly staffed wing, offering constant care.

It is now nine months since Dad died and Mum has aged markedly in that time and her Alzheimer's condition, her sight and her physical condition have all deteriorated. She grieves deeply for Dad, day by day. Occasionally she can still forget, even if momentarily, that Dad has gone, and the heartache returns with a vengeance when she realises all over again that he is not there.

Comfortingly, she is less often truly distressed than she was in her first few months in Orongo. But if left alone for more than five minutes, is still apt to panic. She is still lonely, and there are still tears, and she still "wants to come home". It is very rare to see her smile from within: there are few moments of real joy for her. Perhaps, the truth is, if we face it, there are none.

In the space of a few months, Mum has become "a very old lady" - so much so the family can hardly credit the rapidity of her decline. She now has to depend on the nurses for absolutely everything. She has "given up" in many ways and sits and sleeps the day away. Conversations she does have are always polite but they are short, often confused and out of context.

Two months ago she had a bad fall. She now no longer uses her stick but depends on a walking frame. She also got the flu and a very bad cough settled on her chest. I think she had about 3 rounds of anti-biotics but the cough remained. There is a slight improvement at last, now, I think.

The family visit her often and take her home for meals, but she is always much more relaxed in the company of only one or two. She gets agitated easily and anxious, mainly, I think, because she cannot see and forgets who is in the room with her. We used to take her to church nearly every Sunday, but this is not quite as easy any more because of her physical condition.

In her loneliness Mum seems to crave physical affection for reassurance. One day at church, she stroked my arm. I looked at her. "I just want to know I belong to someone", she said. "You belong to me, to all of your family, and we belong to you, Mum" I replied quickly. But the loneliness for her is real. It is hard, very hard.

On the other hand, we wait for those little gems which only she can come up with. Some are genuinely witty "Mum-isms" and some are funny because of her confused mind – in the nicest possible way. She is utterly convinced it is 1999 – in which case she is bound to be around for the new millennium!

I was just getting her back in the car one Sunday afternoon and before I could close her door she suddenly leaned forward, turned to me, and with some urgency said, "Well, I have made up my mind about one thing. I am definitely not going to get married again."

I was highly relieved to hear it!! Fancy having to organise a wedding on top of everything else! But keep your eye on the "Engagements Announced" columns – just in case.

With love from Mum and from me – and although the rest of the family have not read this, I'll send you theirs as well.

Sincerely

Godfrey

God's Christmas Blessings from Rae

12 December 1994

Dear friend(s) of Mum's

Thank you for the warm thoughts and Christmas greetings so many of you continue to send to Mum. On her behalf I would like to send her thanks and her Christmas greetings to you.

Mum has deteriorated suddenly and markedly in the last three weeks. In that time she was admitted to hospital twice - where she often did not know what time of day it was. She is now back, once again, in Orongo but she has aged terribly and for some inexplicable reason can hardly walk any more - even with her walking frame. She eats and drinks very little and her loss of weight is as astonishing as it is upsetting. It is true that her condition seems to vary with each visit but the changes are only slight. At this point I cannot see that she will ever be able to come to our homes again. Mind you, two weeks ago my brothers and I thought she would not come out of hospital again and we were wrong. It has been a difficult year. I did not know it could get worse. But it has. I have a photo of her and Dad together taken just a few weeks before Dad died. That is little more than fifteen months ago and the contrast between Mum as she was even then and as she is now, is stark. I am glad that Dad has not had to see her like this.

It is just on three years since I returned to New Zealand after more than 20 years living in London. I had not planned to settle here again, but looking back now, I wonder if the Great Designer had! I am deeply grateful that circumstances made it inevitable that I stayed on. I had the chance to get to know Dad again before he died last year. And since his death, Mum's great unhappiness and deterioration in physical and mental health has challenged me (and all the family) to care with a compassion that brings no reward. Our visits to Mum, listening to her pleas to come back home (but is that her childhood home she is referring to?), seeing – and sharing – her distress, have not become any easier as the year has past. And they bring no lasting joy to her. As we walk out the door, she does not remember we have been. The sadness of growing old like this and witnessing her feelings of desertion are tragic. Having to face up to the harshness of losing a loved one to senile dementia - and to despair, is a tough lesson for me. I would have missed it all had I still been in England. But I needed the lesson – even if it was only to learn that there is utter futility in asking of life, "Why must it end like this?" And somehow humility is imposed on all of us who share the experience of watching the suffering in someone you love. I thought I might have had the answers. I have none.

Since her return from hospital (just last week) her distress seems to have been replaced with a depression and flatness that is almost worst, even unbearable. Mum now stares blankly at, and even through, you. Today, Riley held one hand and I held the other. Riley was sitting directly in front of her, staring at her. He asked her if she could see him. , "Can you see me, Mum? Can you see Riley?" "No" she said, "where is he?" A moment later she adds, "When are you taking me home?" – the fifth time in as many minutes.

But deep down, she has given up. And in that resignation we are keenly aware that she feels a sense of betrayal as she continually begs us not to leave her or to take her home – and we coldly, it must appear to her, continually ignore her. This still cuts us up. We have not been able to harden to it no matter how we rationalise it time after time after time.

I am sorry to tell you how bad Mum has become. But so many of you have written to me and told me that you appreciate knowing how she is. I wish I could be brighter! But as there seems to be less and less we can do for her, it is WONDERFUL to know that she has not been forgotten and that she still has friends who care so much. Your cards are read and they are put up in her bedroom. We can only hope that the support your cards and letters offer *us*, somehow, deep down in her subconscious, carry a message of joy for her too. We do not know. But we hope so. And that is all we have.

The family join me in sending Christmas greetings and love to you.

Sincerely

Godfrey

Godfrey: PO Box 31333, Milford, Auckland 1309; Tel 09 486 0811

Rae: "Orongo", 60 Park Rise, Campbells Bay, Auckland 1310; *Mum's private phone line next to her bed has been disconnected. The main switchboard number for Orongo is 09 479 5211.*

The last letter sent to Mum's friends on her behalf:

Godfrey Bell
PO Box 31333 Milford Auckland 1309 New Zealand
Tel 09 486 0811 Fax 09 486 0776

25 January 1995

Dear family and friend(s) of Mum
This is to let you know that Mum returned to North Shore Hospital last week: this has been her third admission since November. Her condition has deteriorated and the decision has been made that she is beyond Rest Home care now and she cannot return to Orongo.
North Shore Hospital cannot keep Mum in a public bed and today she was moved by ambulance to a private hospital where she will stay permanently.
Her new address, from today, is:
Attwell Ward, Wesley Village Hospital, 227 Mt Eden Road
Mt Eden, Auckland 3; Tel 09 638 9089
When we were visiting private hospitals which could take Mum, we were absolutely delighted to spot in Wesley Village, the same photograph of Reverend Ashleigh Petch hanging in the chapel there, as Mum and Dad had in their lounge in Tauranga. Underneath the photo a plaque commemorated Ashleigh's loving chaplaincy there. As Ashleigh was a close family friend (he even baptised me), the presence of this particular photograph added a special significance to our acceptance that Mum would move into that hospital. Somehow, suddenly, Wesley Village was personalised for us: Ashleigh is there caring for Mum. Dad would have been delighted about that too, I know. Friends stay with you even long after they have gone. . .
So many of you responded to my Christmas letter and continue to send greetings to Mum. Every letter and phone call is much appreciated.
Sincerely
Godfrey

Death Notices in all the national newspapers

DEATHS

BELL Hilda Rae On March 16, 1995, peacefully in her sleep, at Wesley Village Hospital, Mt. Eden, Auckland. Aged 86 years. Beloved and devoted wife of the late Reverend Charles Bell and deeply loved mother of Weston, Riley and Godfrey. Loved mother-in-law of Anne and Kathy, grandmother of Andrew, Nicky, Bryan, Hilary, Simon and Michael and great-grandmother of Victoria and Catherine. A funeral service will be held at Wesley Methodist Church, 13th Avenue, Tauranga on Monday, March 20, 1995 at 11am, followed by private cremation. Correspondence to 9B Garden Road, Remuera, Auckland.

Home at last, Praise God Almighty, Home at last.

BELL Hilda Rae On March 16, 1995. Dearly loved twin sister of Charles Barrell (Woodville, ex Christchurch) and half sister of Annette Luxton (nee Barrell) (Christchurch). So deeply loved, so deeply mourned.

BELL Hilda Rae On March 16, 1995. Much loved sister-in-law of Len and Gwen Jago (New Plymouth), Evelyn Hickling (Hamilton), Jean and Don McDowall (New Plymouth). Loved Auntie Rae of all her nieces and nephews and families. Will be sadly missed.

Mum's funeral order of service

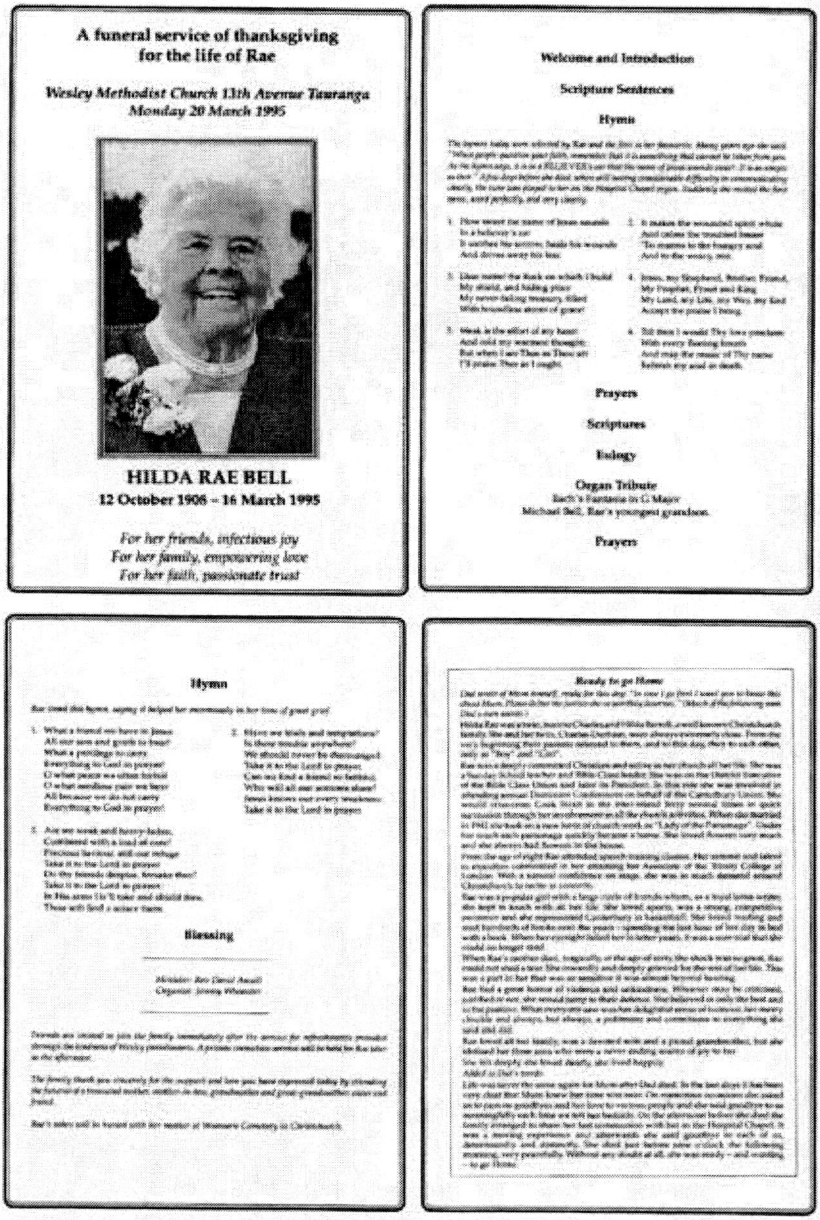

A funeral service of thanksgiving for the life of Rae

Wesley Methodist Church 13th Avenue Tauranga
Monday 20 March 1995

HILDA RAE BELL
12 October 1906 – 16 March 1995

For her friends, infectious joy
For her family, empowering love
For her faith, passionate trust

Welcome and Introduction

Scripture Sentences

Hymn

Prayers

Scriptures

Eulogy

Organ Tribute
Bach's Fantasia in G Major
Michael Bell, Rae's youngest grandson.

Prayers

Hymn

Blessing

Ready to go Home

Extract from Mum's Funeral Order of Service

Ready to go Home

Dad wrote of Mum himself, ready for this day: "In case I go first I want you to know this about Mum. Please do her the justice she so worthily deserves. " (Much of the following uses Dad's own words.)

Hilda Rae was a twin, born to Charles and Hilda Barrell, a well known Christchurch family. She and her twin, Charles Durham, were always extremely close. From the very beginning their parents referred to them, and to this day, they to each other, only as "Boy" and "Girl".

Rae was a deeply committed Christian and active in her church all her life. She was a Sunday School teacher and Bible Class leader. She was on the District Executive of the Bible Class Union and later its President. In this role she was involved in attending annual Dominion Conferences on behalf of the Canterbury Union. She would criss-cross Cook Strait in the inter-island ferry several times in quick succession through her involvement in all the church activities. When she married in 1942 she took on a new form of church work as "Lady of the Parsonage". Under her touch each parsonage quickly became a home. She loved flowers very much and she always had flowers in the house.

From the age of eight Rae attended speech training classes. Her interest and talent in elocution culminated in her attaining her Associate of the Trinity College of London. With a natural confidence on stage, she was in much demand around Christchurch to recite at concerts.

Rae was a popular girl with a large circle of friends whom, as a loyal letter writer, she kept in touch with all her life. She loved sports, was a strong, competitive swimmer and she represented Canterbury in basketball. She loved reading and read hundreds of books over the years – spending the last hour of her day in bed with a book. When her eyesight failed her in latter years, it was a sore trial that she could no long read.

When Rae's mother died, tragically, at the age of sixty, the shock was so great, Rae could not shed a tear. She inwardly and deeply grieved for the rest of her life. This was a part in her that was so sensitive it was almost beyond bearing.

Rae had a great horror of violence and unkindness. Whoever may be criticised, justified or not, she would jump to their defence. She believed in only the best and in the positive. What everyone saw was her delightful sense of humour, her merry chuckle, and always, but always, a politeness and correctness in everything she said and did.

Rae loved all her family, was a devoted wife and a proud grandmother, but she idolised her three sons who were a never ending source of joy to her.
She felt deeply, she loved dearly, she lived happily.
Added to Dad's words:
Life was never the same again for Mum after Dad died. in the last days it has been very clear that Mum knew her time was near. On numerous occasions she asked us to pass on goodbyes and her love to various people and she said goodbye to us meaningfully each time we left her bedside. On the afternoon before she died, the family arranged to share her last communion with her in the Hospital Chapel. It was a moving experience and afterwards she said goodbye to each of us, determinedly and distinctly. She died just before nine o'clock the following morning, very peacefully. Without any doubt at all, she was ready – and wanting – to go Home.

The pallbearers at Mum's funeral were:
Andrew Bell (grandson)
Bryan Bell (grandson)
Simon Bell (grandson)
Jack Armit (friend)
Don McDowall (brother-in-law by marriage)
Graeme Barrell.(nephew)

Mum's funeral photo card which accompanied the Order of Service

1993

HILDA RAE BELL

1908 - 1995

1940

1971

Transcript of Mum's Funeral Service
Wesley Methodist Church, Tauranga, Monday March 20th 1995

Rev David Ansell:

Welcome. Welcome to Wesley Church today. We gather as family, as church family and friends, to remember and to celebrate the life of Hilda Rae Bell, a woman of the church, a woman known and loved by many. We come to reflect on her life, especially to remember her as she was in the days of her strength and to give thanks to God for her life.

As we anchor ourselves in the affirmations of the Christian faith, we hear words of scripture. Jesus said, Blessed are those who mourn, for they shall be comforted. God so loved the world he gave his only son, that everyone who has faith in him may not die but have eternal life. Praise be to the God and Father of our Lord Jesus Christ who in his mercy gave us new birth into a living hope through the resurrection of Jesus Christ from the dead. The inheritance to which we are born is one that nothing can destroy, or spoil, or wither. There is nothing in death or life, in the world as it is or the world as it shall be, nothing in all creation, that can separate us from the love of God in Christ Jesus our Lord.

We stand to sing a hymn of faith, words which express deep personal meaning for Rae.

[Hymn: How sweet the name of Jesus sounds in a believer's ear]

We continue in prayer.

Ever loving and ever gracious God, we thank you for these words of faith, words which remind us that in Jesus your love watches over us and keeps us throughout the days of our life. We thank you that Jesus has come as the one who expresses the divine love, that his spirit continually reaches out to declare your love, your compassion, your forgiveness and your truth. We thank you that his is the love that is able to take away the anxiety and fear. That he is the rock with whom we can stand secure. That he is the one who is able to meet every yearning and every need in our lives. Lord Jesus, we praise you this day, we thank you for your goodness and love, a love which continues beyond this life, into the life that is beyond. Gracious Lord, be with us as we come together today, open our minds and hearts, that we would be thankful for Rae's life, that we would celebrate today, and where there is a sense of sorrow and loss, where there is any measure of regret, we pray that you will offer understanding and healing. Hear this our prayer, we ask it in Christ's name, who taught us when we pray together, to say [Lord's Prayer]

There are many things that we want to share this morning as we remember Rae and her life of love and faith. So we move now to a sharing of scriptures and of family tribute offered by her three sons, Weston, Riley and Godfrey and her grandsons Bryan and Andrew.

Riley:
Our first reading this morning is taken from Revelations 21. [Reading]

Weston:
Mum was a dedicated Christian. Her life was given in service to her Church, her husband and her family. Her loyalty knew no bounds and she would defend her family and friends against any criticism, however well merited it might have been. I cannot ever recall her saying a bad word about anyone. She was selfless to the extreme and would have given her last cent to any of us in the family if we had said we needed it and never asked why. Through a combination of being practical and frugal she saw to it that the family was always well provided for even in some very difficult times. In all, her life epitomised the ideal of loving Christian service and throughout she remained cheerful, with great warmth and a welcome for everyone. She had strength and she had charisma.

A few days before she died, my wife came across her Bible which had been carefully stored away, probably after she had lost the ability to read it. She had labelled it "My precious Bible". Inside, the caption was "To our dear Rae from Father and Mother, 12 October 1929" – which was her twenty-first birthday. Over the years she had written inside some odd pieces of poetry of a spiritual nature which were obviously very meaningful to her. Last week Kathy spent some time with Mum and read the poems back to her and she much appreciated this. As an adjunct to the scripture readings this morning, we thought it would be nice to share one or two of these with you. I will read one now. Two of her grandsons Bryan and Andrew will also read a short verse following. The first one speaks of the call to Christian service, which is certainly a call she heeded and fulfilled. The title is "Thy Will Be Done".

I said, Let me walk in the fields.
He said, No walk in town.
I said, There are no flowers there.
He said, No flowers, but a crown.
I said, But the skies are black,

There is nothing but noise and din.
And he wept as he sent me back,
There is more, he said, there is sin.
I said, But the air is thick
And the fogs are veiling the sun.
He answered, Yet souls are sick
And the souls in the dark, undone.
Then I cast one look at the fields
And turned my face to the town
Then into his hand went mine
And into my heart came he
And I walk in the light divine
The path I had feared to see.

Bryan Bell:
This poem is entitled "Silence".
If you stand very still in the heart of the wood
You will hear many wonderful things
The snap of a twig, and the wind in the trees
And the whirl of invisible wings.
If you stand very still in the turmoil of life
And wait for the voice from within
You will be led down a quiet way
Of wisdom and peace
In a mad world of chaos and din.
If you stand very still and hold on to your faith
You will get all the help that you ask
You will draw from the silence
All the things that you need
Hope, courage and strength, for your task

Andrew Bell:
The first part is an extract from F W H Myers, St Paul
Yea, thro life, death,
Thro sorrow, thro sinning
He shall suffice me
For he hath sufficed
Christ is the end, for Christ was the beginning
Christ the beginning, for the end is Christ.

The next passage only had a date, April 1930
Let the beauty of Jesus be seen in me
And all His wonderful passion and purity
Oh thou spirit divine will nature refine
Till the beauty of Jesus be seen in me.

Godfrey:
This reading is from John Chapter 14 which includes the line, "In my father's house, are many mansions". This particular line had a special significance for Mum. She used to quote it when sharing views on what heaven and hell was all about it. She did not believe in any kind of fiery hell, but she used to say, I do believe that there are many mansions in our Lord's house. And that being so, my darling mother, we all know that God must have surely prepared the finest mansion of them all for someone as special as you.
Mum was utterly devoted and deeply loyal to her mother and their relationship made an enormous impact on Mum's life. One of Mum's most precious things was her mother's Bible, given to her by her father after her mother had died. In recognition of the deep love for her mother and her long grieving for her, today Mum is being buried with her mother's Bible in her hands. For this very special reason, this reading which Mum knew so well, is quoted directly from that particular Bible, my grandmother's, using of course the old English which is not so commonly heard these days.

St John, Chapter 14 [Reading] Here endeth the reading from St John.

And as part of the family tribute, I would like to share one or two thoughts with you.
Mum's passing must have been a fulfilling and beautiful moment for her. Earlier last week, Riley faxed a message to Weston and to me. It said, "I may be being sentimental but all day today I could see Dad and Mum's mother standing just there, waiting in the wings." I am sure you were right Riley. They would have been getting ready to welcome her home. She died only two days later.
I want to tell you a tale about my mum not just now as my mother, but as a twin. She dearly loved her twin brother, Boy and there were many a tale to tell. On one occasion, when still very young, the twins were to

sing a duet in church. Mum and Uncle Charlie went together up to the front of the church and turned to face the congregation, holding each other's hands tightly such was their concentration. They proceeded to sing in perfect harmony, something like "Jesus Bids Us Shine", although I cannot quite remember what it was. They sang in unison, that is until verse 3. At that point one started singing verse 3 and the other started singing verse 4. They stopped precisely at the end of the first line realising that something was very wrong. Without turning to look at each other, they remained staring straight ahead of them at the congregation with one saying to the other, "You're wrong" and the other replying "No you're wrong", "You're wrong", "No, you're wrong", repeatedly and without resolution. Their mother had to intervene. She walked up the aisle from the back of the church, knelt down in front of them, whispered in their ear and returned to her pew. The twins proceeded with verse 3 in unison and thankfully finished also In unison. As the twins returned to their places walking back up the aisle, one was heard to say to the other, "Anyway you *were* wrong."

On another occasion, a lady who did not know they were twins, asked which child was the older. "I am", said Mum proudly. "No, I am", said Uncle Charlie. Trying to settle the matter, the lady asked Mum how much older she was than her brother. This was the moment Mum had been waiting for. She could now prove her claim to her rightful status. She had the facts ready. She puffed out her little chest and announced triumphantly, "Three minutes."

And now my mum, as my mum. A friend of mine, whom I used to go to school with, and who stayed with my parents occasionally when we were teenagers and now lives in London, faxed me when I told him about Mum. "I will remember your mum most for her sense of humour and, oh, for her pavlovas." Her pavlovas were indeed fantastic, but so were her banana cakes.

But I shall remember my mother most dearly for her warmth and for the fact that we seemed to share exactly the same sense of humour. She could reduce me to tears of laughter. Dad used to look on slightly puzzled as to what she had said and what I had found so very funny. It was indeed, which she shared with all her friends, an *infectious* joy.

But most of all she loved deeply and cared deeply. Dad wrote that Mum idolised her three sons. Funny, but somehow I knew that. But here she was very clever. She never had a favourite son but each of us could well have believed we were the favourite, so passionately did she love us all. It was an empowering love, one which inspired us to try always to be our best, to love, to laugh, and most importantly of all, to be a close family.

And as for her faith. It was an unquestioning faith. She simply *believed*. She had a trust in her faith that was immovable and that might have left some of us slightly in awe of how deeply she trusted. It was a passionate trust that the Lord was there at any time and always. If anyone has given themselves to their Lord totally and utterly, without pause, doubt or hesitation, it is this person here today, to whom we have come to say goodbye.

As for her sensitivity and kindness. which were great, it would be summed up best with something she used to say to me: if you are ever in doubt as to what to do or say dear, choose the kinder thing.

When I left for England many years ago, she and Dad came to farewell me on the ship. After the goodbyes and the broken streamers and the New Zealand shores were fading from sight, I returned to my cabin. There on my bed was a card from her. It said, "We will miss you. Do not forget what you stand for. Remember no matter where you go, there you are."

I can hear her saying it again today. I think it would be her final wish that we the family remember just that now that both she and Dad have gone. Remember what we stand for, no matter where we go, there we are. Our parents and our grandparents living on through us.

What more can one say of our Mum? Only this and this I suppose is all that matters. She was a lovely, lovely, lovely mother.

Rev David Ansell:

Just before we hear the organ tribute, some more words that I guess take us back to the beginnings of Rae's life, a woman whom we have already begun to hear shared our life, who lived within the family of the church all her life and who for a number of years shared our life in this place. When I arrived in Tauranga a number of years ago, Rae and Charlie were an older couple firmly entrenched in this congregation, but I think with Rae just a little in the background. She was mostly bright and cheery but her worsening sight made it difficult for her to be as active as she might have wished and she became increasingly dependent upon Charlie and her friends to enable her to cope. She also began to have problems with her memory as Alzheimer's disease started to affect her and she became a shadow of her former self. So it is good that we can gather today to pay tribute to a woman whose life story has in fact been one of warmth and energy and a zest for living, a woman of faith, whom we have already heard, gave out so much during her life.

As we look at some of the family history, born in 1908 into the heart of New Zealand Methodism in Christchurch. Her parents, Charles and Hilda Barrell prominent in Christchurch and in the Durham Street Methodist Church. And along with her twin brother Charles, they were a close and devoted family. Her father was a well to do businessman and active lay preacher, who ran what was then the largest funeral directing business in New Zealand at the time. So that for Rae, these were major influences in her growing up years. She was much loved by her family, and her family wealth and support and social standing coloured her upbringing and her achievements. In a letter that he wrote sometime before he died, Charlie commented that she was a reasonably good scholar and managed to cope with all the exams she was required to pass. That rings some bells somewhere doesn't it? In fact she became a highly competent shorthand typist but her real love and achievement in those days was in the world of sport. And for those of us who came on the scene later on in Rae's life it is something of an eye opener to hear her husband-to-be describe her as "strong, fit and fast". In fact Rae was a strong, competitive swimmer and became a Canterbury representative at basketball and in this field she developed some of her leadership skills, captain to the Gregg's team for which she played. When she was only eight years old she was sent off to speech training classes, developing for her a lifetime interest in speech, in drama and in English literature: always an avid reader. She developed her knowledge and skills finally achieving an ATCL in speech and only just falling short of obtaining an LTCL. Much in demand around Christchurch for her ability to recite and to entertain at social functions and concerts. In many ways, and I guess I saw glimpses of this, a natural actress, who with her confident personality and ready humour was able to reach out and touch many people. And I gather there are still people in Matamata who have a stage image of Rae bewailing the fate of her missing dog Fifi, who turned out to be male instead of female.

As a young woman Rae was part of a lively, energetic group of women around Christchurch, very much the centre of attraction, and with the use of father's swept up Essex, was able regularly to blitz the streets of

Christchurch. And can't you imagine the occasion when she and the girls packed into the Essex late at night, much later than was proper for young women of the day, and drove a number of times around Cathedral Square, no doubt hooting and making all sorts of noise, until finally stopped by a Traffic Officer. But far from being upset about it, she fronted him up and said, "Yes Officer, how can we help you, have you got a problem?" "Are you having fun, Miss?" "Oh yes, hope you are too." "I'd have more fun Miss if you turned your car lights on. You've been around the Square four times already. Might I suggest you turn them on." And can't you just hear Rae responding, "What a jolly good idea" as they drove off into the night.

But Rae was far from being an empty headed socialite. She was already a committed Christian, a young woman who had moved through the Sunday School and Bible Class life of the Church, who became heavily involved in the Methodist Church of Riccarton accepting leadership as Sunday School Teacher, Bible Class leader, member of Quarterly Meeting and no doubt other things as well. She was committed to the work of the old Bible Class Union, on the Canterbury Union as executive member and as President, involved in the summer schools and Easter camps of the day, giving time and energy travelling widely to offer leadership and encouragement. Then in 1939 Rae attended a summer school in Stratford which was to shape the rest of her life. It was there apparently that she was marked down by Charlie's sister Jean who seemingly acted as his talent scout. Rae's self confidence, good humour and general attractiveness were almost too much for Charlie to handle, especially when he plucked up the courage to have a conversation with her and discovered that she disagreed with him totally on every issue he brought up. Then the story moves on to Auckland seven or eight months later, Charlie at Theological College, down with the flu, and in came Eileen Armit, the matchmaker, complete with Rae Barrell, who had temporarily transferred to Auckland with her employer The Public Trust. Now Eileen, as we all know was never one to be backward, and I quote, verbatim, said Eileen, "She obviously wanted to meet you again Charlie, didn't you Rae?" And when Rae turned down Charlie's invitation to go to the pictures on the grounds that she would be working a lot, again Eileen struck, "Nonsense, Rae, you are not going to be busy every night for the next two months. You will go with Charlie. Of course she will Charlie." And so it came to pass. Father Barrell said no, at least once. And

Charlie had to wait for some time before his Taranaki pigs fattened sufficiently that they could be sold to provide an engagement ring.

The move from a well to do family in Christchurch to a struggling life of a 1940s parsonage must have been quite traumatic. And I believe it says a great deal about Rae's strength of character and Christian commitment that she fronted up with all the energy and gifts that she possessed. A good homemaker, loved her flowers, very self disciplined and organised, and if I get the picture right, she was the one who made very sure that her three sons were always in the right place at the right time doing the right thing. I gather that is largely true except for a story I heard last night which related to Riley out late at night in the family car driving straight past his father who was on a push bike looking for him.

So then, Rae loved her family as we have heard, thought that her three sons were just the best and included their families in that same love and care. Perhaps it is significant that all the family have gathered today which as I think we heard is Simon's 22nd birthday, the day after what would have been Charlie's 83rd birthday, I am sure Rae celebrates with us this morning. There is much more that we might say about a woman of strongly committed faith, a woman of strong standards and values, expressed through the Church, through her commitment to the Women's Christian Temperance Union, a concern which she shared with her mother and followed in her mother's footsteps. Rae was a woman of tender heart, had a real horror of violence and unkindness and was always ready to spring to the defence of anyone who was being criticised. She had a warm positive outlook on life, a life lived strongly in will, a life of certain faith, knowing without a shadow of doubt, as Godfrey shared with us before, that Christ went before her to prepare a place.

So today we gladly celebrate her life and witness and we release her into the hands of God.

To Weston, to Riley and to Godfrey and to your whole family circle, we acknowledge the loving care with which you surrounded your mother, especially in this last year or two and for the care that you gave to her. We honour you for that. And to the whole family circle we offer you our love, our prayers and our friendship as you face your personal sense of loss and the reality of Rae's death. And our hope is that her life and witness will continue to be a strength and a guide for each one of you.

I finish with some words from her family:
Life was never the same again for Mum after Dad died. In the last days it has been very clear that Mum knew that her time was near. On numerous occasions she asked us to pass on goodbyes and her love to various people and she said goodbye to us meaningfully each time we left her bedside. On the afternoon before she died the family arranged to share her last communion with her in the hospital chapel. It was a moving experience and afterwards she said goodbye to each of us determinedly and distinctly. She died just before nine o'clock the following morning, very peacefully. Without any doubt at all, she was ready - and wanting - to go Home.
Rae Bell, thank you for a life well lived. You have gone to meet your Lord who loved you and whom you loved and served all your life. Go in peace and receive the blessing that has been prepared for you from the beginning. Amen.

[Organ Tribute by Rae's youngest grandson, Michael Bell, playing Bach's Fantasia in G Major]

Thank you Michael.
We offer our prayers. Let us pray.
Loving God from whom all life comes and to whom it returns, we thank you again for the words of faith and hope that you give, for the life of Jesus Christ who came to share our life, and to call each of us to follow Him. We thank you today, for Rae's life as mother, mother-in-law. grandmother, great grandmother, sister and friend. We thank you for her life and love, for her warmth and bright personality and for her sense of humour which brightened many lives. We thank you for her committed life of faith, for her strong leadership skills and for her unwavering sense of values and of right and wrong. We thank you especially for all that she meant within her family circle, for her deep love and concern for each member and for everything in her life that reflected your goodness and love. Oh God give us grace to release Rae into your care to release her spirit to you, knowing that she is free at last, free from the restrictions of limited sight and struggling mind and that in your keeping she is now safe, happy and complete, united with all those loved ones who have gone on before. Be with her family, with Weston and Kathy, with Riley and Anne, and Godfrey, and their families. Encourage and strengthen them, even as we ask that you will

bless and encourage each one of us. Hear these our prayers, we offer them in Christ's name. Amen.
We stand to sing our closing hymn, a hymn of great significance in Rae's life, *What a friend we have in Jesus.*
[Hymn: What a friend we have in Jesus]

We leave this place in the knowledge and faith of these words, words of comfort and encouragement to all who will listen. And now may the grace of our Lord Jesus Christ, the love of God and the fellowship of the Holy Spirit, be with you and keep you, now and always.
Amen.

The thank you card after Mum's funeral

In Loving Memory

HILDA RAE BELL

12 October 1908 – 16 March 1995

For her friends, infectious joy,
For her family, empowering love
For her faith, passionate trust.

"How sweet the name of Jesus sounds
In a believer's ear
It soothes his sorrows, heals his wounds
And drives away his fear."

(from Rae's favourite hymn)

Weston and Kathy, Riley and Anne
and Godfrey

thank you sincerely
for your kind expressions of sympathy
on the passing of their deeply loved mother

Loss teaches us sensitivity that makes us whole:
vulnerability is forced upon us.
Everything we want or love is tenuous.
We learn we own nothing.
We learn life offers only its moments.

Extract from *Elegy Written in a Country Churchyard*
- Thomas Gray (1751)

Selected verses were read at the burial of Mum's ashes
Waimarie Cemetery, Christchurch, 20 Apr 1995

The Curfew tolls the knell of parting day,
The lowing herd wind slowly o'er the lea,
The plowman homeward plods his weary way,
And leaves the world to darkness and to me.

Now fades the glimmering landscape on the sight,
And all the air a solemn stillness holds,
Save where the beetle wheels his droning flight,
And drowsy tinklings lull the distant folds;

Save that from yonder ivy-mantled tow'r
The moping owl does to the moon complain
Of such, as wand'ring near her secret bow'r,
Molest her ancient solitary reign.

Beneath those rugged elms, that yew-tree's shade,
Where heaves the turf in many a mould'ring heap,
Each in his narrow cell for ever laid,
The rude Forefathers of the hamlet sleep.

The breezy call of incense-breathing Morn,
The swallow twitt'ring from the straw-built shed,
The cock's shrill clarion, or the echoing horn,
No more shall rouse them from their lowly bed.

For them no more the blazing hearth shall burn,
Or busy housewife ply her evening care:
No children run to lisp their sire's return,
Or climb his knees the envied kiss to share.

Mum's final resting place with her mother
Waimarie Cemetery, Christchurch, 20 April 1995

Mum's ashes in her father's handmade fuchsia box, resting on her mother's grave, prior to being buried next to her.

Riley, Godfrey and Weston with their mother's ashes at their grandmother's grave just before the private burial. Photo Annette Luxon (nee Barrell)

SACRED TO THE MEMORY OF
HILDA
6TH OCT 1885 – 13TH FEB 1946
DEARLY LOVED MOTHER OF
RAE AND CHARLES

Rae's mother Hilda's grave today with the dates of her birth and death and her twin children's names added – details that were previously and deliberately omitted. (See story of original stone Chapter 15.) Rae's grave, originally intended for her father, is at the head of her mother's grave. Photos Hilary Donaldson (nee Bell) 2004

Mum's ashes were buried with her mother 49 years after her mother was laid to rest in the same spot. Mum's headstone was added to the double head-to-head grave.

TREASURED MEMORIES OF

HILDA RAE BELL

12 OCTOBER 1908 – 16 MARCH 1995

ADORED AND DEVOTED WIFE OF

REVEREND CHARLES HARRISON BELL

AND BELOVED MOTHER OF

WESTON, RILEY AND GODFREY

AT REST HERE WITH HER "DARLING MOTHER" HILDA BARRELL

HOME AT LAST, PRAISE GOD ALMIGHTY, HOME AT LAST

Mum's silver ribbon brooch – one of her favourites and spotted in many photographs of her

Mum's watch – worn most of her life – and always with a tiny white handkerchief tucked under the strap. It stopped working about twenty years before she died but she kept on wearing it: "It's just perfect for my hanky."

One of many 1942 wedding presents which Mum kept "for best" – an occasion which rarely, if ever, arrived. This present, from Daisie Fairweather, like many others, still had the tissue paper and the gift card inside – fifty years later.

The gold chain and locket of Rae's great aunt Lil or Lily, Jane Lydia Fitzer, 1871 (London) – 1963 (Dunedin)

APPENDICES

APPENDIX I
The county and country codes used in family trees and charts

ABD	Aberdeenshire
AKD	Auckland
ARG	Argentina
AUS	Australia
AVN	Avon
BDF	Bedfordshire
BEL	Belgium
BEW	Berwickshire
BOP	Bay of Plenty
BRK	Berkshire
BWI	British West Indies
CAM	Cambridgeshire
CAN	Canada
CBY	Canterbury
CLA	County Clare
CMA	Cumbria
CON	Cornwall
CHS	Cheshire
CUB	Cuba
DBY	Derbyshire
DEU	Germany
DEV	Devon
DOR	Dorset
DUR	Durham
EGY	Egypt
ENG	England
ESP	Spain
ESS	Essex
FRA	France
GIS	Gisborne
GLS	Gloucestershire
GRC	Greece
HAM	Hampshire
HBY	Hawkes Bay
HEF	Herefordshire
IL	Illinois
IND	India
IOM	Isle of Man
IRL	Ireland
ITL	Italy
KEN	Kenya
KNT	Kent
LAN	Lancashire
LDY	Londonderry

LEI	Leicestershire
London	*includes:* London, Greater London; and parts of Essex, Middlesex, Surrey, or Kent
MBH	Marlborough
MDX	Middlesex
MEX	Mexico
MON	Monmouthshire
MSY	Merseyside
MWT	Manawatu
MYS	Malaysia
NFK	Norfolk
NIL	Northern Ireland
NLD	Northland
NLN	Nelson
NSW	New South Wales
NT	Northern Territory
NTH	Northamptonshire
NV	Nevada
NZ or NZL	New Zealand
OTG	Otago
OXF	Oxfordshire
PA	Pennsylvania
PNG	Papua New Guinea
QLD	Queensland
RUT	Rutlandshire
SAL or SHR	Shropshire (SAL comes from Salop, a former official name for Shropshire)
SCT	Scotland
SLD	Southland
SLI	Sligo
SGP	Singapore
SOM	Somerset
South Africa	*See ZAP*
Spain	*See ESP*
SRY	Surrey
SSX	Sussex
STS	Staffordshire
SUF	Suffolk
SXW	West Sussex
TMN	Tasman
TNK	Taranaki
TUR	Turkey
USA	United States of America
VIC	Victoria
WA	Western Australia
WAN	Wanganui
WAR	Warwickshire
WIL	Wiltshire

WKT	Waikato
WLD	Westland
WLS	Wales
WMD	West Midlands
WOR	Worcestershire
WsM	Weston-super-Mare
WTN	Wellington
WYK	West Yorkshire
YKS	Yorkshire
ZAF	South Africa
ZWE	Zimbabwe

APPENDIX II
Ships in the family story

The Ship	Sailed	With	Voyage
Thomas Harrison Built 1834, Sunderland barque, 355 tons	London to Nelson 26 May 1842 to 25 Oct 1842	John Riley 38yo Mary Riley 36yo William C. 9yo Mary Ann 5yo John Bolton 1yo	4 mo. 29 days 65 chln died on voyage. Did not stop en route
Berkshire Built 1836, Sunderland Home port London barque, 587 tons	London to Nelson 4 Oct 1849 to 30 Jan 1850	Robert Strange 21yo (assumed on board but not listed) Blanche Crooke 17yo (married Robert Strange) and her sister Mary Crooke 19yo (married Thomas Hooper)	3 mo. 26 days Crooke sisters in assisted steerage. Called at New Plymouth. As entered Nelson harbour ran on to Arrow Reef, floated off on following tide.
Tiptree Built 1851, New Brunswick (Canada) 1,650 tons Sank 1867 at Liverpool	London to Lyttelton 20 Oct 1863 to 20 Jan 1864	Frank Perrott 41yo Harriet Perrott 36yo Emily Perrott 12yo Eleanora Perrott 11yo Frank Perrott 8yo Edwin Perrott 5yo Gilbert Perrott 1yo	Exactly 3 mo. (92 days)
Caribou Built 1864, Quebec (Canada) 1,160 tons	Glasgow to Port Chalmers 1 Apr 1865 to 14 Jul 1865	Bridget Ann Casey 29yo (married Andrew Diamond exactly 3 months after her arrival in Dunedin)	3 mo. 13 days
Maori Built 1851, Sunderland 703 tons	London to Lyttelton 26 Mar 1858 to 14 Jul 1858	John George Bell[1] 26yo	3 mo. 18 days (110 days)

[1] The evidence that he was on the *Maori* on this voyage has recently been brought into question.

The Ship	Sailed	With	Voyage
Geraldine Paget Built 1870, Glasgow 1,200 ton clipper	London to Lyttelton (1st of only 2 trips to NZ) 18 Sep 1874 to 27 Dec 1874	George Barrell 20yo Ophelia Barrell 19yo	3 mo. 9 days (exactly 100 days). Left London with 380 Govt immigrants. One immigrant, John White, lost overboard just before reaching Lyttelton.
Caroline Coventry	London to Lyttelton Arrived 8 Jun 1869	Rebecca (Perrott) (Charles's great great aunt) and husband Thomas Young	
Blue Jacket	London to Lyttelton 18 Jul – 14 Oct 1866	Alicia Clifford, 20yo, domestic servant. (Rebecca Perrott's daughter)	
Ganymede Hulk	Prison ship moored at Sheerness, Kent 1837	Charles Clifford for stealing one ship, in Hulks prior to transportation to Australia	
Coromandel 111	Sheerness to Tasmania 1838	Charles Clifford transported to Australia as convict	

APPENDIX III
Memorials: Where are they buried or remembered?

Visit their final resting places: cemeteries, battlefields and memorials

Maiden name in brackets; relationships given are to Godfrey.

AUSTRALIA
Melbourne Coburg Cemetery Anna Maria Diamond (McDonnell), 1916, 69yo, 2xgt grandmother. *Died only 3 weeks before her daughter Mary Catherine Fitzer, also buried in Melbourne.* **Melbourne General Cemetery** Vera Catherine Fitzer, 1892, 1yo, gt aunt. Mary Catherine Fitzer (Diamond), 1916, 51yo, gt grandmother **Perth Karrakatta Cemetery** Harry F Diamond, 1917, 19yo, 1st cousin 2x removed Charles Diamond, 1954, 86yo, 2xgt uncle Lillian Diamond (Fothergill) , 1954, 82yo, 2xgt aunt Dudley F Diamond, 1962, 52yo, 1st cousin 2x removed
BELGIUM
Buttes New British Cemetery (NZ) Memorial, Polygon Wood Sgt William Walker, 1917, 31yo, 2nd cousin, 1x removed
ENGLAND
Bristol Canford Cemetery Emily Twiggs (Barrell), 1930, 83yo, 2xgt aunt Lord Mayor of Bristol, HW Twiggs, 1932, 76yo, 2xgt uncle by marriage **Hayes and Harlington Cemetery** Kate Barrell (Brooks), 1930, 73yo, 2xgt aunt by marriage Alfred Barrell, 1938, 80yo, 2xgt uncle

Horsham Hills Cemetery
Rose Symonds (Barrell), 1961, 70yo, 1st cousin 2x removed
Dorothy Grace Symonds, 1993, 71yo, 2nd cousin 1x removed

Liverpool Necropolis Cemetery, West Derby Rd
(Now a public garden) (Riley family vault)
Sarah Ann Riley, 1841, 20yo, 3xgt aunt
William Quail, 1846, 32yo, 3xgt uncle by marriage
Rev Calverley Riley, 1850, 71yo, 3xgt grandfather
Sarah Riley (Crawshaw), 1856, 76yo, 3xgt grandmother
Elizabeth Ann Riley, 1869, 30yo, 1st cousin 3x removed
Martha Riley, 1871, 58yo, 3xgt aunt by marriage
George Willis Riley, 1882, 69yo, 3xgt uncle

London Highgate Cemetery
John A Strange, 1875, 1yo, 1st cousin 3x removed
Dr William HEATH Strange, 1907, 69yo, 3xgt uncle
Anna Jane Strange (Pirrie), 1919, 79yo, 3xgt aunt by marriage
Mary Rose Strange, 1945, 74yo, 1st cousin 3x removed
Dr Robert G Strange, 1947, 75yo, 1st cousin 3x removed
William Pirrie H Strange, 1953, 84yo, 1st cousin 3x removed

Ripponden, Ryburn Valley, West Yorkshire
(These two ancestors died in Ripponden but their graves have not been found.)
Abraham Riley, 1758, 36yo, 5xgt grandfather
Sarah Riley (Lum), 1760, 39yo, 5xgt grandmother

Swindon, Newport St Chapel
(Now demolished) (Strange family vault)
James Strange, 1826, 64yo, 2xgt grandfather

Weston-super-Mare Cemetery
Edwin Barrell, 1908, 85yo, 2xgt uncle
Corp Henry W Barrell, 1886, 64yo, 2xgt grandfather
Hubert W Barrell, 1945, 69yo, 1st cousin 2x removed
Florence Barrell (Smith), 1974, 93yo, 1st cousin 2x removed by marriage
Matilda Ann (Tilly) Barrell, 1924, 61yo, 2xgt aunt
William B Barrell, 1879, 27yo, 2xgt uncle
Louisa Barrell (Brewer), 1897, 73yo, 2xgt grandmother

Edward Brooks, abt 1878, father-in-law of Alfred Barrell
Maria Brooks (Harse), 1889, 54yo, mother-in-law of Alfred Barrell
Sarah Ann Sully (Carter), 1890, 65yo, 2xgt grandmother
Walter G Slocombe, 1919, 71yo, half 2xgt uncle by marriage
Emily Slocombe (nee Sully), 1923, 77yo, half 2xgt aunt
Ernest W Sully, 1936, 73yo, 2xgt uncle
John Sully, 1867, 18yo, half 2xgt uncle
William Sully, 1886, 71yo, 2xgt grandfather
Cecil S Westacott, 1968, 77yo, 1st cousin, 1x removed
Hedley S Westacott, 1938, 44yo, 1st cousin, 1x removed

EGYPT

El Alamein
Killed in action WWII:
Rivers Wright, 1942, 35yo, 1st cousin 1x removed by marriage

FRANCE

Battle of the Somme 1916
Killed in action WWI:
Lt Harry Bolton Riley, 1916, 20yo, 1st cousin 2x removed

Peronne Communal Cemetery Extension, Peronne Somme
Killed in action WWI:
Pte Walter J Styles, 1918, brother of Eileen Fitzer (Styles) gt aunt by marriage

GERMANY

Kiel British Military Cemetery
Killed in action WWI:
PO Maurice Bell, 1942, 26yo, 1st cousin 1x removed

ITALY

Faenza. Emilia-Romagna Faenza War Cemetery
Killed in action WWII:
William Miles, 1945, 27yo, 2nd cousin, 1x removed

NEW ZEALAND

Christchurch Addington Cemetery
Alicia Booth (Clifford), 1882, 36yo, 1st cousin 3x removed
Christchurch Linwood Cemetery
George Barrell, 1921, 66yo, gt grandfather Block 35 plot 151
Ophelia Barrell (Sully) 1946, 91yo, gt grandmother Block 36 plot 152
Ruby Barrell (Brown), 1920, 23yo, gt aunt by marriage
Lucy Barrell, 1932, 57yo, gt aunt
Kate Barrell, 1933, 56yo, gt aunt
Eva Barrell, 1969, 88yo, gt aunt

Christchurch Waimarie Cemetery
Hilda Barrell (Fitzer), 1946, 60yo, grandmother
Charles Weston Barrell, 1965, 82yo, grandfather
Hilda Rae Bell (Barrell), 1995, 86yo, mother
Charles Durham Barrell, 1996, 87yo, uncle
Ray Durham Barrell, 1961, 15yo, 1st cousin
Ira J Barrell (Hedges), 1973, 63yo, aunt by marriage
Madge Barrell (Pengelly) , 1983, 72yo, step grandmother by marriage
Valerie Mary Barrell, 1967, 49yo, 1st cousin 1x removed

Collingwood Settlers' Cemetery
Mary Riley (Bolton), 1871, 65yo, 2xgt grandmother
John Riley, 1879, 76yo, 2xgt grandfather
Mary Ann Scrimgeour (Riley) 1889, 53yo, 2xgt aunt
Robert James Strange, 1875, 47yo, 2xgt grandfather
Blanche Strange (Crooke), 1884, 51yo, 2xgt grandmother

Dunedin Southern Cemetery
*Capt William H Fitzer, 1886, 49yo, 2xgt grandfather, *no headstone*
*William Henry Fitzer, 1923, 62yo, gt grandfather, *no headstone*
*Johanna Fitzer (Streeter) , 1924, 85yo, 2xgt grandmother, *no headstone*
*Jane Lydia Fitzer, 1963, 91yo, 2xgt aunt, *no headstone*
(*Block 138, Lot 8 – a bare site with a small tree)
Henry James Diamond, 1868, 31yo, 2xgt grandfather Block 19, Lot 12
Pte Henry James (Harry) Diamond, 1925, 58yo, 2xgt uncle Block 19, Lot 13
Andrew Diamond, 1901, 67yo, 3xgt uncle
Bridget Diamond (Casey), 1912, 76yo, 3xgt aunt by marriage

Hamilton Newstead Cemetery
Evelyn Hickling (Bell) , 2004, 88yo, aunt

Hawera Cemetery
Laura Bell (Riley), 1951, 75yo, grandmother
Thomas Bell, 1959, 83yo, grandfather

Huirangi Cemetery, Taranaki
Edwin George Perrott, 1920, 62yo, 2xgt uncle

Hurunui, Balcairn Cemetery, Canterbury
Mary Isabel Perrott, 1889, 5mo, 1st cousin 1x removed, *no headstone*
(Frank's granddaughter died almost exactly a year after Frank)

Hurunui, Waikari Cemetery, Canterbury
(see Waikari)

Matamata Historic Village Church, Tower Hill, Waikato
Rev Charles H Bell, 1993, 81yo, father, plaque in church

Midhirst Cemetery, Taranaki
William Thirlwall (Bill) Bell, 1996, 84yo, 1st cousin 1x removed
Mary Gwendolyn Jago (Bell), 2006, 92yo, aunt
(Buried next to her cousin Bill Bell)
Leonard Charles Timaru Jago, 1999, 88yo, uncle by marriage
(ashes with his wife Gwen)
Florence Edith (Edie) Jago, 1950, 49yo, no relation (Len's sister)
Walter John Jago, 1957, 50yo, no relation (Len's brother)

Midhirst Old Cemetery, Taranaki
Eleanora Bell (Perrott), 1924, 72yo, gt grandmother
Mary Bell (Thirlwall), 1927, 51yo, gt aunt by marriage
George John Bell, 1954, 83yo, gt uncle

Nelson Cemetery
William Calverley Riley, 1903, 71yo, 2xgt uncle
Susan Riley (Trist) , 1903, 65yo, 2xgt aunt by marriage

New Plymouth Awanui Cemetery
McDowall, Donald, 1999, 81yo, uncle by marriage

Raetihi Cemetery
Harriett Perrott (Reeve), ("Little Grandma"), 1913, 85yo, 2xgt grandmother

Stratford Regan Street Old Cemetery
John George Bell, 1903, 71yo, gt grandfather

Te Henui Cemetery, Taranaki
Mary F Eveline Riley (Strange), 1922, 71yo, gt grandmother
John Bolton ("JB") Riley. 1926, 86yo, gt grandfather 4th row on left from gates, 6th grave in, Primitive Methodist section

Waikari Cemetery, Hurunui, Canterbury
Frank Perrott, 1888, 66yo, 2xgt grandfather *(fallen headstone)*

SCOTLAND

Duns
Margaret Scott (Bell/Lidgate), 1879, 67yo, 2xgt aunt
Leopold Scott, 1889, 72yo, 2xgt uncle by marriage

Edrom Churchyard
Helen Trotter (Bell), 1898, 72yo, 2xgt aunt
Robert Trotter, 1891, 72yo, 2xgt uncle by marriage

Edrom Cemetery
Robert George Trotter, 1927, 63yo, 1st cousin 2x removed
(buried next to son Robert below)
Robert Trotter, 1910, 13yo, 2nd cousin 1x removed

Whitsome graveyard *(Near church but not church graveyard)*
George John Bell, 1833, 44yo, 2xgt grandfather
Elizabeth Bell (Lidgate), 1860, 73yo, 2xgt grandmother
Mary Bell, 1862, 48yo, 2xgt aunt
Catherine (Kate) Bell, 1894, 74yo, 2xgt aunt
Alice Bell, 1901, 72yo, 2xgt aunt
Jane Bell, 1896, 66yo, 2xgt aunt

John George Bell, 1903, 71yo, gt grandfather *(Memorial only. Buried in NZ.)*
Elizabeth Younger (Bell), 1913, 85yo, 2xgt aunt
John Younger, 1888, 75yo, 2xgt uncle by marriage

SINGAPORE

Krani War Cemetery
Killed in action WWII:
WO Dennis Scrimgeour, 1942, 22yo, 2nd cousin 1x removed

TURKEY

Gallipoli
Killed in action WWI:
Sgt Walter Riley, 1915, 33yo, 1st cousin 2x removed

Chunuk Bair NZ Memorial
Sgt Walter Riley, 1915, 33yo (as above)

Lone Pine Memorial
Pte Walter Styles, 1915, 23yo (as above – see France)

APPENDIX IV
Dad's Cars

Dad was always interested in his cars, aspiring to grander cars than he could ever afford. Second-hand would do – even if just for the sheer joy of driving an Armstrong Siddeley, but mostly he contented himself with small cars, occasionally new ones. One often remembers family chapters in terms of the car at the time. The following is a summary of the cars he bought and sold, as far as I can complete it.

Bike/Car/Truck	Col/No. plate	Bought	Place
Harley Davidson motorbike	1919 Flat twin	1929	NLD
Ariel motorbike		1930	TNK & NLD
Ford V8 Coupe		(c1934 model)	OTG, CBY
Ford Prefect	Cream	c1949	WTN & NLN
Ford Consul	2-tone grey	1953	NLN & WKT
Ford Consul	aqua- marine	1957 (new, £400)	WKT
Armstrong Siddeley 1954 model	Grey/dark racing green; 215 658	1959 (used 60,000 miles, £450)	WKT
Volkswagen beetle		Feb 1962	WKT & CBY
Volkswagen beetle	Green; AM5335	1963	CBY, WAN
Truck		Jul 1969 $600	WAN
Tractor		Jul 1969 $120	WAN
Holden			WAN
BMW	White	1973	WAN
Ford Cortina	Red	Nov 82 ?	BOP
Ford Escort	Beige	Sep 1983	BOP
Ford Laser	Blue; Nov 81 model	Jul 1985	BOP

While in Britain:

Volkswagen beetle	Dark blue 1970 model XEA 582H	Mar 76	UK trip

APPENDIX V
Dad's Birthday Book: "People I have known"

A birthday book of Dad's, *Selections of Poetry and Prose,* dated 1927, included the following names of his family and friends at the time. It is unfortunate that we do not know when he stopped using it but I imagine most names were relevant in his single days even if he lost touch later on. However, it is intriguing to note that there is a 1954 entry. I think some names have been written in by Mum. Others have been written in, it seems, by the people themselves. Perhaps it was used for many years. There are one or two strange entries (e.g. February 11th and 7th June – Riley and Weston entries – but these days are not their birthdays) which do not seem to make any sense. Question marks indicate puzzlement or uncertainty and dots indicate indecipherable handwriting. As a source of reference and further insight into Dad's life it has proved far more useful than anticipated (e.g. validation of some dates): a neat summary of "lives he touched" at one point in time and each name must surely carry its own story. Who are all these people? How did he know them? Why are they entered in this precious little book? As I read through the names, some rang bells, as they are included here in his story.

Inscription:
Charles H Bell, 7th December 1927, Form IV, New Plymouth

January

1	Wm Ernest Russell, A Martin, William H Woods
2	G M Jones, H Fr Lawrence
3	Edith J Lane, Rawene
5	Snowy Inwood, Tamaling Nuoura (?), E Dyer
7	Frank Hoskin, Frank Bateup
9	L Jones, 1919
13	Esmay McKavanagh
14	Millie Lawrence, Scivier Lawrence, Mavis R Skipper
15	J H Woods
16	F Green, R Skipper
17	Mrs M Shaw
18	Glenys Holland, Henry J Tozer 1910
19	Beatrice Bulmer 1919, Ruth Jones 1921, J C Geldard

20	M G Bell 1914, L C T Jago, Jack? Sanderson
25	D Haylock, R W Mayson, Clifford A Lane
26	Grace D Craig, Te Rangisohoora Rogers (Batete)
27	E M Keen, Frank M Shepherd
28	E Gager
29	J C Keen
31	Leonard Brown
February	
1	Weno K Tahiwi
3	E G Cauty
4	Boyd Palmer, S P Wilson
6	M Corcoran, H Choat
9	Alice Clara Pearson 1925[1]
11	R H Carey 1885, R C Bell April 22nd 1954 ???
12	Charles Lawrence, Ropu Watson, Florence Fox
13	Ina Porter, G Porter
14	Walter J Jago, ?? . . . atch, Dora A Sheaf ??
15	Joan Porter, Stewart Ferguson
16	Colin Black
17	Minnie Anderson
18	Reginald Grice
19	J Browning, Ruby Casey
21	M J Hilder 1890, A Choat
22	Dorothy Wood, H ? Dupen ?
23	E Grace Bennett, Florence C Grounds
25	C H Lawrence
27	Anne (Nan) Holland 1920, Mereana Wi Kaitaia 1918, Jean Humphreys
28	Ted Robinson
29	Don Hickmann
March	
1	J C Draper, J E Pearson 1923
3	Hilda Keen
5	Norman Ferguson
7	Beryl Keen
10	Capt Geo Martin, Ivy Florence Griffin, Les H Thomas
11	Ivan Laurence

1 Interesting that this date, Feb 9th, did not include Honor's name – suggesting the birthday book was not in use in 1937 (see 1937 diary Chapter 9).

13	Frances May Rushton
15	J Burton 1902
16	Dorothy Lane 1911
17	Thos Gager 1850
19	C Harrison Bell
21	Miriamar Larkins, Nancy Wells 1910
24	J K Watson
27	E J Skuse 1917, E A Garton, Grace Hikuroa
28	T S Eane?/Lane?
31	C Barrow, J F Choat 1854 (died 24 Dec 1933)
April	
2	M M Fletcher
4	E R Bulmer 1879
5	Morva Gunn, Sealey St, Thames
6	Joseph Pearson 1884, Mori Ellison
9	R Green
11	P Poole
14	L Hensley
17	Edmund D Grounds
18	S A Hilder, Mary Martin
19	R R Bennett
20	Lois Brookes
21	John Holt
22	Doris Baldwin
23	Maisie Porter
24	George Cloke, Nola Lane
25	Edith Harrison, Maurice Humphreys
26	Jean Holland
27	Alice B Dixon 1881
29	Pearl Kelly, A J Sharland
30	Margaret Shaw, J B C. . . ?ty
May	
2	Phyllis May Emmett, Marion Wilson, June Robinson, Laurie Greenslade
3	William T Grounds
4	E J Baldwin, C E Bickers?
5	Flora Cobbald
7	E M Bay
8	Marjorie Keen

10	P Griffey, G Wellington
11	Elsie Shepherd
13	Archdeacon J Sands
14	Walter S Riley, Nelson McKnight
15	Elsie Giles
18	Thos Moor, L B Keen
20	Reg N S. . ?en, Keith B Ronald
21	E Merrifield, Sealie. ? R Gilmore
23	May Hensley, Eunice Rushton 1919, Grace Rushton 1919
24	Bessie E Bulmer 1887
26	Gerard Grounds
27	Stanley L Luxton, Amy Jackson 1915, S B Choat 1863, F H Perrott 1855, A J Craig
28	Jack Green
30	Charles Shaw
31	Sybil Neumann
June	
4	Owen Keen (Jock), M Green, Ella Yorke
7	W T Bell [???], Ruth A Hilder 1919, Les S Pearson 1915
9	R Bird, C H Craig
11	E Ladbrook
15	Fred Barnard, Allan McDonald
19	Aldwyn Williams 1912
22	G G Bell
23	G L Vivian
26	Cedric A Verry, D A Cauty
27	Les Foster
28	Andrew J Johnston, Arthur F Grounds
30	Reg Wellington 1894
July	
1	C Holland, F Lawrence, G M Grice
2	E A Freeman
3	G E Bedggood, Eric Baldwin
5	E Humphreys
10	Joy Cotterell
11	Eliza Richards
12	D W Jones
13	M J Jenkin 1912

14	George Skuse 1904, Jessie Hilder 1916
15	Amy Yorke 1908
20	Myrtle Hilder
24	Peter Norman Hensley,, R ? Whitehead
26	Ken Gunty?
28	Michael Frank Griffin, Owen Scotter Williams
29	L R Moor
30	W A Thomas
31	A Baldwin
August	
1	T E Bell
3	M J E Bell
9	Gladys Woods, Gilbert Ferguson, Harold? W Burley?
10	J Thomason
11	V H Hensley, I M Raynor
12	M L Dixon 1918, L E Cleave
14	Grace Carter
15	S E Hensley
17	Florence Mays 1911
19	C Jago?
20	J M Blight, G Bay, Geo C Studd
21	Christina A Brookes
22	May Woods
24	Maurice P Bell, Betty Moor, J Martin, C D Penning, Harold K Brown 1914
25	E M Gubb
26	Ruby L Thomas - Okaihau 1933
31	U Downs, O E Jones
September	
3	Bruce MacKay, W R Francis
6	L Bird
8	Blanche L Skipper, J Henry Woolford
9	A Chapman, Howell Jones
12	N Holland, G V Cauty
13	E H Cotterell
14	Ethel Greenhatch 1912, T K Burgess 1916
17	Laura F Bell
18	F E Jago[1], Thelma E Penny

[1] Florence Edith (Edie) Jago, 1900-1950, Len Jago's older sister

21	A Russell
22	S Kerrisk, Albert T Field
23	John Churchill
24	R F McFarland
25	George C Tempero, Ena M Miller, John J Craig
27	Herbert Neal
28	C H Skuse
29	?? Parlane 1906, M Winiata, J Rainey
30	E L Bell, M C Jones
October	
1	Elsie M Carey, Pat Humphreys
3	E C Bennett, H C Bennett
4	J B Dawson
7	G E Merrifield, W Graham Brown, C M M Scott, E A Harwood
9	E D Patchett[1], E Magee
11	Kate Cobbald
12	HRB (Rae)
15	C E Donelle - Puketona, ? Bendall
17	Molly J Thomas
18	Hugh Gallagher, M Cauty
19	N C Parlane
20	Mrs M Woods
21	Florence A Holt, Effie N Ferraby, Fred Copeland[2]
22	. . ?angi Hikjuroa?, Doris E Moat?, Hector Holland
25	Margaret A Hilder
26	. . . . ? . . . ean?
27	R L Gibbins
29	N Wigmore
30	A S Eaddy, Patricia Keen, Rhys Williams
November	
3	Lily Pearson
5	G W Choat, L H Parlane
6	Annie H Owen
9	H J Bird 1885
10	Mrs Allan
11	Jean Wilson

1 Assumed to be Rev Ernest D Patchett 1878-1958

2 Assumed to be Rev Fred Copeland 1880-1970

12	Zilla Rushton 1917
13	C A Lucas
14	Charles H Lane, J H A Skipper 1878
16	Ronald K Davison
17	Mavis Pope, Ethel E Craig
18	I G Moor
19	P [or D?] Field
20	Geo Bell, Joan? [Jean?] Brookes
21	E J Penning
22	H Moore 1914
23	Edith O Harris?
24	Agnes Graham, W Stabler, Trev Mallindine?
25	A Mahon, B R H Davey, John Moor, H Corcoran
26	Joyce Grace Mills
28	Thos Skuse 1890
29	Edna Hilder 1921
December	
3	J A MacKay
4	Harry P Carey, J Warren Taylor, G? Simpson Beer?
5	Gordon L Lawrence
7	C L Duder - Kaikohe 1935
9	M Fergusson
11	H W Lacy
12	T W Bennet ? - Mt Albert ?, Isabella Stolter
4	W G Coplestone
15	W H Bedggood
17	Janet Ida Lucy Scott, Wi Perahama Te Mahauariki
18	Eileen Stannard
22	Jackie Woods
23	Olive E Craig
25	Ivy E Craig
27	A E Filleul 1856
28	Gladwyn R Pearson 1919
29	D M Mail

APPENDIX VI
Dad's Autograph Book

Interesting extracts from Dad's Autograph Book, found after he died.

To my friend, Charlie, With Best Wishes for your 19th birthday
March 19th 1931. Harold C Bennett

This book is like a garden patch, Where every old hen must have a scratch.
B Widmer. Dec 5 1931

Good, better, best, Never let it rest
Till your good is better, And your better best.
HCB

For two pins I'd write something
C H Skuse, 28 March 1931

Remember this and bear in mind, A faithful friend is hard to find
But when you find one good and true, Change not the old one for the new
Len Jago, March 22 1931

Clean hands, clean face and tidy hair, Are better than fine clothes to wear
Thos Skuse, Stratford, 28 March 1931

Smile, once in a while, 'Twill make your heart seem lighter
Smile once in a while, 'Twill make life's pathway brighter
F E Jago[1]*, "Merleswood", Wharehuia*

Love many, trust a few, But always paddle your own canoe.
E L Bell, "Coldstream" Wharehuia

Blessed is the man that sitteth on a tack, For he will surely rise.
L C T Jago[2] *22 March 1931*

1 Florence Edith (Edie) Jago, 1900-1950, Len Jago's older sister

2 It is interesting that Len Jago signed his name using his middle initial "T" (for Timaru). This name was dropped for most of his life.

APPENDIX VII
Mum's 1942 Diary

After both Mum and Dad had died, we found several small diaries stacked away. Most delightful was to find Mum's diary, every day written up in the year of her marriage, 1942. We also have her 1940 diary. However, mostly she wrote in shorthand[1], none more so than on the actual day of her wedding, when she suddenly took up two or three small pages to cover the entry!

What was interesting, shorthand or no shorthand, was to see the names that were entered (she always referred to her mother as "Mother", preferring to write "Mother and Dad" than "Mum") and it was impossible to ignore her visits to Bible Class camps, her church meetings and activities and her sporting events. It is also interesting to note that she wrote her name as Rae H Barrell rather than the correct H Rae Barrell.

A sample of some of the more interesting days follows. All of them are in shorthand and I have extracted only names and the odd word when suddenly Mum reverted to longhand.

By the number of visits to the dentist, she obviously decided to work on her teeth before she got married! And she was clearly delighted to hand in her resignation to the Public Trust with a big star marking the day and her enthusiasm manifested in the capital letters! And we learn of at least one thing they did on their honeymoon – went to the pictures to see a Laurel & Hardy comedy *Saps at Sea* .

---

[1] I tried to get Mum's shorthand deciphered. It proved surprisingly difficult. First of all finding anyone at all who knew shorthand or used it "any longer" was a task in itself. Eventually a teacher at a secretarial college agreed to TRY to do it. It failed. The diaries were returned: "Sorry, most unsuccessful. Was your mother left handed? Cannot translate." [Mum was naturally left handed but trained at school to write right handed.] Anne, my sister in law, also tried, but decided that Mum, perhaps like her, developed her own style. Perhaps she *deliberately* developed her own secret style! Anyway, her secrets, it seems, are firmly locked away for eternity.

Extracts from Rae's small pocket diary

Inside cover:

Rae H Barrell	130 Clarence Road, Christchurch
Telephone no	30 965

1942 (sh = shorthand entry)

Mon Jan 5	Sadie, Hilda, Charl & I
Tue Jan 6	Quarterly Mtg Clarence Rd 7. 30pm
Wed Jan 7	Lil's at New Brighton
Thu Jan 8	Charl & Arch NB: Quarterly Mtg
Fri Jan 9	Mother & Charl
Wed Jan 21	Mother, Richmond Church; 2. 30 Mrs Straw's funeral
Thu Jan 22	*[A big star marks this day]* Win , May & Kiddies Dunedin PUT IN MY RESIGNATION TODAY *[Mum's caps]*
Wed Jan 28	Val, Doreen, dressmaker
Sun Feb 8	Graeme Weston [Barrell] baptised at Durham St by Rev Raymond Dudley; Miss Hedges & Ula , Oamaru
Mon Feb 9	4. 45pm Dentist
Sat Feb 14	Richmond SS picnic; Mother & Dad sh West Coast, Moana, 10am
Mon Feb 16	Dentist, dressmaker
Tue Feb 17	Dressmaker
Wed Feb 18	Dentist
Thu Feb 19	Dentist
Sun Feb 22	Mr Bell, Hawera, 1030
Mon Feb 23	Grandma *[Ophelia Barrell, nee Sully]*
Fri Feb 27	LEFT PTO (Public Trust Office)
Mon Mar 2	PTO Junior Girls trousseau
Tue Mar 3	PTO Senior Girls trousseau
Sat Mar 14	Gwen & Ash's wedding
Wed Mar 18	Harold Brown, Henry Woolford
Thu Mar 19	*[The day she married: ALL in sh - darn!! except for:]* 2. 30pm Mother & Dad *[Did she have an appt with her parents on her wedding day?! Maybe it was for photographs.]*
Fri Mar 20	Una - a son
Sun Mar 22	Molly's

Wed Mar 25	sh. . to USS Co. . . Harewood aerodrome. Left by plane at 10.15am and arrived Wgtn 11.40am. Met A Katie . . sh. . saw Dorothy Harwood . . Harold Brown's at Johnsonville. . . . caught railcar at 5. 15pm to Hawera.
Tue Mar 31	. . . pictures "Saps at Sea" *[a Laurel & Hardy comedy]*
Fri Apr 3	Good Friday. Left Hawera 10am for Wgtn
Sun Apr 5	Easter Day. Doctor.
Apr 6-25	*[No entries – for first time in whole year: ill. – GB]*
Mon May 11	Engaged two years today. *[Odd to note this now she was married?]* Cold wintry day. Shifted to Edgeware Rd
Tue May 12	Charl & I, to Rangiora, Ministers' Retreat. A very wet day.
	[Obviously lost interest after marriage: no more entries for rest of year! – GB]

Notes:

1. The reference to her Grandma, Mon Feb 23, is interesting. I wonder what that day was about.
2. The day before, Sun Feb 22, she saw Mr Bell, Hawera. Was she in Hawera but back in Christchurch to see her grandmother the following day? (Unlikely.) If she was in Christchurch, why the Hawera reference? It can only be a reference to her future father-in-law Tom Bell?
3. She saw a doctor on Easter Sunday (Apr 5th) – she must have been quite ill.

APPENDIX VIII
Mum's box of papers

Mum kept a small box in which she crammed things she wanted to keep. It was really her writing box and all over the lid and down the sides, inside and outside, and even on the bottom – in every last square inch, or indeed centimetre, was nothing less than her entire address book. The phone numbers, addresses and birthdays of friends and family, were written here, on her box.

Inside were letters, little newspaper cuttings, Mum and Dad's birth certificates, marriage certificate, typed poems, devotions and prayers, some of our own school reports and references, cuttings from birthday cards she received. In there was even her Christchurch High School Old Girls' Association Membership Card - for 1925! I discovered too that she often cut out the personal message from birthday cards and kept them. On some of the envelopes were little messages in her own broad, round, handwriting – nearly always in ink – that appeared to be intended for those who found them after she died: for example, "This is my darling mother's".

Her memorabilia and the messages she chose to keep, told a lot about her. All of the messages and memoirs related, in some way or other, to her faith, her family, her friends. She liked little sayings on kindnesses and love, and lines on the meaning of friendship. In amongst all the papers, carefully folded and tucked away, in envelopes, or on their own tucked down the side of the box, were prayers and favourite lines of hymns. There were also obituaries and even a description of a friend's wedding, which she must have kept for 50 odd years.

As I unfolded these little pieces of paper, and opened the dozens of envelopes containing her little treasures, I realised how all must have been very special to her. She must have spotted something, sat at the typewriter to type it up, grabbing any piece of handy paper; cut something out of the newspaper, cut out the personal greetings of special birthday cards to her, and popped them in her box, where they stayed for decades. To remember.

On one piece of paper, yet another colour, yet another size, folded over four or six times, was the following poem. We wish we had found it in time to read at her funeral.

My Resolution

I won't look back; God knows the fruitless efforts,
The wasted hours, the sinning, the regrets;
I'll leave them all with Him who blots the record,
And mercifully forgives, and then forgets.

I won't look forward; God sees all the future,
The road that, short or long, will lead me Home,
And He will face with me its every trial.
And bear with me, the burden that may come.

But I'll look up…into the face of Jesus,
For there my heart can rest, my fears are stilled;
And there is joy and love, and light for darkness,
And perfect peace, and every hope, fulfilled.

APPENDIX IX
Dad's Sermons

Out of the thousand plus sermons Dad wrote, all carefully written in longhand, enveloped and stored neatly in shoe boxes, I have selected a couple to publish extracts from – not for the quality or otherwise of the sermons as sermons, but more for the significance of the occasions on which he delivered them and for the insights they may offer into Dad as a person.

Each of his sermons was written on one side of used paper, A4 paper torn in half and written in A5 portrait format. Just as Dad did not choose to number any of the pages of notes he originally sent me when I said I would write his story, I now discover, fascinatingly, that neither did he number any of the many thousands of pages of his sermons. I cannot imagine why he did not do this and I find myself wondering how he coped if he ever dropped or misplaced even one or two pages while he was in the pulpit.

Some of my Convictions
2 Timothy 2/19; 1 Corinthians 3/5-7

18th December 1966 Rangiora (Farewell)
5th February 1978 Turakina, Fordell (Final services)

"Nevertheless the foundations of God standeth sure" (2 Tim 2/19)

[Extract only:]
Dr C H Lucas was one of the Prince of Preachers of my father's generation. In one of his few published sermons, he dealt with the text "Go thou thy way until the end be" and in the course of it he said, "Life has its end for you and for me and we are nearer to it than when we arose this morning. For a thousand times the minister expands the truth from the open Book to his people and then there comes a last time and he speaks to them no more. For a thousand times, the student works among his books that surround him like a host of friends and there comes a last time and he is gone where they know even as they are known. For a thousand times the workman passes down the street to his familiar employ and there comes a last day and the well worn

tools are needed no more. For many, many times, you and I meet and part at the House of God or elsewhere and then the shadows fall and we are lost to each other *until we meet to part no more*[1] [my italics]. The hastening years move one and our pilgrimage with time is done. But be careful here. The word "end" has a double meaning. It may mean merely a termination, the ceasing to be of what was. It may also mean a fulfilment, a completion, the attainment of what has been kept in view."
Both meanings are present this morning. We are all rather conscious that it has its first meaning. This is an end – a termination – some years ahead of what we had planned – and I, for my part, am sad it is so, and regret it.
But I am not cast down for I believe it has the other meaning too. We believe that all that happens is under the hand of God and the truth we proclaim is eternal truth – living truth – that goes on in strength and vitality in the souls of men.
"The foundation of God standeth sure". This is my confidence and assurance. I want to share with you one or two convictions that have come to me over the years. I believe they belong to the foundations and remain unchanged. And because I believe this I have had the strength to hold to my course.
First is my certainty that this is God's world and it will work only God's way. This to me is so fundamental that no life can be a good life without acknowledging it. It came to me out of the study of ethics at Trinity College. Right conduct for man must be that which is natural or suitable to such as being a man really and truly is. Not suitable merely to me or to you or to any third person, but to such as being a man is. Clearly, what is right for an animal, what it ought to eat, how it ought to be housed, how it should behave, is settled by its physical nature. You would not feed a lion on roots, or expect a web footed duck to leap from crag to crag. In other words, what an animal does and how it feeds, is decided for it by nature and to ignore that nature and expect it to behave some other way will lead, if not to its death, certainly to its suffering and pain.
Once, I inadvertently filled my car with the wrong petrol. I had gone only a couple of miles down the road when the car coughed and spluttered and stopped. Why did my car break down? Because it was

---

[1] Interestingly these are the very words (in italics) that John Riley (1803-1879) repeated in several letters when he wrote in the 1850s & 1860s from Nelson to his mother and brother in Liverpool.

not made to run on diesel. You know as well as I do, that a car can break down for a dozen other reasons but a car is made a certain way and will carry out its function as a motorcar only if we acknowledge these built-in requirements and work within the limits they impose. It is no use saying we have no money to buy the right petrol, or saying we are miles away from a petrol station. The car just stops and nothing else will make it go.

How like human life all this is. God has made us a certain way and life will succeed only as we acknowledge this and work within the framework of that pattern. We might not like what it requires of us, but surely it is not ours to make or change the rules – they are built in. Like with the motorcar, we make excuses for not doing what God requires of us – but also like the motorcar, life will grind to a halt: it won't go along just because we have found some reason not to give it the right fuel.

We have wars and revolutions and plagues and famines, ill health, broken homes and delinquency. It is easy to cry out against God and ask Why does this happen? Every time it happens, should we not rather ask, What rule did we break? Where did we fail to follow God? This is God's world and it will work only God's way.

But perhaps the truth is, we don't break rules: they break us. From these unalterable truths the pattern of life is determined. What of people who do play by the rules but suffer innocently as a result of those who do not. No man is an island ("There is no difference between the man who sows and the man who waters: God will reward each one according to the work he has done" - Corinthians 3).

I guess all of you have seen shows or parades where a clown rides a bicycle with a wheel designed deliberately off centre. Both rider and bicycle move along like a hiccoughing horse. The rider could never stand up to it if it was anything more than a short distance or for a short time. If the action was sped up the bicycle would surely disintegrate no matter how well made and how strong any of the individual parts may be.

People belong together in an integrated whole. As such we inherit a lot of good we might not individually deserve: we also inherit some bad we individually do not deserve. When this unit of people proceeds as a bicycle that is off centre, it is quite possible that some innocent parts will suffer in the shaking, straining, breaking down process that goes on. This may be illustrated with the situation where missionaries who go to do good are tortured and killed, not necessarily because of them but because the natives rebel against the cruelties and injustices of the past, even a hundred years earlier, when unscrupulous traders or slavemasters left festering resentment.

But if we retaliate in kind we are adding to the world's evil – we are adding to the disintegrating process that is going on and other people, some of them innocent ones, are going to be caught in the process, perhaps even a hundred years from now. If we can rise to it, if we can hold to the good, we slow up the disintegration processes, we bring the world that much nearer to its true centre and save other and future generations that much innocent suffering, even if we are hurt badly in doing so.

This I believe is what happened to our Lord, but He showed us what is the true centre of the world – though He Himself was destroyed in the process.

I said that what is right for man is what is natural or suitable to his nature. The trouble is that sin has taken such a deep hold in our nature and has been with us or rather in us so long, we no longer know what our true nature is. We have to look beyond ourselves to find out what kind of person God intended us to be – stripped of all our pervasiveness, twists and distortions. That working model of what man ought to be as God intended him to be is found in Jesus Christ.

So as we listen to Him and are guided to live His kind of life – filled with prayer, worship, loving kindness, outreaching concern, under His ideals and standards, we are moving to our true selves, back to our true centre and helping to correct the imbalance of the world and leading it away from the destruction that threatens to destroy its very existence.

But this imperfection and imbalance runs so deep in our nature that there is nothing good enough left in us to correct it, and even by trying ever so hard, we cannot get back to the state that God intended us to be in. Our very goodness is tarnished; our best intentions are tainted with evil; sin is ingrained and we are under its power. So that the good I would do, I do not, and the evil that I would not, I do. As someone humourously put it: everything I like doing is either illegal, immoral or fattening.

For this dilemma, God has provided a great corrective. In a very simple way, He puts to right the evil that is wrecking the world and our personal lives. All He asks of us is to have faith in Jesus Christ. It has been said in a thousand different ways and manifested in hundreds of other ways but at heart, this is the truth of what is said. Believe in Jesus

Christ. Link yourself to Him through faith. As it were marry yourself to Him; let Him adopt you. From henceforth God no longer sees you and regards you as you are, a sinner deserving the deserts of your sin, but as one in Christ.

From henceforth you are regarded and treated as a Christian person. It is too simple, you say, you cannot believe it. You feel you ought to do something, You ought to wait until you are better than you have been. But nowhere does God say any such thing. He accepts you for He regards you as in Christ. Just as a child adopted into a family is accepted as a child of the family by the family and everybody else.

This is what makes our message Gospel-good news. We have sinned grievously, we are sinning, we will go on sinning – just because we are human and sin has such a hold over our lives. But God accepts us – not waiting for us to get better – but helping us to be better in the future.

This for me vindicates the Christian religion. It does not consist in activities, such as pilgrimages to holy places, sacrifices and rituals difficult to perform and other things that are beyond the reach of some people who might be poor or maimed or too young or too old to perform them.

This makes ours a universal faith and an all available faith and an all correcting faith: where there is a heart to believe, there God can come and does come and make one His child.

God saves. He is love. This is why I have preached for over thirty years. It is a glorious privilege to have been called to such a task. No one is more aware of my limitations for this great task than I am. I wish to God I was adequate enough to do it so well that people everywhere would listen and heed and respond. There is nothing grander to tell, I would [pray?] to God that everybody knew it, for this is life and joy and peace and deliverance – and everything in life that is good.

And in the end, despite everything, "nevertheless the foundations of God standeth sure".

I commend these thoughts to your earnest consideration.

Eph 3/7 Eph 3/7-21; Isaiah 10/1-9; Amos 7/10

14 Nov 1982 Aromoho (Wanganui)
10 April 1983 Trinity Wanganui

"Whereof I was made a minister according to the gift of the grace of God" (Eph 3/7)

[Extract only:]

50 years - it is a long time in anticipation, a short time in retrospect

Friend - "I've decided that a hundred years is not a very long time after all."

Three months ago, Alan Jones completed his fifty years of ministry. He finished it with a bang. Mine is finishing with a whimper. I've always regretted that ill health has prevented me going at top speed right to the end. But retirement has not entirely stopped me from preaching and I am learning a lot, even in retirement.

First and foremost I must pay tribute to my wife who has stood loyally by me for over forty of these fifty years. Her own record in the service of the church is a worthy one in its own right. She always took a leading role in the church of her childhood and later was President of the Canterbury Bible Class Union and then held office at Dominion level. She worked, usually as leader, in untold numbers of Bible Class camps and conferences. She has loved and served her church without stint all her life and not least as the lady of the parsonage. By nature she is an organiser and loves to have everything planned and in place, so the endless interruptions of parsonage life must have been an anathema to her. But she never let it show. She was always gracious, the perfect hostess and to me a great encourager and tireless helper.

Next I must apologise if my references to myself appear too regular in what follows. The pulpit is the last place where one should speak about oneself, but the very nature of this sermon will require it today. Next I must confess to a problem. Thinking back, memories come flooding in and it is impossible to put into these minutes all I would like to recount of my years serving the church.

My ministry began in the midst of social upheaval and the beginning of a technical revolution. Radios, telephones, motor cars, were far from being universally owned and television was unheard of. The newspapers of the day were full of reports of revolts in India and the activities of Mahatma Gandhi. Communism was less than twenty years old. Hitler came into power the very year I began my ministry. While my influence on the world stage was less shattering than his, at least I am still alive!

Society of course, was dominated by a depression, *the* depression – and it affected all our thinking for years afterwards in the church as well as outside it. All these things together meant that democracy which had been taken for granted for a century or more, was being challenged and the world of ideas was coming to the boil. Among the new ideas was pacifism. A book hit the market called "Cry Havoc" by Beverley Nichols and along with other books like "Peace with Honour" it was causing a stir and marked the beginning of a new revolutionary idea. Our church, always blessed with an acute social conscience (some people would say cursed by it) over the years of my ministry, tore herself in shreds over the issue.

As a youth I found myself coming under the influence of such men as L D Weatherhead and his books on "Transforming Friendship" and other people like H E Fosdick and E Stanley Jones. My mind was stirred and challenged by them and years later they were still influencing and changing my thinking.

It was in this atmosphere of economic depression mixed with revolutionary thinking and social change that I felt a call to the ministry. Not because of them, but in the midst of them. It came to me at the age of thirteen when I was having to decide what course I would take at secondary school. I was young, but of course it was the right time. It came a lot like the voice that spoke to Samuel, but not quite so audible. It was rather in my mind than in my ear. But it certainly was the last thing I wanted to hear. I put it from me and in going to secondary school I chose to do a non-academic course in agriculture. For two years I was miserable fighting all the time the call to the church – and hating the battle within me. I then gave in and knew some peace. But it was time to leave school and so I went home to the farm, not scholastically prepared for the ministry at all, but glad enough to have a farm to go to, both because I liked it and also because it was a job (although without pay) when thousands of school leavers couldn't get any work of any sort.

Four years later a minister came to Stratford who took me under his wing (Rev Tom Skuse). He put me through the hoops to become a lay preacher and prepared me to be a candidate for the ministry. And it was here in Wanganui that I appeared before the Synod Committee in what I think you called the Parlour, and I preached a trial sermon in the old church before a handful of people, three of them ministers. Can you imagine it?! The depression was being felt in the church too and they were turning down more candidates than they were accepting and I was one of the turned-down ones. That suited me and I felt I could turn to the farm again with a clear conscience. But the voice came back to haunt me and so after another unsuccessful offer, I put myself down for Home Mission work.

The ensuing Conference appointed me to Ohaeawai. Do you know where that is? I didn't and neither did anybody else until someone got the AA map and found it was a place of about one hundred inhabitants in the Bay of Islands. In 1933, one Sunday night, fifty years ago today, or rather last Sunday, I helped my family milk fifty cows by hand and next morning said goodbye to them from that same cowshed and threw my leg over my motorbike and headed north. I was just 21.

The next Sunday I was wearing a clerical collar and taking services in a scattered area that embraced thirteen preaching places and there was not one Methodist church among them. I preached in Presbyterian churches, in an Anglican church, in school halls, wool sheds, private homes. On the first Sunday morning after church they asked me, "Have you got the collection?" When I said no they explained that I had better get it as that was my pay. At the end of the quarter when I was chairing the Quarterly Meeting, I had to present the balance sheet. I alone had a record of the collections. There was no other income of any sort: that was it. In the first quarter we had twelve wet Sundays out of thirteen which did my collections no good at all. My pay for the whole of my first year was £85! Despite the importance of the collection as my entire livelihood, in my childhood the taking up of collection in church at all was not welcomed. It was almost an embarrassment with many ministers adopting an attitude of "Hurry up and get it over with". The fact that today it is a dedicated offering and an integral part of the service could hardly have been imagined.

Things change. We no longer even have Home Missionaries. And probably that is one of the features of my 50 years ministry: living as I have, it has seemed, on the crest of a wave of change. I have seen so much change – things that we thought once were immovable, unchanging, eternal.

Fifty years ago it would have nearly caused a riot if a minister wore a gown and it would have been even worse had the choir been gowned. The communion service was tacked on to the end of the service after the non-communicants had been given an opportunity to leave. Women always wore hats in church and men always wore their best suits. Eleven o'clock for morning service was almost sacrosanct.

One of the other more subtle changes has been the movement from the evening to the morning service. As Quarterly Meetings debate today the value of retaining the evening service, so fifty years ago they debated the value of keeping the morning service. I remember evening services when the congregations were so large chairs had to be put in the aisle and people had to sit in the vestry. No more!

That sort of thing belonged to the day when people listened to preachers just because they were preachers first and foremost. If there was a special occasion and one wanted to boost the congregation numbers, you sought out a preacher with a reputation – and the people came – in large numbers. Today, visiting preachers are more likely to reduce normal congregation sizes, not increase them!

The morning service has become the strong one. I believe it is the worship when the family comes to church (not that they sit in "the family pew" any longer – but they used to do that too). But they are there in church and Sunday School and Bible Class and the preacher in the pulpit is the family minister – often very much part and parcel of the family experience. He is pastor and as pastor the congregation they tend to feel a bond with him and they attend the service because of that.

There has been a move in theological thinking too. When I first talked about going into the ministry, I had religiously minded relatives, some of whom were horrified that I would have to go to Trinity College. They warned of the terrible "modern theology" that was taught there – and they feared for my soul. I was brought up on the Sankey hymn book. The new Methodist hymn book was treated with suspicion and the love we have for it now only grew after a long time.

But in those early days, when I started to do some reading, I had a feeling that what I had been brought up on was not adequate. Somehow, somewhere, there were other answers to my theological doubts. In my Home Missionary days I fell foul of Brethren that associated with some of my congregations. We spent hours on theological arguments concerned with the increasing influence of new sects. It was a great relief to me when I got to Trinity College to learn of their truths. Those Trinity years proved to be exciting, stimulating, expansive and I have been eternally grateful to the Methodist Church for giving me those years of training. They did worlds for me in expanding my horizons and building up my self confidence and my appreciation of the greatness of God and the wonder of his love and grace and my appreciation and understanding of the Bible.

But imagine my surprise as I moved out into further studies and the active ministry. I discovered there was one great gap in that teaching. When I wanted to know what the Church is in New Testament thinking, what is her nature and structure, I could not find any chapter on it in any text books we had studied. The great debate of church union was surely a sign of the times in which I began my ministry. As proposals for church union came thick and fast, I found I had to know what the nature of the church was and what the teachings of the Bible in that regard were.

In my box of sermons at home, I have a dozen or so on the subject of the church which I wrote as I thought and read my way through the different debates in establishing my understanding of her. That leads me to state a couple of great convictions that have been born out of these fifty years of ministry.

The first is that the church is one of the great realities of life. We can understand the Bible and the Christian life only as we see it as the family or people of God. It is made up of those who have responded to God's call to discipleship and who are linked together as fellow believers, caring for one another in love and striving together to live the life of God, to which we are all called. There are no hard and fast rules that are more important than the people who make up the family. When we use these rules and laws to beat the people, we are defeating the very spirit of the family.

The second is that I believe with all my heart that this is God's world and will work only in God's way. As the Creator, God is very much like the inventor of, say, the car. He knows what makes it go and He tells us how it goes through his instructions. Men and women are free-will agents and God lets them ignore his guidelines if they want to. But the consequences are sure! As with the car, so life too will, in the end, break down, if we ignore what God has to say.

So I read with appreciation what the Bible has to say, for it is God speaking to me, of what is His intention for the people of the world. I have no hesitation in preaching with certainty and conviction for I am convinced that our salvation from self destruction, our hope for a full and satisfying life, are to be found in those words. Sooner or later we have to come round to taking heed of those truths and living by them. Jesus spoke much more truly than many realise. "Come unto me, for I have the words of eternal life." If we don't come of our own free will, life itself will drive us to it, whether we like it or not. So I have great confidence in proclaiming the Word of God.

One of the changes I have seen in my fifty years of ministry is the role of the minister's work. The pastoral work has grown immensely in importance and our College training recognises it in its new training and study programmes. It is good that people are turning more and more to our ministers as counsellors and this has become an enormously time consuming part of the minister's work. I found it consumed more and more of my time towards the end of my ministry and made increasingly heavy demands on my strength, resources and nervous energy until it well nigh exhausted me. But somehow, I still believe that the unique task of the minister is preaching. There is nothing quite like it in any other walk of life.

As I left to start Home Mission work, my minister said that three things were essential to make a minister's work effective:

1. good organisation
2. good pastoral [care]
3. good preaching

- and in that order. There is a lot of truth in that, but to me the really unique task is preaching. Others can be effective organisers and counsellors, but the task of preaching is very special.

- It is not entertainment, although it must be done with some form of presentation.
- It is not teaching, although that must be present.
- It is not lecturing (presenting facts on a take it or leave it basis) – although one has to expound that.
- It is not oratory, although the power of oratory encourages people to listen

It is all of these things, but most of all, it is

- a presentation of God to the people and a presentation of the people to God.

It requires the skill to plead, persuade, convince. It takes all the skills a man is capable of: it is somehow drawing back the veil and letting the people see God. In the end, the people have to see past the preacher to find and see God for themselves. But in the end, God, in his own ways, speaks His own message: "He who has ears, let him hear". I could not have been a preacher if I could not have believed in this.

I have preached because I was convinced God called me to do it – why, I will never know. But He has been good to me. He has given me rich rewards and I am eternally grateful. It has involved doing many things I did not want to do. But I have learned that I have gained far more from doing what I ought to do than I have from doing what I wanted to do. In Richard Attenborough's recent film [1982] *Gandhi,* Ben Kingsley who played the part of Gandhi said after the film was completed, "The part stretched me beyond what I was before and I won't shrink back from what I am now." I feel like that about going into the ministry.

The compensations have been enormous. I would plead with you, do not be afraid of God. He calls you to be his servant too. It will bring joy and satisfaction beyond all believing. Will you give Him your love and service too?

APPENDIX X
Dad's 100th birthday letter for his family: 19th March 2012

In amongst Dad's things which we found only after Mum had also died, was a small envelope marked by Dad. He asked for it to be opened on his 100th birthday. Curiosity conquered my self discipline. In light of this book, which I hope will serve as a complete and permanent record of Dad's life, I wanted to read it and to publish it now. He wrote it thirty years ago and it is already of great interest to us. I am sure Dad would be pleased, not disappointed, that we did not wait just another six years to read it (his hundredth birthday would have been 19th March 2012) – and in so doing miss this opportunity to make it a long lasting record.

NB: It is important to realise that Dad wrote this in 1976 – before he had any idea that later a whole book would be written on his life.

August 1976

To Weston, Riley and Godfrey
To be opened on my 100th birthday, 19th March 2012
Dad

I am inspired to write this by the fact that my own father's 100th birthday has just passed (1st August 1976). At the moment I am with my greatly loved wife in London on holiday in the United Kingdom, the first trip we have had outside New Zealand (apart from a trip to Australia by Rae in her single days).
On the morning of 1st August, I went to church at the Central Hall Westminster, on a lovely summer's day. As I did so, I fell to contemplating what sort of world this is, compared to the kind of world into which my father was born one hundred years ago. It would have been the most revolutionary century in the history of mankind. He was born in New Zealand in Canterbury (Ashley or Ashley Gorge) when it was a colony of Britain and was just being broken in. The total population would have been less than one million. Free, compulsory and non-sectarian education was introduced the year of his birth. This did not prevent him from leaving school after one week in Standard 3

and going out to work to help the family purse. There were no pensions or age benefits of any sort as far as I know. Mechanisation was almost unknown and most work was done manually and by the sweat of one's brow. With axe and cross-cut saw he felled hundreds of acres of native bush in central Taranaki as a young man.

During my life time (which of course was part of his) the motor car and allied motor vehicles have been developed until today nearly every family has one and often (in New Zealand anyway) more than one. The four wheel drive has been developed and is essential equipment for coping with roadless terrain. In like manner, the aeroplane has been developed from its earliest forms, until today it is possible to travel commercially at faster than sound speeds. The Concorde has come into service. Heathrow Airport has develop from a paddock into a complex centre into and out of which thousands of people move daily and where aeroplanes arrive and depart something like every forty seconds.

The Olympic Games have just concluded at Montreal. It was possible to see them as they happened on the colour television. I have seen tapes and tape-recorders invented, telephones in homes and telephones in cars, radar as a means of communication and control. There are satellites (man made) in orbit around the earth and used to beam television pictures to all points of the world. Several landings have been made on the moon and spaceships have sent pictures of the moon's surface <u>away</u> from the earth. This week for the first time, a manmade spaceship landed on Mars and sent photographs back to earth.

There have been many by-products produced from petroleum. Plastic is one that we use in every day life e.g. bags, string, coverings, shoes, clothes, etc. The biro with which I write this, like plastic, was unknown before the last world war. Likewise, the transistor which has transformed radio.

Socially and politically great changes have taken place. At this moment there is a strong movement for the equality of women and recent legislation in England has made it compulsory that <u>all</u> positions advertised as vacant must state that women as well as men may apply. One of the manifestations of this is "unisex" clothes. Abortion is a much debated social issue and so is homosexuality with a move to legalise sexual acts between consenting male adults.

At the Games, over 20 black nations walked out because New Zealand had an All Black rugby team playing in South Africa which practices apartheid. Tensions are high over the issue of racism. Rhodesia is being threatened by an internal war (already some shooting has started) because they will not grant majority rule. There is a strong national movement abroad and state after state in Africa has been gaining independence, the latest being Angola. Communism is spreading and has succeeded in expelling USA from South Vietnam. There has newly emerged what is called the Third World – consisting mainly of black nations committed neither to Communism nor to Western civilisation. Democracy is being severely tested.

New Zealand's good name as a fair, just and racially integrated society is being put under a cloud because the new National Government under Rob Muldoon has condoned the Rugby tour of South Africa claiming that the Rugby Union has the right to play matches against whom it chooses. There are strong feelings and much discussion and severe division between New Zealanders themselves over the issue.

The churches still function and are accepted as institutions of the modern world, but there are difficulties as the Western world is very materialistic in its outlook. Sunday is very secularised. It is the day for sports, picnics, gatherings of all sorts and, over here in England, shops remain open for business. Church attendance has fallen to a hard core of loyal supporters with a tolerant acceptance of the church by the rest but with a feeling she should not interfere in things political. However, still a goodly proportion of the civic leaders have church connections and much of the inspiration for social concern institutions, such as old people's homes, "Life Line", homes for unmarried mothers, citizens' advice centres, charities of all sorts, stems from church people. There is a good deal of natural human concern which carries along such things as old age pensions, free medical care at all levels, and people accept that governments should back all such enterprises at least financially and even to manning them. In the world, which is experiencing a population explosion, vast numbers are near starvation and some help is forthcoming. Recently governments have made grants of up to 1% of Gross National Income to this end. But the inspiration and drive for it comes mainly from church people and (organisationally) from the National Council of Churches and the World Council of Churches with some help from United Nations organisations. Internally there is a movement within the main stream churches to form united churches. At the moment, the Pentecostal movement flourishes and is growing apace.

Another burning issue is the matter of birth control, with the Roman Catholic church opposing it most strongly while in such countries as India, governments are trying to educate the people to practice it.

A new development has been very rich Arabs who have pushed out into Western countries and taken over the very rich oil fields. They have formed an alliance of oil producing countries and are becoming very shrewd at dictating prices and thus gaining considerable control of oil dependent nations into which category fall many of the powerful Western countries. As a result the Arabs have become fabulously rich as illustrated by a deal here in London last month when an individual Arab bought a hotel for £5 million cash! There is some concern in this country over the increasing number of black skinned and dark races that are settling here. It is generating some feeling.

To give a real comparison over a hundred year span, I ought to go back to my earliest childhood. This is somewhat vague now but a few things might be useful to recall.

My earliest recollections are of the farm at Raetihi which we left when I was four years of age. We retained ownership of it for a number of years and leased it to various people until it was finally sold. I visited it again only once. It was when I was sixteen years old and in my first suit of long trousers. A party of our neighbours at Wharehuia (Mr Will Hosking, Mr Reg Wellington and Mum and Dad and myself) did a trip there in Mr Wellington's Model T Ford. While the roads in Taranaki were tar sealed they were far in advance of most roads and on our trip to Raetihi we travelled the un-metalled road, let alone unsealed, of the Parapara ranges. The trip from Wanganui by this road was regarded with some horror, but we had a dry road, a fine day, but even so it took us from Wanganui something like eight hours. The farm was much as I remembered it from my toddler days, still fairly littered with fallen trees. I recall these being sawn up and heaped up and burnt by my father prior to clearing for the plough and sowing in pasture. Raetihi was only a clearing in dense native trees and after we left to reside at Stratford, a bush fire destroyed part of the town, including our farm house and out-buildings.

At the time of this trip there were a number of our neighbours who had cars, but earlier on this was rare. I recall the excitement when Will Hosking bought his first one, a Morris. Then there was a Willy's

Knight[1] (owner Mr Will Wellington) in the district and another car owned by Mr Vivian, and possibly one or two others which I don't remember. Everybody else travelled by horse and gig or trap. We ourselves owned a buggy with a buck seat (a kind of duckey-seat) and this was regarded as quite something in that day. Later on, my mother inherited from her parents a quiet pony and a phaeton – a low slung open horse-drawn carriage with four wheels and two double seats facing inwards. There were very few of these about. Market day in the provincial towns was the occasion to get the horses shod and it was a common sight to see both sides of the street lined with gigs and such like while the horses were tethered in the blacksmith's yard, many of them taking their turn to be shod.

A horse and cart or dray was the common mode to shift produce to and from the farm. Manure would arrive at the station at Midhirst and this would be the signal for a hectic few hours. A ton would be the limit of the dray so it would mean a round trip of about one to one and a half hours, five or ten times, to get the manure home. As waiting time was charged for the rail truck, it was a case of getting it emptied as quickly as possible and a later arrival of the truck at the station would mean working into the night. Later on, as cars became more common, this was not exactly a pleasant experience. The milk from the farm was carted by the same horse and dray to the creamery – a factory where the separating was done, with the cream going to a control factory to be made into butter and the milk made into casein. Or, if the farmer required it for his calves and pigs, he carted it home again for them. The creamer was a popular place to hear news of the district. At this stage, most milking was done by machines, but hand milking was not unknown and inventors of milking machines were still living – indeed they were not even old.

For working the farm, most farmers aimed to own (otherwise they had to borrow from neighbours) a plough, a set of discs, harrows, a drill, a roller, a mower, a rake, a sledge and of course a dray. Those who farmed on a larger scale would own a wagon or brake and possibly a tether, a hay-sweep and a hay-stacker. These were the aristocrats of the farming community and they were looked up to. Contractors for cultivating or haymaking were almost unknown and the only way to lighten the burden was for neighbours to help each other. In our particular case, a group purchased harvesting equipment between

[1] e.g. a popular car of the time was the 1926 Willy's Knight Model 66 Tourer

them, while each member of the group planned to own his own mowing machine and do his own mowing. When they called on each other for help, such as did happen with hay-mowing, the repayment was usually in the form of return labour and rarely in cash.

To move any distance, one was dependent on the railways. Outings usually were limited to a once or twice weekly trip by horse and gig to town. Trap journeys beyond ten miles were rare as were visits to relations or friends outside one's immediate district, and even then, not very often at night.

Even telephones were the privilege of the better off and often they had to tolerate the visit of neighbours to use their phones when occasion demanded. Post Office sub-stations existed in most local areas, meaning one every three miles or so and were often to be found in a shop or even in a private home – a source of some supplementary income. Telegrams would be phoned from these small Post Offices to a nearby larger Post Office from where they would be sent on by Morse code.

Radios were unheard of until later. As a lad of about twelve to fourteen, I recall visiting an uncle and family at Tuna to hear our first radio. It had to be an evening visit. The radio was a massive affair with multiple dials. We listened in turn through headphones to what proved to be more noise and static than music or voices. It had to be constantly tuned in and re-tuned in, to catch the constantly fading station. If I recall correctly, we gave up finally and spent the time chatting and enjoying the company of each other. Television was unheard of as were aeroplanes – well, not quite. About the time I was nine years old, we watched all day for the sight of our first aeroplane which, it was reported, would be flying to New Plymouth. While they were not unknown, standing all day looking to the sky was the measure to which they belonged within the experience of ordinary people.

In shopping, self help was unheard of. Things were asked for at the counter and weighed out or measured off, while you waited. Articles were put in brown paper bags or wrapped in brown paper and tied with string (sellotape was unknown). Bacon would be cut with a knife off a roll and even lollies would be shovelled out of tins and weighed while you waited. Most grocers had delivery services and butchers would load up with a range of meat and call at the houses (more especially farm houses). The housewife would go to the gate and decide on her meat. It would be cut off, weighed on scales that hung at the back of the cart, and placed on the plate which the housewife took with her to the gate. Quite a lot of skill was required in buying as there were no refrigerators in the houses and no chance of buying additional supplies before the next visit from the butcher. Bread was often sold the same sort of way. Many farmers, of course, were as good as butchers themselves and killed their own beasts for home consumption. This did involve sharing with neighbours as there was the problem of keeping the meat fresh. With sheep it wasn't so bad, but a beef animal was quite an occasion. Most farmers kept at least one pig for home consumption. It wasn't easy to get the right quantity of water at the right temperature to do the job of removing the hairs from the animal. Then came the task of curing the bacon. It was not an uncommon sight in farm houses to see the carcass of a quite massive pig, cut up into various joints and hanging from the kitchen ceiling where it was getting a smoking from the daily use of the kitchen fire. This was the basic supply of the farmer's breakfast for the next twelve months.

Talking of shopping, people bought in larger supplies. Flour was often purchased in bags of 25lbs, sometimes 100lbs. Sugar was normally in 70lb bags. Milk was measured at the door of each house, into a billy. Some people baked their own bread and in a few cases, churned their own butter. In our family we purchased it through the factory, generally 5lbs at a time, and collected it from the factory on a Thursday when delivering milk. We bought tea in 5lb tins, while some people bought a chest of tea. The tins and sacks from these goods were generally utilised for an array of uses: sugar sacks to make aprons. Flour sacks were even used for underclothes.

Electric power was used to light and heat homes in larger towns, but most country areas were dependent on kerosene lamps and wood burning stoves and open fires. Toilets were deep wells in the ground and bed chambers were used throughout the house. An early morning first job was to collect and empty them. Water supplies came from tanks and wells for which few had any aids to draw the water, other than a bucket and rope. For baths, water was heated on the stove and carried to the baths, or, in some cases, to tubs. Hot water cylinders were not unknown but belonged mainly only to the more financially fortunate. Dishes were washed in a basin with hot water from the same source. Washing day was a hard day's work. It was done in a detached wash-house (if not completely outside) where the wood-fed copper had to be brought to the boil and the clothes put through rinses in a double

wooden tub and rung out either manually or with the aid of a hand turned wringer. Monday was traditional wash-day.
To play sport on a Sunday was severely frowned on and if one was so bold as to have a game of tennis on that day, one would try and hide the racquet on the way to the court. There were practically no organised games of any sort and shops and commercial places were closed. Only a very occasional confectionery shop might remain open. In the very earliest days of my childhood, there was no half day holiday, but this did come later with each town deciding which day of the week would be their half day closing. Later still, it was universally adopted that it would be Saturday and finally it became a full day closing on Saturday.
Carpets on the floor were for the very rich only. Usually linoleum was used but in my time I have seen bare boards remain bare (and not polished) with fertiliser sacks used as door mats. Generally walls were papered but I have seen some rooms where pictures from old copies of *The Auckland Weekly* were effectively (and interestingly) used in lieu of manufactured wallpapers.

I wonder what sort of a world it will be in 2012.

Love,
Dad

BIBLIOGRAPHY

Alphabetical by title

A History of New Zealand	Keith Sinclair, Penguin revised 1969 England
Around Weston-super-Mare	Sharon Poole, Frith 2001 England
Beyond the Waimakariri	D N Hawkins
Ferntown to Farewell Spit	Carol Dawber & Cheryl Win, October Enterprises 2003 New Zealand
G R Macdonald Dictionary of Canterbury Biographies	G R Macdonald, Canterbury Museum, New Zealand A unique collection of handwritten biographies on index cards, presented to Canterbury Museum in 1964 by George Macdonald after 12 years of voluntary research on early Canterbury settlers and covering 22,000 entries.
Images of England Central Liverpool	David Paul, Tempus 1997 England
Swindon An Illustrated History	Mark Child, Breedon 2002 England
Swindon Fifty Years Ago More or Less	William Morris, The Swindon Advertiser 1885 England Now the (Swindon) Evening Advertiser. The author was the newspaper's editor and founder, and used many of his own published articles from the newspaper in compiling the book.
Swindon Living Memories Francis Frith	Brian Bridgeman, Frith 2003 England
The Barrells of Durham Street	Margaret Scott, Caxton Press New Zealand
The Bell Family A Record compiled for the Family Reunion January 1985	Evelyn Hickling (nee Bell) New Zealand

The Bell Family Supplement 1998	Jack Orchard, New Zealand
The History of Methodism in New Zealand	Rev William Morley McKee & Co, Wellington 1900
The Riley Family *A record compiled for the Family Reunion Easter 1979*	Evelyn Hickling (1916-2004), New Zealand
The Story of New Zealand	W H Oliver, Faber & Faber 1960 reprinted 1968 England
Weston-super-Mare *A Pictorial History*	Sharon Poole, Phillimore 1995 England
Weston-super-Mare with Worle & Uphill *Somerset's Holiday Gem*	Sharon Poole, Halsgrove 2004 England
Wiltshire Churches	David Parker, Frith 2001 England
Wiltshire Living Memories	Tony Cornish, Frith 2000 England

INDICES

Time Line Index (1)
of direct line ancestors

(including historical reference points)

&

Alphabetical Index

Guidance Notes for the use of the Index

1. In the Time Line Index preceding the alphabetical index, only references to Charles's and Rae's direct line ancestors are included down to the death of Rae & Charles's parent. Additionally, some time line historical reference points are given to contextualise the ancestor entries.
2. In the Time Line Index, the births, marriages and deaths of *Charles's great grandparents* (only) are highlighted in bold.
3. Rev Charles Harrison Bell is indexed under "Charles"
4. Rae Barrell (single) and Rae Bell (married) are both indexed under "Rae".
5. *Italics* indicate: titles (e.g. of books, newspapers, films, etc), names (e.g. sailing ships) photos, line drawings, engravings, cartoons, images of advertisements, etc.
6. Graves, headstones, plaques & monuments are indexed by the prefix "Memorials".
7. Maps are indexed by the prefix "Maps".
8. Family trees and charts are indexed by the prefix "Chart".
9. Names of ships are indexed by the prefix "Ships".
10. Newspapers are indexed by the prefix "Newspapers".

1

— 1801 Mary Clark born Streatley, Berkshire, 222
— 1802 (abt) Frances Colledge born Kilsby, Northamptonshire, 227
— **1803 John Riley** born, Halifax, Yorkshire, 174, 186
— 1804 Sarah Strange (nee Ayers) dies, Swindon, 207
— 1805 Thomas Perrott promoted to Corporal in East Somerset Militia, 142
— **1806 Mary Bolton** born, York, 174

1810s

— 1811 Calverley Riley ordained in St Vincent, West Indies, 176, 177
— **1813 George John Bell** marries **Elizabeth Lidgate** in Scotland, 104, 105
— 1814 (bef) Andrew Diamond born, Northern Ireland, 31
— 1815 William Sully Jr born, Stogursey, Somerset, 574
— 1818 Calverley Riley moves to Isle of Man, 177

1820s

— 1821 Henry William Barrell born, Bristol, 573, 575
— **1822 F T Perrott** born Shepton Mallet, 143
— 1822 Robert Strange marries Mary Clark, Streatley, Berkshire, 222
— 1824 Louisa Brewer born, Bristol, 574
— 1825 (abt) Sarah Ann Carter born, Cheddar, Somerset, 574
— 1825 Calverley Riley moves to Liverpool, 177
— 1826 James Strange dies Swindon, 215
— **1827 Harriett Reeve (m Perrott)**, born Shepton Mallet, 143
— **1828 Robert James Strange** born, Devizes, Wiltshire, 220
— **1829 John Riley** marries **Mary Bolton**, Birmingham, 174, 188

1830s

— **1832 Blanche Crooke** born Kilsby, Northamptonshire, 8, 227
— 1832 John George Bell born in Whitsome, Scotland, 107
— **1833 George John Bell** dies in Scotland, 103, 126, 127, 1040
— 1837 Henry J Diamond born Londonderry, Northern Ireland, 587
— 1838 Johanna Streeter born, Brighton, 587

1840s

— 1840 John Bolton Riley born, Leeds, 174, 188
— 1840 Treaty of Waitangi signed, 174
— 1842 Nelson's first year of settlement under The NZ Company, 189
— 1842 Riley family emigrate to NZ, 174, 188
— 1842 William Sully Sr dies, 574
— 1843 Wairau Massacre, 174
— 1844 Henry William Barrell marries Louisa Brewer, Bristol, 575, 577
— 1846 John Clark dies, Streatley, 221
— 1847 Anna Maria McDonnell born, Ireland, 574
— **1848 F T Perrott** marries **Harriett Reeve**, 143

1850s

— 1850 (abt) William Henry Barrell dies, Bristol, 26, 574
— 1850 Blanche Crooke emigrates to NZ on the *Berkshire*, 29, 227
— 1850 Calverley Riley dies, Liverpool, 173, 178
— 1850 Robert J Strange emigrates to NZ (sailing ship/date not proven), 29
— **1850 Robert J Strange** marries **Blanche Crooke**, Nelson, 29
— 1851 Mary Frances Eveline Strange born, Nelson, 87

A

B

C

D

E

F

G

H

I

J

K

L

M

N

O

P

Q

R

S

T

U

V

W

Y

Z